IP Quality of Service

Srinivas Vegesna

Cisco Press

Cisco Press
201 W 103rd Street
Indianapolis, IN 46290 USA

IP Quality of Service

Srinivas Vegesna

Copyright© 2001 Cisco Press

Published by:
Cisco Press
201 West 103rd Street
Indianapolis, IN 46290 USA

Printed in the United States of America 5 6 7 8 9 0 04 03

Fifth Printing January 2003

Library of Congress Cataloging-in-Publication Number: 98-86710

ISBN: 1-57870-116-3

Warning and Disclaimer

This book is designed to provide information about IP Quality of Service. Every effort has been made to make this book as complete and as accurate as possible, but no warranty or fitness is implied.

The information is provided on an "as is" basis. The author, Cisco Press, and Cisco Systems, Inc., shall have neither liability nor responsibility to any person or entity with respect to any loss or damages arising from the information contained in this book or from the use of the discs or programs that may accompany it.

The opinions expressed in this book belong to the author and are not necessarily those of Cisco Systems, Inc.

Trademark Acknowledgments

All terms mentioned in this book that are known to be trademarks or service marks have been appropriately capitalized. Cisco Press or Cisco Systems, Inc., cannot attest to the accuracy of this information. Use of a term in this book should not be regarded as affecting the validity of any trademark or service mark.

Feedback Information

At Cisco Press, our goal is to create in-depth technical books of the highest quality and value. Each book is crafted with care and precision, undergoing rigorous development that involves the unique expertise of members from the professional technical community.

Readers' feedback is a natural continuation of this process. If you have any comments regarding how we could improve the quality of this book, or otherwise alter it to better suit your needs, you can contact us through e-mail at feedback@ciscopress.com. Please make sure to include the book title and ISBN in your message.

We greatly appreciate your assistance.

Publisher	John Wait
Editor-in-Chief	John Kane
Cisco Representative	Anthony Wolfenden
Cisco Press Program Manager	Sonia Torres Chavez
Cisco Marketing Communications Manager	Tom Geitner
Cisco Marketing Program Manager	Edie Quiroz
Production Manager	Patrick Kanouse
Acquisitions Editor	Tracy Hughes
Development Editors	Kitty Jarrett
	Allison Johnson
Senior Editor	Jennifer Chisholm
Copy Editor	Audrey Doyle
Technical Editors	Vijay Bollapragada Sanjay Kalra
	Kevin Mahler Erick Mar
	Sheri Moran
Cover Designer	Louisa Adair
Composition	Argosy
Proofreader	Bob LaRoche
Indexer	Larry Sweazy

CISCO SYSTEMS

Corporate Headquarters
Cisco Systems, Inc.
170 West Tasman Drive
San Jose, CA 95134-1706
USA
http://www.cisco.com
Tel: 408 526-4000
      800 553-NETS (6387)
Fax: 408 526-4100

European Headquarters
Cisco Systems Europe
11 Rue Camille Desmoulins
92782 Issy-les-Moulineaux
Cedex 9
France
http://www-europe.cisco.com
Tel: 33 1 58 04 60 00
Fax: 33 1 58 04 61 00

Americas Headquarters
Cisco Systems, Inc.
170 West Tasman Drive
San Jose, CA 95134-1706
USA
http://www.cisco.com
Tel: 408 526-7660
Fax: 408 527-0883

Asia Pacific Headquarters
Cisco Systems Australia,
Pty., Ltd
Level 17, 99 Walker Street
North Sydney
NSW 2059 Australia
http://www.cisco.com
Tel: +61 2 8448 7100
Fax: +61 2 9957 4350

Cisco Systems has more than 200 offices in the following countries. Addresses, phone numbers, and fax numbers are listed on the Cisco Web site at www.cisco.com/go/offices

Argentina • Australia • Austria • Belgium • Brazil • Bulgaria • Canada • Chile • China • Colombia • Costa Rica • Croatia • Czech Republic • Denmark • Dubai, UAE • Finland • France • Germany • Greece • Hong Kong Hungary • India • Indonesia • Ireland • Israel • Italy • Japan • Korea • Luxembourg • Malaysia • Mexico The Netherlands • New Zealand • Norway • Peru • Philippines • Poland • Portugal • Puerto Rico • Romania Russia • Saudi Arabia • Scotland • Singapore • Slovakia • Slovenia • South Africa • Spain • Sweden Switzerland • Taiwan • Thailand • Turkey • Ukraine • United Kingdom • United States • Venezuela • Vietnam Zimbabwe

About the Author

Srinivas Vegesna, CCIE #1399, is a manager in the Service Provider Advanced Consulting Services program at Cisco Systems. His focus is general IP networking, with a special focus on IP routing protocols and IP Quality of Service. In his six years at Cisco, Srinivas has worked with a number of large service provider and enterprise customers in designing, implementing, and troubleshooting large-scale IP networks. Srinivas holds an M.S. degree in Electrical Engineering from Arizona State University. He is currently working towards an M.B.A. degree at Santa Clara University.

Acknowledgments

I would like to thank all my friends and colleagues at Cisco Systems for a stimulating work environment for the last six years. I value the many technical discussions we had in the internal e-mail aliases and hallway conversations. My special thanks go to the technical reviewers of the book, Sanjay Kalra and Vijay Bollapragada, and the development editors of the book, Kitty Jarrett and Allison Johnson. Their input has considerably enhanced the presentation and content in the book. I would like to thank Mosaddaq Turabi for his thoughts on the subject and interest in the book. I would also like to remember a special colleague and friend at Cisco, Kevin Hu, who passed away in 1995. Kevin and I started at Cisco the same day and worked as a team for the one year I knew him. He was truly an all-round person.

Finally, the book wouldn't have been possible without the support and patience of my family. I would like to express my deep gratitude and love for my wife, Latha, for the understanding all along the course of the book. I would also like to thank my brother, Srihari, for being a great brother and a friend. A very special thanks goes to my two-year old son, Akshay, for his bright smile and cute words and my newborn son, Karthik for his innocent looks and sweet nothings.

Dedication

To my parents, Venkatapathi Raju and Kasturi.

About the Technical Reviewers

Vijay Bollapragada, CCIE #1606, is currently a manager in the Solution Engineering team at Cisco, where he works on new world network solutions and resolves complex software and hardware problems with Cisco equipment. Vijay also teaches Cisco engineers and customers several courses, including Cisco Router Architecture, IP Multicast, Internet Quality of Service, and Internet Routing Architectures. He is also an adjunct professor in Duke University's electrical engineering department.

Erick Mar, CCIE #3882, is a Consulting Systems Engineer at Cisco Systems with CCIE certification in routing and switching. For the last 8 years he has worked for various networking manufacturers, providing design and implementation support for large Fortune 500 companies. Erick has an M.B.A. from Santa Clara University and a B.S. in Business Administration from San Francisco State University.

Sheri Moran, CCIE #1476, has worked with Cisco Systems, Inc., for more than 7 years. She currently is a CSE (Consulting Systems Engineer) for the Northeast Commercial Operation and has been in this role for the past 1 1/2 years. Sheri's specialities are in routing, switching, QoS, campus design, IP multicast, and IBM technologies. Prior to this position, Sheri was an SE for the NJ Central Named Region for 6 years, supporting large Enterprise accounts in NJ including Prudential, Johnson & Johnson, Bristol Meyers Squibb, Nabisco, Chubb Insurance, and American Reinsurance. Sheri graduated Summa Cum Laude from Westminster College in New Wilmington, PA, with a B.S. in Computer Science and Math. She also graduated Summa Cum Laude with a Masters degree with a concentration in finance from Monmouth University in NJ (formerly Monmouth College). Sheri is a CCIE and is also Cisco CIP Certified and Novell Certified. Sheri currently lives in Millstone, NJ.

Contents at a Glance

Part I   **IP QoS 3**

Chapter 1   Introducing IP Quality of Service 5

Chapter 2   Differentiated Services Architecture 21

Chapter 3   Network Boundary Traffic Conditioners: Packet Classifier, Marker, and Traffic Rate Management 33

Chapter 4   Per-Hop Behavior: Resource Allocation I 67

Chapter 5   Per-Hop Behavior: Resource Allocation II 105

Chapter 6   Per-Hop Behavior: Congestion Avoidance and Packet Drop Policy 127

Chapter 7   Integrated Services: RSVP 147

Part II   **Layer 2, MPLS QoS—Interworking with IP QoS 167**

Chapter 8   Layer 2 QoS: Interworking with IP QoS 169

Chapter 9   QoS in MPLS-Based Networks 211

Part III   **Traffic Engineering 245**

Chapter 10   MPLS Traffic Engineering 247

Part IV   **Appendixes 277**

Appendix A   Cisco Modular QoS Command-Line Interface 279

Appendix B   Packet Switching Mechanisms 287

Appendix C   Routing Policies 301

Appendix D   Real-time Transport Protocol (RTP) 313

Appendix E   General IP Line Efficiency Functions 315

Appendix F   Link-Layer Fragmentation and Interleaving 319

Appendix G   IP Precedence and DSCP Values 323

Index   327

Table of Contents

Part I   **IP QoS 3**

Chapter 1   Introducing IP Quality of Service 5

Levels of QoS   6

IP QoS History   8

Performance Measures   9
    Bandwidth   10
    Packet Delay and Jitter   10
    Packet Loss   11

QoS Functions   12
    Packet Classifier and Marker   12
    Traffic Rate Management   12
    Resource Allocation   12
    Congestion Avoidance and Packet Drop Policy   13
    QoS Signaling Protocol   13
    Switching   13
    Routing   13

Layer 2 QoS Technologies   14

Multiprotocol Label Switching   14

End-to-End QoS   15

Objectives   15

Audience   16

Scope and Limitations   16

Organization   17
    Part I   17
    Part II   17
    Part III   18
    Part IV   18

References   18

Chapter 2   Differentiated Services Architecture 21

Intserv Architecture   21

Diffserv Architecture   22
    Network Boundary Traffic Conditioners   25
    PHB   26

Resource Allocation Policy   28

Summary   30

References   31

Chapter 3   Network Boundary Traffic Conditioners: Packet Classifier, Marker, and Traffic Rate Management 33

Packet Classification   34

Packet Marking   34
IP Precedence   34
DSCP   36
The QoS Group   36
Case Study 3-1: Packet Classification and Marking Using IP Precedence   37
Case Study 3-2: Packet Classification and Marking Using QoS Groups   39
Case Study 3-3: Enforcing IP Precedence Setting   41

The Need for Traffic Rate Management   42
The Token Bucket Scheme   42

Traffic Policing   43
Case Study 3-4: Limiting a Particular Application's Traffic Rate at a Service Level   48
Case Study 3-5: Limiting Traffic Based on IP Precedence Values   49
Case Study 3-6: Subrate IP Services   50
Case Study 3-7: Web Hosting Services   51
Case Study 3-8: Preventing Denial-of-Service Attacks   51
Case Study 3-9: Enforcing Public Exchange Point Traffic   52

Traffic Shaping   53
Traffic Measuring Instrumentation   54
Case Study 3-10: Shaping Traffic to the Access Rate   56
Case Study 3-11: Shaping Incoming and Outgoing Traffic for a Host to a Certain Mean Rate   59
Case Study 3-12: Shaping Frame Relay Traffic on Receipt of BECNs   60

Summary   62

Frequently Asked Questions   63

References   64

Chapter 4   Per-Hop Behavior: Resource Allocation I 67

Scheduling for Quality of Service (QoS) Support   67
FIFO Queuing   68
The Max-Min Fair-Share Allocation Scheme   69
Generalized Processor Sharing   71

Sequence Number Computation-Based WFQ   72

Flow-Based WFQ   75
   WFQ Interaction with RSVP   79
   WFQ Implementation   79
   Case Study 4-1: Flow-Based WFQ   80
   Case Study 4-2: Bandwidth Allocation by Assigned Weights   82
   Case Study 4-3: WFQ Scheduling Among Voice and FTP Flow Packets   82

Flow-Based Distributed WFQ (DWFQ)   83
   Case Study 4-4: Flow-Based DWFQ   84

Class-Based WFQ   85
   Case Study 4-5: Higher Bandwidth Allocation for Critical Traffic   86
   Case Study 4-6: Higher Bandwidth Allocation Based on Input Interface   87
   Case Study 4-7: Bandwidth Assignment per ToS Class   88
   CBWFQ Without Modular CLI   89
   Case Study 4-8: Bandwidth Allocation Based on the QoS Group Classification Without
    Using Modular QoS CLI   91

Priority Queuing   91
   Case Study 4-9: IP Traffic Prioritization Based on IP Precedence   92
   Case Study 4-10: Packet Prioritization Based on Size   93
   Case Study 4-11: Packet Prioritization Based on Source Address   94

Custom Queuing   94
   How Byte Count Is Used in Custom Queuing   95
   Case Study 4-12: Minimum Interface Bandwidth for Different Protocols   95

Scheduling Mechanisms for Voice Traffic   98
   CBWFQ with a Priority Queue   98
   Case Study 4-13: Strict Priority Queue for Voice   100
   Custom Queuing with Priority Queues   100

Summary   101

Frequently Asked Questions   102

References   103

Chapter 5   Per-Hop Behavior: Resource Allocation II 105

Modified Weighted Round Robin (MWRR)   105
   An Illustration of MWRR Operation   106
   MWRR Implementation   112
   Case Study 5-1: Class-Based MWRR Scheduling   113

Modified Deficit Round Robin (MDRR)   114
   An MDRR Example   115

MDRR Implementation   119
    Case Study 5-2: Bandwidth Allocation and Minimum Jitter Configuration for Voice
    Traffic with Congestion Avoidance Policy   121

Summary   124

Frequently Asked Questions   124

References   124

Chapter 6   Per-Hop Behavior: Congestion Avoidance and Packet Drop Policy 127

TCP Slow Start and Congestion Avoidance   127

TCP Traffic Behavior in a Tail-Drop Scenario   129

RED—Proactive Queue Management for Congestion Avoidance   130
    The Average Queue Size Computation   131
    Packet Drop Probability   132

WRED   133
    WRED Implementation   133
    Case Study 6-1: Congestion Avoidance to Enhance Link Utilization by Using
     WRED   133
    Case 6-2: WRED Based on Traffic Classes Using Modular QoS CLI   135

Flow WRED   136
    Case Study 6-3: Congestion Avoidance for Nonadaptive Flows   138

ECN   139

SPD   139
    Case Study 6-4: Preventing Bad IP Packet Smurf Attacks by Using SPD   141

Summary   143

Frequently Asked Questions   144

References   145

Chapter 7   Integrated Services: RSVP 147

RSVP   147
    RSVP Operation   148
    RSVP Components   150
    RSVP Messages   151

Reservation Styles   152
    Shared Reservations   153

Service Types   155

Controlled Load   155
Guaranteed Bit Rate   155

RSVP Media Support   156

RSVP Scalability   156

Case Study 7-1: Reserving End-to-End Bandwidth for an Application Using RSVP   157

Case Study 7-2: RSVP for VoIP   162

Summary   163

Frequently Asked Questions   164

References   165

Part II   **Layer 2, MPLS QoS—Interworking with IP QoS 167**

Chapter 8   Layer 2 QoS: Interworking with IP QoS 169

ATM   169
ATM Cell Format   169
ATM QoS   172
ATM Service Classes   172
Cell Discard Strategies   173
VP Shaping   174
Case Study 8-1: A PVC with ABR Service   175
Case Study 8-2: VP Traffic Shaping   175

ATM Interworking with IP QoS   178
Case Study 8-3: Differentiated IP Packet Discards at ATM Edges   180
Case Study 8-4: Differentiated Services   183
Case Study 8-5: Setting an ATM CLP Bit Based on IP Precedence   185

Frame Relay   185
Frame Relay Congestion Control   186
Frame Relay Traffic Shaping (FRTS)   187
Frame Relay Fragmentation   190

Frame Relay Interworking with IP QoS   192
Case Study 8-6: Frame Relay Traffic Shaping with QoS Autosense   192
Case Study 8-7: Adaptive Traffic Shaping and BECN/FECN Integration   194
Case Study 8-8: Using Multiple PVCs to a Destination Based on Traffic Type   196
Case Study 8-9: Per-VC WFQ   198

Case Study 8-10: Mapping Between Frame Relay DE Bits and IP Precedence Bits   198
Case 8-11: Frame Relay Fragmentation   199

The IEEE 802.3 Family of LANs   200
Expedited Traffic Capability   200

Summary   206

Frequently Asked Questions   207

References   208

Chapter 9   QoS in MPLS-Based Networks 211

MPLS   211
Forwarding Component   212
Control Component   213
Label Encapsulation   216

MPLS with ATM   218

Case Study 9-1: Downstream Label Distribution   219

MPLS QoS   223

End-to-End IP QoS   225
Case Study 9-2: MPLS CoS   225
LER   227
LSR   227

MPLS VPN   227

Case Study 9-3: MPLS VPN   229

MPLS VPN QoS   237
Differentiated MPLS VPN QoS   237
Guaranteed QoS   238
RSVP at VPN Sites Only   239
RSVP at VPN Sites and Diff-Serv Across the Service Provider Backbone   240
End-to-End Guaranteed Bandwidth   240

Case Study 9-4: MPLS VPN QoS   240

Summary   241

Frequently Asked Questions   242

References   242

Part III   **Traffic Engineering 245**

Chapter 10   MPLS Traffic Engineering 247

The Layer 2 Overlay Model   247

RRR   248

TE Trunk Definition   251

TE Tunnel Attributes   251
  Bandwidth   251
  Setup and Holding Priorities   251
  Resource Class Affinity   252
  Path Selection Order   253
  Adaptability   253
  Resilience   253

Link Resource Attributes   253
  Available Bandwidth   253
  Resource Class   253

Distribution of Link Resource Information   254

Path Selection Policy   254

TE Tunnel Setup   255

Link Admission Control   256

TE Path Maintenance   256

TE-RSVP   256

IGP Routing Protocol Extensions   257
  IS-IS Modifications   258
  OSPF Modifications   258

TE Approaches   258

Case Study 10-1: MPLS TE Tunnel Setup and Operation   258

Summary   273

Frequently Asked Questions   274

References   275

Part IV   **Appendixes 277**

Appendix A   Cisco Modular QoS Command-Line Interface 279

Traffic Class Definition   280

Policy Definition   281

Policy Application   282
   Hierarchical Policies   283

Order of Policy Execution   284
   Inter-Policy Feature Ordering   284
   Intra-Feature Execution Order   284

Appendix B   Packet Switching Mechanisms 287

Process Switching   287

Route-Cache Forwarding   287

CEF   289
   CEF Advantages   289
   Distributed CEF (DCEF)   291
   Case Study B-1: Deploying CEF in a Backbone Router   291
   Route-Cache Switching and CEF Switching Compared   297

Summary   298

Appendix C   Routing Policies 301

Using QoS Policies to Make Routing Decisions   301
   QoS-Based Routing   301
   Policy-Based Routing   302
   Case Study C-1: Routing Based on IP Precedence   303
   Case Study C-2: Routing Based on Packet Size   305

QoS Policy Propagation Using BGP   306
   Case Study C-3: QoS for Incoming and Outgoing Traffic   307

Summary   310

References   311

Appendix D   Real-time Transport Protocol (RTP) 313

Reference   313

Appendix E   General IP Line Efficiency Functions 315

The Nagle Algorithm   315

Path MTU Discovery   315

TCP/IP Header Compression   316

RTP Header Compression   316

References   316

Appendix F   Link-Layer Fragmentation and Interleaving 319

Reference   321

Appendix G   IP Precedence and DSCP Values 323

Index   327

IP QoS

Chapter 1   Introducing IP Quality of Service

Chapter 2   Differentiated Services Architecture

Chapter 3   Network Boundary Traffic Conditioners: Packet Classifier, Marker, and Traffic Rate Management

Chapter 4   Per-Hop Behavior: Resource Allocation I

Chapter 5   Per-Hop Behavior: Resource Allocation II

Chapter 6   Per-Hop Behavior: Congestion Avoidance and Packet Drop Policy

Chapter 7   Integrated Services: RSVP

CHAPTER 1

Introducing IP Quality of Service

Service providers and enterprises used to build and support separate networks to carry their voice, video, mission-critical, and non-mission-critical traffic. There is a growing trend, however, toward convergence of all these networks into a single, packet-based Internet Protocol (IP) network.

The largest IP network is, of course, the global Internet. The Internet has grown exponentially during the past few years, as has its usage and the number of available Internet-based applications. As the Internet and corporate intranets continue to grow, applications other than traditional data, such as Voice over IP (VoIP) and video-conferencing, are envisioned. More and more users and applications are coming on the Internet each day, and the Internet needs the functionality to support both existing and emerging applications and services. Today, however, the Internet offers only *best-effort* service. A best-effort service makes no service guarantees regarding when or whether a packet is delivered to the receiver, though packets are usually dropped only during network congestion. (Best-effort service is discussed in more detail in the section "Levels of QoS," later in this chapter.)

In a network, packets are generally differentiated on a flow basis by the five flow fields in the IP packet header—source IP address, destination IP address, IP protocol field, source port, and destination port. An individual flow is made of packets going from an application on a source machine to an application on a destination machine, and packets belonging to a flow carry the same values for the five IP packet header flow fields.

To support voice, video, and data application traffic with varying service requirements from the network, the systems at the IP network's core need to differentiate and service the different traffic types based on their needs. With best-effort service, however, no differentiation is possible among the thousands of traffic flows existing in the IP network's core. Hence, no priorities or guarantees are provided for any application traffic. This essentially precludes an IP network's capability to carry traffic that has certain minimum network resource and service requirements with service guarantees. IP quality of service (QoS) is aimed at addressing this issue.

IP QoS functions are intended to deliver guaranteed as well as differentiated Internet services by giving network resource and usage control to the network operator. QoS is a set of service requirements to be met by the network in transporting a flow. QoS provides end-to-end service guarantees and policy-based control of an IP network's performance measures, such as resource allocation, switching, routing, packet scheduling, and packet drop mechanisms.

The following are some main IP QoS benefits:

- It enables networks to support existing and emerging multimedia service/application requirements. New applications such as Voice over IP (VoIP) have specific QoS requirements from the network.

- It gives the network operator control of network resources and their usage.

- It provides service guarantees and traffic differentiation across the network. It is required to converge voice, video, and data traffic to be carried on a single IP network.

- It enables service providers to offer premium services along with the present best-effort *Class of Service (CoS)*. A provider could rate its premium services to customers as Platinum, Gold, and Silver, for example, and configure the network to differentiate the traffic from the various classes accordingly.

- It enables application-aware networking, in which a network services its packets based on their application information within the packet headers.

- It plays an essential role in new network service offerings such as Virtual Private Networks (VPNs).

Levels of QoS

Traffic in a network is made up of flows originated by a variety of applications on end stations. These applications differ in their service and performance requirements. Any flow's requirements depend inherently on the application it belongs to. Hence, understanding the application types is key to understanding the different service needs of flows within a network.

The network's capability to deliver service needed by specific network applications with some level of control over performance measures—that is, bandwidth, delay/jitter, and loss—is categorized into three service levels:

- **Best-effort service**—Basic connectivity with no guarantee as to whether or when a packet is delivered to the destination, although a packet is usually dropped only when the router input or output buffer queues are exhausted.

  Best-effort service is not really a part of QoS because no service or delivery guarantees are made in forwarding best-effort traffic. This is the only service the Internet offers today.

Most data applications, such as File Transfer Protocol (FTP), work correctly with best-effort service, albeit with degraded performance. To function well, all applications require certain network resource allocations in terms of bandwidth, delay, and minimal packet loss.

- **Differentiated service**—In differentiated service, traffic is grouped into classes based on their service requirements. Each traffic class is differentiated by the network and serviced according to the configured QOS mechanisms for the class. This scheme for delivering QOS is often referred to as COS.

  Note that differentiated service doesn't give service guarantees per se. It only differentiates traffic and allows a preferential treatment of one traffic class over the other. For this reason, this service is also referred as *soft QOS*.

  This QoS scheme works well for bandwidth-intensive data applications. It is important that network control traffic is differentiated from the rest of the data traffic and prioritized so as to ensure basic network connectivity all the time.

- **Guaranteed service**—A service that requires network resource reservation to ensure that the network meets a traffic flow's specific service requirements.

  Guaranteed service requires prior network resource reservation over the connection path. Guaranteed service also is referred to as *hard QoS* because it requires rigid guarantees from the network.

  Path reservations with a granularity of a single flow don't scale over the Internet backbone, which services thousands of flows at any given time. Aggregate reservations, however, which call for only a minimum state of information in the Internet core routers, should be a scalable means of offering this service.

  Applications requiring such service include multimedia applications such as audio and video. Interactive voice applications over the Internet need to limit latency to 100 ms to meet human ergonomic needs. This latency also is acceptable to a large spectrum of multimedia applications. Internet telephony needs at a minimum an 8-Kbps bandwidth and a 100-ms round-trip delay. The network needs to reserve resources to be able to meet such guaranteed service requirements.

Layer 2 QoS refers to all the QoS mechanisms that either are targeted for or exist in the various link layer technologies. Chapter 8, "Layer 2 QoS: Interworking with IP QoS," covers Layer 2 QoS. Layer 3 QoS refers to QoS functions at the network layer, which is IP. Table 1-1 outlines the three service levels and their related enabling QoS functions at Layers 2 and 3. These QoS functions are discussed in detail in the rest of this book.

Table 1-1 *Service Levels and Enabling QoS Functions*

Service Levels	Enabling Layer 3 QoS	Enabling Layer 2 QoS
Best-effort	Basic connectivity	Asynchronous Transfer Mode (ATM), Unspecified Bit Rate (UBR), Frame Relay Committed Information Rate (CIR)=0
Differentiated	CoS Committed Access Rate (CAR), Weighted Fair Queuing (WFQ), Weighted Random Early Detection (WRED)	IEEE 802.1p
Guaranteed	Resource Reservation Protocol (RSVP)	Subnet Bandwidth Manager (SBM), ATM Constant Bit Rate (CBR), Frame Relay CIR

IP QoS History

IP QoS is not an afterthought. The Internet's founding fathers envisioned this need and provisioned a Type of Service (ToS) byte in the IP header to facilitate QoS as part of the initial IP specification. It described the purpose of the ToS byte as follows:

> The Type of Service provides an indication of the abstract parameters of the quality of service desired. These parameters are to be used to guide the selection of the actual service parameters when transmitting a datagram through the particular network.[1]

Until the late 1980s, the Internet was still within its academic roots and had limited applications and traffic running over it. Hence, ToS support wasn't necessarily important, and almost all IP implementations ignored the ToS byte. IP applications didn't specifically mark the ToS byte, nor did routers use it to affect the forwarding treatment given to an IP packet.

The importance of QoS over the Internet has grown with its evolution from its academic roots to its present commercial and popular stage. The Internet is based on a connectionless end-to-end packet service, which traditionally provided best-effort means of data transportation using the Transmission Control Protocol/Internet Protocol (TCP/IP) Suite. Although the connectionless design gives the Internet its flexibility and robustness, its packet dynamics also make it prone to congestion problems, especially at routers that connect networks of widely different bandwidths. The congestion collapse problem was discussed by John Nagle during the Internet's early growth phase in the mid-1980s[2].

The initial QoS function set was for Internet hosts. One major problem with expensive wide-area network (WAN) links is the excessive overhead due to small Transmission Control Protocol (TCP) packets created by applications such as telnet and rlogin. The Nagle algorithm, which solves this issue, is now supported by all IP host implementations[3]. The Nagle algorithm heralded the beginning of Internet QoS-based functionality in IP.

In 1986, Van Jacobson developed the next set of Internet QoS tools, the congestion avoidance mechanisms for end systems that are now required in TCP implementations. These mechanisms—slow start and congestion avoidance—have helped greatly in preventing a congestion collapse of the present-day Internet. They primarily make the TCP flows responsive to the congestion signals (dropped packets) within the network. Two additional mechanisms—fast retransmit and fast recovery—were added in 1990 to provide optimal performance during periods of packet loss[4].

Though QoS mechanisms in end systems are essential, they didn't complete the end-to-end QoS story until adequate mechanisms were provided within routers to transport traffic between end systems. Hence, around 1990 QoS's focus was on routers. Routers, which are limited to only first-in, first-out (FIFO) scheduling, don't offer a mechanism to differentiate or prioritize traffic within the packet-scheduling algorithm. FIFO queuing causes tail drops and doesn't protect well-behaving flows from misbehaving flows. WFQ, a packet scheduling algorithm[5], and WRED, a queue management algorithm[6], are widely accepted to fill this gap in the Internet backbone.

Internet QoS development continued with standardization efforts in delivering end-to-end QoS over the Internet. The Integrated Services (intserv) Internet Engineering Task Force (IETF) Working Group[7] aims to provide the means for applications to express end-to-end resource requirements with support mechanisms in routers and subnet technologies. RSVP is the signaling protocol for this purpose. The Intserv model requires per-flow states along the path of the connection, which doesn't scale in the Internet backbones, where thousands of flows exist at any time. Chapter 7, "Integrated Services: RSVP," provides a discussion on RSVP and the intserv service types.

The IP ToS byte hasn't been used much in the past, but it is increasingly used lately as a way to signal QoS. The ToS byte is emerging as the primary mechanism for delivering diffserv over the Internet, and for this purpose, the IETF differentiated services (diffserv) Working Group[8] is working on standardizing its use as a diffserv byte. Chapter 2, "Differentiated Services Architecture," discusses the diffserv architecture in detail.

Performance Measures

QoS deployment intends to provide a connection with certain performance bounds from the network. Bandwidth, packet delay and jitter, and packet loss are the common measures used to characterize a connection's performance within a network. They are described in the following sections.

Bandwidth

The term *bandwidth* is used to describe the rated throughput capacity of a given medium, protocol, or connection. It effectively describes the "size of the pipe" required for the application to communicate over the network.

Generally, a connection requiring guaranteed service has certain bandwidth requirements and wants the network to allocate a minimum bandwidth specifically for it. A digitized voice application produces voice as a 64-kbps stream. Such an application becomes nearly unusable if it gets less than 64 kbps from the network along the connection's path.

Packet Delay and Jitter

Packet delay, or *latency*, at each hop consists of serialization delay, propagation delay, and switching delay. The following definitions describe each delay type:

- **Serialization delay**—The time it takes for a device to clock a packet at the given output rate. Serialization delay depends on the link's bandwidth as well as the size of the packet being clocked. A 64-byte packet clocked at 3 Mbps, for example, takes about 171 µs to transmit. Notice that serialization delay depends on bandwidth: The same 64-byte packet at 19.2 kbps takes 26 ms. Serialization delay also is referred to as *transmission delay*.

- **Propagation delay**—The time it takes for a transmitted bit to get from the transmitter to a link's receiver. This is significant because it is, at best, a fraction of the speed of light. Note that this delay is a function of the distance and the media but not of the bandwidth. For WAN links, propagation delays of milliseconds are normal. Transcontinental U.S. propagation delay is in the order of 30 ms.

- **Switching delay**—The time it takes for a device to start transmitting a packet after the device receives the packet. This is typically less than 10 µs.

All packets in a flow don't experience the same delay in the network. The delay seen by each packet can vary based on transient network conditions.

If the network is not congested, queues will not build at routers, and serialization delay at each hop as well as propagation delay account for the total packet delay. This constitutes the minimum delay the network can offer. Note that serialization delays become insignificant compared to the propagation delays on fast link speeds.

If the network is congested, queuing delays will start to influence end-to-end delays and will contribute to the delay variation among the different packets in the same connection. The variation in packet delay is referred to as *packet jitter*.

Packet jitter is important because it estimates the maximum delays between packet reception at the receiver against individual packet delay. A receiver, depending on the application, can offset the jitter by adding a receive buffer that could store packets up to the jitter bound. Playback applications that send a continuous information stream—including applications such as interactive voice calls, videoconferencing, and distribution—fall into this category.

Figure 1-1 illustrates the impact of the three delay types on the total delay with increasing link speeds. Note that the serialization delay becomes minimal compared to propagation delay as the link's bandwidth increases. The switching delay is negligible if the queues are empty, but it can increase drastically as the number of packets waiting in the queue increases.

Figure 1-1   *Delay Components of a 1500-byte Packet on a Transcontinental U.S. Link with Increasing Bandwidths*

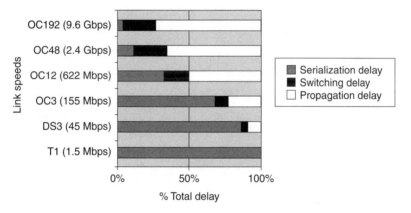

Packet Loss

Packet loss specifies the number of packets being lost by the network during transmission. Packet drops at network congestion points and corrupted packets on the transmission wire cause packet loss. Packet drops generally occur at congestion points when incoming packets far exceed the queue size limit at the output queue. They also occur due to insufficient input buffers on packet arrival. Packet loss is generally specified as a fraction of packets lost while transmitting a certain number of packets over some time interval.

Certain applications don't function well or are highly inefficient when packets are lost. Such loss-intolerant applications call for packet loss guarantees from the network.

Packet loss should be rare for a well-designed, correctly subscribed or under-subscribed network. It is also rare for guaranteed service applications for which the network has already reserved the required resources. Packet loss is mainly due to packet drops at network congestion points with fiber transmission lines, with a Bit Error Rate (BER) of 10E-9 being relatively loss-free. Packet drops, however, are a fact of life when transmitting best-effort traffic, although such drops are done only when necessary. Keep in mind that dropped packets waste network resources, as they already consumed certain network resources on their way to the loss point.

QoS Functions

This section briefly discusses the various QoS functions, their related features, and their benefits. The functions are discussed in further detail in the rest of the book.

Packet Classifier and Marker

Routers at the network's edge use a classifier function to identify packets belonging to a certain traffic class based on one or more TCP/IP header fields. A marker function is then used to color the classified traffic by setting either the IP precedence or the Differentiated Services Code Point (DSCP) field.

Chapter 3, "Network Boundary Traffic Conditioners: Packet Classifier, Marker, and Traffic Rate Management," offers more detail on these QoS functions.

Traffic Rate Management

Service providers use a policing function to meter the customer's traffic entering the network against the customer's traffic profile. At the same time, an enterprise accessing its service provider might need to use a traffic shaping function to meter all its traffic and send it out at a constant rate such that all its traffic passes through the service provider's policing functions. *Token bucket* is the common traffic-metering scheme used to measure traffic.

Chapter 3 offers more details on this QoS function.

Resource Allocation

FIFO scheduling is the widely deployed, traditional queuing mechanism within routers and switches on the Internet today. Though it is simple to implement, FIFO queuing has some fundamental problems in providing QoS. It provides no way to enable delay-sensitive traffic to be prioritized and moved to the head of the queue. All traffic is treated exactly the same, with no scope for traffic differentiation or service differentiation among traffic.

For the scheduling algorithm to deliver QoS, at a minimum it needs to be able to differentiate among the different packets in the queue and know the service level of each packet. A scheduling algorithm determines which packet goes next from a queue. How often the flow packets are served determines the bandwidth or resource allocation for the flow.

Chapter 4, "Per-Hop Behavior: Resource Allocation I," covers QoS features in this section in detail.

Congestion Avoidance and Packet Drop Policy

In traditional FIFO queuing, queue management is done by dropping all incoming packets after the packets in the queue reach the maximum queue length. This queue management technique is called *tail drop*, which signals congestion only when the queue is completely full. In this case, no active queue management is done to avoid congestion, or to reduce the queue sizes to minimize queuing delays. An active queue management algorithm enables routers to detect congestion before the queue overflows.

Chapter 6, "Per-Hop Behavior: Congestion Avoidance and Packet Drop Policy," discusses the QoS features in this section.

QoS Signaling Protocol

RSVP is part of the IETF intserv architecture for providing end-to-end QoS over the Internet. It enables applications to signal per-flow QoS requirements to the network. Service parameters are used to specifically quantify these requirements for admission control.

Chapter 7 offers more detail on these QoS functions.

Switching

A router's primary function is to quickly and efficiently switch all incoming traffic to the correct output interface and next-hop address based on the information in the forwarding table. The traditional cache-based forwarding mechanism, although efficient, has scaling and performance problems because it is traffic-driven and can lead to increased cache maintenance and poor switching performance during network instability.

The topology-based forwarding method solves the problems involved with cache-based forwarding mechanisms by building a forwarding table that exactly matches the router's routing table. The topology-based forwarding mechanism is referred to as Cisco Express Forwarding (CEF) in Cisco routers. Appendix B, "Packet Switching Mechanisms," offers more detail on these QoS functions.

Routing

Traditional routing is destination-based only and routes packets on the shortest path derived in the routing table. This is not flexible enough for certain network scenarios. Policy routing is a QoS function that enables the user to change destination-based routing to routing based on various user-configurable packet parameters.

Current routing protocols provide shortest-path routing, which selects routes based on a metric value such as administrative cost, weight, or hop count. Packets are routed based on the routing table, without any knowledge of the flow requirements or the resource availability along the route. QoS routing is a routing mechanism that takes into account a flow's QoS requirements and has some knowledge of the resource availability in the network in its route selection criteria.

Appendix C, "Routing Policies," offers more detail on these QoS functions.

Layer 2 QoS Technologies

Support for QoS is available in some Layer 2 technologies, including ATM, Frame Relay, Token Ring, and recently in the Ethernet family of switched LANs. As a connection-oriented technology, ATM offers the strongest support for QoS and could provide a specific QoS guarantee per connection. Hence, a node requesting a connection can request a certain QoS from the network and can be assured that the network delivers that QoS for the life of the connection. Frame Relay networks provide connections with a minimum CIR, which is enforced during congestion periods. Token Ring and a more recent Institute of Electrical and Electronic Engineers (IEEE) standard, 802.1p, have mechanisms enabling service differentiation.

If the QoS need is just within a subnetwork or a WAN cloud, these Layer 2 technologies, especially ATM, can provide the answer. But ATM or any other Layer 2 technology will never be pervasive enough to be the solution on a much wider scale, such as on the Internet.

Multiprotocol Label Switching

The Multiprotocol Label Switching (MPLS) Working Group[9] at the IETF is standardizing a base technology for using a label-swapping forwarding paradigm (label switching) in conjunction with network-layer routing. The group aims to implement that technology over various link-level technologies, including Packet-over-Sonet, Frame Relay, ATM, and 10 Mbps/100 Mbps/1 Gbps Ethernet. The MPLS standard is based mostly on Cisco's tag switching [11].

MPLS also offers greater flexibility in delivering QoS and traffic engineering. It uses labels to identify particular traffic that needs to receive specific QoS and to provide forwarding along an explicit path different from the one constructed by destination-based forwarding. MPLS, MPLS-based VPNs, and MPLS traffic engineering are aimed primarily at service provider networks. MPLS and MPLS QoS are discussed in Chapter 9, "QoS in MPLS-Based Networks." Chapter 10, "MPLS Traffic Engineering," explores traffic engineering using MPLS.

End-to-End QoS

Layer 2 QoS technologies offer solutions on a smaller scope only and can't provide end-to-end QoS simply because the Internet or any large scale IP network is made up of a large group of diverse Layer 2 technologies. In a network, end-to-end connectivity starts at Layer 3 and, hence, only a network layer protocol, which is IP in the TCP/IP-based Internet, can deliver end-to-end QoS.

The Internet is made up of diverse link technologies and physical media. IP, being the layer providing end-to-end connectivity, needs to map its QoS functions to the link QoS mechanisms, especially of switched networks, to facilitate end-to-end QoS.

Some service provider backbones are based on switched networks such as ATM or Frame Relay. In this case, you need to have ATM and Frame Relay QoS-to-IP interworking to provide end-to-end QoS. This enables the IP QoS request to be honored within the ATM or the frame cloud.

Switched LANs are an integral part of Internet service providers (ISPs) that provide Web-hosting services and corporate intranets. IEEE 802.1p and IEEE 802.1Q offer priority-based traffic differentiation in switched LANs. Interworking these protocols with IP is essential to making QoS end to end. Chapter 8 discusses IP QoS interworking with switches, backbones, and LANs in detail.

MPLS facilitates IP QoS delivery and provides extensive traffic engineering capabilities that help provide MPLS-based VPNs. For end-to-end QoS, IP QoS needs to interwork with the QoS mechanisms in MPLS and MPLS-based VPNs. Chapter 9 focuses on this topic.

Objectives

This book is intended to be a valuable technical resource for network managers, architects, and engineers who want to understand and deploy IP QoS-based services within their network. IP QoS functions are indispensable in today's scalable, IP network designs, which are intended to deliver guaranteed and differentiated Internet services by giving control of the network resources and its usage to the network operator.

This book's goal is to discuss IP QoS architectures and their associated QoS functions that enable end-to-end QoS in corporate intranets, service provider networks, and, in general, the Internet. On the subject of IP QoS architectures, this book's primary focus is on the diffserv architecture. This book also focuses on ATM, Frame Relay, IEEE 802.1p, IEEE 802.1Q, MPLS, and MPLS VPN QoS technologies and on how they interwork with IP QoS in providing an end-to-end service. Another important topic of this book is MPLS traffic engineering.

This book provides complete coverage of IP QoS and all related technologies, complete with case studies. Readers will gain a thorough understanding in the following areas to help deliver and deploy IP QoS and MPLS-based traffic engineering:

- Fundamentals and the need for IP QoS

- The diffserv QoS architecture and its enabling QoS functionality

- The Intserv QoS model and its enabling QoS functions

- ATM, Frame Relay, and IEEE 802.1p/802.1Q QoS technologies—Interworking with IP QoS

- MPLS and MPLS VPN QoS—Interworking with IP QoS

- MPLS traffic engineering

- Routing policies, general IP QoS functions, and other miscellaneous QoS information

QoS applies to any IP-based network. As such, this book targets all IP networks—corporate intranets, service provider networks, and the Internet.

Audience

The book is written for internetworking professionals who are responsible for designing and maintaining IP services for corporate intranets and for service provider network infrastructures. If you are a network engineer, architect, planner, designer, or operator who has a rudimentary knowledge of QoS technologies, this book will provide you with practical insights on what you need to consider to design and implement varying degrees of QoS in the network.

This book also includes useful information for consultants, systems engineers, and sales engineers who design IP networks for clients. The information in this book covers a wide audience because incorporating some measure of QoS is an integral part of any network design process.

Scope and Limitations

Although the book attempts to comprehensively cover IP QoS and Cisco's QoS functionality, a few things are outside this book's scope. For example, it doesn't attempt to cover Cisco platform architecture information that might be related to QoS. Although it attempts to keep the coverage generic such that it applies across the Cisco platforms, some features relevant to specific platforms are highlighted because the current QoS offerings are not truly consistent across all platforms.

One of the goals is to keep the coverage generic and up-to-date so that it remains relevant for the long run. However, QoS in general and Cisco QoS features in particular, are seeing a lot of new developments, and there is always some scope for a few details to change here and there as time passes.

The case studies in this book are designed to discuss the application and provide some configuration details on enabling QoS functionality to help the reader implement QoS in his network. It is not meant to replace the general Cisco documentation. Cisco documentation is still the best resource for complete details on a particular QoS configuration command.

The case studies in this book are based on a number of different IOS versions. In general, most case studies are based on 12.0(6)S or a more recent 12.0S IOS version unless otherwise noted. In case of the MPLS case studies, 12.0(8)ST or a more recent 12.0ST IOS version is used.

Organization

This book consists of four parts: Part I, "IP QoS," focuses on IP QoS architectures and the QoS functions enabling them. Part II, "Layer 2, MPLS QoS—Interworking with IP QoS," lists the QoS mechanisms in ATM, Frame Relay, Ethernet, MPLS, and MPLS VPN and discusses how they map with IP QoS. Part III, "Traffic Engineering," discusses traffic engineering using MPLS. Finally, Part IV, "Appendixes," discusses the modular QoS command-line interface and miscellaneous QoS functions and provides some useful reference material.

Most chapters include a case study section to help in implementation, as well as a question and answer section.

Part I

This part of the book discusses the IP QoS architectures and their enabling functions. Chapter 2 introduces the two IP QoS architectures: diffserv and intserv, and goes on to discuss the diffserv architecture.

Chapters 3, 4, 5, and 6 discuss the different functions that enable diffserv architecture. Chapter 3, for instance, discusses the QoS functions that condition the traffic at the network boundary to facilitate diffserv within the network. Chapters 4 and 5 discuss packet scheduling mechanisms that provide minimum bandwidth guarantees for traffic. Chapter 6 focuses on the active queue management techniques that proactively drop packets signaling congestion. Finally, Chapter 7 discusses the RSVP protocol and its two integrated service types.

Part II

This section of the book, comprising Chapters 8 and 9, discusses ATM, Frame Relay, IEEE 802.1p, IEEE 802.1Q, MPLS, and MPLS VPN QoS technologies and how they interwork to provide an end-to-end IP QoS.

Part III

Chapter 10, the only chapter in Part III, talks about the need for traffic engineering and discusses MPLS traffic engineering operation.

Part IV

This part of the book has useful information that didn't fit well with previous sections but still is relevant in providing IP QoS.

Appendix A, "Cisco Modular QoS Command-Line Interface," details the new user interface that enables flexible and modular QoS configuration.

Appendix B, "Packet Switching Mechanisms," introduces the various packet-switching mechanisms available on Cisco platforms. It compares the switching mechanisms and recommends CEF, which also is a required packet-switching mechanism for certain QoS features.

Appendix C, "Routing Policies," discusses QoS routing, policy-based routing, and QoS Policy Propagation using Border Gateway Protocol (QPPB).

Appendix D, "Real-Time Transport Protocol (RTP)," talks about the transport protocol used to carry real-time packetized audio and video traffic.

Appendix E, "General IP Line Efficiency Functions," talks about some IP functions that help improve available bandwidth.

Appendix F, "Link Layer Fragmentation and Interleaving," discusses fragmentation and interleaving functionality with the Multilink Point-to-Point protocol.

Appendix G, "IP Precedence and DSCP Values," tabulates IP precedence and DSCP values. It also shows how IP precedence and DSCP values are mapped to each other.

References

[1] RFC 791: "Internet Protocol Specification," J. Postel, 1981

[2] RFC 896: "Congestion Control in IP/TCP Internetworks," J. Nagle, 1984

[3] RFC 1122: "Requirements for Internet Hosts—Communication Layers," R. Braden, 1989

[4] RFC 2001: "TCP Slow Start, Congestion Avoidance, Fast Retransmit, and Fast Recovery Algorithms," W. Stevens, 1997

[5] S. Floyd and V. Jacobson. "Random Early Detection Gateways for Congestion Avoidance." *IEEE/ACM Transactions on Networking*, August 1993

[6] A. Demers, S. Keshav, and S. Shenkar. "Design and Analysis of a Fair Queuing Algorithm." *Proceedings of ACM SIGCOMM '89*, Austin, TX, September 1989

[7] IETF Intserv Working Group, www.ietf.org/html.charters/intserv-charter.html

[8] IETF DiffServ Working Group, www.ietf.org/html.charters/diffserv-charter.html

[9] IETF MPLS Working Group, www.ietf.org/html.charters/mpls-charter.html

CHAPTER 2

Differentiated Services Architecture

The aim of IP Quality of Service (QoS) is to deliver guaranteed and differentiated services on the Internet or any IP-based network. Guaranteed and differentiated services provide different levels of QoS, and each represents an architectural model for delivering QoS.

This chapter primarily focuses on Differentiated Services (diffserv) architecture for delivering QoS in the Internet. The other architectural model, Integrated Services (intserv) is introduced. Intserv is discussed in Chapter 7, "Integrated Services: RSVP." An operational QoS model for a network node is also presented.

Intserv Architecture

The Internet Engineering Task Force (IETF) set up the intserv Working Group (WG) in 1994 to expand the Internet's service model to better meet the needs of emerging, diverse voice/video applications. It aims to clearly define the new enhanced Internet service model as well as to provide the means for applications to express end-to-end resource requirements with support mechanisms in routers and subnet technologies. It follows the goal of managing those flows separately that requested specific QoS.

Two services—guaranteed[1] and controlled load[2]—are defined for this purpose. *Guaranteed service* provides deterministic delay guarantees, whereas *controlled load service* provides a network service close to that provided by a best-effort network under lightly loaded conditions. Both services are discussed in detail in Chapter 7.

Resource Reservation Protocol (RSVP) is suggested as the signaling protocol that delivers end-to-end service requirements[3].

The intserv model requires per-flow guaranteed QoS on the Internet. With the thousands of flows existing on the Internet today, the amount of state information required in the routers can be enormous. This can create scaling problems, as the state information increases as the number of flows increases. This makes intserv hard to deploy on the Internet.

In 1998, the diffserv Working Group was formed under IETF. Diffserv is a bridge between intserv's guaranteed QoS requirements and the best-effort service offered by the Internet today. Diffserv provides traffic differentiation by classifying traffic into a few classes, with relative service priority among the traffic classes.

Diffserv Architecture

The diffserv approach[4] to providing QoS in networks employs a small, well-defined set of building blocks from which you can build a variety of services. Its aim is to define the differentiated services (DS) byte, the Type of Service (ToS) byte from the Internet Protocol (IP) Version 4 header and the Traffic Class byte from IP Version 6, and mark the standardized DS byte of the packet such that it receives a particular forwarding treatment, or per-hop behavior (PHB), at each network node.

The diffserv architecture provides a framework[5] within which service providers can offer customers a range of network services, each differentiated based on performance. A customer can choose the performance level needed on a packet-by-packet basis by simply marking the packet's Differentiated Services Code Point (DSCP) field to a specific value. This value specifies the PHB given to the packet within the service provider network. Typically, the service provider and customer negotiate a profile describing the rate at which traffic can be submitted at each service level. Packets submitted in excess of the agreed profile might not be allotted the requested service level.

The diffserv architecture only specifies the basic mechanisms on ways you can treat packets. You can build a variety of services by using these mechanisms as building blocks. A service defines some significant characteristic of packet transmission, such as throughput, delay, jitter, and packet loss in one direction along a path in a network. In addition, you can characterize a service in terms of the relative priority of access to resources in a network. After a service is defined, a PHB is specified on all the network nodes of the network offering this service, and a DSCP is assigned to the PHB. A PHB is an externally observable forwarding behavior given by a network node to all packets carrying a specific DSCP value. The traffic requiring a specific service level carries the associated DSCP field in its packets.

All nodes in the diffserv domain observe the PHB based on the DSCP field in the packet. In addition, the network nodes on the diffserv domain's boundary carry the important function of conditioning the traffic entering the domain. Traffic conditioning involves functions such as packet classification and traffic policing and is typically carried out on the input interface of the traffic arriving into the domain. Traffic conditioning plays a crucial role in engineering traffic carried within a diffserv domain, such that the network can observe the PHB for all its traffic entering the domain.

The diffserv architecture is illustrated in Figure 2-1. The two major functional blocks in this architecture are shown in Table 2-1.

Figure 2-1 *Diffserv Overview*

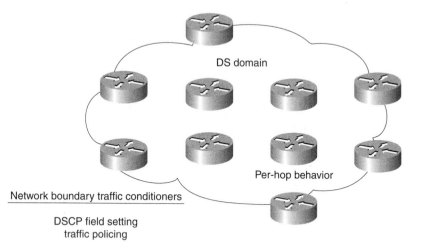

Table 2-1 *Functional Blocks in the diffserv Architecture*

Functional Blocks	Location	Enabling Functions	Action
Traffic Conditioners	Typically, on the input interface on the diffserv domain boundary router	Packet Classification, Traffic Shaping, and Policing *(Chapter 3)*	Polices incoming traffic and sets the DSCP field based on the traffic profile
PHB	All routers in the entire diffserv domain	Resource Allocation *(Chapters 4 and 5)* Packet Drop Policy *(Chapter 6)*	PHB applied to packets based on service characteristic defined by DSCP

Apart from these two functional blocks, resource allocation policy plays an important role in defining the policy for admission control, ratio of resource overbooking, and so on.

NOTE Cisco introduced modular QoS command-line interface (CLI) (discussed in Appendix C, "Routing Policies") to provide a clean separation and modular configuration of the different enabling QoS functions.

A general QoS operational model is shown in Figure 2-2.

Figure 2-2 *General QoS Operational Model*

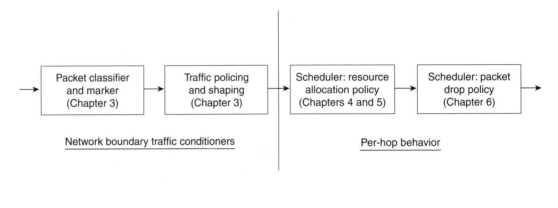

DSCP

The IETF diffserv group is in the process of standardizing an effort that enables users to mark 6 bits of the ToS byte in the IP header with a DSCP. The lowest-order 2 bits are currently unused (CU). DSCP is an extension to 3 bits used by IP precedence. Like IP precedence, you can use DSCP to provide differential treatment to packets marked appropriately. Figure 2-3 shows the ToS byte[6]. The ToS byte is renamed the DS byte with the standardization of the DSCP field. Figure 2-4 shows the DS byte.

Figure 2-3 *ToS Byte as of RFC 1349*

IP precedence: 3 bits (P2-P0)
Type of service (ToS): 4 bits (T3-T0)
Currently unused (CU): 1 bit

Figure 2-4 *DS Byte*

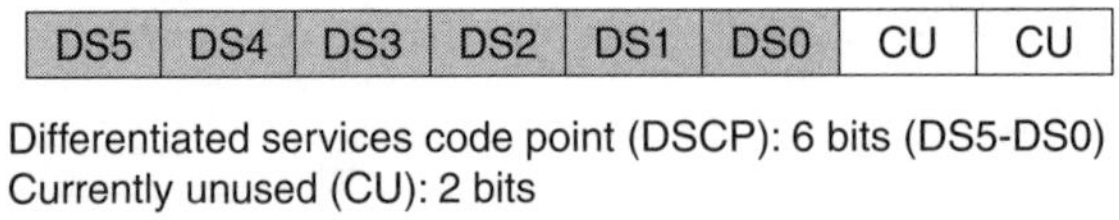

| DS5 | DS4 | DS3 | DS2 | DS1 | DS0 | CU | CU |

Differentiated services code point (DSCP): 6 bits (DS5-DS0)
Currently unused (CU): 2 bits

The DSCPs defined[1] thus far by the IETF Working Group are as follows:

— **Default DSCP**—It is defined to be 000 000.

— **Class Selector DSCPs**—They are defined to be backward-compatible with IP precedence and are tabulated in Table 2-2.

Table 2-2   *Class Selector DSCP*

Class Selectors	DSCP
Precedence 1	001 000
Precedence 2	010 000
Precedence 3	011 000
Precedence 4	100 000
Precedence 5	101 000
Precedence 6	110 000
Precedence 7	111 000

— **Expedited Forwarding (EF) PHB**—It defines premium service. Recommended DSCP is 101110.

— **Assured Forwarding (AF) PHB**—It defines four service levels, with each service level having three drop precedence levels. As a result, AF PHB recommends 12 code points, as shown in Table 2-3.

Table 2-3   *AF PHB*

Drop Precedence	Class 1	Class 2	Class 3	Class 4
Low	001010	010010	011010	100010
Medium	001100	010100	011100	100100
High	001110	010110	011110	100110

Network Boundary Traffic Conditioners

Traffic conditioners are various QoS functions needed on a network boundary. The edge functions classify or mark traffic by setting the DSCP field and monitor incoming traffic into the network for profile compliance.

DSCP is the field indicating what treatment the packet should receive in a diffserv domain. The function can be that of packet classifier, DSCP marker, or traffic metering function, with either the shaper or dropper action. These functions are described in the following sections; however, they are more fully discussed in Chapter 3, "Network Boundary Traffic Conditioners: Packet Classifier, Marker, and Traffic Rate Management."

Classifier

The classifier selects a packet in a traffic stream based on the content of some portion of the packet header. The most common way to classify traffic is based on the DSCP field, but you can classify traffic based on the other fields in the packet headers. This function identifies a packet's traffic class.

Marker

This function helps write/rewrite the DSCP field of a packet based on its traffic class.

Metering

The metering function checks compliance to traffic profile, based on a traffic descriptor such as a token bucket, and passes the result to the marker function and either a shaper or dropper function to trigger particular action for in-profile and out-of-profile packets.

Shaper

The shaper function delays traffic by buffering some packets so that they comply with the profile. This action is also referred to as traffic shaping.

Dropper

The dropper function drops all traffic that doesn't comply with the traffic profile. This action is also referred to as traffic policing.

PHB

Network nodes with diffserv support use the DSCP field in the IP header to select a specific PHB for a packet. A PHB is a description of the externally observable forwarding behavior of a diffserv node applied to a set of packets with the same DSCP.

You can define a PHB in terms of its resource priority relative to other PHBs, or to some observable traffic service characteristics, such as packet delay, loss, or jitter. You can view a PHB as a black box, as it defines some externally observable forwarding behavior without mandating a particular implementation.

In a diffserv network, best-effort behavior can be viewed as the default PHB. Diffserv recommends specific DSCP values for each PHB, but a network provider can choose to use a different DSCP than the recommended values in his or her network. The recommended DSCP for best-effort behavior is 000000.

The PHB of a specific traffic class depends on a number of factors:

- **Arrival rate or load for the traffic class**—This is controlled by the traffic conditioning at the network boundary.

- **Resource allocation for the traffic class**—This is controlled by the resource allocation on the nodes in the diffserv domain. Resource allocation in the network nodes is discussed in Chapter 4, "Per-Hop Behavior: Resource Allocation I," and Chapter 5, "Per-Hop Behavior: Resource Allocation II."

- **Traffic loss**—This depends on the packet discard policy on the nodes in the diffserv domain. This function is covered in Chapter 6, "Per-Hop Behavior: Congestion Avoidance and Packet Drop Policy."

Two PHBs, EF and AF, are standardized. They are discussed in the following sections.

EF PHB

You can use the EF PHB to build a low-loss, low-latency, low-jitter, assured-bandwidth, end-to-end service through diffserv domains.[8] EF PHB targets applications such as Voice over IP (VoIP) and video conferencing, and services such as virtual leased line, as the service looks like a point-to-point connection for a diffserv network's end nodes. Such service is also often termed as *premium service*.

The main contributors to high packet delays and packet jitter are queuing delays caused by large, accumulated queues. Such queues are typical at network congestion points. Network congestion occurs when the arrival rate of packets exceeds their departure rate. You can essentially eliminate queuing delays if the maximum arrival rate is less than the minimal departure rate. The EF service sets the departure rate, whereas you can control the traffic arrival rate at the node by using appropriate traffic conditioners at the network boundary.

An EF PHB needs to assure that the traffic sees no or minimal queues and, hence, needs to configure a departure rate for traffic that is equal to or more than the packet arrival rate. The departure rate or bandwidth should be independent of the other traffic at any time. The packet arrival and departure rates are typically measured at intervals equal to the time it takes for a link's maximum transmission unit (MTU)-sized packet to be transmitted.

A router can allocate resources for a certain departure rate on an interface by using different EF functionality implementations. Packet scheduling techniques—such as Class-Based Weighted Fair Queuing (CBWFQ), Weighted Round Robin (WRR), and Deficit Round Robin (DRR)—provide this functionality when the EF traffic can be carried over a highly weighted queue; that is, a weight that allocates a much higher rate to EF traffic than the actual EF traffic arrival rate. Further, you can modify these scheduling techniques to include a priority queue to carry EF traffic. The scheduling techniques are discussed in detail in Chapter 5.

When EF traffic is implemented using a priority queue, it is important to ensure that a busy EF priority queue does not potentially starve the remaining traffic queues beyond a certain configurable limit. To alleviate this problem, a user can set up a maximum rate against which the traffic serviced by the priority queue is policed. If the traffic exceeds the configured rate limit, all excess EF traffic is dropped. The network boundary traffic conditioners should be configured such that the EF traffic never exceeds its maximum configured rate at any hop in the network.

The recommended DSCP to be used for EF traffic in the network is 101110.

AF PHB

AF PHB[9] is a means for a service provider to offer different levels of forwarding assurances for IP packets received from a customer diffserv domain. It is suitable for most Transmission Control Protocol (TCP)-based applications.

An AF PHB provides differentiated service levels among the four AF traffic classes. Each AF traffic class is serviced in its own queue, enabling independent capacity management for the four traffic classes. Within each AF class are three drop precedence levels (Low, Medium, and High) for Random Early Detection (RED)-like queue management.

Resource Allocation Policy

The last section discussed the defined diffserv PHBs in a network. How is the traffic conditioned at the edge and the resources allocated in the network to achieve the desired PHB? Three solutions are suggested: network provisioning, signaled QoS, and policy manager.

Network Provisioning

One resource allocation solution is to provision resources within the network using heuristic methods or systematic modeling techniques. This method can work only in a small network environment where the QoS policies and network traffic profile don't change often.

Signaled QoS

In this method, applications signal QoS requests using a signaling protocol such as RSVP. For RSVP, the diffserv domain is treated as another link in the network for admission control. QoSes are mapped between RSVP and diffserv classes. You can map RSVP guaranteed service to diffserv EF service, for example.

Signaled QoS can be a scalable solution in a large-scale network environment because RSVP is run only at the network edges with diffserv used in the network core, as shown in Figure 2-5. Mapping between RSVP reservation and a diffserv class happens at the edge of the diffserv network. With widespread RSVP support (for instance, the Microsoft Windows 2000 operating system supports RSVP), policy-aware applications at the network edges can use RSVP to signal QoS across the network without any scalability concerns. The solution suits well in some large-scale enterprise networks.

Figure 2-5   *RSVP Signaling Across a Differentiated Services Network*

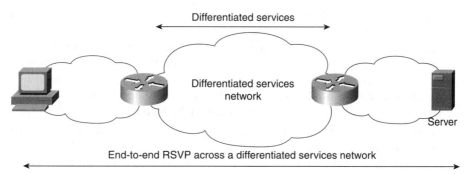

RSVP can scale well to support a few thousand per-flow sessions running in parallel. In addition, work is ongoing to provide aggregated RSVP. Multiple RSVP reservations are aggregated into a single aggregate reservation for large-scale RSVP deployment across a core network backbone that requires topology-aware admission control. Aggregated RSVP reservation is a fat, slowly adjusting reservation state that results in a reduced state signaling information in the network core. As a normal RSVP reservation, you can map the aggregate reservation to a diffserv class.

QoS Policy Manager

The policy definition determines the QoS applied on a traffic flow. The policy identifies the critical application traffic in the network and specifies its QoS level. Policy is simply the configuration needed in all the individual network nodes to enable QoS. How does a QoS node get its policy?

In simple terms, a network engineer can configure the policies by making changes to a router's configuration. On a large-scale network, however, the process becomes tedious and unmanageable. To deliver end-to-end QoS on a large-scale network, the policies applied across all the individual nodes in the network should be consistent. As such, a centralized policy manager to define policies makes the task less daunting. This policy manager can distribute the policy to all the network devices.

Common Open Policy Service (COPS) is an IETF protocol for distributing policy. In COPS terminology, the centralized policy server is called the Policy Decision Point (PDP). The network node implementing or enforcing the policy is called the Policy Enforcement Point (PEP). The PDP uses the COPS protocol for downloading the policies into the PEPs in the network. A PEP device can generate a message informing the PDP if it cannot implement a policy that it was given by PDP.

IP Precedence Versus DSCP

As discussed in this chapter, diffserv architecture needs traffic conditioners at the network boundary and resource allocation and packet discard functions in the network core to provide EF and AF services. Because DSCP field definitions were not fully clear until recently, the diffserv architecture was initially supported using the 3-bit IP precedence because historically, the IP precedence field is used to mark QoS or precedence in IP packets. Cisco IOS is fully aligned with the diffserv architecture and provides all required network edge and core QoS functions based on the 3-bit IP precedence field.

Both 3-bit IP precedence and 6-bit DSCP fields are used in exactly the same purpose in a diffserv network: for marking packets at the network edge and triggering specific packet queuing/discard behavior in the network. Further, the DSCP field definition is backward-compatible with the IP precedence values. Hence, DSCP field support doesn't require any change in the existing basic functionality and architecture. Soon, all IP QoS functions will support the DSCP field along with IP precedence.

Cisco introduced modular QoS CLI to provide a clean separation and modular configuration of the different enabling QoS functions. Modular QoS CLI is discussed in Appendix C. DSCP support for the various QoS functions is part of the modular QoS architecture.

Summary

Two Internet QoS architectures, intserv and diffserv, are introduced in this chapter. intserv architecture is defined to enable applications to request end-to-end network resource requirements. RSVP is suggested as a signaling protocol to request end-to-end resource requirements. This architecture can run into scalability issues in large networks, especially on the Internet, where the number of traffic flows can run in the order of tens of thousands. Intserv is discussed in detail in Chapter 7.

The chapter focuses on the diffserv architecture. Diffserv defines the architecture for implementing scalable service differentiation on the Internet. Diffserv uses the newly standardized DSCP field in the IP header to mark the QoS required by a packet, and a diffserv-enabled network delivers the packet with a PHB indicated by the DSCP field. Traffic is policed and marked appropriately at the edge of the diffserv-enabled network. A PHB is an externally observable forwarding behavior given by a network node to all packets carrying a specific DSCP value. You can specify PHBs in terms of their relative priority in access to resources, or in terms of their relative traffic performance characteristics. Two PHBs, EF and AF, are defined. EF is targeted at real-time applications, such as VoIP. AF provides different forwarding assurance levels for packets based on their DSCP field.

COPS is a new IETF protocol for distributing QoS policy information across the network.

References

[1] "Specification of the Controlled-Load Network Element Service," J. Wroclawski, RFC 2211.

[2] "Specification of Guaranteed Quality of Service," S. Shenker, C. Partridge, R. Guerin, RFC 2212.

[3] "The Use of RSVP with IETF Integrated Services," J. Wroclawski, RFC 2210.

[4] IETF Differentiated Services Working Group.

[5] "Type of Service in the Internet Protocol Suite," P. Almquist, RFC 1349.

[6] "A Framework for Differentiated Services," Y. Bernet, and others, Internet Draft.

[7] "Definition of the Differentiated Services Field (DS Field) in the IPv4 and IPv6 Headers," K. Nichols, and others, RFC 2474.

[8] Expedited Forwarding (EF) PHB. RFC2598.txt.

[9] Assured Forwarding (AF) PHB. RFC2597.txt.

Network Boundary Traffic Conditioners: Packet Classifier, Marker, and Traffic Rate Management

Traffic conditioning functions at the network boundary are vital to delivering differentiated services within a network domain. These functions provide packet classifier, marker, and traffic rate management.

In a network, packets are generally differentiated on a flow basis by the five flow fields in the Internet Protocol (IP) packet header: source IP address; destination IP address; IP protocol field; and source and destination ports. An individual flow is made of packets going from an application on a source machine to an application on a destination machine, and packets belonging to a flow carry the same values for the five packet header flow fields. Quality of service (QoS) applied on an individual flow basis, however, is not scalable because the number of flows can be large. So, routers at the network boundary perform classifier functions to identify packets belonging to a certain traffic class based on one or more Transmission Control Protocol/Internet Protocol (TCP/IP) header fields. A marker function is used to color the classified traffic by setting either the IP Precedence or the Differentiated Services Code Point (DSCP) field. Within the network core, you can apply a per-hop behavior (PHB) to the packets based on either the IP Precedence or the DSCP field marked in the packet header.

Another important traffic conditioner at the network boundary is traffic rate management. It enables a service provider to meter the customer's traffic entering the network against the customer's traffic profile using a policing function. Conversely, an enterprise accessing its service provider can meter all its traffic to shape the traffic and send out at a constant rate such that all its traffic passes through the service provider's policing functions.

Network boundary traffic conditioners are essential to delivering differentiated services in a network.

Packet Classification

Packet classification is a means of identifying packets to be of a certain class based on one or more fields in a packet. The identification function can range from straightforward to complicated. The different classification support types include:

- IP flow identification based on the five flow parameters: Source IP Address, Destination IP Address, IP protocol field, Source Port Number, and Destination Port number.

- Identification based on IP Precedence or DSCP field.

- Packet identification based on other TCP/IP header parameters, such as packet length.

- Identification based on source and destination Media Access Control (MAC) addresses.

- Application identification based on port numbers, Web Universal Resource Locator (URL) addresses, and so on. This functionality is available in Cisco products as Network Based Application Recognition (NBAR).

You can use access lists to match packets based on the various flow parameters. Access lists can also identify packets based on the IP Precedence or DSCP field. NBAR enables a router to recognize traffic flows as belonging to a specific application enabling packet classification based on application.

Packet classification also can be done based on information internal to the router. Examples of such classification are identification based on the arrived input interface and the QoS group field in the internal packet data structure. All the preceding classification mechanisms are supported across all QoS functions as part of Modular QoS command-line interface (CLI). Modular QoS CLI is discussed in Appendix A, "Cisco Modular QoS Command-Line Interface."

The classification action is referred to as *packet marking* or *packet coloring*. Packets identified to belong to a class are colored accordingly.

Packet Marking

You can mark classified packets to indicate their traffic class. You can color packets by marking the IP Precedence or the DSCP field in the packet's IP header, or the QoS group field in the packet's internal data structure within a router.

IP Precedence

The IP Precedence field in the packet's IP header is used to indicate the relative priority with which a particular packet should be handled. It is made up of three bits in the IP header's Type of Service (ToS) byte. Apart from IP Precedence, the ToS byte contains ToS bits. ToS bits were designed to contain values indicating how each packet should be handled in a network, but this particular field is never used much in the real world. The ToS byte[1] showing both the IP Precedence and ToS bits is illustrated in Figure 2-3 in Chapter 2, "Differentiated Services Architecture." Table 3-1 shows the different IP Precedence bit values and their names[2].

Table 3-1   *IP Precedence Values and Names*

IP Precedence Value	IP Precedence Bits	IP Precedence Names
0	000	Routine
1	001	Priority
2	010	Immediate
3	011	Flash
4	100	Flash Override
5	101	Critical
6	110	Internetwork Control
7	111	Network Control

NOTE   All routing control traffic in the network uses IP Precedence 6 by default. IP Precedence 7 also is reserved for network control traffic. Hence, use of IP Precedences 6 and 7 is not recommended for user traffic.

Packet coloring by setting the IP Precedence field can be done either by the application originating the traffic or by a node in the network. Cisco QoS features supporting this function include Committed Access Rate (CAR), Policy-Based Routing (PBR), and QoS Policy Propagation using Border Gateway Control (BGP) (QPPB). Case study 3-1, later in this chapter, discusses the IP Precedence setting using different QoS features. CAR is discussed in the "Traffic Policing" section of this chapter. PBR and QPPB are discussed in Appendix C, "Routing Policies."

NOTE   PBR is primarily a feature to route packets based on policy, though it has functionality for marking packets with IP Precedence. As such, PBR is recommended only for marking packets when either CAR or QPPB support is unavailable, or when IP Precedence needs to be marked while routing packets based on a policy.

DSCP

DSCP field is used to indicate a certain PHB in a network. It is made up of 6 bits in the IP header and is being standardized by the Internet Engineering Task Force (IETF) Differentiated Services Working Group. The original ToS byte containing the DSCP bits has been renamed the DSCP byte. The DSCP byte is shown in Figure 2-4 in Chapter 2. The DSCP field definitions[3] and the recommended DSCP values for the different forwarding behaviors are also discussed in Chapter 2.

The DSCP field is part of the IP header, similar to IP Precedence. In fact, the DSCP field is a superset of the IP Precedence field. Hence, the DSCP field is used and is set in ways similar to what was described with respect to IP Precedence.

Note that the DSCP field definition is backward-compatible with the IP Precedence values.

The QoS Group

The QoS group is a field in the packet data structure internal to the router. The QoS group is used to mark packets matching certain user-specified classification criteria. It is important to note that a QoS group is an internal label to the router and is not part of the IP packet header.

Packet coloring internal to the router is done using QoS groups. Cisco QoS features supporting this function include CAR and QPPB. Case study 3-2, later in this chapter, discusses QoS group settings using the different QoS features.

Modular QoS CLI enables packet marking by any of the three mechanisms discussed in this section. Table 3-2 compares packet coloring using IP Precedence, DSCP, and QoS groups.

Table 3-2   *Marking Traffic Using IP Precedence, DSCP, and QoS Groups*

Attributes	IP Precedence	DSCP	QoS Groups
Scope of the Classification	Entire network. Carried within the packet's IP header.	Entire network. Carried within the packet's IP header.	Internal to the router only. Not carried within the IP packet.
Number of Classes	8 classes (0–7)	64 classes (0–63)	100 classes (0–99)

Often, packets arrive at a network boundary carrying a set IP Precedence or DSCP field. Even in such situations when the packet arriving into the network is already marked, a network operator wants to enforce the right marking at the network edge based on the packet's class and its offered service level before the traffic enters the network. Case study 3-3, later in this chapter, discusses an example of IP Precedence enforcement.

Case Study 3-1: Packet Classification and Marking Using IP Precedence

An Internet service provider (ISP) offers different levels of premium services using IP Precedence for customer traffic, which assures preferential treatment within its network backbone. An enterprise customer purchases two levels of service from the ISP. It likes its traffic from network 215.215.215.0/24 to have a service level of IP Precedence 5 and the rest of the traffic a service level of IP Precedence 4, as in Figure 3-1.

Figure 3-1   *An Enterprise Network's Connection to Its ISP*

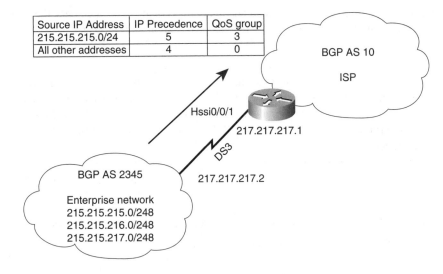

Source IP Address	IP Precedence	QoS group
215.215.215.0/24	5	3
All other addresses	4	0

This case study discusses the IP Precedence setting function using CAR, PBR, and QPPB.

On the ISP router's High-Speed Serial Interface (HSSI) connecting to the enterprise customer, you should configure CAR, PBR, or QPPB commands to set IP Precedence values based on the source IP address for all incoming traffic.

IP Precedence Using CAR

Listing 3-1 is a sample configuration to enable traffic based on IP Precedence using CAR.

Listing 3-1   *Using CAR to Classify Traffic Based on IP Precedence*

```
interface Hssi 0/0/1
rate-limit access-group 1 input 45000000 22500 22500 conform-action
set-prec-transmit 5 exceed-action set-prec-transmit 5
rate-limit input 45000000 22500 22500 conform-action set-prec-transmit 4
```

continues

Listing 3-1   *Using CAR to Classify Traffic Based on IP Precedence (Continued)*

```
exceed-action set-prec-transmit 4

access-list 1 permit 215.215.215.0 0.0.0.255
```

Two rate-limit statements are defined to set the IP Precedence values. The first statement sets IP Precedence 5 for all traffic carrying a source address in the 215.215.215.0/24 address space. The rest of the traffic arriving on the Hssi0/0/1 interface is set with an IP Precedence of 4.

Note that though rate-limit parameters are defined in the two statements, the purpose is not to rate-limit but simply to set IP Precedence based on an IP access list.

NOTE   CAR provides two functions in a single statement: rate limiting and IP Precedence setting. In this case study, the purpose is to set only the IP Precedence, but a CAR statement requires both rate-limiting and IP Precedence functions to be configured. In the future, with the support for modular QoS CLI, setting IP Precedence will not require enabling rate-limiting functions.

IP Precedence Using PBR

Listing 3-2 is a sample configuration to enable traffic based on IP Precedence using PBR.

Listing 3-2   *Using PBR to Classify Traffic Based on IP Precedence*

```
interface Hssi 0/0/1
ip policy route-map tasman

route-map tasman permit 10
match ip address 1
set ip precedence 5

route-map tasman permit 20
set ip precedence 4

access-list 1 permit 215.215.215.0 0.0.0.255
```

The route map tasman is used to set IP Precedence 5 for traffic with a source address in the 215.215.215.0/24 address space and IP Precedence 4 for the rest of the traffic.

IP Precedence Using QPPB

The ISP router receives a BGP route of 215.215.215.0 from the enterprise network. Within the ISP router's BGP configuration, a table map tasman is defined to tag the route 215.215.215.0 with a precedence of 5. The rest of the BGP routes of the enterprise are tagged with IP Precedence 4. BGP installs the BGP route in the routing table with its associated IP Precedence value. Cisco Express Forwarding (CEF) carries the IP Precedence value along with the forwarding information from the routing table. CEF is discussed in Appendix B, "Packet Switching Mechanisms."

When CEF switching incoming traffic on the Hssi0/0/1 interface, check the packet's source address and tag the associated IP Precedence value from the matching CEF entry before transmitting the packet on the outgoing interface. The configuration for this purpose is shown in Listing 3-3.

Listing 3-3   *Using QPPB to Classify Traffic Based on IP Precedence*

```
interface Hssi 0/0/1
ip address 217.217.217.1 255.255.255.252
bgp source ip-prec-map

router bgp 10
table-map tasman
neighbor 217.217.217.2 remote-as 2345

route-map tasman permit 10
match ip address 1
set ip precedence 5

route-map tasman permit 20
set ip precedence 4

access-list 1 permit 215.215.215.0 0.0.0.255
```

Case Study 3-2: Packet Classification and Marking Using QoS Groups

In case study 3-1, assume that the ISP prefers to use QoS groups to indicate different traffic service levels on its routers that connect to customers. In case study 2, the enterprise customer traffic from network 215.215.215.0/24 gets a QoS group 3 service level, and the rest of the traffic a service level of QoS group 0, as shown in Figure 3-1.

NOTE	You can choose to classify packets by QoS group rather than IP Precedence either when you want more than eight traffic classes, or when you don't want to change the original packets' IP Precedence values.

This case study discusses packet classification based on the QoS group using CAR and QPPB. It shows sample CAR and QPPB configurations on the ISP router to classify and mark packets using QoS group values.

QoS Groups Using CAR

Listing 3-4 is a sample configuration to enable traffic based on QoS groups using CAR.

Listing 3-4   *Using CAR to Classify Traffic Based on QoS Groups*

```
interface Hssi 0/0/1
rate-limit access-group 1 input 45000000 22500 22500 conform-action set-qos-transmit
3 exceed-action drop
rate-limit input 45000000 22500 22500 conform-action set-qos-transmit 0 exceed-
action drop

access-list 1 permit 215.215.215.0 0.0.0.255
```

QoS Groups Using QPPB

Listing 3-5 is a sample configuration to enable traffic based on QoS groups using QPPB.

Listing 3-5   *Using QPPB to Classify Traffic Based on QoS Groups*

```
interface Hssi 0/0/1
ip address 217.217.217.1 255.255.255.252
bgp source ip-qos-map

router bgp 10
table-map tasman
neighbor 217.217.217.2 remote-as 2345

route-map tasman permit 10
match ip address 1
set ip qos-group 3

route-map tasman permit 20
set ip qos-group 0

access-list 1 permit 215.215.215.0 0.0.0.255
```

Figure 3-4 *Standard Token Bucket for CAR*

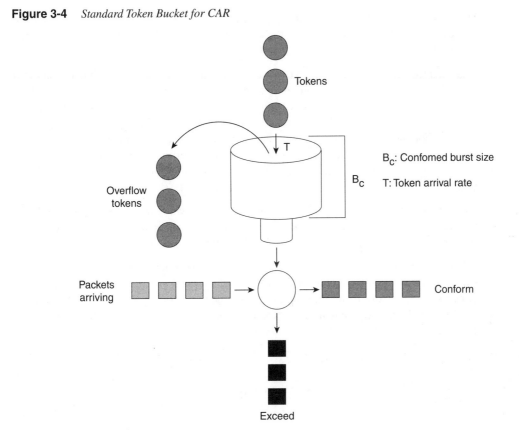

D_A is the number of tokens the stream currently borrowed. This is reduced at regular intervals, determined by the configured committed rate by the accumulation of tokens. Say you borrow 100 tokens for each of the three packets you send after the last packet drop. The D_A is 100, 200, and 300 after the first, second, and third packets are sent, respectively.

D_C is the sum of the D_A of all packets sent since the last time a packet was dropped. Unlike D_A, which is an actual count of the borrowed tokens since the last packet drop, D_C is the sum of the actual debts for all the packets that borrowed tokens since the last CAR packet drop. Say, as in the previous example, you borrow 100 tokens for each of the three packets you send after the last packet drop. D_C equals 100, 300 (= 100 + 200), and 600 (= 100 + 200 + 300) after the first, second, and third packets are sent, respectively. Note that for the first packet that needs to borrow tokens after a packet drop, D_C is equal to D_A.

The D_C value is set to zero after a packet is dropped, and the next packet that needs to borrow has a new value computed, which is equal to the D_A. In the example, if the fourth packet gets dropped, the next packet that needs to borrow tokens (for example, 100) has its

$D_C = D_A = 400 \ (= 300 + 100)$. Note that unlike D_C, D_A is not forgiven after a packet drop. If D_A is greater than the extended limit, all packets are dropped until D_A is reduced through accumulation of tokens.

The need for a token bucket with extended burst capability is not to immediately enter into a tail-drop scenario such as a standard token bucket, but rather, to gradually drop packets in a more Random Early Detection (RED)-like fashion. RED is discussed in Chapter 6, "Per-Hop Behavior: Congestion Avoidance and Packet Drop Policy." If a packet arrives and needs to borrow some tokens, a comparison is made between B_E and D_C. If D_C is greater than B_E, the packet is dropped and D_C is set to zero. Otherwise, the packet is sent, and D_A is incremented by the number of tokens borrowed and D_C with the newly computed D_A value.

Note that if a packet is dropped because the number of available tokens is less than the packet size (in bytes), tokens will not be removed from the bucket (for example, dropped packets do not count against any rate or burst limits).

It is important to note that CIR is a rate expressed in bytes per second. The bursts are expressed in bytes. A burst counter counts the current burst size. The burst counter can either be less than or greater than the B_C. When the burst counter exceeds B_C, the burst counter equals $B_C + D_A$. When a packet arrives, the burst counter is evaluated, as shown in Figure 3-5.

Figure 3-5 *Action Based on the Burst Counter Value*

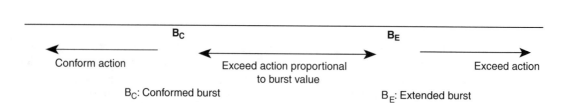

For cases when the burst counter value is between B_C and B_E, you can approximately represent the exceed action probability as:

$$(\text{Burst counter} - B_C) \div (B_E - B_C)$$

Based on this approximation, the CAR packet drop probability is shown in Figure 3-6. The concept of exceed action packet drop probability between the conformed and extended burst is similar to the packet drop probability of RED between the minimum and maximum thresholds.

Figure 3-6   *CAR Packet Drop Probability*

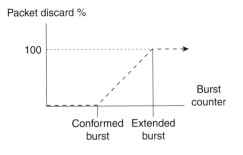

NOTE   The discussion in this section assumes packet transmission and packet drop as conform and exceed actions, respectively, for simplicity. In reality, a number of options are available to define both conform and exceed actions. They are discussed in the next section, "The Action Policy."

In a simple rate-limit statement where the B_C and B_E are the same value, no variable drop probability exceed region exists.

CAR implementation puts the following constraints on the token bucket parameters:

- Rate (bps) should be in increments of 8 Kbps, and the lowest value allowed for conformed and extended burst size is 8000 bytes.
- The minimum value of B_C size is Rate (bps) divided by 2000. It should be at least 8000 bytes.
- The B_E is always equal to or greater than the B_C value.

The Action Policy

You can define separate action policies for conforming and exceeding traffic for each rate-limit statement. A **conform-action** or **exceed-action** could be one of the following:

- Transmit
- Drop
- *Continue* (go to next rate limit statement in the list)
- Set precedence and transmit
- Set precedence and *continue*

- Set **qos-group** and transmit
- Set **qos-group** and *continue*

Case study 3-9 discusses how you can use action *continue*. Note that classification using **qos-group** functionality is available only in Versatile Interface Processor (VIP)-based 7500 series routers.

NOTE Per-Interface Rate Configuration (PIRC) is a limited-scope feature implementation of CAR targeted for the Cisco 12000 series routers. PIRC fits within the micro code space of the packet-switching application-specific integrated circuit (ASIC) on certain line cards of the router. You can apply only one CAR rule to the interface to rate-limit and/or set IP Precedence. PIRC is supported only in the ingress direction.

Case Study 3-4: Limiting a Particular Application's Traffic Rate at a Service Level

A service provider has one of its premium customers define its traffic service level. All customer traffic except Hypertext Transfer Protocol (HTTP) (Web) traffic over a rate of 15 Mbps is marked with an IP Precedence of 4. HTTP traffic over a rate of 15 Mbps is transmitted with an IP Precedence of 0. The customer has a 30-Mbps service from the service provider.

On the service provider boundary router connecting the premium customer, you enable CAR as shown is Listing 3-7.

Listing 3-7 *Limiting HTTP Traffic at a Service Level to a Specific Rate*

```
Interface Hssi1/0/0
rate-limit input 30000000 15000 15000 conform-action
continue exceed-action drop
rate-limit input access-group 101 15000000 10000 10000 conform-action
set-prec-transmit 4 exceed-action set-prec-transmit 0
rate-limit input 30000000 15000 15000 conform-action
set-prec-transmit 4 exceed-action set-prec-transmit 4
!
access-list 101 permit tcp any any eq www
access-list 101 permit tcp any eq www any
```

The first CAR statement is used to rate-limit all incoming traffic to 30 Mbps. It uses a *continue* action so that you continue to the next rate-limit statement. The second rate-limit statement is used to set the IP Precedence value for HTTP traffic based on its traffic rate.

The last rate-limit statement is used to set the IP Precedence value to 4 for all non-HTTP traffic. Listings 3-8 and 3-9 give the output of some relevant **show** commands for CAR.

Listing 3-8   *CAR Parameters and Packet Statistics*

```
#show interface hssi1/0 rate
Hssi1/0/0
  Input
matches: all traffic
      params:  30000000 bps, 15000 limit, 15000 extended limit
      conformed 0 packets, 0 bytes; action: continue
      exceeded 0 packets, 0 bytes; action: drop
      last packet: 338617304ms ago, current burst: 0 bytes
      last cleared 00:11:11 ago, conformed 0 bps, exceeded 0 bps
    matches: access-group 101
      params:  15000000 bps, 10000 limit, 10000 extended limit
      conformed 0 packets, 0 bytes; action: set-prec-transmit 4
      exceeded 0 packets, 0 bytes; action: set-prec-transmit 0
      last packet: 338617201ms ago, current burst: 0 bytes
      last cleared 00:11:11 ago, conformed 0 bps, exceeded 0 bps
    matches: all traffic
      params:  15000000 bps, 10000 limit, 10000 extended limit
      conformed 0 packets, 0 bytes; action: set-prec-transmit 4
      exceeded 0 packets, 0 bytes; action: set-prec-transmit 4
      last packet: 338617304ms ago, current burst: 0 bytes
      last cleared 00:03:30 ago, conformed 0 bps, exceeded 0 bps
```

The **show interface rate** command displays the CAR configuration parameters as well as CAR packet statistics. With the display, current burst gives a snapshot of the value in the token bucket at the time the value is printed. The conformed bps is obtained by dividing the total conformed traffic passed by the elapsed time since the counters were cleared the last time.

Listing 3-9   *Input and Output IP Precedence Accounting Information on Interface Hssi1/0/0*

```
#show interface hssi1/0/0 precedence
Hssi1/0/0
  Input
    Precedence 4:  10 packets, 1040 bytes
  Output
    Precedence 4:  10 packets, 1040 bytes
```

The **show interface precedence** command shows input and output packet accounting on an interface when IP accounting precedence input/output is applied on the interface.

Case Study 3-5: Limiting Traffic Based on IP Precedence Values

A service provider rate-limits low-precedence traffic coming on partner DS3 connections. Traffic with precedence values of 0, 1, and 2 are rate-limited to 10 Mbps, but no rate-limiting constraints are placed on high-precedence traffic, as in Figure 3-7.

Figure 3-7 *Limiting Customer Traffic Based on IP Precedence Value*

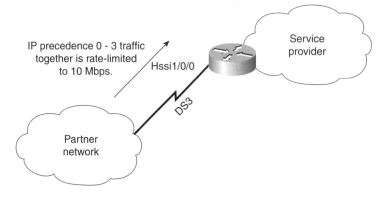

On the HSSI interface going to the partner network, the service provider adds the configuration shown in Listing 3-10 for this functionality.

Listing 3-10 *Rate-Limiting Traffic Based on Packet Precedence Values*

```
interface Hssi1/0/0
rate-limit input access-group rate-limit 1 10000000 10000 10000
conform-action transmit exceed-action drop

access-list rate-limit 1 mask 07
```

To match a range of precedence values, you use a mask of 8 bits, where each bit refers to a precedence value. Precedence 7 is 10000000, precedence 6 is 01000000, precedence 5 is 0010000, and so on. In this example, the mask 07 is in hex, which is 00000111 in decimal. Hence, the mask matches precedence values 0, 1, and 2.

We use a rate-limit access list statement to match the precedence values 0, 1, and 2. IP-precedence-based rate-limit access lists range from 1 to 99. The rate-limit statement limits all traffic with precedence 0, 1, and 2 to 10 Mbps.

Case Study 3-6: Subrate IP Services

A service provider delivers a physical T3 to its customer but offers a less expensive subrate service (for example, 10 MB, 20 MB, or 30 MB on a T3). The customer pays for only the subrate bandwidth; however, he or she can upgrade to additional access bandwidth over time based on demand. CAR limits the traffic rate available to the customer and delivered to the network to the agreed-upon rate limit (plus the ability to temporarily burst over the limit). The network operator can upgrade the service without any physical network rearrangement.

The service provider can configure an inbound rate-limit statement on the T3 interface to limit the traffic rate to the subrate the T3 customer subscribed. In the configuration example in Listing 3-11, you are limiting the input rate of traffic to 20 Mbps. Any traffic that exceeds the 20 Mbps rate is dropped.

Listing 3-11   *Delivering Subrate IP Service*

```
interface Hssi0/0/0
rate-limit input rate-limit 20000000 40000 40000 conform-action
transmit exceed-action drop
```

Case Study 3-7: Web Hosting Services

Say a service provider hosts a web server farm providing outsourcing services for its customers. Customer payment levels are set based on the assured bandwidth capacity and the level of service offered to the customer traffic in the service provider network. An e-business customer buys 5 Mbps of assured bandwidth with premium service from the service provider for its web server. The service provider marks all the e-business web server (IP address 209.11.212.1) traffic with an IP Precedence value of 4 for up to the purchased rate of 5 Mbps. An IP Precedence of 4 within the packets indicates premium service within the network in case of network congestion. Traffic beyond 5 Mbps from the web server is still sent in a best-effort fashion and tagged with an IP Precedence of 0. Listing 3-12 shows an example on how you can enable a service provider router connecting the web farms for such a network scenario.

Listing 3-12   *Web Hosting Service Example*

```
interface FastEthernet4/0/0
rate-limit input access-group 2 rate-limit 5000000 40000 40000
conform-action set-prec-transmit 4 exceed-action set-prec-transmit 0

access-list 2 permit  209.11.212.1
```

All packets being sent by the web server with an IP address of 209.11.212.1 are set with an IP Precedence value based on the traffic rate. All traffic within the 5-Mbps rate gets an IP Precedence of 4, and the rest get an IP Precedence of 0.

Case Study 3-8: Preventing Denial-of-Service Attacks

Service providers are often hit by malicious attacks using Internet Control Message Protocol (ICMP) packets aimed at bringing an important machine such as a mail or web server down by blasting packets at them at a high rate.

In this case, though the router itself is not being attacked, you can use CAR to limit the exposure of the internal network to such attacks by rate-limiting ICMP packets to a level that is needed for normal operations and to detect a malicious attack.

Listing 3-13 shows ways you can enable a router with a DS3 interface to limit its incoming ICMP traffic to 256 Kbps.

Listing 3-13 *Limiting Denial-of-Service Attacks*

```
interface Hssi1/0
 rate-limit input access-group 100 256000 8000 8000 conform-action
transmit exceed-action drop

access-list 100 permit icmp any any
```

Case Study 3-9: Enforcing Public Exchange Point Traffic

Say a Tier-1 ISP offers transit services to downstream ISP peers X and Y through a public exchange connectivity point provided by a Fiber Distributed Data Interface (FDDI) switch. The upstream Tier-1 provider utilizes MAC-address rate limits provided by CAR to enforce bandwidth usage limitations on the downstream ISPs. The Tier-1 ISP wants to assure that the non-peering ISPs on the switch don't send any traffic to it, as in Figure 3-8.

Figure 3-8 *Enforcing Public Exchange Point Traffic*

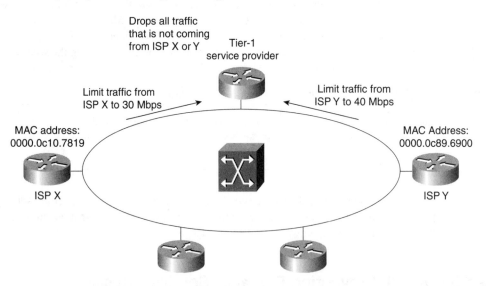

The Tier-1 ISP wants to rate-limit all traffic received from the ISP X and ISP Y routers to a mean rate of 30 Mbps and 40 Mbps, respectively. Any traffic exceeding the mean rate is dropped.

The Tier-1 ISP drops any packets arriving from non-peers on the FDDI (other than ISPs X and Y).

Listing 3-14 show ways you can enable the Tier-1 ISP router for this functionality.

Listing 3-14 *Enforcing Public Exchange Point Traffic Example*

```
interface Fddi1/0/0
 ip address 162.111.10.1 255.255.255.192
rate-limit input access-group rate-limit 110 30000000 15000 15000
                conform-action transmit exceed-action drop
rate-limit input access-group rate-limit 120 40000000 40000 40000
conform-action transmit exceed-action drop
rate-limit input access-group 100  4000000 40000 40000
conform-action drop exceed-action drop
access-list rate-limit 110 0000.0c10.7819
access-list rate-limit 120 0000.0c89.6900
access-list 100 permit ip any any
```

0000.0c10.7819 and 0000.0c89.6900 are the MAC addresses on the FDDI interface of ISP X's and ISP Y's routers, respectively.

Rate-limit access lists ranging from 100 to 199 are used to match traffic by MAC addresses. A rate-limit access list of 110 limits the traffic coming from ISP X to 30 Mbps. A rate-limit access list of 120 is used to rate-limit the traffic from ISP Y to 40 Mbps.

The last rate-limit statement is a "catch-all" statement that drops any traffic arriving from non-peer routers connected on the FDDI.

Traffic Shaping

TS is a mechanism to smooth the traffic flow on an interface to avoid congestion on the link and to meet a service provider's requirements. TS smoothes bursty traffic to meet the configured CIR by queuing or buffering packets exceeding the mean rate. The queued packets are transmitted as tokens become available. The queued packets' transmission is scheduled in either the first-in, first-out (FIFO) or Weighted Fair Queuing (WFQ) order. TS operation is illustrated in Figure 3-9.

Figure 3-9 *Traffic Shaping Operation*

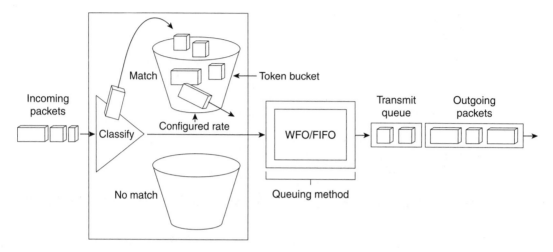

TS also can be configured in an adaptive mode on a frame-relay interface. In this mode, TS estimates the available bandwidth by Backward Explicit Congestion Notification (BECN)/ Forward Explicit Congestion Notification (FECN) field and Discard Eligible(DE) bit integration (discussed in Chapter 8, "Layer 2 QoS: Interworking with IP QoS").

This section covers traffic shaping on all interfaces/subinterfaces, regardless of the interface encapsulation. Traffic-shaping on an individual Frame Relay permanent virtual circuit (PVC)/switched virtual circuit (SVC) is covered in Chapter 8.

Traffic Measuring Instrumentation

TS uses a token bucket to measure traffic to classify a packet to be either conforming or nonconforming.

The maximum size of the token bucket is set to be the sum of conformed burst size, B_C and the extended burst size, B_E. Tokens equivalent to B_C are added to the bucket every measuring interval T, where $T = B_C \div CIR$. CIR is the allowed mean rate of traffic flow. If the bucket becomes full, any added tokens overflow. When a packet arrives, the token bucket is checked to see if enough tokens are available to send the packet. If enough tokens are available, the packet is marked compliant, and the tokens equivalent to the packet size are removed from the bucket. If enough tokens are not available, the packet is marked non-compliant and is queued for later transmission. The TS token bucket is depicted in Figure 3-10.

Figure 3-10 *The Token Bucket Scheme for the Traffic Shaping Function*

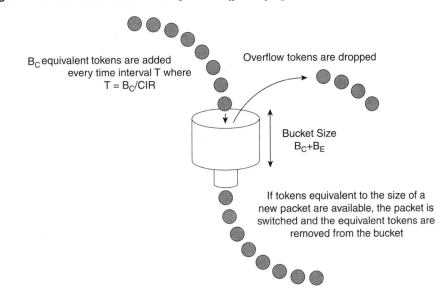

B_C equivalent tokens are added every time interval T where $T = B_C/CIR$

Overflow tokens are dropped

Bucket Size $B_C + B_E$

If tokens equivalent to the size of a new packet are available, the packet is switched and the equivalent tokens are removed from the bucket

You can accomplish traffic shaping on any generic interface using one of two implementations—Generic Traffic Shaping (GTS) and Distributed Traffic Shaping (DTS). Table 3-4 compares the two TS implementations.

NOTE   TS works only for outbound traffic; hence, TS cannot be applied on the inbound traffic to an interface.

Table 3-4   *Comparison of TS implementations: GTS and DTS*

Feature Attributes	GTS	DTS
Order of Transmission of Buffered Packets	Uses WFQ as a scheduling algorithm.	Can use either FIFO or Distributed WFQ (DWFQ) as a scheduling algorithm.
Traffic Matching Specification	Has two modes: either all traffic, or traffic matched by a simple or extended IP access list.	Traffic classes as defined by a user by means of one of the classification features (CAR or QPPB).

continues

Table 3-4   *Comparison of TS implementations: GTS and DTS (Continued)*

Feature Attributes	GTS	DTS
Per Frame Relay Data-Link Connection Identifier (DLCI) Support	Doesn't support per-PVC/SVC traffic-shaping on a Frame Relay interface.	Supports per-PVC/SVC traffic-shaping on a Frame Relay interface.
Availability	All single-processor (non-distributed) router platforms.	VIP-based 7500 series routers.
Protocol Support	All protocols.	IP only.

Case Study 3-10: Shaping Traffic to the Access Rate

An enterprise connects to a service provider's network at a 256 Kbps access rate using a T1. The enterprise's network administrator wants to constrain the amount of data going over the T1 link to 256 Kbps on average, as in Figure 3-11.

Figure 3-11   *Traffic Shaping to an Access Rate of 256K*

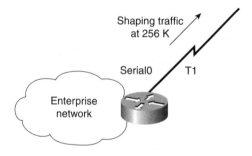

The serial interface of the enterprise's router that connects to the service provider has an access rate of 256 Kbps. Traffic shaping by both GTS and DTS features is discussed in the following sections.

Shaping Traffic Using GTS

Listings 3-15 through 3-18 show a sample configuration to shape traffic using GTS to an access rate of 256 Kbps, and some of the relevant **show** commands to monitor the shaping operation.

Listing 3-15   *Shaping Traffic to 256 Kbps on Average Using GTS*

```
interface Serial0
  traffic-shape rate 256000
```

Note that in the configuration, only the desired CIR is provided. The appropriate sustained and B_E values, which are shown in Listing 3-16, are picked automatically.

Listing 3-16 *GTS Parameters on Interface Serial0*

```
#show traffic shape serial0
     Access Target Byte  Sustain  Excess   Interval Increment Adapt
I/F  List   Rate   Limit bits/int bits/int (ms)     (bytes)   Active
Se0         256000 1984  7936     7936     31       992       -
```

The **show traffic-shape** command shows the traffic shaping configuration and the token bucket parameters.

Listing 3-17 *Information on the GTS shaping queue*

```
#show traffic serial queue
Traffic queued in shaping queue on Serial0
  Queueing strategy: weighted fair
  Queueing Stats: 0/1000/64/0 (size/max total/threshold/drops)
    Conversations  4/8/256 (active/max active/max total)
    Reserved Conversations 0/0 (allocated/max allocated)

(depth/weight/discards/tail drops/interleaves) 9/585/0/0/0
  Conversation 118, linktype: ip, length: 70
  source: 199.199.199.199, destination: 2.2.2.1, id: 0x212D, ttl: 255,
  TOS: 192 prot: 6, source port 60568, destination port 711

  (depth/weight/discards/tail drops/interleaves) 6/1365/0/0/0
  Conversation 84, linktype: ip, length: 60
  source: 254.6.140.76, destination: 172.16.1.3, id: 0x45C0, ttl: 213,
prot: 158

  (depth/weight/discards/tail drops/interleaves) 8/4096/0/0/0
  Conversation 124, linktype: ip, length: 114
  source: 172.16.69.115, destination: 2.2.2.1, id: 0x0079, ttl: 254,
prot: 1

  (depth/weight/discards/tail drops/interleaves) 5/4096/26/0/0
  Conversation 257, linktype: cdp, length: 337
```

The **show traffic-shape queue** command shows the WFQ information as well as the WFQ queued packets on the interface.

Listing 3-18 *GTS Statistics on Interface Serial0*

```
#show traffic serial0
     Access Queue  Packets Bytes  Packets Bytes   Shaping
I/F  List   Depth                 Delayed Delayed Active
Se0         4      2000    185152 20      1281    yes
```

The **show traffic-shape statistics** command shows the GTS packet statistics. Queue depth shows the number of packets in the WFQ queue at the moment the command is issued. Packets and Bytes show the total traffic switched through the interface. Packets Delayed and Bytes Delayed show the part of the total traffic transmitted that was delayed in the WFQ queue. Shaping Active shows if traffic shaping is active or not. Shaping is active if packets are to be shaped in the WFQ queue before transmitting them.

Shaping Traffic Using DTS

A class-map classifies all IP traffic into the class myclass. A policy-map applies the policy mypolicy to shape the traffic to an average rate of 256 Kbps on the traffic class myclass. The mypolicy policy is then applied on the interface to shape the outgoing traffic.

Note that the serial interface is Serial0/0/0 in Figure 3-11 for the purpose of the DTS discussion. DTS applies only to VIP-based 7500 routers.

Listings 3-19 and 3-20 are sample configurations and relevant **show** command output for shaping traffic to 256 Kbps using DTS.

Listing 3-19   *Shaping Traffic to 256 Kbps Using DTS*

```
class-map myclass
match any

policy-map mypolicy
class myclass
shape average 256000 16384 0

interface Serial0/0/0
service-policy output mypolicy
```

The **shape average** command is used to send traffic at the configured CIR of 256000 bps without sending any excess burst bits per interval. The conformed burst (B_C) is 16384 bits. Hence, the interval is 64 ms. The command allows only B_C bits of data to be sent per interval. The excess burst is not allowed at all, even if it is configured to a value other than 0. The **shape peak** command is used to peak to a burst of $B_C + B_E$ bits per interval while keeping a CIR.

Listing 3-20   *DTS Parameters and Queue Statistics*

```
#show interface shape
Serial0/0/0 nobuffer drop 0
 Serial0/0/0 (class 2):
    cir 256000,  Bc 16384,  Be 0
    packets output 0, bytes output 0
    queue limit 0, queue size 0, drops 0
    last clear = 00:01:39 ago,  shape rate = 0 bps
```

The **show interface shape** command shows the packet and queue statistics along with the configured DTS parameters.

Case Study 3-11: Shaping Incoming and Outgoing Traffic for a Host to a Certain Mean Rate

At a large company's remote sales office, Host A with an IP address of 200.200.200.1 is connected to the network on an Ethernet interface. It connects to the corporate office through a router using a T1. The network administrator wants to shape Host A's incoming and outgoing traffic to 128 K, as in Figure 3-12.

Figure 3-12 *Traffic Shaping Incoming and Outgoing Traffic of Host A*

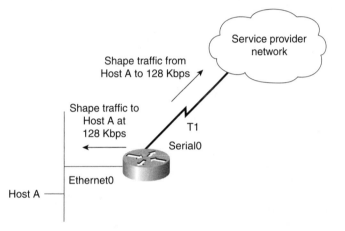

Host A is connected to the remote sales office router using interface ethernet0. The router's interface serial0 connects to the corporate network through a T1. The following configuration shows how to shape Host A's to and from traffic using GTS and DTS.

Listings 3-21 and 3-22 show samples of the configuration required for GTS and DTS, respectively, to achieve this functionality.

Shaping Incoming and Outgoing Traffic of a Host Through GTS

Listing 3-21 shows a sample configuration for GTS.

Listing 3-21 *Shaping Traffic to 128 Kbps Using GTS*

```
interface serial 0
 traffic-shape group 101 128000

interface ethernet 0
 traffic-shape group 102 128000

access-list 101 permit ip host 200.200.200.1 any
access-list 102 permit ip any host 200.200.200.1
```

The access lists 101 and 102 match host 200.200.200.1's outgoing and incoming traffic, respectively. The outgoing traffic is shaped on interface serial0 to 128 Kbps. The incoming traffic is shaped similarly on the ethernet0 interface.

Shaping Incoming and Outgoing Traffic of a Host Through DTS

Listing 3-22 shows a sample configuration for DTS. Note that the serial interface and the ethernet interface in Figure 3-12 are Serial0/0/0 and Ethernet1/0/0 for the purpose of the DTS discussion. DTS applies only to VIP-based 7500 routers.

Listing 3-22 *Shaping Traffic to 128 Kbps Using DTS*

```
class-map FromHostA
  match ip access-list 101

class-map ToHostA
  match ip access-list 102


policy-map frompolicy
  class FromHostA
    shape peak 128000 8192 1280

policy-map topolicy
class ToHostA
    shape peak 128000 8192 1280

interface serial0/0/0
service-policy output frompolicy

interface ethernet1/0/0
service-policy output topolicy
```

The class maps FromHostA and ToHostA are used to match the from and the to traffic to Host A, respectively. On both traffic classes, a policy to shape the traffic to 128 Kbps is applied. The service-policy commands are used to activate the policies on the interface output traffic.

The **shape peak 128000 8192 1280** shapes traffic providing output traffic at an average rate of 128 Kbps with packet bursts of 9472 (8192 + 1280) per interval.

Case Study 3-12: Shaping Frame Relay Traffic on Receipt of BECNs

Say an e-business site connects to the Internet using Frame Relay at a physical rate of T1. The access rate provided by the service provider is 256 Kbps and the CIR is 64 Kbps. The e-business site wants to send traffic at the access rate of 256 Kbps and throttle back to the CIR of 64 Kbps if it receives BECNs.

In this case study, we will go over the configuration required on the e-business site router's interface to the service provider.

Listings 3-23 and 3-24 show samples of the configuration required for GTS and DTS, respectively, to achieve this functionality.

Shaping Frame Relay Traffic Through GTS

Listing 3-23 shows a sample configuration for GTS.

Listing 3-23 *Shaping Traffic to 256 Kbps Using GTS*

```
interface Serial0/0/0.1 point-to-point
 traffic-shape rate 256000
 traffic-shape adaptive 64000
```

The **traffic-shape adaptive** command makes the router adapt its traffic-shaping rate to the incoming BECNs. The outgoing traffic on the interface is shaped at 256 Kbps (as configured by the **traffic-shape rate** command) on average when it receives no BECNs. The CIR is throttled to 64 Kbps, however, if it receives a series of BECNs, as in Figure 3-13.

Figure 3-13 *Adaptive Traffic Shaping on a Frame Relay Interface*

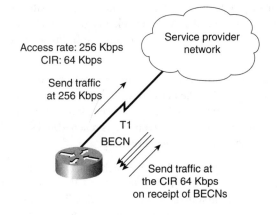

Shaping Frame Relay Traffic Through DTS

Listing 3-24 shows a sample configuration for DTS.

Listing 3-24 *Shaping Traffic to 256 Kbps Using DTS*

```
class-map myclass
 match any
```

continues

Listing 3-24   *Shaping Traffic to 256 Kbps Using DTS (Continued)*

```
policy-map mypolicy
  class myclass
    shape peak 256000 16384 1280
    shape adaptive 64000

interface serial0/0/0.1 point-to-point
service-policy output mypolicy
```

The **shape adaptive** command makes the router adapt its traffic-shaping rate to the incoming BECNs. The outgoing traffic on the interface is shaped at 256 Kbps (as configured by the **shape peak** command) on average when it receives no BECNs. The CIR is throttled to 64 Kbps, however, if it receives a series of BECNs.

Summary

Network boundary traffic conditioners provide packet classifier, marker, and traffic rate management functions.

Packets are classified at the network boundary so that they receive differentiated service within the network. Packet classification is necessary to identify different classes of traffic based on their service level. You can perform packet classification based on one or more fields in the packet's IP header. After a packet is identified to be of a certain class, a marker function is used to color the packet by setting the IP Precedence, the DSCP, or the QoS group value.

Traffic rate management on network boundary routers is essential to ensure resource availability and QoS within the network core. CAR is used to rate-limit any traffic trying to go over the configured rate. CAR can send some burst of traffic at up to the line rate and then start dropping packets after a given rate is reached. TS smoothes the traffic by queuing packets and sending them at a configured rate.

TS is more TCP-friendly than CAR, as a packet drop can cause a TCP stream to lower the window size to 1. This can lower the rate taken by the TCP stream below the allowed rate. By choosing the right burst parameters, which can vary from one TCP implementation to another, a TCP stream can take up the entire configured rate.

Frequently Asked Questions

Q — *Can I use IP access lists to match packets based on their DSCP field?*

A — Yes. Support for DSCP within IP access lists is initially introduced in Cisco IOS Version 12.0(7)T. As an example, access list 101 matches all IP packets with a DSCP field set to Expedited Forwarding (101110).

```
access-list 101 permit ip any any dscp EF
```

Q — *On a router, how can I mark Telnet packets destined to or originating from it to be set a certain IP Precedence value?*

A — You can mark Telnet packets from or to the router to a certain IP Precedence value by using the **ip telnet tos** command. As an example, you can set Telnet packets with an IP Precedence 6 by using the **ip telnet tos C0** command.

Q — *I am rate-limiting for 1 Mbps of traffic. Why do I see exceed traffic when the conformed traffic is as low as 250 Kbps?*

A — The exceed traffic might have happened for a short period of time. On average, the traffic seen by CAR is only 250 Kbps.

Q — *How do I choose the right B_C parameter for CAR?*

A — No right answer exists. It depends on the type of flows and how accommodating you want to be to traffic burstiness.

For IP and ICMP traffic flows, the burst parameters don't matter as they only lead to more short- or long-term bursty behavior. It isn't a big concern, as over time, the rate is limited to the configured CIR.

For protocols such as TCP, however, which use adaptive window-based rate control, a drop leads to a retransmission timer timeout at the sender and causes its window size to be reduced to 1. Though the right burst parameters for TCP flow vary based on the TCP implementations on the flow's sender and receiver, in general the best choices for CAR burst parameters are

conformed_burst = CIR $\times$ (1 byte $\div$ 8 bits) $\times$ 1.5 seconds, where CIR is configured rate

extend_burst = 2 $\times$ **conformed_burst**

Q — *How big are the CAR traffic counters?*

A — CAR uses 64-bit counters.

Q — *How does CAR penalize flows that continually exceed the B_C value?*

A — When a packet is dropped, you set the D_C to zero, but the D_A is left untouched. The next time a packet needs to borrow some tokens, the cumulative debt becomes equal to the D_A. If the flow continually borrows tokens, the D_A can continue to grow quickly to a value above the extended limit such that even compounding is not necessary to cause the packet to get dropped. You continue to drop packets until the D_A is reduced because of token accumulation.

Q — *How can a network administrator enable traffic rate limiting to be active during a certain time period of the day only?*

A — A network administrator can make this possible by using time-based IP access lists within CAR or modular QoS. Please refer to Cisco documentation for more information on time-based IP access lists.

Q — *What amount of processor resources is taken by CAR on a router?*

A — The amount of processor resources taken by CAR depends on the match condition and the depth of the rate-limit statements.

A match condition using a complicated extended IP access list takes more processor power relative to one using a basic IP access list. In general, the new precedence and MAC address access lists need less processor resources compared to the IP access lists.

The rate limits are evaluated sequentially, so the amount of processor resources used increases linearly with the number of rate limits checked.

References

[1] "Type of Service in the Internet Protocol Suite," P. Almquist, RFC 1349.

[2] "Internet Protocol Specification," Jon Postel, RFC 791.

[3] "Definition of the Differentiated Services Field (DS Field) in the IPv4 and IPv6 Headers," K. Nichols, and others, RFC 2474.

CHAPTER 4

Per-Hop Behavior: Resource Allocation I

At times of network congestion, resource allocation for a flow on a router is determined by the router's scheduling discipline for the packets queued in the queuing system. The scheduling behavior determines which packet goes next from a queue. How often a flow's packets are served determines its *bandwidth*, or *resource allocation*.

The traditional packet scheduling mechanism on the Internet has been first-in, first-out (FIFO) scheduling, by which packets are transmitted in the same order in which they arrive in the output queue. FIFO is simple and easy to implement but cannot differentiate among the many flows; hence, FIFO cannot allocate specific performance bounds for a flow, or prioritize one flow over the others.

Weighted Fair Queuing (WFQ) is a scheduling discipline in which flow differentiation occurs in scheduling. In WFQ, each flow or traffic class is assigned a weight, and the rate at which a flow or a traffic class is serviced is proportional to its assigned weight. WFQ provides prioritization among unequally weighted traffic flows and fairness and protection among equally weighted traffic flows as per the max-min fair-share allocation scheme. This chapter discusses max-min fair-share allocation and how Fair Queuing (FQ) simulates this allocation scheme. It also covers WFQ in detail. Other related scheduling disciplines—Modified Weighted Round Robin (MWRR) and Modified Deficit Round Robin (MDRR)—are covered in Chapter 5, "Per-Hop Behavior: Resource Allocation II."

Later in this chapter, priority queuing and custom queuing schemes are discussed. Priority queuing and custom queuing also help define flows into different packet flows and schedule them based on an absolute priority and round-robin basis, respectively.

The chapter ends with a section on scheduling disciplines for voice. Note that this chapter covers only packet scheduling issues that decide which packet is served next. The queue management component of scheduling, which defines the packet drop policy, is covered in Chapter 6, "Per-Hop Behavior: Congestion Avoidance and Packet Drop Policy."

Scheduling for Quality of Service (QoS) Support

Packet dynamics in a network can make the network prone to occasional or constant congestion, especially at routers connecting networks of widely different bandwidths. At times when a network doesn't see traffic congestion, any scheduling scheme works, because no queues build at the routers. When some network congestion exists, however, queues build upon the routers, and the scheduling mechanism on a router determines the order in which the packets in the queue are serviced.

For the scheduling algorithm to deliver QoS, at a minimum it needs to be able to differentiate among the different packets in the queue and know each packet's service level. Such a scheduling algorithm should allow guarantees on performance bounds by allocating resources on a flow basis and/or by prioritizing one flow over the other. You can do this at a granularity of a single flow or a traffic class that might be made up of packets from different traffic flows. Traffic classification is discussed in Chapter 3, "Network Boundary Traffic Conditioners: Packet Classifier, Marker, and Traffic Rate Management."

In addition, a scheduling algorithm is needed that provides fairness and protection among the flows with the same priority, such as all best-effort traffic flows.

Other requirements for such a scheduling algorithm include ease of implementation and admission control for flows requiring resource guarantees.

Although WFQ is more difficult to implement than FIFO queuing, it supports all the other requirements for QoS support that FIFO cannot deliver. WFQ also can work in conjunction with Resource Reservation Protocol (RSVP) to provide admission control for flows signaling resource requirements using RSVP. RSVP is discussed in detail in Chapter 7, "Integrated Services: RSVP."

NOTE   It is important to keep in mind the conservation law from queuing theory, which states that any scheduling discipline can only reduce a flow's mean delay at another flow's expense.

Occasionally, latency is traded for bandwidth. Some flows are delayed to offer a particular bandwidth to other flows. When someone gets preferential treatment, someone else will suffer.

FIFO Queuing

FIFO queuing is a queuing mechanism in which the order of the packets coming into a queue is the same as the order in which they are serviced or transmitted out of the queue. Figure 4-1 illustrates a FIFO queue.

Figure 4-1   *FIFO Queue*

In FIFO queuing, the order in which packets arrive in a queue is the same as the order in which they are transmitted from the queue. FIFO, the most common scheduling mechanism in routers today, is easy to implement. It has no mechanism to differentiate between flows, however, and hence cannot prioritize among them. Not only can FIFO queuing not prioritize one flow over the other, but it also offers neither protection nor fairness to equal-priority traffic flows because a large, badly behaving flow can take the share of resources of well-behaving flows with end-to-end, adaptive flow-control schemes, such as Transmission Control Protocol (TCP) dynamic window control. With FIFO, flows receive service approximately in proportion to the rate at which they send data into the network. Such a scheme is obviously not fair, because it rewards greedy flows over well-behaved ones. Any fairness algorithm by its nature offers protection against greedy flows.

The Max-Min Fair-Share Allocation Scheme

If FIFO doesn't do fair-share allocation among flows, how do you define a fair allocation scheme in which each flow gets its fair share of resources? A widely accepted fair-share allocation scheme is called the *max-min fair-share scheme*.

Various users' demands for a resource usually differ. So it is possible to classify users in the order of their increasing demand for a resource. The max-min fair-share allocation is defined as follows[1]:

- Resources are allocated in order of increasing demand.
- No user gets a resource share larger than its demand.
- Users with unsatisfied demands get an equal share of the resource.

Consider an example in which a resource has a capacity of 14, servicing five users, A, B, C, D, and E, with demands 2, 2, 3, 5, and 6, respectively. Initially, the source with the smallest demand is given a resource equal to the resource capacity divided by the total number of users. In this case, User A and User B are given a resource of 14 ÷ 5 = 2.8. But Users A and B actually need only 2. So the unused excess, 1.6 (0.8 each from Users A and B), is distributed evenly among the other three users. So Users C, D, and E each get a resource of 2.8 + (1.6 ÷ 3) = 3.33. Now, the user with the next-smaller demand is serviced. In this case, it is User C. The resource allocated to User C is 0.33 units in excess of its demand for 3. This unused excess is distributed evenly between Users D and E so that each now has a resource of $3.33 + (0.33 \div 2) = 3.5$.

We can calculate fair allocation as follows:

Fair allocation = (resource capacity – resource capacity already allocated to users) ÷ number of users who still need resource allocation

This example is illustrated in Figures 4-2, 4-3, and 4-4. In Step 1, shown in Figure 4-2, the demands of Users A and B are fully allocated because their resource requests fall within the fair allocation. In this step, the demands of C, D, and E exceed fair allocation of 2.8 and, hence, cannot be allocated. In the next step, the unused excess bandwidth of A and B's fair allocation is equally distributed among the three remaining users, C, D, and E.

Figure 4-2   *Resource Allocation for Users A and B*

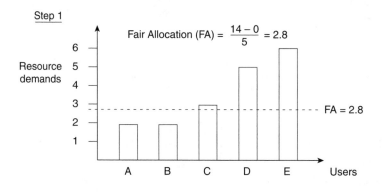

In Step 2, shown in Figure 4-3, the demand of User C is fully allocated because its resource request falls within the fair allocation. In this step, the demands of D and E exceed fair allocation of 3.33 and, hence, cannot be allocated. In the next step, the unused excess bandwidth of C's fair allocation is equally distributed between the two remaining users, D and E.

In Step 3, shown in Figure 4-4, the fair allocation of 3.5 falls below the requests of both Users D and E, which are each allocated 3.5 and have unsatisfied demands of 1.5 and 2.5, respectively.

This scheme allocates resources according to the max-min fair-share scheme. Note that all users with unsatisfied demands (beyond what is their max-min fair share) get equal allocation. So, you can see that this scheme is referred to as max-min fair-share allocation because it maximizes the minimum share of a user whose demand is not fully satisfied.

Consider an extension to the max-min fair-share allocation scheme in which each user is assigned a weight. Such a scheme is referred to as *weighted max-min fair-share allocation*, in which a user's fair share is proportional to its assigned weight.

Figure 4-3   *Resource Allocation forUser C*

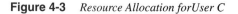

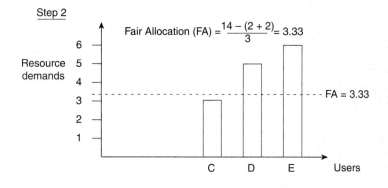

Step 2

Fair Allocation (FA) = $\dfrac{14 - (2 + 2)}{3}$ = 3.33

Resource demands

FA = 3.33

C   D   E   Users

Figure 4-4   *Resource Allocation forUsers D and E*

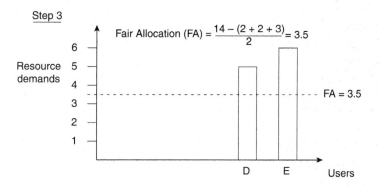

Step 3

Fair Allocation (FA) = $\dfrac{14 - (2 + 2 + 3)}{2}$ = 3.5

Resource demands

FA = 3.5

D   E   Users

Generalized Processor Sharing

For best-effort traffic flows and other equally weighted flow classes, the right scheduling discipline is one that provides fairness as described by the max-min fair-share allocation. Generalized processor sharing (GPS) is an ideal scheduling mechanism that achieves this objective.

GPS puts each flow in its own logical queue and services an infinitesimally small amount of data from each nonempty queue in a round-robin fashion. It services only an infinitesimally small amount of data at each turn so that it visits all the nonempty queues at any finite time interval, thus being fair at any moment in time.

If you assign a weight per flow, in each round of service, GPS services an amount of data from a flow in proportion to the assigned weight. This GPS extension provides weighted max-min fair share.

GPS, though an ideal model for max-min fair share, is not possible to implement. The right scheduling algorithm for practical purposes is one that approximates GPS and can be implemented.

Sequence Number Computation-Based WFQ

WFQ is an approximation of the GPS scheme, because it attempts to simulate a GPS scheduler behavior without making its impractical infinitesimal packet size assumption[2]. Sequence number computation-based WFQ simulates a GPS server that services 1 byte at a time. WFQ works well with variable-size packets, because it doesn't need to know a flow's mean packet size in advance. FQ is a WFQ technique that considers all flows to be the same—that is, to be of equal weight.

FQ simulates GPS by computing a sequence number for each arriving packet. The assigned sequence numbers are essentially service tags, which define the relative order in which the packets are to be serviced. The service order of packets using sequence number computation emulates the service order of a GPS scheduler.

To intuitively understand how GPS simulation is done, consider a variable called *round number*, which denotes the number of rounds of service a byte-by-byte round-robin scheduler has completed at a given time. The computation of a sequence number depends on the round number.

To illustrate how GPS is simulated by FQ, consider three flows, A, B, and C, with packet sizes 128, 64, and 32 bytes, respectively. Packets arrive back-to-back on a busy FQ server in the order A1, A2, A3, B1, C1, with A1 arriving first, followed by A2, and so on.

A flow is said to be *active* if any outstanding packets of that flow are awaiting service, and *inactive* otherwise.

For this example, assume Packet A1 arrived on an inactive flow in the FQ system. Assuming service by a byte-by-byte round-robin scheduler, an entire 128-byte packet is sent when the scheduler completes 128 rounds of service since the packet arrived. If the round number at the time Packet A1 arrived is 100, the entire packet is transmitted when the round number becomes $100 + 128 = 228$. Hence, the sequence number of a packet for an inactive flow is calculated by adding the round number and the packet size in bytes. Essentially, it is the round in which the last byte of the packet is transmitted. Because, in reality, a scheduler transmits a packet and not 1 byte at a time, it services the entire packet whenever the round number becomes equal to the sequence number.

When Packet A2 arrives, the flow is already active with A1 in the queue, waiting for service, with a sequence number of 228. The sequence number of Packet A2 is 228 + 128 = 356, because it needs to be transmitted after A1. Hence, the sequence number of a packet arriving on an active flow is the highest sequence number of the packet in the flow queue, plus its packet size in bytes.

Similarly, Packet A3 gets a sequence number of 356 + 128 = 484. Because Packets B1 and C1 arrive on an inactive flow, their sequence numbers are 164 (that is, 100 + 64) and 132 (that is, 100 + 32), respectively.

Sequence Number (SN) assignment for a packet is summarized based on whether it arrives on an active or an inactive flow as follows:

Packet arrives on an inactive flow:

> SN = size of the packet in bytes + the round number at the time the packet arrived (The round number is the sequence number of the last packet serviced.)

Packet arrives on an active flow:

> SN = size of the packet in bytes + the highest sequence number of the packet already in the flow queue

Packets in their flow queues, along with their computed sequence numbers, are shown in Figure 4-5 to illustrate how the FQ scheduler emulated GPS. A GPS scheduler will have completed scheduling the entire Packet A1 in the 228th round. The sequence number denotes the relative order in which the packets are served by the scheduler. The FQ scheduler serves the packets in the following order: C1, B1, A1, A2, and A3.

Round numbers are used only for calculating sequence numbers if the arriving packet belongs to a new flow. Otherwise, the sequence number is based on the highest sequence number of a packet in that flow awaiting service. If Packet A4 arrives at any time before A3 is serviced, it has a sequence number of 484 + 128 = 612.

Note that the round number is updated every time a packet is scheduled for transmission to equal the sequence number of the packet being transmitted. So if Packet D1 of size 32 bytes, belonging to a new flow, arrives when A1 is being transmitted, the round number is 228 and the sequence number of D1 is 260 (228 + 32). Because D1 has a lower sequence number than A2 and A3, it is scheduled for transmission before A2 and A3. Figure 4-6 depicts this change in scheduling order.

Figure 4-5 *An Example Illustrating the Byte-by-Byte Round-Robin GPS Scheduler Simulation for FQ*

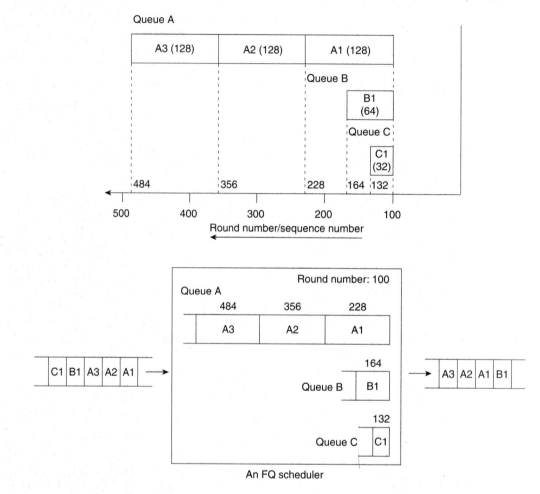

An FQ scheduler

Most often, some flows are considered more important or mission-critical than others. Such flows need to be preferred over the others by the scheduler. You can expand the FQ concept to assign weights per flow so that each flow is serviced in proportion to its weight. Such a fair queuing system is called flow-based WFQ and is discussed in the next section.

Figure 4-6   *Illustration of FQ Scheduler Behavior; Packet D1 Arriving After Packet A1 Is Scheduled*

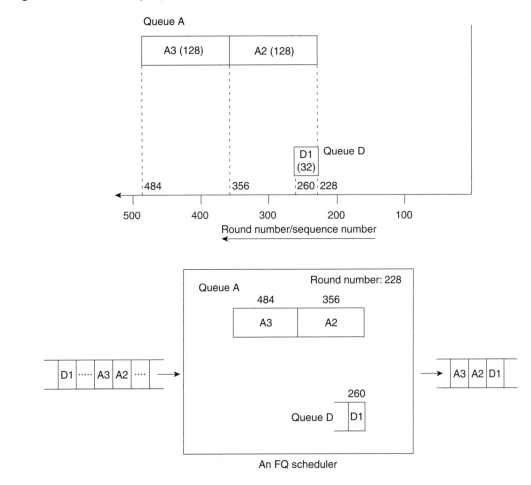

An FQ scheduler

Flow-Based WFQ

In WFQ, weights are assigned based on their precedence value in the Internet Protocol (IP) header. They are calculated as follows:

Weight = 4096 ÷ (IP precedence + 1)

NOTE	With the recent changes in WFQ implementation, the preceding WFQ flow weight calculation formula applies only when running IOS Versions 12.0(4)T or lower. The changes are made to enable class guarantees for Class-Based Weighted Fair Queuing (CBWFQ). CBWFQ is discussed later in this chapter.

For IOS Versions 12.0(5)T and higher, the WFQ flow weights discussed in this chapter are multiplied by 8. Hence, the WFQ weight for best-effort (IP precedence 0) traffic becomes

$$4096 \times 8 = 32768$$

and the equation for weight calculation becomes

Weight = $32768 \div$ (IP precedence + 1)

Table 4-1 tabulates a packet's weight based on its IP precedence and Type of Service (ToS) byte value.

Table 4-1 *Weights Assigned Based on the IP Precedence Value of a Packet Belonging to an Unreserved (Non-RSVP) Flow*

IP Precedence	ToS Byte Value	Weight	
		IOS Versions Prior to 12.0(5)T	**IOS Versions 12.0(5)T and Higher**
0	0 (0x00)	4096	32768
1	32 (0x20)	2048	16384
2	64 (0x40)	1365	10920
3	96 (0x60)	1024	8192
4	128 (0x80)	819	6552
5	160 (0xA0)	682	5456
6	192 (0xC0)	585	4680
7	224 (0xE0)	512	4096

The weight of an RSVP flow with the largest bandwidth reservation is 4 until IOS Version 12.0(5)T and is 6 for 12.0(5)T and higher. The weight of all other RSVP flow reservations is derived based on the largest bandwidth reservation, as shown here:

Weight for RSVP flow or conversation = highest bandwidth reservation on the link × (greatest bandwidth reservation on the link ÷ conservation bandwidth)

For the purpose of the discussion in the remainder of this section, weights prior to 12.0(5)T are used. It is important to note that the exact weight calculation scheme used doesn't matter in illustrating the working of WFQ.

WFQ uses two packet parameters to determine its sequence number. Like FQ, WFQ uses the packet's byte size. In addition, however, WFQ uses the weight assigned to the packet. The packet's weight is multiplied by its byte size for calculating the sequence number. This is the only difference between WFQ and FQ.

Note that the direct correlation between a byte-by-byte round-robin scheduler and FQ is lost with WFQ, because the packet's byte count is multiplied by its weight before its sequence number is calculated. Consider a sequence number in WFQ as a number calculated to determine the relative order of a packet in a WFQ scheduler, and consider the round number as the sequence number of the last packet served in the WFQ scheduler.

Using the same example discussed in the FQ section, assume that packets of Flow A have precedence 5, whereas Flows B and C have precedence 0. This results in a weight of 683 for packets in Flow A and 4096 for packets in Flows B and C. Table 4-2 shows all the flow parameters in this example. The sequence number of Packet A1 is calculated as $100 + (683 \times 128) = 87524$. Similarly, you can calculate sequence numbers for packets A2, A3, B1, and C1 as 174948, 262372, 262244, and 131172, respectively. So the order in which the scheduler services them is A1, C1, A2, B1, and A3, as illustrated in Figure 4-7.

Table 4-2   *Flow-Based WFQ Example*

Queue	Packet Size	Precedence	Weight = 4096 ÷ (Precedence + 1)
Queue A	128	5	683
Queue B	64	0	4096
Queue C	32	0	4096

Note that with WFQ, you can prioritize Flow A, but you can't accommodate Flows B and C fairly. A WFQ scheduler simulates a max-min weighted GPS.

If Packets A4 and D1 (a new flow with a precedence 0 and size 32 bytes) arrive after A1 is scheduled, A4 and D1 get a sequence number of 349,796 $((683 \times 128) + 262,372)$ and 218,596 $((4096 \times 32) + 87,524)$, respectively. The discussion of calculating the sequence numbers for A4 and D1 with FQ still applies here. Now, the scheduling order of the remaining packets is changed to C1, A2, D1, B1, A3, and A4. This is shown in Figure 4-8.

In Figure 4-8, packet D1 comes closely after packet A1 has been scheduled for transmission. Packet D1 is transmitted before packets A3 and A4, which arrived in the queue early.

Figure 4-7 *Illustration of the Flow-Based WFQ Example*

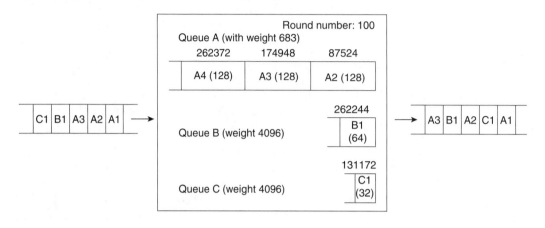

Sequence number calculation for a packet arriving on an interface occurs only when congestion is on the outbound interface (no buffer is available in the interface hardware queue). When no congestion is on the outbound interface, the scheduling behavior is FIFO—an arriving packet is simply queued to the outbound interface hardware queue for transmission.

The length of interface hardware transmit queues determines the maximum queuing delay for real-time traffic in a WFQ scheduler. Real-time traffic such as voice has to wait until the packets already queued in the hardware queue are sent before it can be transmitted. Excessive queuing delays can result in jitter, a problem for real-time traffic such as voice. Typical hardware interface buffers can hold from one to five packets. In IOS implement-ation, most interfaces automatically reduce their hardware transmit queues to 2 when WFQ is enabled. A network operator should be able to modify the length of the interface hardware transmit queues based on the delay requirements for the traffic in the network. This is especially true for voice and other real-time traffic. You can modify the interface transmit queue size by using the **tx-queue-limit** command.

Figure 4-8   *Illustration of the Flow-Based WFQ Example (continued).*

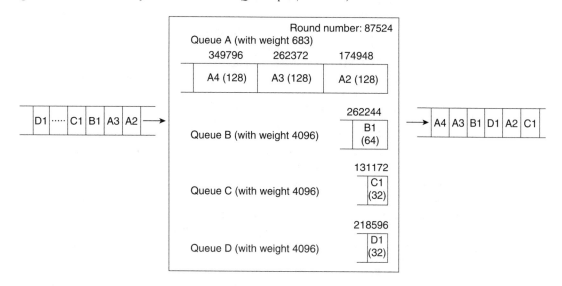

WFQ Interaction with RSVP

RSVP requires scheduler support to guarantee bandwidth reservations. WFQ interacts with RSVP reservation request (RESV) messages requesting resource allocations. WFQ maintains reserved conversation queues with weights assigned to match the bandwidth allocation reserved based on RSVP requests. RSVP is discussed in detail in Chapter 7. The number of reserved conversations allowed is a configurable parameter.

WFQ Implementation

In flow-based WFQ implementation, weights are based strictly on precedence and cannot be changed. Though FQ in itself is not available, WFQ becomes FQ for all practical purposes when all traffic arriving at the scheduler carries the same precedence value.

With flow-based WFQ, packets with different IP precedence in a single flow are not scheduled out of order. In this regard, a flow is implemented as a hash defined by source and destination IP addresses, IP protocol field, Transmission Control Protocol/User Datagram Protocol (TCP/UDP) port numbers and the 5 bits (excluding the 3 IP precedence bits) in the ToS byte. Due to this flow description, packets of the same flow, but with different precedence values, fall into the same queue. Packets within a flow queue are serviced in FIFO order.

In general, WFQ limits its drops to the most active flows, whereas FIFO might drop from any flow. Therefore, WFQ should encourage the most active flows to scale back without affecting the smaller flows. Because the median flow duration in the Internet is 10–20 packets in length, a fairly small percentage of the flows should be taking the lion's share of the drops with WFQ, while FIFO drops should be distributed across all flows. Hence, the effects of global synchronization with FIFO are less pronounced with WFQ for traffic with adaptive flow control such as TCP traffic. Global synchronization and proactive drop policies are detailed in Chapter 6.

In general, a flow-based WFQ uses a subqueue for each flow. As such, flow-based WFQ queues are referred to as *conversation queues*. Because memory is a finite resource, the default number of conversation queues allocated is restricted to 256. This parameter is configurable when enabling the **fair-queue** interface command, however. Note that increasing the number of queues increases the memory taken by the queue data structures and the amount of state information maintained by the router. If the number of flows is greater than the number of queues, multiple flows can share a single queue. Configuring a large number of queues increases the chances of having only one flow per queue.

Flow-based WFQ can also work in conjunction with Weighted Random Early Detection (WRED), a proactive packet drop policy to avoid congestion. WRED is discussed in Chapter 6.

Flow-based WFQ implementation is done using list sorting. The complexity is of the order of O(n), where n is the number of packets waiting for service from a WFQ scheduler. List sorting can become prohibitively expensive on high-bandwidth links where the number of flows and the number of packets to be serviced per second is high.

NOTE   Flow-based WFQ is available on most Cisco router platforms. One notable exception is Cisco 12000 series routers. It is the default queuing mechanism in all interfaces with a bandwidth less than 2 Mbps.

Case Study 4-1: Flow-Based WFQ

Important traffic is occasionally delayed by low-priority traffic within a network, because packets from all active flows look the same in the output queue of a router doing FIFO queuing. To help differentiate packets by their service requirements, the network administrator for the site starts to tag IP precedence within the packet based on the importance of the traffic at the ingress and implements flow-based WFQ such that

- Active flows with the same IP precedence traffic get the same amount of interface bandwidth.

- Active flows with high-precedence traffic get a larger amount of interface bandwidth than active flows with lower-precedence traffic.

After IP precedence is set at the ingress, you can deploy flow-based WFQ on the routers to achieve the preceding objectives. Packet classification based on IP precedence is discussed in case studies in Chapter 3.

You can set up flow-based WFQ on an interface by using the **fair-queue** interface command. The **show queue** command, shown in Listing 4-1, describes the active flows along with the queue depth, weight, and other queue statistics as well as the queue parameters in the WFQ system.

Listing 4-1   *show queue serial0 Command Output*

```
Router#show queue serial0
Input queue: 0/75/0 (size/max/drops); Total output drops: 0
Queueing strategy: weighted fair
Output queue: 9/1000/120/0 (size/max total/threshold/drops)
    Conversations  1/4/256 (active/max active/threshold)
    Reserved Conversations 0/1 (allocated/max allocated)

(depth/weight/discards/tail drops/interleaves) 2/4096/0/0/0
Conversation 1044, linktype: ip, length: 1504
source: 172.26.237.58, destination: 172.26.237.2, id: 0xC4FE, ttl:126,
TOS: 0 prot: 6, source port 1563, destination port 4665
```

In Listing 4-1, max total is a per-interface, global limit on the number of buffers for WFQ, whereas threshold is the maximum number of buffers allowed per conversation. Note that max total is the same as the output hold queue, and you can change it using the **hold-queue** *<queue length>* **out** interface command. A conversation with nonzero queue depth is said to be *active*. active and max active show the present and the maximum number of active conversations. Reserved Conversations shows RSVP flow reservations.

In the second part of Listing 4-1, depth shows the number of packets in the conservation queue (which is defined below this line of queue statistics) waiting service, and weight shows the weight assigned to this flow. A discard is done by WFQ logic when the number of packets in a conversation queue exceeds the threshold. Tail drops happen when the WFQ buffer surpasses the max total. At that time, any packet arriving on the tail of a full queue gets dropped. Interleaves happen when link layer fragmentation and interleaving are configured to allow small packets to be interleaved between fragments of big packets, lowering the delay jitter seen by the small packet flows.

NOTE   Queues are displayed only if one or more packets are in the queue at the time the **show queue** is issued. Otherwise, the conversation is inactive and no output is displayed. Hence, the **show queue** interface command does not give any output if the interface is lightly loaded.

The **show queueing fair** command is used to check the WFQ parameters on an interface. Listing 4-2 displays the output of the **show queueing fair** command.

Listing 4-2 *show queueing fair Command Output*

```
Router#show queueing fair
Current fair queue configuration:

Interface          Discard      Dynamic        Reserved
                   threshold    queue count    queue count
Serial0            64           256            0
```

Case Study 4-2: Bandwidth Allocation by Assigned Weights

A serial interface with flow-based WFQ carries eight flows, one flow at each of the eight precedence values. How does the bandwidth allocation for each flow change if there are 25 flows—18 precedence 1 flows and one flow for each remaining precedence value?

As discussed earlier in this chapter, bandwidth allocated to a flow is inversely proportional to its weight. Further, in the case of flow-based WFQ:

$$\text{weight} = 4096 \div (1 + \text{precedence})$$

Hence, the share of bandwidth of a flow becomes directly proportional to $(1 + \text{precedence})$.

Each flow gets a link bandwidth proportional to $(P + 1)$, where P denotes the IP precedence value of the packets in that flow. The amount of bandwidth a flow gets depends on the other flows sharing the link.

In the first scenario, say there are eight flows, with one flow at each precedence level. Precedence 0 traffic gets $1 \div (1 + 2 + 3 + 4 + 5 + 6 + 7 + 8) = 1/36$ of the link bandwidth, precedence 1 traffic gets 2/36, precedence 2 traffic gets 3/36, and so on.

In the second scenario, there are 25 flows with 18 precedence 1 flows, and seven other flows belonging to each remaining precedence value. In this scenario, precedence 0 gets $1 \div (1 + 2(18) + 3 + 4 + 5 + 6 + 7 + 8) = 1/70$ of the link bandwidth, each precedence 1 flow gets 2/70, and so on.

Case Study 4-3: WFQ Scheduling Among Voice and FTP Flow Packets

A DS3 link at an Internet service provider (ISP) carries voice traffic along with the File Transfer Protocol (FTP) traffic. The voice traffic is seeing varying delays because of the relatively large and variably sized FTP packets. The network engineering group believes that replacing the default FIFO queuing with classic WFQ helps, but it isn't sure how it will get fair treatment competing with FTP traffic.

The voice traffic is made up of 64 bytes and is represented as V1, V2, V3, and so on, and FTP traffic consists of 1472-byte packets and is represented as F1, F2, F3, and so on. The following scenarios discuss the resource allocation for voice traffic (when run in conjunction with FTP traffic) in the FQ and WFQ situation.

In the first scenario, IP precedence is not set in any packet. All traffic carries the default precedence value of 0. The voice traffic of 64-byte packets gets a fair treatment competing with an FTP flow. When both flows are active, the voice traffic gets the same bandwidth as the FTP traffic, effectively scheduling one FTP packet for 23 (= $1472 \div 64$) voice packets, on average.

In the second scenario, voice packets carry precedence 5 and FTP traffic has a precedence of 0. The voice traffic is weighted lower than the FTP traffic. The voice traffic and FTP get 6/7 percent and 1/7 percent of the link bandwidth, respectively. Hence, the voice traffic flow gets six times the bandwidth of the FTP flow. Taking packet size differences into consideration, when both flows are active, one FTP packet is scheduled for 138 (= 23×6) voice packets!

NOTE   WFQ in itself doesn't give absolute priority to a particular traffic flow. It can give only a higher weight in the share of resources or certain guaranteed bandwidth, as shown in this case study. Hence, it might not be ideal for interactive, real-time applications, such as voice, in all circumstances. WFQ can work for voice when little background traffic is in the network. On a loaded network, however, WFQ cannot achieve the low-jitter requirements for interactive voice traffic. For applications such as voice, WFQ is modified with a priority queue (PQ). WFQ with a PQ is discussed toward the end of this chapter.

Flow-Based Distributed WFQ (DWFQ)

Flow-based DWFQ operates in a distributed mode in the 7500 series routers supporting Versatile Interface Processor (VIP) line cards with built-in processors. When flow-based DWFQ is enabled on an interface, the feature runs on the interface's individual VIP line card, unlike flow-based WFQ, which runs on the router's central processor. Distributed Cisco Express Forwarding (DCEF) switching is required to run DWFQ. DCEF switching is discussed in Appendix B, "Packet Switching Mechanisms."

Flow-based WFQ uses a sorted linked list to maintain packets, and newly arriving packets are inserted into the sorted list based on the sequence number assigned to the packet. In contrast, flow-based DWFQ uses calendar queues to perform the sorting function required by WFQ. Flow-based DWFQ implements calendar queues that approximate GPS with a less-complex algorithm than simple list sorting. Calendar queues do an O(1) insertion, which is important for higher-speed interfaces, as opposed to O(n) algorithms. Calendar queues are more efficient in terms of CPU utilization, but calendar queues have larger memory requirements. It is a trade-off between the larger memory costs versus limitations imposed by a smaller set of calendar queues.

Timestamps are computed for each arriving packet and are sorted using a calendar queue. Any calendar queue-based implementation has its timestamp granularity constrained by the number of calendar queues in the system. For the calendar queue system to behave the same as the flow-based WFQ implementation, you need $4096 \times$ maximum transmission unit (MTU)-size calendar queues!

Because the number of calendar queues prevents the timestamp granularity from allowing unique timestamp values for packets ranging from 1 byte to MTU bytes, packets with different sizes from flows/classes with the same weight can have the same timestamp. To serve these variable-size packets with the same timestamp, it is necessary to run a deficit-like algorithm on the calendar queues to ensure proper bandwidth allocation. Thus, part of the DWFQ implementation has Deficit Round Robin (DRR)-like characteristics. The DRR algorithm is described in Chapter 5.

DWFQ implementation has an individual queue limit and an aggregate queue limit across all the individual queues. The individual queue limits are enforced only when the aggregate queue limit is reached.

Flow-based DWFQ is actually FQ. Under FQ, all flows are the same, and flows are not weighted. In the case of flow-based DWFQ, a flow is described by a hash function consisting of the source and destination IP addresses, IP field, and TCP/UDP port numbers. All non-IP traffic is treated as a single flow and, therefore, placed in the same queue.

Because of the reasons discussed in the section on flow-based WFQ, the number of subqueues allowed in flow-based DWFQ is restricted. The total number of subqueues for a flow-based DWFQ is 512. If more than 512 flows exist on an interface, some flows will share the same subqueue.

Case Study 4-4: Flow-Based DWFQ

In a network that is yet to start using IP precedence based on the packet's importance, a large company finds that an active data-transfer flow with large packet sizes affects the performance of transactional traffic made up of small packet sizes. The company's network engineer wants to isolate a flow's performance and likes all flows to be treated the same way, each getting its fair share of bandwidth.

Flow-based DWFQ provides both isolation and protection among the active flows. In this case, all active flows get an equal share of bandwidth.

To achieve this functionality, enable flow-based DWFQ using the interface command **fair-queue** on VIP-based 7500 series routers in the network. The **show interface** command displays a line showing VIP-based fair queuing as the queuing or scheduling strategy being used. Listing 4-3 shows information on the flow-based DWFQ.

Listing 4-3   *Flow-Based DWFQ Information*

```
Router#show interface fair
POS0/0/0 queue size 0
      packets output 2, wfq drops 1, nobuffer drops 0
WFQ: aggregate queue limit 5972, individual queue limit 2986
      max available buffers 5972
```

The **show interface fair** command displays packet statistics for the number of packets transmitted as well as packet drops due to DWFQ and buffer pool depletion.

NOTE   The number of available buffers for DWFQ, individual, and aggregate limits is derived based on the VIP Static Random Access Memory (SRAM) capacity, the number of interfaces on the VIP, and the speed of those interfaces.

Class-Based WFQ

The last two sections discussed flow-based WFQ mechanisms running on the IOS router platforms' central processor, and flow-based DWFQ mechanisms running on the 7500 platform's VIP line cards. This section studies a CBWFQ mechanism that is supported in both nondistributed and distributed operation modes.

CBWFQ allocates a different subqueue for each traffic class compared with a subqueue per each flow in the flow-based versions of WFQ. So, you can use the existing flow-based implementations of WFQ to deliver CBWFQ in both nondistributed and distributed modes of operation by adding a traffic classification module in which each WFQ subqueue carries a traffic class rather than a traffic flow. Hence, CBWFQ is still based on sequence number computation when run on the router's central processor and on calendar queue implementation when run on the 7500 platform's VIP line cards.

The CBWFQ mechanism uses the modular QoS command-line interface (CLI) framework discussed in Appendix A, "Cisco Modular QoS Command-Line Interface." As such, it supports all classes supported under this framework. You can base traffic classes on a variety of traffic parameters, such as IP precedence, Differentiated Services Code Point (DSCP), input interface, and QoS groups. Appendix A lists the possible classifications.

CBWFQ enables a user to directly specify the required minimum bandwidth per traffic class. This functionality is different from flow-based WFQ, where a flow's minimum bandwidth is derived indirectly based on the assigned weights to all active flows in the WFQ system.

NOTE	Note that CBWFQ also can be used to run flow-based WFQ. In CBWFQ, the default-class traffic class appears as normal WFQ flows on which you can apply flow-based WFQ by using the **fair-queue** command.

DWFQ and CBWFQ differ in that you can run FQ within any DWFQ class, but in the case of CBWFQ, only default classes can run WFQ.

Case Study 4-5: Higher Bandwidth Allocation for Critical Traffic

A Fortune 500 company finds that its critical database application traffic is getting a slow performance on its wide-area network (WAN) link, and upon doing some traffic analysis it confirms that network congestion caused by the other traffic, such as Web, FTP, and video/audio downloads, is the culprit. It has entrusted its networking department to prioritize database application traffic such that the application traffic is preferred, but at the same time, it doesn't want to totally starve the other traffic.

All critical database application traffic is classified under the class *gold* by using a **class-map**. Then a policy named *goldservice* is defined on the *gold* traffic class. Finally, the policy *goldservice* is applied on the output traffic of interface serial0 to apply specific bandwidth allocation for the outgoing critical traffic. Listing 4-4 gives the sample configuration.

Listing 4-4 *Allocating Bandwidth for Critical Traffic*

```
class-map gold
  match access-group 101

policy-map goldservice
  class gold
    bandwidth 500

interface serial0
service-policy output goldservice
access-list 101 permit ip any any udp range 1500 1600
```

CBWFQ can directly specify a minimum bandwidth per class by using the **bandwidth** command.

The access-list 101 matches all critical database application traffic in the network. The **show policy** and **show class** commands display all policy and class map information on the router, respectively.

Listings 4-5 and 4-6 display the output of the policy *goldservice* and the *gold* traffic class, respectively.

Listing 4-5   *Information on the goldservice Policy*

```
Router#show policy goldservice
 Policy Map goldservice
  Weighted Fair Queueing
    Class gold
      Bandwidth 500 (kbps) Max Thresh 64 (packets)
```

Listing 4-6   *Information on the gold Traffic Class*

```
Router#show class gold
 class Map gold
 match access-group  101
```

As in Case Study 4-1, you use **show queueing fair** for the WFQ information and the **show queue serial0** command to see packets waiting in the queue.

Case Study 4-6: Higher Bandwidth Allocation Based on Input Interface

A network engineer at a service provider wants to allocate 30 Mbps bandwidth on an Internet router's DS3 link for traffic coming from a server on the Internet router's Fast Ethernet segment.

The initial step is to classify traffic that needs to go over the DS3 link based on the incoming interface of Fast Ethernet1/1 on the Internet router. The class map used for this purpose is named server. Then a policy-map *febandwidth* is used to configure the policy desired on the *server* traffic class. The *febandwidth* policy is then enabled on the outgoing traffic of the DS3 (Hssi0/0) interface by using the command **service-policy output febandwidth**. Listing 4-7 shows a sample configuration.

Listing 4-7   *Bandwidth Allocation Based on Input Interface*

```
class-map server
match input-interface FastEthernet1/1

policy-map febandwidth
class server
bandwidth 30000

interface Hssi0/0
service-policy output febandwidth
```

Case Study 4-7: Bandwidth Assignment per ToS Class

A large ISP decides to categorize its traffic into four classes in the network backbone based on IP precedence, as shown in Table 4-3. Each class is assigned traffic belonging to two IP precedence values—one precedence value each for normal and excess traffic. Classes 1–3 need to be allocated 15 percent, 30 percent, and 40 percent of the link bandwidth of a High-Speed Serial Interface (HSSI) interface, respectively. Class 0 takes the leftover available bandwidth (15 percent).

Table 4-3   *IP Precedence Allocation Based on Traffic Class*

	Critical (Class 3)	Expensive (Class 2)	Moderate (Class 1)	Cheap (Class 0)
Normal Traffic	Precedence 7	Precedence 6	Precedence 5	Precedence 4
Excess Traffic	Precedence 3	Precedence 2	Precedence 1	Precedence 0

Assume here that packet classification into IP precedence based on traffic rate was already done on the network boundary routers or interfaces connecting to the customer traffic. See Chapter 3 for details regarding packet classification.

On an HSSI interface, ToS classes 0–3 are given 6750 Kbps, 13500 Kbps, 18000 Kbps, and 6750 Kbps, respectively, based on the link bandwidth percentage allocations, as shown in Listing 4-8.

Listing 4-8   *Enabling CBWFQ for ToS Classes*

```
class-map match-any class0
  match ip precedence 4
  match ip precedence 0
class-map match-any class1
  match ip precedence 1
  match ip precedence 5
class-map match-any class2
  match ip precedence 2
  match ip precedence 6
class-map match-any class3
  match ip precedence 3
  match ip precedence 7

policy-map tos-based
  class class0
    bandwidth 6750
  class class1
    bandwidth 13500
  class class2
    bandwidth 18000
  class class3
    bandwidth 6750

interface hssi0/0/0
 service-policy output tos-based
```

NOTE	Although bandwidth specification as a percentage of the total link bandwidth is not allowed at the time of this writing, this option will be available soon.

CBWFQ Without Modular CLI

You can enable certain class-based distributed WFQ mechanisms—namely, ToS-based DWFQ and QoS-group-based DWFQ—on VIP-based 7500 series routers without using the modular QoS CLI.

ToS-Based DWFQ

ToS-based DWFQ is a class-based WFQ by which the two low-order precedence bits are used to choose the queue. Only four possible queues exist. Table 4-4 shows the ToS class allocation based on the IP precedence bits.

Table 4-4   *ToS-Based Classification*

IP Precedence Bits	ToS Class Bits	ToS Class Assigned
000	00	0
001	01	1
010	10	2
011	11	3
100	00	0
101	01	1
110	10	2
111	11	3

ToS-based DWFQ is enabled by using the **fair-queue tos** command.

As an example, Case Study 4-7 is shown here, redone using ToS-based CBWFQ without the modular QoS CLI. Listing 4-9 lists the required configuration for this functionality.

Listing 4-9   *Assigning Bandwidth per ToS Class on an Interface*

```
interface Hssi0/0/0
fair-queue tos
fair-queue tos 1 weight 15
fair-queue tos 2 weight 30
fair-queue tos 3 weight 40
```

NOTE	The weight parameter is used differently in DWFQ implementation when compared to flow-based WFQ. Weights in DWFQ implementation indicate the percentage of link bandwidth allocated.

Note that the default weights of ToS classes 1, 2, and 3 are 20, 30, and 40, respectively. In this case, the intended weight assignments for classes 2 and 3 are their default values and hence, they need not be configured at all. Class 1 is assigned a weight of 15. Listing 4-10 displays information on ToS-based DWFQ and its packet statistics.

Listing 4-10   *ToS-Based DWFQ Information*

```
Router#show interface fair
HSSI0/0/0 queue size 0
        packets output 20, wfq drops 1, nobuffer drops 0
 WFQ: aggregate queue limit 5972, individual queue limit 2986
       max available buffers 5972

      Class 0: weight 15 limit 2986 qsize 0 packets output 0 drops 0
      Class 1: weight 15 limit 2986 qsize 0 packets output 0 drops 0
      Class 2: weight 30 limit 2986 qsize 0 packets output 0 drops 0
      Class 3: weight 40 limit 2986 qsize 0 packets output 0 drops 0
```

weight indicates a percentage of the link bandwidth allocated to the given class. A ToS class 3 has a weight of 40, for example, which means it is allocated 40 percent of the link bandwidth during times when the queues for all four classes (0, 1, 2, and 3) are simultaneously backlogged.

The weight for ToS class 0 is always based on the weights of the other classes and changes when weights for any one of the classes 1–3 change. Because the total weight is 100, the bandwidth allotted to ToS class 0 is always 100 - (weights of classes 1–3). Note the sum of the class 1–3 weights should not exceed 99.

QoS Group-Based DWFQ

In addition to the ToS-based DWFQ, you can configure QoS group-based DWFQ without modular QoS CLI in VIP-based 7500 series routers.

The QoS group is a number assigned to a packet when that packet matches certain user-specified criteria. It is important to note that a QoS group is an internal label to the router and not a field within the IP packet, unlike IP precedence. Without using modular QoS CLI, the QoS group-based DWFQ feature is enabled by using a **fair-queue qos-group** command.

Case Study 4-8: Bandwidth Allocation Based on the QoS Group Classification Without Using Modular QoS CLI

The ISP wants to allocate four times the bandwidth for traffic classified with QoS group 3 when compared to traffic classified with QoS group 0 on a router's HSSI0/0/0 interface. Assume that packets were already assigned the QoS group label by a different application, and packets with only QoS group labels 0 and 3 are allowed in the ISP router.

Listing 4-11 shows how to enable QoS group-based WFQ without using modular QoS CLI.

Listing 4-11   *Allocate 80 Percent of the Bandwidth to QoS Group 3 Traffic*

```
interface hssi0/0/0
  fair-queue qos-group
  fair-queue qos-group 3 weight 80
```

The bandwidth is allocated in a ratio of 4:1 between QoS groups 3 and 0. Because the weight indicates the percentage of bandwidth, the ratio of the weights to get the bandwidth allocation desired is 80:20 for QoS groups 3 and 1.

Listing 4-12 shows the information on DWFQ parameters and operation on the router.

Listing 4-12   *DWFQ Information*

```
Router#show interface fair
HSSI0/0/0 queue size 0
    packets output 3142, wfq drops 32, nobuffer drops 0
 WFQ: aggregate queue limit 5972, individual queue limit 2986
    max available buffers 5972

  Class 0: weight 20  limit 2986 qsize 0 packets output 11 drops 1
  Class 3: weight 80  limit 2986 qsize 0 packets output 3131 drops 31
qsize 0 packets output 0 drops
```

Priority Queuing

Priority queuing maintains four output subqueues—high, medium, normal, and low—in decreasing order of priority. A network administrator can classify flows to fall into any of these four queues. Packets on the highest-priority queue are transmitted first. When that queue empties, traffic on the next-highest-priority queue is transmitted, and so on. No packets in the medium-priority queue are serviced if packets in the high-priority queue are waiting for service.

Priority queuing is intended for environments where mission-critical data needs to be categorized as the highest priority, even if it means starving the lower-priority traffic at times of congestion. During congestion, mission-critical data can potentially take 100 percent of the bandwidth. If the high-priority traffic equals or exceeds the line rate for a period of time, priority queuing always lets the highest-priority traffic go before the next-highest-priority traffic and, in the worst case, drops important control traffic.

Priority queuing is implemented to classify packets into any of the priority queues based on input interface, simple and extended IP access lists, packet size, and application.

Note that unclassified traffic, which isn't classified to fall into any of the four priority queues, goes to the normal queue. The packets within a priority queue follow FIFO order of service.

Case Study 4-9: IP Traffic Prioritization Based on IP Precedence

An Internet firm classifies its traffic with IP precedence values 0, 1, 2, and 3 based on their importance. The more important the traffic, the higher the precedence value it gets. High-precedence traffic has a strict priority over all lower-precedence traffic.

Use of remaining IP precedence values is left for future application traffic with more stringent needs and is not supported today. If unsupported precedence values are used, such traffic gets the priority of a precedence 0 packet.

As discussed previously, priority queuing offers four priority queues that are serviced strictly in the order of their priority. The priority queues of high, medium, normal, and low are mapped to precedence values 3, 2, 1, and 0, respectively. Listing 4-13 is a sample configuration on the router to achieve this functionality.

Listing 4-13 *Priority Queuing Based on IP Precedence*

```
interface Serial0
 ip address 201.201.201.2 255.255.255.252
 priority-group 1


access-list 100 permit ip any any precedence routine
access-list 101 permit ip any any precedence priority
access-list 102 permit ip any any precedence immediate
access-list 103 permit ip any any precedence flash
priority-list 1 protocol ip high list 103
priority-list 1 protocol ip medium list 102
priority-list 1 protocol ip normal list 101
priority-list 1 protocol ip low list 100
priority-list 1 default low
```

Listings 4-14 and 4-15 show the current priority queuing configuration and interface queuing strategy information, respectively. The **show queueing priority** command shows the current priority queue configuration on the router. The **show interface serial0** command shows the priority list configured on the interface as well as packet statistics for the four priority queues.

Listing 4-14 *Information on Priority Queuing Parameters*

```
Router#show queueing priority
Current priority queue configuration:
List   Queue  Args
1      low    default
1      high   protocol ip        list 103
1      medium protocol ip        list 102
1      normal protocol ip        list 101
1      low    protocol ip        list 100
```

Listing 4-15 *Interface Queuing Strategy Information*

```
Router#show interface serial0
<top portion deleted>
Queueing strategy: priority-list 1
  Output queue (queue priority: size/max/drops):
     high: 2/20/0, medium: 0/40/0, normal: 0/60/0, low: 4/80/0
<bottom portion deleted>
```

Case Study 4-10: Packet Prioritization Based on Size

An enterprise firm often sees large and varying delays over its WAN link for its mission-critical transactional traffic and Voice over IP (VoIP) traffic whose packet sizes fall below 100 bytes. The firm likes the router to process traffic with packet sizes below 100 bytes whenever it arrives, without regard for the rest of the traffic waiting to be scheduled. The router can send the rest of the traffic only if no traffic with a packet size of 100 bytes or below is waiting in the queue.

Listing 4-16 gives a sample configuration to enable priority queuing based on packet size.

Listing 4-16 *Priority Queuing Based on Packet Size*

```
interface serial 0
 priority-group 1

priority-list 1 protocol ip high lt 100
priority-list 1 default low
```

Case Study 4-11: Packet Prioritization Based on Source Address

A large corporate branch office connects to the head office using a T1 link. One of the subnets, 213.13.13.0/28 at the branch site, hosts critical applications and servers. The network administrator for the field office wants to prioritize any traffic coming from this subnet over the user traffic generated by the rest of the branch office network.

Listing 4-17 lists the configuration to enable priority queuing based on the source IP address.

Listing 4-17 *Priority Queuing Based on Source Address*

```
interface serial 0
 priority-group 1


priority-list 1 protocol ip high list 1
priority-list 1 default low

access-list 1 permit 213.13.13.0 0.0.0.15
```

Custom Queuing

Whereas priority queuing potentially guarantees the entire bandwidth for mission-critical data at the expense of low-priority data, custom queuing guarantees a minimum bandwidth for each traffic classification.

This bandwidth reservation discipline services each nonempty queue sequentially in a round-robin fashion, transmitting a configurable percentage of traffic on each queue. Custom queuing guarantees that mission-critical data is always assigned a certain percentage of the bandwidth, while assuring predictable throughput for other traffic. You can think of custom queuing as CBWFQ with lots of configuration details.

You can classify traffic into 16 queues. Apart from the 16 queues is a special 0 queue, called the *system queue*. The system queue handles high-priority packets, such as keepalive packets and control packets. User traffic cannot be classified into this queue. Custom queuing is implemented to classify IP packets into any of the 16 queues based on input interface, simple and extended IP access lists, packet size, and application type.

A popular use of custom queuing is to guarantee a certain bandwidth to a set of places selected by an access list. To allocate bandwidth to different queues, you must specify the byte count for each queue.

How Byte Count Is Used in Custom Queuing

In custom queuing, the router sends packets from a particular queue until the byte count is exceeded. Even after the byte count value is exceeded, the packet currently being transmitted is completely sent. Therefore, if you set the byte count to 100 bytes and your protocol's packet size is 1024 bytes, every time this queue is serviced, 1024 bytes are sent, not 100 bytes.

Assume that one protocol has 500-byte packets, another has 300-byte packets, and a third has 100-byte packets. If you want to split the bandwidth evenly across all three protocols, you might choose to specify byte counts of 200, 200, and 200 for each queue. This configuration does not result in a 33/33/33 ratio, however. When the router services the first queue, it sends a single 500-byte packet; when it services the second queue, it sends a 300-byte packet; and when it services the third queue, it sends two 100-byte packets. The effective ratio is 50/30/20. Thus, setting the byte count too low can result in an unintended bandwidth allocation.

Large byte counts produce a "jerky" distribution, however. That is, if you assign 10 KB, 10 KB, and 10 KB to three queues in the example given, each protocol is serviced promptly when its queue is the one being serviced, but it might be a long time before the queue is serviced again. A better solution is to specify 500-byte, 600-byte, and 500-byte counts for the queue. This configuration results in a ratio of 31:38:31, which might be acceptable.

To service queues in a timely manner, and to ensure that the configured bandwidth allocation is as close as possible to the required bandwidth allocation, you must determine the byte count based on each protocol's packet size. Otherwise, your percentages might not match what you configure.

Case Study 4-12: Minimum Interface Bandwidth for Different Protocols

A network administrator wants to allocate bandwidth among protocols A, B, and C as 20 percent, 60 percent, and 20 percent, respectively. It was found that on average, the packet size for protocol A is 1086 bytes, protocol B is 291 bytes, and protocol C is 831 bytes.

To use custom queuing to achieve this functionality, it is necessary to find the right byte-count values for each protocol queue leading to the intended bandwidth allocation.

To determine the correct byte counts, perform the following tasks:

Step 1   For each queue, divide the percentage of bandwidth you want to allocate to the queue by the packet size, in bytes. The ratios are

20:1086, 60:291, 20:831

or

0.01842, 0.20619, 0.02407

Step 2 Normalize the numbers by dividing by the lowest number:

1, 11.2, 1.3

The result is the ratio of the number of packets that must be sent so that the percentage of bandwidth each protocol uses is approximately 20, 60, and 20 percent.

Step 3 A fraction in any of the ratio values means an additional packet is sent. Round up the numbers to the next whole number to obtain the actual packet count.

In this example, the actual ratio is 1 packet, 12 packets, and 2 packets.

Step 4 Convert the packet number ratio into byte counts by multiplying each packet count by the corresponding packet size.

In this example, the number of packets sent is one 1086-byte packet, twelve 291-byte packets, and two 831-byte packets, or 1086, 3492, and 1662 bytes, respectively, from each queue. These are the byte counts you would specify in your custom queuing configuration.

Step 5 To determine the bandwidth distribution this ratio represents, first determine the total number of bytes sent after all three queues are serviced:

$(1 \times 1086) + (12 \times 291) + (2 \times 831) = 1086 + 3492 + 1662 = 6240$

Step 6 Then determine the percentage of the total number of bytes sent from each queue:

$1086 \div 6240$, $3492 \div 6240$, $1662 \div 6240 = 17.4\%$, 56%, and 26.6%

As you can see, this is close to the desired ratio of 20:60:20.

Step 7 If the actual bandwidth is not close enough to the desired bandwidth, multiply the original ratio of 1:11.2:1.3 in Step 2 by the best value, in order to get the ratio as close to three integer values as possible. Note that the multiplier you use need not be an integer. If you multiply the ratio by 2, for example, you get 2:22.4:2.6. You would now send two 1086-byte packets, twenty-three 291-byte packets, and three 831-byte packets, or 2172:6693:2493, for a total of 11,358 bytes. The resulting ratio is 19:59:22 percent, which is much closer to the desired ratio you achieved.

Listing 4-18 is the sample configuration needed to stipulate the byte count of the three protocol queues and the assignment of each protocol traffic to its appropriate queue. The configured custom Queue 1 is enabled on interface Serial0/0/3.

Listing 4-18   *Enabling Custom Queuing*

```
interface Serial0/0/3
 custom-queue-list 1

queue-list 1 protocol ip 1 tcp <protocolA>
queue-list 1 protocol ip 2 tcp <protocolB>
queue-list 1 protocol ip 3 tcp <protocolC>
queue-list 1 queue 1 byte-count 2172
queue-list 1 queue 2 byte-count 6693
queue-list 1 queue 3 byte-count 2493
```

Listings 4-19 and 4-20 show information on the custom queuing configuration and the interface queuing strategy, respectively. The **show queueing custom** command is used to display the custom queuing configuration.

Listing 4-19   *Information on Custom Queuing Configuration*

```
Router#show queueing custom
Current custom queue configuration:

List    Queue   Args
1       1       protocol ip          tcp port <protocolA>
1       2       protocol ip          tcp port <protocolB>
1       3       protocol ip          tcp port <protocolC>
1       1       byte-count 2172
1       2       byte-count 6693
1       3       byte-count 2493
```

Listing 4-20   *Interface Queuing Strategy and Queue Statistics*

```
Router#show interface serial0/0/3
<top portion deleted>
Queueing strategy: custom-list 1
  Output queues: (queue #: size/max/drops)
      0: 0/20/0 1: 0/20/0 2: 0/20/0 3: 0/20/0 4: 0/20/0
      5: 0/20/0 6: 0/20/0 7: 0/20/0 8: 0/20/0 9: 0/20/0
      10: 0/20/0 11: 0/20/0 12: 0/20/0 13: 0/20/0 14: 0/20/0
      15: 0/20/0 16: 0/20/0
<bottom portion deleted>
```

The **show interface** command gives the maximum queue size of each of the 16 queues under custom queuing, along with the instantaneous queue size and packet drop statistics per queue at the time the command is issued.

Also, note that window size affects the bandwidth distribution as well. If the window size of a particular protocol is set to 1, that protocol does not place another packet into the queue until it receives an acknowledgment. The custom queuing algorithm moves to the next queue if the byte count is exceeded or if no packets are in that queue.

Therefore, with a window size of 1, only one packet is sent each time. If the byte count is set to 2 KB and the packet size is 256 bytes, only 256 bytes are sent each time this queue is serviced.

NOTE	Although custom queuing allows bandwidth reservation per traffic class, as does CBWFQ, CBWFQ has many advantages over custom queuing. Some are listed here:

  • Setting up CBWFQ is far easier and straightforward compared to enabling custom queuing for bandwidth allocations.

  • RSVP depends on CBWFQ for bandwidth allocation.

  • With CBWFQ, you can apply packet drop policies such as Random Early Detection (RED) on each traffic class, in addition to allocating a minimum bandwidth.

  • You are no longer limited to 16 custom queues. CBWFQ supports 64 classes.

Scheduling Mechanisms for Voice Traffic

Voice traffic requires minimum delay and jitter (delay variation) to be intelligible to the listener. Although CBWFQ and custom queuing scheduling mechanisms can give bandwidth guarantees for voice, they cannot provide the jitter bounds acceptable for voice traffic. Voice has relatively low bandwidth demands (typically 64 kbps) but more stringent delay and jitter needs. Hence, CBWFQ and custom queuing are modified to implement a strict priority queue(s) to carry voice and thereby minimize drastically delay and jitter for voice traffic. A strict priority queue is also called a *low latency queue*.

Apart from voice, you can use the strict priority queues to carry other real-time, delay-sensitive application traffic.

CBWFQ with a Priority Queue

CBWFQ with a priority queue affords a scheduling mechanism providing a strict priority queuing scheme for delay-sensitive traffic, such as voice, and CBWFQ scheduling for differentiation and bandwidth guarantees among the other traffic classes. CBWFQ with a priority queue is also called *low latency queuing (LLQ)*.

A voice priority queue in CBWFQ provides a single priority queue behaving similar to the high-priority queue discussed in the priority queuing section of this chapter. The remaining queues are CBWFQ queues (one queue per traffic class) delivering differentiation and bandwidth guarantees among the queues based on the configured weight or the bandwidth allocated for each queue.

You can identify voice traffic by its Real-time Transport Protocol (RTP) port numbers and classify it into a priority queue by using the **ip rtp priority** command on an output interface. RTP is discussed in Appendix D, "Real-time Transport Protocol."

A busy priority queue can potentially starve the remaining queues on an interface, making the performance seen by the CBWFQ queues less than desirable. To alleviate this problem, a user can set up a maximum bandwidth against which the traffic serviced by the priority queue is policed. If the traffic exceeds the configured bandwidth, all excess traffic is dropped. Note that this might not always be the right way of policing traffic, because it is based on bandwidth rather than voice calls.

The sum of the bandwidths for the priority queue and the CBWFQ queues is not allowed to exceed 75 percent of the interface bandwidth. This is done to provide room for other unclassified traffic and Layer 2 encapsulations. However, using the **max-reserved-bandwidth** command, you can modify the default maximum reservable bandwidth.

Even with the priority queue in CBWFQ, the queuing system can't service and transmit a voice packet arriving on an empty priority queue immediately, because it needs to finish scheduling the packet it is already servicing and transmit it on the wire. Voice packets are small in size, but the data packet sizes carried in the CBWFQ queues can potentially be large. The larger the packet sizes, the greater the possible delay seen by the packets in the voice traffic.

This delay can be more perceivable on low-speed interfaces. To reduce voice traffic delay, Multilink Point-to-Point (MLPP) fragmentation needs to be configured for low-speed interfaces to fragment the large data packets so that you can interleave the small voice packets between the data fragments that make up a large data packet. MLPP is discussed in Appendix E, "General IP Line Efficiency Functions."

NOTE   You can enable the voice priority queue in conjunction with not only CBWFQ, but also flow-based WFQ.

Case Study 4-13: Strict Priority Queue for Voice

Enable a router interface to service all voice traffic up to a rate of 640 Kbps with strict priority.

Listings 4-21 and 4-22 discuss enabling a strict priority queue for voice traffic using flow-based WFQ and CBWFQ, respectively.

Listing 4-21   *Enabling a Strict Priority Queue for Voice Traffic up to 640 Kbps*

```
interface Serial0
 ip rtp priority 16384 16383 640
```

On a serial interface, flow-based WFQ is on by default. On an interface with bandwidth higher than 2 Mbps, you can turn on flow-based WFQ using the **fair-queue** command. In the previous configuration, the entire voice port range is specified; from 16384 to 32767 applies to Cisco VoIP devices to ensure that all voice traffic is given strict priority service by using the **ip rtp priority** command. In flow-based WFQ, a priority queue is assigned a special weight of 0.

Listing 4-22   *Enabling a Strict Priority Queue for Voice Traffic up to 640 Kbps Using CBWFQ*

```
class-map premium
 match <premium voice traffic>

policy-map premiumpolicy
 class premium
 priority 640

interface serial0
 service-policy output premiumpolicy
```

On interface serial0, CBWFQ allocates a minimum bandwidth of 640 Kbps to the premium voice traffic using CBWFQ. CBWFQ services the voice traffic on a strict priority queue based on the **priority** command under the **policy-map** configuration.

Custom Queuing with Priority Queues

As discussed earlier in this chapter, custom queuing is used to allocate minimum interface bandwidth for a certain traffic class. Although custom queuing can give bandwidth guarantees, it still can cause unacceptable delays for the queue with voice or other delay-sensitive traffic, because it needs to wait while the other queues are serviced based on their byte-count allocations.

To service voice traffic with minimum delays, you can modify some or all of the custom queues of the normal custom queuing scheduling mechanism to act as priority queues, similar to the priority queues of the priority queuing scheme.

Custom queuing supports up to 16 queues per interface. To support priority queue(s), one of the 16 queues can be set up as the lowest-custom queue. This modifies all queues before the lowest-custom queue to be priority queues. If Queue 6 is configured as a lowest-custom queue, for example, Queues 1–5 act as priority queues and queues 6–16 act as custom queues. Queues 1–5 are in decreasing order of priority. Queue 1 is the highest-priority queue and Queue 5 the lowest.

If a custom queue is being serviced when the priority queues are empty, a newly arrived packet in a priority queue needs to wait until the custom queue is serviced according to its byte-count allocation. So the byte counts need to be kept low to avoid large delays for priority packets.

NOTE   Note that MWRR and MDRR scheduling can also support voice when one of their queues is made a strict priority queue. MWRR and MDRR algorithms are discussed in Chapter 5.

Summary

At times of network congestion, a scheduling discipline can allocate a specific bandwidth to a certain traffic flow or packet class by determining the order in which the packets in its queue get serviced. In flow-based WFQ, all flows with the same weight are treated fairly based on the max-min fair-share algorithm, and flows with different weights get unequal bandwidth allocations based on their weights. The CBWFQ algorithm is a class-based WFQ mechanism using modular QoS CLI. It is used to allocate a minimum guaranteed bandwidth to a traffic class. Each traffic class is allocated a different subqueue and is serviced according to its bandwidth allocation.

Priority and custom queuing algorithms service queues on a strict priority and round-robin basis, respectively. Voice traffic can be serviced on a strict priority queue in CBWFQ and custom queuing so that voice traffic sees low jitter.

Frequently Asked Questions

Q — *Explain the queuing mechanisms using the frequently used airline industry analogy.*

A — Comparing the queuing analogy to the airline industry, a FIFO queue is analogous to an airline queuing model whereby passengers belonging to all classes—first, business, and economy—have a single queue to board the plane. No service differentiation exists in this queuing model.

CBWFQ, MWRR, and MDRR are analogous to an airline queuing service that assigns a separate queue for each class of passengers, with a weight or bandwidth assigned to each queue. A passenger queue is serviced at a rate determined by its weight or bandwidth allocation.

In an airline model analogous to priority queuing, a separate queue for first, business, and economy is used, and they are served in strict priority—in other words, those in the first-class queue are served first. An airline model serving ten passengers from first class, six from business class, and four from economy class on a round-robin basis is similar to the custom queuing model.

Q — *How is the bandwidth used in CBWFQ when one class is not using its allocated bandwidth?*

A — The bandwidth specified for a traffic class in CBWFQ is its minimum guaranteed bandwidth at times of congestion. If a traffic class is not using its allocated bandwidth to its fullest, the other traffic classes in the queuing system can use any leftover bandwidth in proportion to their assigned bandwidth.

Q — *Are there any exceptions to the precedence-based weight assignment procedure in flow-based WFQ?*

A — Yes. Weight is based on IP precedence for IP traffic unless any of the following four conditions applies:

- RSVP has negotiated a specific weight for a specific flow.

- The traffic is voice and Local Frame Interleave is on.

- The traffic is a locally generated packet, such as a routing update packet set with an internal packet priority flag.

- A strict priority queue for voice is enabled by using the **ip rtp priority** command.

In each of those cases, a weight specific to the application is used.

Q — *How does flow-based WFQ treat non-IP traffic?*

A — There are separate classification routines for non-IP flows based on the packet's data link layer type (for example, IPX, AppleTalk, DECnet, BRIDGE, RSRB). All these non-IP flows are assigned a weight similar to an IP precedence 0 packet. Each non-IP conversation has a separate flow and is based on the data link layer type. Thus, even though you treat non-IP flows as precedence 0 packets, you provide fairness among the non-IP protocols.

Q — *I have WFQ scheduling on my interface. But the actual bandwidth usage between the various traffic classes is different from the theoretical allocation. Why?*

A — You use the **show interfaces fair** or **show queueing fair** command to observe queue depths and drop counts for each traffic class. In this way, you can determine whether the load is such that you can expect achieved bandwidth ratios to equal configured ratios. If the load is not sufficient to keep all class queues nonempty, the achieved bandwidth allocation does not match the theoretical allocation because the WFQ algorithm is a work-conserving algorithm and allows classes to use all available bandwidth.

References

[1] "An Engineering Approach to Computer Networking," S. Keshav, Reading, MA: Addison-Wesley, 1997.

[2] "A classical self-clocked WFQ algorithm," A. Demers, S. Keshav, and S. Shenker, SIGCOMM 1989, Austin, TX, September 1989.

CHAPTER 5

Per-Hop Behavior: Resource Allocation II

The right packet scheduling mechanism for a router depends on its switching architecture. Weighted Fair Queuing (WFQ) is a scheduling algorithm for resource allocation on Cisco router platforms with a bus-based architecture. Cisco platforms using a switch fabric for packet switching tend to use a scheduling algorithm that better suits that architecture. In particular, the Cisco Catalyst family of switches and 8540 routers use the Modified Weighted Round Robin (MWRR) algorithm, and the Cisco 12000 series routers use the Modified Deficit Round Robin (MDRR) algorithm. Both MWRR and MDRR are similar in scheduling behavior to WFQ because they, too, simulate Generalized Processor Sharing (GPS).

The next two sections provide a detailed discussion of the MWRR and MDRR algorithms.

Modified Weighted Round Robin (MWRR)

Round-robin scheduling that serves a packet rather than an infinitesimal amount from each nonempty queue is the simplest way to simulate GPS. It works well in representing a GPS scheduler if all packets are the same size. Weighted Round Robin (WRR) is an extension of round-robin scheduling in which each flow is assigned a weight[1]. WRR serves a flow in proportion to its weight.

WRR scheduling is well suited when an Asynchronous Transfer Mode (ATM) switch fabric is used for switching. Internally, the switch fabric treats packets as cells, and WRR is used to schedule the cells in the queues. WRR is essentially a cell-based round robin, whereby the weight determines how many cells are scheduled in each round robin. Hence, each queue shares the interface bandwidth of the ratio of the weights independent of packet sizes.

You can schedule only packets, not cells. Therefore, all cells of a packet are served in the same pass, even when you need to borrow some weight from the future. To support variable-size packets, MWRR uses a deficit counter associated with each WRR queue. This gives MWRR some characteristics of the Deficit Round Robin (DRR) algorithm described in the next section.

Before a queue is serviced, its deficit counter is initialized to the queue's weight. A packet from a queue is scheduled only if the deficit counter is greater than zero. After serving the n-cell packet, the resulting counter is decremented by n. Packets are scheduled as long as the counter is greater than 0. Otherwise, you skip to the next queue. In each coming round, the queue's deficit counter is incremented by the queue's weight. No packet is scheduled, however, if the deficit counter is still not greater than 0. If the counter becomes greater than 0, a packet is scheduled. After serving the packet, the deficit counter is decremented by the number of cells in the packet. By using a deficit counter, MWRR works independent of the variable-length packet sizes in the long run.

The effective bandwidth for each queue is proportional to its weight:

Effective queue bandwidth = (Queue weight × Interface bandwidth) ÷ Sum of all active queue weights)

An Illustration of MWRR Operation

In this example, consider three queues with the assigned weights shown in Table 5-1. Figure 5-1 depicts the queues along with their deficit counters. Deficit counters are used to make WRR support variable packet sizes.

Table 5-1   *Weights Associated with Each Queue*

Queue	Weight
2	4
1	3
0	2

The queues show the cells queued, and the cells making up a packet are marked in the same shade of black. Queue 2, for example, has a 2-cell, 3-cell, and 4-cell packet in its queue.

Queue 0 is the first queue being served. The deficit counter is initialized to 2, the queue's weight. At the head of the queue is a 4-cell packet. Therefore, the deficit counter becomes $2 - 4 = -2$ after serving the packet. Because the deficit counter is negative, the queue cannot be served until it accumulates to a value greater than zero, as in Figure 5-2.

Queue 1 is the next queue to be served. Its deficit counter is initialized to 3. The 3-cell packet at the head of the queue is served, which makes the deficit counter become $3 - 3 = 0$. Because the counter is not greater than zero, you skip to the next queue, as in Figure 5-3.

Figure 5-1   *WRR Queues with Their Deficit Counters Before Start of Service*

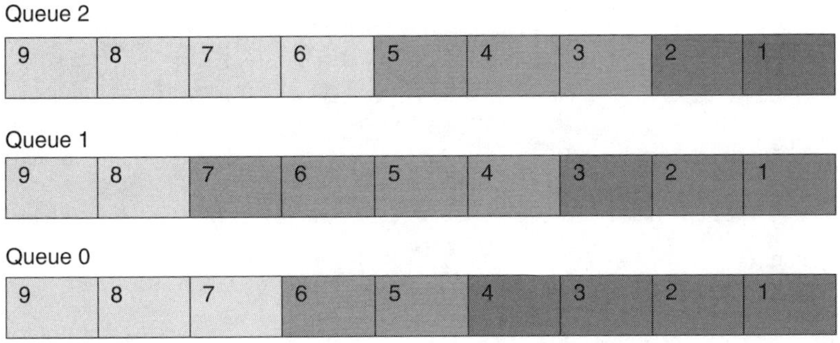

Queue 2

| 9 | 8 | 7 | 6 | 5 | 4 | 3 | 2 | 1 |

Queue 1

| 9 | 8 | 7 | 6 | 5 | 4 | 3 | 2 | 1 |

Queue 0

| 9 | 8 | 7 | 6 | 5 | 4 | 3 | 2 | 1 |

Queue	Deficit counter
0	0
1	0
2	0

Figure 5-2   *MWRR After Serving Queue 0 in the First Round*

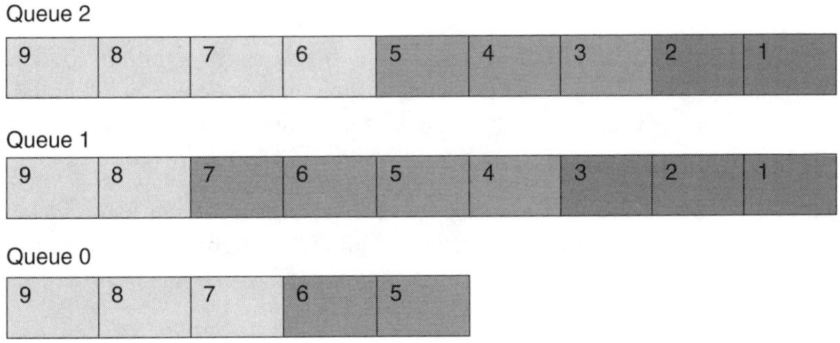

Queue 2

| 9 | 8 | 7 | 6 | 5 | 4 | 3 | 2 | 1 |

Queue 1

| 9 | 8 | 7 | 6 | 5 | 4 | 3 | 2 | 1 |

Queue 0

| 9 | 8 | 7 | 6 | 5 |

Queue	Deficit counter
2	0
1	0
0	-2

Figure 5-3   *MWRR After Serving Queue 1 in the First Round*

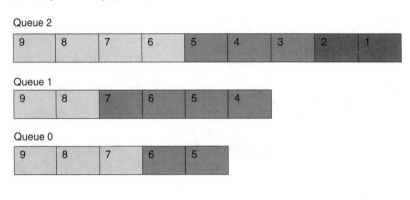

Queue	Deficit counter
2	0
1	0
0	-2

Now it is Queue 2's turn to be serviced. Its deficit counter is initialized to 4. The 2-cell packet at the head of the queue is served, which makes the deficit counter $4 - 2 = 2$. The next 3-cell packet is also served, as the deficit counter is greater than zero. After the 3-cell packet is served, the deficit counter is $2 - 3 = -1$, as in Figure 5-4.

Queue 0 is now served in the second round. The deficit counter from the last round was –2. Incrementing the deficit counter by the queue's weight makes the counter $-2 + 2 = 0$. No packet can be served because the deficit counter is still not greater than zero, so you skip to the next queue, as in Figure 5-5.

Queue 1 has a deficit counter of zero in the first round. For the second round, the deficit counter is $0 + 3 = 3$. The 4-cell packet at the head of the queue is served, making the deficit counter $3 - 4 = -1$, as in Figure 5-6.

Figure 5-4   *MWRR After Serving Queue 2 in the First Round*

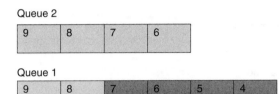

Queue 2

9	8	7	6	

Queue 1

9	8	7	6	5	4

Queue 0

9	8	7	6	5

Queue	Deficit counter
2	-1
1	0
0	-2

Figure 5-5   *MWRR After Serving Queue 0 in the Second Round*

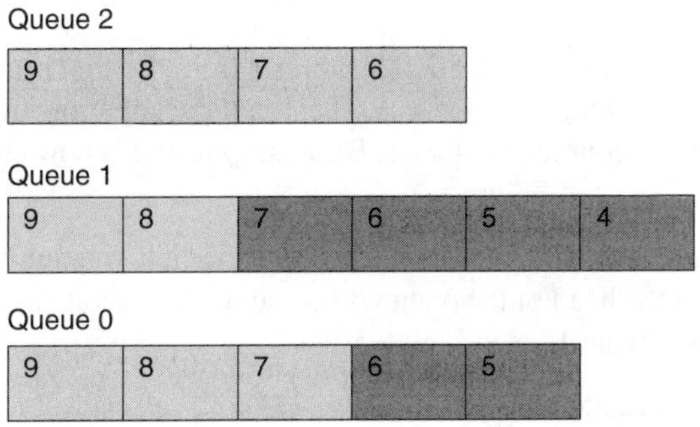

Queue 2

9	8	7	6	

Queue 1

9	8	7	6	5	4

Queue 0

9	8	7	6	5

Queue	Deficit counter
2	-1
1	0
0	0

Figure 5-6 *MWRR After Serving Queue 1 in the Second Round*

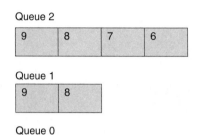

Queue	Deficit counter
2	-1
1	-1
0	0

In the second round, Queue 2's deficit counter from the first round is incremented by the queue's weight, making it $-1 + 4 = 3$. The 4-cell packet at the head of Queue 2 is served, making the deficit counter $3 - 4 = -1$. Because Queue 2 is now empty, the deficit counter is initialized to zero, as in Figure 5-7.

Now, it is again Queue 0's turn to be served. Its deficit counter becomes $0 + 2 = 2$. The 2-cell packet at the head of the queue is served, which results in a deficit counter of $2 - 2 = 0$. Now skip to Queue 1, as in Figure 5-8.

Queue 1's new deficit counter is $-1 + 3 = 2$. The 2-cell packet at the head of Queue 1 is served, resulting in a deficit counter of $2 - 2 = 0$. The resulting Queue 1 is now empty. Because Queue 2 is already empty, skip to Queue 0, as in Figure 5-9.

Figure 5-7   *MWRR After Serving Queue 2 in the Second Round*

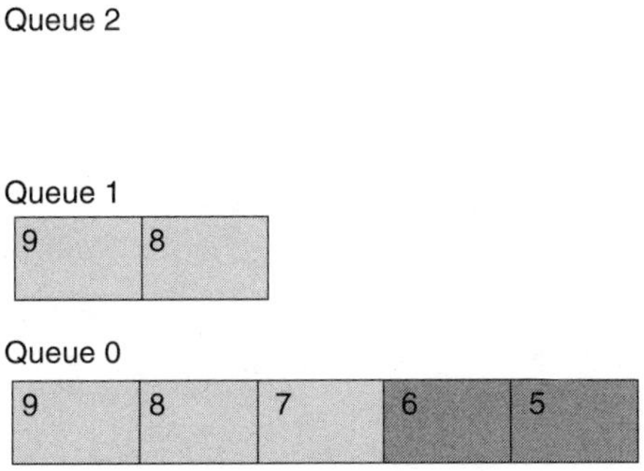

Queue 2

Queue 1

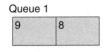

Queue 0

Queue	Deficit counter
2	0
1	-1
0	0

Figure 5-8   *MWRR After Serving Queue 0 in the Third Round*

Queue 2

Queue 1

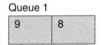

Queue 0

Queue	Deficit counter
2	0
1	-1
0	0

Figure 5-9 *MWRR After Serving Queue 1 in the Third Round*

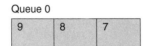

Queue 2

Queue 1

Queue 0

9	8	7

Queue	Deficit counter
2	0
1	0
0	0

Queue 0's deficit counter in the fourth round becomes 2. The 3-cell packet is served, which makes the deficit counter equal to −1. Because Queue 0 is now empty, reset the deficit counter to zero.

MWRR Implementation

MWRR is implemented in the Cisco Catalyst family of switches and the Cisco 8540 routers. These switches and routers differ in terms of the number of available MWRR queues and in the ways you can classify traffic into the queues.

MWRR in 8540 routers offers four queues between any interface pair based on Type of Service (ToS) group bits. Table 5-2 shows the ToS class allocation based on the IP precedence bits.

Table 5-2 *MWRR ToS Class Allocation*

IP Precedence Bits	ToS Class Bits	ToS Class Assigned
000	00	0
001	00	1
010	01	2
011	01	3

Table 5-2   *MWRR ToS Class Allocation (Continued)*

IP Precedence Bits	ToS Class Bits	ToS Class Assigned
100	10	0
101	10	1
110	11	2
111	11	3

NOTE   8500 ToS-based MWRR is similar to ToS-based Distributed WFQ (DWFQ), discussed in Chapter 4, "Per-Hop Behavior: Resource Allocation I," but differs in terms of which precedence bits are used to implement it. ToS-based DWFQ uses the two low-order precedence bits, whereas 8500 ToS-based MWRR uses the two high-order precedence bits.

Catalyst 6000 and 6500 series switches use MWRR with two queues, Queue 1 and Queue 2, based on the Layer 2 Institute of Electrical and Electronic Engineers (IEEE) 802.1p Class of Service (CoS) field. Frames with CoS values of 0–3 go to Queue 1, and frames with CoS values of 4–7 go to Queue 2. 802.1p CoS is discussed in Chapter 8, "Layer 2 QoS: Interworking with IP QoS."

6500 series switches also implement strict priority queues as part of MWRR to support the low-latency requirements of voice and other real-time traffic.

Case Study 5-1: Class-Based MWRR Scheduling

A large Internet service provider (ISP) decides to categorize its traffic into four classes in a network backbone made up of a Cisco 8540 router based on IP precedence, as shown in Table 5-3. Each class is assigned traffic belonging to two IP precedence values—one precedence value each for normal and excess traffic. Classes 0–3 need to be allocated 15 percent, 15 percent, 30 percent, and 40 percent of the link bandwidth, respectively.

Table 5-3   *IP Precedence Allocation Based on Traffic Class*

	Critical (Class 3)	Expensive (Class 2)	Moderate (Class 1)	Cheap (Class 0)
Normal Traffic	Precedence 7	Precedence 5	Precedence 3	Precedence 1
Excess Traffic	Precedence 6	Precedence 4	Precedence 2	Precedence 0

You can enable Quality of Service (QoS)-based forwarding in an 8540 router by using the global command **qos switching**. The default weight allocation for ToS classes 0–3 is 1, 2, 4, and 8, respectively. Hence, ToS classes 0–3 get an effective bandwidth of 1/15, 2/15, 4/15, and 8/15 of the interface bandwidth.

In this case, the bandwidth allocation for classes 0–3 is 15:15:30:40 or 3:3:6:8 because the WRR scheduling weight can only be between 1–15.

Listing 5-1 shows a sample configuration to enable ToS-based MWRR globally on an 8500 router.

Listing 5-1   *Enabling ToS-Based MWRR*

```
qos switching
qos mapping precedence 0 wrr-weight 3
qos mapping precedence 1 wrr-weight 3
qos mapping precedence 2 wrr-weight 6
qos mapping precedence 3 wrr-weight 8
```

The configuration to QoS-switch according to the above criteria for traffic coming into port 1 and going out of port 0 only is given in Listing 5-2.

Listing 5-2   *Enabling ToS-Based MWRR on Specific Traffic*

```
qos switching
qos mapping <incoming interface> <outgoing interface>
    precedence 0 wrr-weight 3
qos mapping <incoming interface> <outgoing interface>
    precedence 1 wrr-weight 3
qos mapping <incoming interface> <outgoing interface>
    precedence 2 wrr-weight 6
qos mapping <incoming interface> <outgoing interface>
    precedence 3 wrr-weight 8
```

Modified Deficit Round Robin (MDRR)

This section discusses the MDRR algorithm for resource allocation available in the Cisco 12000 series routers. Within a DRR scheduler[2], each service queue has an associated *quantum value*—an average number of bytes served in each round—and a deficit counter initialized to the quantum value. Each nonempty flow queue is served in a round-robin fashion, scheduling on average packets of quantum bytes in each round. Packets in a service queue are served as long as the deficit counter is greater than zero. Each packet served decreases the deficit counter by a value equal to its length in bytes. A queue can no longer be served after the deficit counter becomes zero or negative. In each new round, each nonempty queue's deficit counter is incremented by its quantum value.

After a queue is served, the queue's deficit counter represents the amount of debit it incurred during the past round, depending on whether it was served equal to or more than its allocated quantum bytes. The amount the queue is entitled to be served in a subsequent round is reduced from the quantum bytes by a value equal to the deficit counter.

For efficiency, you should make the quantum size equal to the maximum packet size in the network. This ensures that the DRR scheduler always serves at least one packet from each nonempty flow queue.

NOTE   An empty flow queue's deficit counter is reset to zero so that credits are not accumulated indefinitely, as it would eventually lead to unfairness.

The general DRR algorithm described in this section is modified to allow a *low-latency* queue. In MDRR, all queues are serviced in a round-robin fashion with the exception of the low-latency queue. You can define this queue to run in either one of two ways: in strict priority or alternate priority mode.

In *strict priority mode*, the low-latency queue is serviced whenever the queue is nonempty. This allows the lowest possible delay for this traffic. It is conceivable, however, for the other queues to starve if the high-priority, low-latency queue is full for long periods of time because it can potentially take 100 percent of the interface bandwidth.

In *alternate priority mode*, the low-latency queue is serviced alternating between the low-latency queue and the remaining CoS queues. In addition to a low-latency queue, MDRR supports up to seven other queues, making the total number of queues to eight. Assuming that 0 is the low-latency queue, the queues are served in the following order: 0, 1, 0, 2, 0, 3, 0, 4, 0, 5, 0, 6, 0, 7.

In alternate priority mode the largest delay for Queue 0 is equal to the largest single quantum for the other queues rather than the sum of all the quanta for the queues if Queue 0 were served in traditional round-robin fashion.

In addition to being DRR-draining, MDRR is not conventional round-robin scheduling. Instead, DRR is modified in such a way that it limits the latency on one user-configurable queue, thus providing better jitter characteristics.

An MDRR Example

This example, which illustrates an alternate-priority low-latency queue, defines three queues—Queue 2, Queue 1, and Queue 0, with weights of 1, 2, and 1, respectively. Queue 2 is the low-latency queue running in alternate-priority mode. All the queues, along with their deficit counters, are shown in Figure 5-10.

Figure 5-10 *Queues 0–2, Along with Their Deficit Counters*

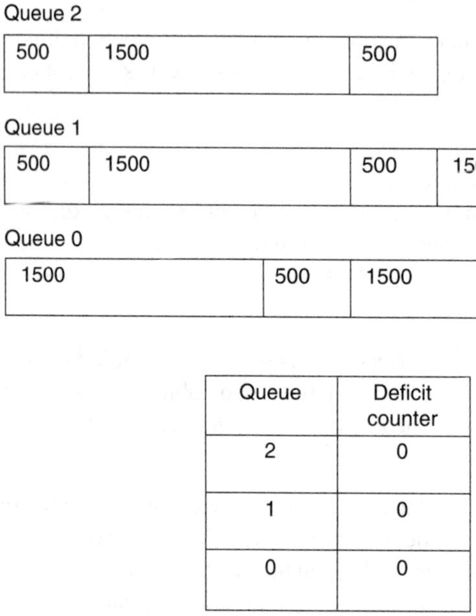

Queue 2

500	1500		500	

Queue 1

500	1500		500	1500

Queue 0

1500		500	1500	

Queue	Deficit counter
2	0
1	0
0	0

Table 5-4 provides the weight and quantum associated with each queue. When MDRR is run on the output interface queue, the interface maximum transmission unit (MTU) is used. When MDRR is run, the fabric queues.

Table 5-4 *Queues 0–2, Along with Their Associated Weights and Quantum Values*

Queue Number	Weight	Quantum = Weight × MTU (MTU = 1500 Bytes)
Queue 2	1	1500
Queue 1	2	3000
Queue 0	1	1500

On the first pass, Queue 2 is served. Queue 2's deficit counter is initialized to equal its quantum value, 1500. Queue 2 is served as long as the deficit counter is greater than 0. After serving a packet, size of the packet that was just transmitted from Queue2 is subtracted from its deficit counter. The first 500-byte packet from the queue gets served because the deficit counter is 1500. Now, the deficit counter is updated as 1500 – 500 = 1000. Therefore, the next packet is served. After the 1500-byte packet is served, the deficit counter becomes –500 and Queue 2 can no longer be served. Figure 5-11 shows the three queues and the deficit counters after Queue 2 is served.

Figure 5-11 *MDRR After Serving Queue 2, Its First Pass*

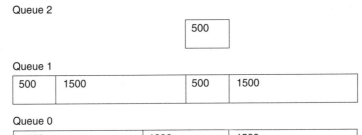

Queue 2

500

Queue 1

500	1500		500	1500

Queue 0

1500	1000	1500

Queue	Deficit counter
2	-500
1	0
0	0

Because you are in alternate-priority mode, you alternate between serving Queue 2 and another queue. This other queue is selected in a round-robin fashion. Consider that in the round robin, it is now Queue 0's turn. The deficit counter is initialized to 1500, the quantum value for the queue. The first 1500-byte packet is served. After serving the first packet, its deficit counter is updated as $1500 - 1500 = 0$. Hence, no other packet can be served in this pass. Figure 5-12 shows the three queues and their deficit counters after Queue 0 is served.

Because you alternate between the low-latency queue and the other queues served in the round robin, Queue 2 is served next. Queue 2's deficit counter is updated to $-500 + 1500 = 1000$. This allows the next packet in Queue 2 to be served. After sending the 500-byte packet, the deficit counter becomes 500. It could have served another packet, but Queue 2 is empty. Therefore, its deficit counter is reset to 0. An empty queue is not attended, and the deficit counter remains 0 until a packet arrives on the queue. Figure 5-13 shows the queues and the counters at this point.

Figure 5-12 *MDRR After Serving Queue 0, Its First Pass*

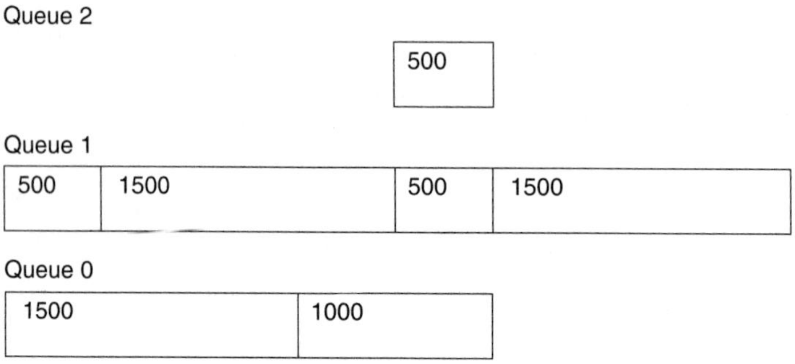

Queue 2

500

Queue 1

500	1500	500	1500

Queue 0

1500	1000

Queue	Deficit counter
2	-500
1	0
0	0

Figure 5-13 *MDRR After Serving Queue 2, Its Second Pass*

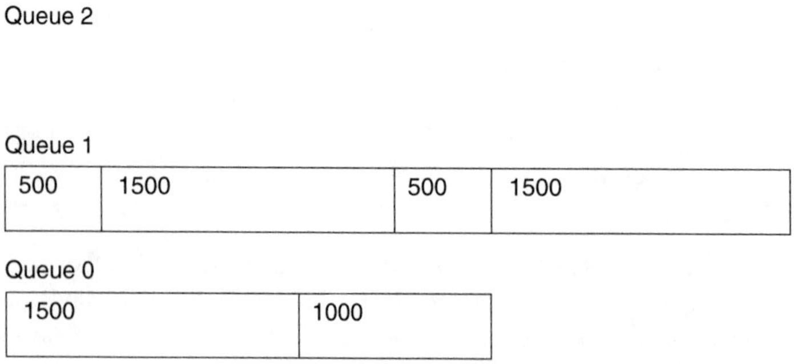

Queue 2

Queue 1

500	1500	500	1500

Queue 0

1500	1000

Queue	Deficit counter
2	0
1	0
0	0

Queue 1 is served next. It deficit counter is initialized to 3000. This allows three packets to be sent, leaving the deficit counter to be 3000 – 1500 – 500 – 1500 = –500. Figure 5-14 shows the queues and the deficit counters at this stage.

Figure 5-14 *MDRR After Serving Queue 1, Its First Pass*

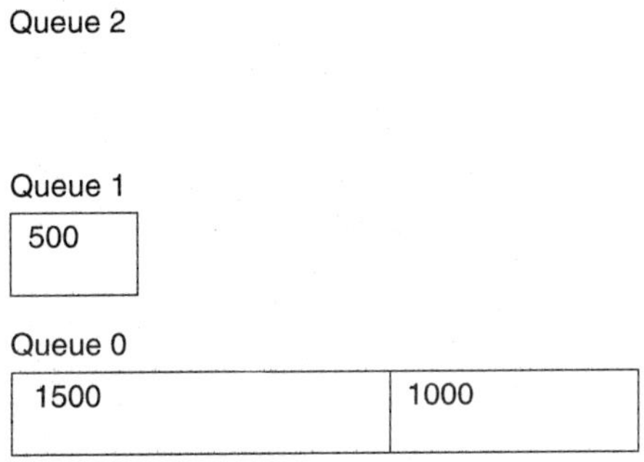

Queue 2

Queue 1

500

Queue 0

1500	1000

Queue	Deficit counter
2	0
1	-500
0	0

Queue 0 is the next queue serviced and sends two packets, making the deficit counter 1500 – 1000 – 1500 = –500. Because the queue is now empty, the deficit counter is reset to 0. Figure 5-15 depicts the queues and counters at this stage.

Queue 1 serves the remaining packet in a similar fashion in its next pass. Because the queue becomes empty, its deficit counter is reset to 0.

MDRR Implementation

Cisco 12000 series routers support MDRR. MDRR can run on the output interface queue (transmit [TX] side) or on the input interface queue (receive [RX] side) when feeding the fabric queues to the output interface.

Different hardware revisions of line cards termed as engine 0, 1, 2, 3, and so on, exist for Cisco 12000 series routers. The nature of MDRR support on a line card depends on the line card's hardware revision. Engine 0 supports MDRR software implementation. Line card hardware revisions, Engine 2 and above, support MDRR hardware implementation.

Figure 5-15 *MDRR After Serving Queue 0, Its Second Pass*

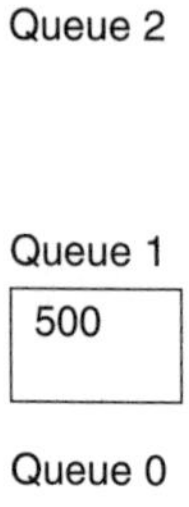

Queue 2

Queue 1

500

Queue 0

Queue	Deficit counter
2	0
1	-500
0	0

MDRR on the RX

MDRR is implemented in either software or hardware on a line card. In a software implementation, each line card can send traffic to 16 destination slots because the 12000 series routers use a 16x16 switching fabric. For each destination slot, the switching fabric has eight CoS queues, making the total number of CoS queues 128 (16 x 8). You can configure each CoS queue independently.

In the hardware implementation, each line card has eight CoS queues per destination interface. With 16 destination slots and 16 interfaces per slot, the maximum number of CoS queues is $16 \times 16 \times 8 = 2048$. All the interfaces on a destination slot have the same CoS parameters.

MDRR on the TX

Each interface has eight CoS queues, which you can configure independently in both hardware- and software-based MDRR implementations.

Flexible mapping between IP precedence and the eight possible queues is offered in the MDRR implementation. MDRR allows a maximum of eight queues so that each IP precedence value can be made its own queue. The mapping is flexible, however. The number of queues needed and the precedence values mapped to those queues are user-configurable. You can map one or more precedence values into a queue.

MDRR also offers individualized drop policy and bandwidth allocation. Each queue has its own associated Random Early Detection (RED) parameters that determine its drop thresholds and DRR quantum, the latter which determines how much bandwidth it gets. The quantum (in other words, the average number of bytes taken from the queue for each service) is user-configurable.

Case Study 5-2: Bandwidth Allocation and Minimum Jitter Configuration for Voice Traffic with Congestion Avoidance Policy

Traffic is classified into different classes so that a certain minimum bandwidth can be allocated for each class depending on the need and importance of the traffic. An ISP implements five traffic classes—gold, silver, bronze, best-effort, and a voice class carrying voice traffic and requiring minimum jitter.

You need four queues, 0–3, to carry the four traffic classes (best-effort, bronze, silver, gold), and a fifth low-latency queue to carry the voice traffic.

This example shows three OC3 Point-to-Point Protocol (PPP) over Synchronous Optical Network (SONET) (PoS) interfaces, one each in slots 1–3. Listing 5-3 gives a sample configuration for this purpose.

Listing 5-3 *Defining Traffic Classes and Allocating Them to Appropriate Queues with a Minimum Bandwidth During Congestion*

```
interface POS1/0
 tx-cos cos-a

interface POS2/0
 tx-cos cos-a

interface POS3/0
 tx-cos cos-a

slot-table-cos table-a
 destination-slot 0 cos-a
 destination-slot 1 cos-a
 destination-slot 2 cos-a

rx-cos-slot 1 table-a
rx-cos-slot 2 table-a
rx-cos-slot 3 table-a

cos-queue-group cos-a
 precedence all random-detect-label 0
 precedence 0 queue 0
 precedence 1 queue 1
```

continues

Listing 5-3 *Defining Traffic Classes and Allocating Them to Appropriate Queues with a Minimum Bandwidth During Congestion (Continued)*

```
precedence 2 queue 2
precedence 3 queue 3
precedence 4 queue low-latency
precedence 5 queue 0
random-detect-label 0 50 200 2
exponential-weighting-constant 8
queue 0 10
queue 1 20
queue 2 30
queue 3 40
queue low-latency strict-priority 20
```

All interfaces for PoS1/0, PoS2/0, and PoS3/0 are configured with TX CoS based on the **cos-queue group** *cos-a* command. The *cos-a* command defines a CoS policy. Traffic is mapped into classes based on their IP precedence value in the packet. Each of the five classes is allocated to its individual queue, and weights are allocated based on the bandwidth allocation for each class. The bandwidth allocation for a class is proportional to its weight. The percentage of interface bandwidth allocation for Queues 0–3 and the low-latency queue is 8.33, 16.67, 25, 33.33, and 16.67, respectively. Voice is delay-sensitive but not bandwidth-intensive. Hence, it is allocated a low-latency queue with strict priority, but it doesn't need a high-bandwidth allocation.

The network supports only IP precedence values of 0–4. IP precedence 5 is allocated to Queue 0 for best-effort service. IP precedence 6 and 7 packets are control packets that a router originates. They are flagged internally and are transmitted first, regardless of the MDRR configuration.

The *cos-a* **cos-queue-group** command defines a Weighted Random Early Detection (WRED), a congestion avoidance policy that applies to all queues as follows:

- Minimum threshold: 50 packets
- Maximum threshold: 200 packets
- Probability of dropping packets at maximum threshold: $\int$ = 50 percent
- Exponential weighting constant to calculate average queue depth: 8

WRED is discussed in Chapter 6, "Per-Hop Behavior: Congestion Avoidance and Packet Drop Policy."

The MDRR algorithm can also be applied on the input interface line card on the fabric queues delivering the packet to the destination line card. The **slot-table-cos** command defines the CoS policy for each destination line card's CoS fabric queues on the receive line card. In the example, the *table-a* **slot-table-cos** command defines the CoS policy for destination line cards 0–2 based on the *cos-a* **cos-queue-group** command. Note that the destination line card can be the same as the receive line card because the input and output interfaces for certain traffic can exist on the same line card.

The **rx-cos-slot** command applies the *table-a* **slot-table-cos** command to a particular slot (line card). Listing 5-4 shows the CoS configuration on the router.

Listing 5-4   *CoS Information*

```
Router#show cos
Interface       Queue Cos Group
PO1/0               cos-a
PO2/0               cos-a
PO3/0               cos-a

Rx Slot         Slot Table
1               table-a
2               table-a
3               table-a

Slot Table Name - table-0
1               cos-a
2               cos-a
3               cos-a

Cos Queue Group - cos-a
precedence all mapped label 0
red label 0
min thresh 100, max thresh 300 max prob 2
...
exponential-weighting-constant 8
queue 0  weight 10
queue 1  weight 20
queue 2  weight 40
queue 3  weight 80
queue 4  weight 10
queue 5  weight 10
queue 6  weight 10
low latency queue weight 20, priority strict
```

Note that Queues 4–6 are not mapped to any IP precedence, so they are empty queues. Only Queues 0–3 and the low-latency queue are mapped to an IP precedence, and bandwidth is allocated proportional to the queue weights during congestion.

From the line card, the **show controllers frfab/tofab cos-queue length/parameters/ variables** command shows information regarding the CoS receive and transmit queues.

Summary

In this chapter, we discuss two new scheduling algorithms, MWRR and MDRR, that are used for resource allocation. MWRR and MDRR are similar to WFQ algorithm in their scheduling behavior. MWRR and MDRR scheduling can also support voice traffic if the voice queue is made a strict priority queue. At this time, MWRR and MDRR are used in the Catalyst family of switches and Cisco 12000 series routers, respectively.

Frequently Asked Questions

Q — *How does a scheduling algorithm determine resource allocation?*

A — A scheduling algorithm determines which packet goes next in a queue. How often a flow's packets are served determines the bandwidth or resource allocation for the flow.

Q — *Can MWRR and MDRR support voice traffic?*

A — Yes. MWRR and MDRR can support voice traffic when one of their queues can be made a *strict priority queue*. A strict priority queue carries voice and other real-time traffic with low latency.

Q — *How do MWRR and MDRR relate to WFQ?*

A — WFQ, MWRR, and MDRR are all scheduling algorithms for resource allocation. Both MWRR and MDRR are similar in scheduling behavior to WFQ because all three algorithms simulate the GPS model. GPS is discussed in Chapter 4.

References

[1] "An Engineering Approach to Computer Networking," S. Keshav, Addison-Wesley, 1997.

[2] "Efficient Fair Queuing using Deficit Round Robin," M. Shreedhar, George Varghese, SIGCOMM 1995, pp. 231-242.

Per-Hop Behavior: Congestion Avoidance and Packet Drop Policy

A *packet drop policy* is a queue management algorithm that manages the packets and queue length in a queuing system. Traditional first-in, first-out (FIFO) queue management uses a simple tail-drop policy, which drops any packet arriving on a full queue.

Transmission Control Protocol (TCP) is currently the dominant transport protocol used on the Internet. This chapter discusses TCP congestion control mechanisms and how TCP traffic reacts in a tail-drop scenario. It calls for an active queue management algorithm, Random Early Detection (RED), that avoids network congestion by dropping packets proactively to signal congestion to the TCP sources with end-to-end adaptive feedback control.

Weighted Random Early Detection (WRED), also discussed in this chapter, allows different RED parameters based on the packet's Internet Protocol (IP) precedence value or traffic class. *Flow WRED*, a WRED extension that applies an increased non-zero drop probability to penalize flows taking more than their fair share of queue resources, and *Explicit Congestion Notification (ECN)*, which enables congestion notification for incipient congestion by marking packets rather than dropping them, are also discussed. The chapter ends with a section on Selective Packet Discard (SPD), a selective packet drop policy on the IP input queue that queues packets for the IP process in a router.

TCP Slow Start and Congestion Avoidance

A TCP source uses a *congestion window (cwnd)* to perform congestion avoidance. When a new TCP session is established, the congestion window is initialized, based on the slow start mechanism, to one segment (the maximum segment size [MSS] is announced by the other end, or set to the default, and is typically 536 bytes or 512 bytes). The congestion window indicates the maximum amount of data the sender can send on a TCP session without receiving an acknowledgment.

When the first packet is acknowledged, the TCP source increases the window size to 2, at which point two packets can be sent. When the two packets are acknowledged, the window size increases to 4. In this manner, the congestion window size grows exponentially. Note that the increase in window size might not be exactly exponential, however, because a TCP receiver need not acknowledge each packet, as it typically uses delayed acknowledgments and sends an acknowledgment for every two packets it receives. The TCP source's behavior follows the slow start algorithm, which operates by sending new packets into the network at a rate of acknowledgments received from the other end. This makes TCP *self-clocking*.

In TCP, packet loss is an indicator of congestion. A TCP source detects congestion when it fails to receive an acknowledgment for a packet within the estimated retransmit timer timeout (RTT) period. In such a situation, it resets the congestion window to one segment and restarts the slow start algorithm. It also decreases the *slow start threshold (ssthresh)* to half the congestion window size at the time the retransmit was required. Note that when the TCP session is established, ssthresh is set to the size of the receiver window announced by the other end, or the default 65,535 bytes.

After an RTT timeout, a sender follows the slow start algorithm until the window size reaches ssthresh. Afterward, the window size increases linearly (by 1/cwnd) per acknowledgment received. The window size is increased slowly after it reaches ssthresh because ssthresh estimates the bandwidth-delay product for the TCP connection. TCP's slow start algorithm and congestion avoidance[1] behavior are depicted in Figure 6-1.

Figure 6-1   *TCP Congestion Window Showing Slow Start and Congestion Avoidance Operations*

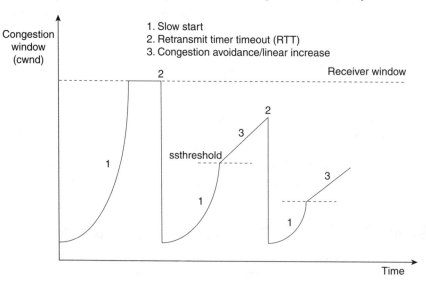

When packet loss occurs for reasons other than network congestion, waiting for the RTT times to expire can have an adverse performance impact, especially in high-speed networks. To avoid this scenario, TCP fast retransmit and recovery algorithms are used.

TCP Traffic Behavior in a Tail-Drop Scenario

Traditionally, packets arriving at the queue when the queue reaches its maximum queue length are dropped. This behavior continues until the queue decreases because of a packet transmission. This queue management technique is called *tail-drop*[2].

Because packet drop signals congestion to a TCP source, the tail-drop mechanism signals congestion only when the queue is completely full. A packet drop causes a TCP source to drop its window size to one segment and enter the slow start mode, which drastically slows down the traffic from the source.

Because many thousands of TCP flows transit a typical core router on the Internet or on a large-scale IP network, a tail-drop scenario will lead to packet loss for a large number of TCP sessions. The TCP sources of all these TCP sessions now slow down simultaneously, resulting in a significant drop in the traffic seen by the queue, and thereby reducing the queue size drastically.

All the TCP sources that went into slow start with a window size set to 1 segment now start to increase their window sizes exponentially, increasing the traffic at the queue. The increased traffic steadily causes the queue to build up again, leading to packet drops. The tail-drops again cause a large number of TCP sources to slow down, provoking an immediate drop in traffic. As these TCP sources increase their window sizes steadily, they can again lead to congestion and packet drops.

This cyclic behavior of significant traffic slowdown and congestion leads to a wave-type effect in the queue size often termed as *global synchronization*. Global synchronization behavior is depicted in Figure 6-2. It is called so because it synchronizes the behavior of a large number of TCP sources leading to undesirable queue fluctuations. It also leads to high delay jitter for the traffic and lowers the network's overall throughput.

Figure 6-2   *Global Synchronization*

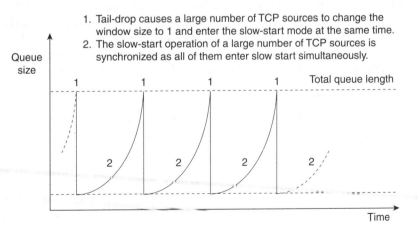

RED—Proactive Queue Management for Congestion Avoidance

The behavior of TCP sources due to tail-drop underscores the need for proactive queue management to signal congestion before the queue is full, and to control queue sizes to minimize queuing delays. RED is a congestion avoidance mechanism proposed by Sally Floyd and Van Jacobson[3]. It is an active queue management technique intended to provide considerable performance advantages over a traditional tail-drop approach.

RED takes a proactive approach to congestion. Instead of waiting until the queue is completely filled up, RED starts dropping packets with a non-zero drop probability after the average queue size exceeds a certain minimum threshold. A drop probability ensures that RED randomly drops packets from only a few flows, avoiding global synchronization. A packet drop is meant to signal the TCP source to slow down. Responsive TCP flows slow down after packet loss by going into a slow-start mode.

If the average queue continues to rise in spite of the random drops, the packet drop probability increases linearly to control the average queue size. As such, the packet drop rate increases linearly as the average queue size increases from the minimum to the maximum threshold. The average queue size is strictly enforced to be the maximum threshold value because you drop all newly arriving packets (with a 100 percent probability, similar to tail-drop) when the average queue size exceeds maximum threshold. Thus, RED aims to reduce the average queue size, hence reducing queuing delay.

The packet drop probability is based on a weighted exponential average queue size, as described in the section "The Average Queue Size Computation," so that RED doesn't have a bias toward transient bursty traffic while controlling prolonged congestion.

If the average queue length is already short, or below the minimum threshold, RED provides no actual benefit. On the other hand, if congestion is sustained for long periods of time, RED—with a deep queue and a high maximum threshold value—still exhibits tail-drop behavior. RED's main purpose is to accommodate temporary bursts and to detect and prevent sustained congestion by signaling sources to slow down. This results in congestion avoidance if the sources cooperate and reduce the traffic. If sources don't cooperate, any packet coming over the queue of maximum threshold length is dropped.

RED's main goals include:

- Minimizing the packets' packet delay jitter by controlling the average queue size
- Avoiding global synchronization for TCP traffic
- Supporting bursty traffic without bias
- Strictly enforcing the upper limit on the average queue limit.

RED is implemented by means of two different algorithms:

- **Average queue size computation**—This determines the degree of burstiness allowed in the queue.
- **Packet drop probability**—For a given average queue size, the probability that a packet is dropped determines how frequently the router drops packets.

These algorithms are discussed in the following sections.

The Average Queue Size Computation

RED calculates an exponentially weighted average queue size, rather than the current queue size, when deciding the packet drop probability. The current average queue length depends on the previous average and on the queue's current actual size. In using an average queue size, RED achieves its goal to not react to momentary burstiness in the network and react only to persistent congestion. The formula is

$$average = (old\_average \times (1-1/2^n) + (current\_queue\_size \times 1/2^n)$$

where n is the exponential weight factor, a user-configurable variable.

The exponential weight factor is the key parameter determining the significance of the old average and the current queue size values in the average queue size computation. A default value of 9 for the exponential weight factor n is seen to show best results. In calculating the average queue size, high values of n increase the significance of the old average queue size over the current queue size in computing the average queue size; low values of n increase the significance of the current queue size over the old average.

With high values of n, the average queue size closely tracks the old average queue size and more freely accommodates changes in the current queue size, resulting in the following RED behavior:

- The average queue size moves slowly and is unlikely to change quickly, avoiding drastic swings in size.
- RED accommodates temporary bursts in traffic, smoothing out the peaks and lows in the current queue size.
- RED is slow to start dropping packets, but it can continue dropping packets for a time after the actual queue size falls below the minimum threshold.
- If n is too high, RED does not react to congestion, as the current queue size becomes insignificant in calculating the average queue size. Packets are transmitted or dropped as if RED were not in effect.

With low values of n, the average queue size closely tracks the current queue size, resulting in the following RED behavior:

- The average queue size moves rapidly and fluctuates with changes in the traffic levels.
- The RED process responds quickly to long queues. When the queue falls below the minimum threshold, the process stops dropping packets.
- If n is too low, RED overreacts to temporary traffic bursts and drops traffic unnecessarily.

Packet Drop Probability

Packet drop probability is a linear function of the average queue size. It also is based on the minimum threshold, maximum threshold, and *mark probability denominator*, which is the fraction of packets dropped when the average queue depth is at the maximum threshold. If the mark probability denominator is 10, for example, 1 out of every 10 packets is dropped when the average queue is at the maximum threshold. The packet drop probability formula is as follows:

$$\text{packet drop probability} = \left(\frac{(\text{average queue length} - \text{minimum threshold})}{(\text{maximum threshold} - \text{minimum threshold})} \right) / \frac{\text{mark probability}}{\text{denominator}}$$

When the average queue depth is above the minimum threshold, RED starts dropping packets. The packet drop rate increases linearly as the average queue size increases, until the average queue size reaches the maximum threshold.

When the average queue size is above the maximum threshold, all packets are dropped. Packet drop probability is illustrated in Figure 6-3.

Figure 6-3   *RED Packet Drop Probability*

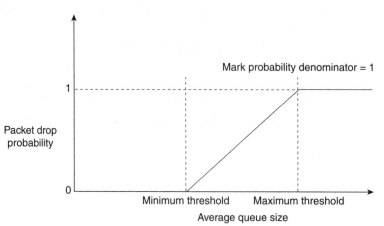

WRED

WRED introduces grades of service among packets based on a packet's drop probability and allows selective RED parameters based on IP precedence. As a result, WRED drops more aggressively for certain-precedence-level packets and less aggressively for other-precedence-level packets.

WRED Implementation

WRED can be run on the central processor of the router or on a distributed mode on Cisco's 7500 series routers with Versatile Interface Processors (VIPs). By default, the maximum threshold is the same for all precedence levels, but the minimum threshold varies with packet precedence. Hence, you drop the lower precedence packets more aggressively than the higher precedence packets. The default minimum threshold value for precedence 0 traffic is half the value of the maximum threshold.

You can enable WRED based on traffic classes by using modular QoS CLI. Modular QoS CLI allows different RED parameters for each traffic class and is discussed in Appendix A, "Cisco Modular QoS Command-line Interface."

In Cisco 12000 series routers, WRED is available in either hardware- or software-based implementations, depending on the hardware revision of the line card. Cisco 12000 series routers allow eight class of service (CoS) queues. You can map a CoS queue to carry packets of one or more precedence value(s). After the CoS queues are defined, RED parameters can be applied independently to the different CoS queues. Because this router platform uses a switch-based architecture, you can enable WRED on both the fabric queues on the receive side and the interface queues on the transmit side. For information on how to enable WRED on a Cisco 1200 series routers, refer to Case Study 5-10 in Chapter 5, "Per-Hop Behavior: Allocation II."

Case Study 6-1: Congestion Avoidance to Enhance Link Utilization by Using WRED

A service provider offers premium services—platinum, gold, silver, and bronze—to its customers and differentiates customer traffic on its backbone by marking the traffic with IP precedence 4, 3, 2, and 1, respectively, based on their premium service level. The service provider offers these premium services along with the best-effort service that sets traffic to a precedence of 0. The service provider's peering connections to the other top-tier Internet service providers are occasionally congested, pointing to a need for a congestion avoidance policy.

Active queue management using WRED is needed on interfaces that peer with the other service providers to control congestion. On the interface connecting a peer service provider, enable WRED by using the **random-detect** command.

Note that the WRED minimum drop threshold parameter needs to be relatively higher for higher-precedence (better service) traffic when compared to the lower-precedence traffic, so lower-precedence packets are dropped before higher-precedence traffic gets affected.

Listings 6-1 and 6-2 show the WRED default parameters and packet drop statistics by using the **show queueing random-detect** command when WRED is running in the central processor and VIP line cards of a Cisco 7500 router, respectively.

Listing 6-1   *WRED Operation on a Low-end 7200 Series Router and on a 7500 Series Router in a Nondistributed Mode*

```
Router#show queueing random-detect
  Hssi3/0/0
    Queueing strategy: random early detection (WRED)
    Exp-weight-constant: 9 (1/512)
mean queue depth: 40
        drops: class   random    tail    min-th   max-th   mark-prob
                 0      13783    174972   20       40       1/10
                 1      14790    109428   22       40       1/10
                 2      14522    119275   24       40       1/10
                 3      14166    128738   26       40       1/10
                 4      13384    138281   28       40       1/10
                 5      12285    147148   31       40       1/10
                 6      10893    156288   33       40       1/10
                 7      9573     166044   35       40       1/10
               rsvp     0        0        37       40       1/10
```

When running on the central processor, WRED is run on the interface transmit queue and its thresholds are determined as follows:

- **min_threshold (i)**—The minimum threshold corresponding to traffic of precedence i, equal to:

  $(1/2 + i/18) \times$ output hold queue

- **max_threshold**—Equal to the output hold queue

The output of the **show queuing red** command gives the following packet statistics:

- **Random Drop**—WRED drops when the mean queue depth falls in between the minimum and maximum WRED thresholds.

- **Tail-drop**—WRED drops when the mean queue depth exceeds the maximum threshold.

- **Mark Probability**—The drop probability when the mean queue depth is equal to the maximum threshold.

Listing 6-2   *WRED Operation on a VIP-Based 7500 Series Router*

```
Router#show queueing random-detect
Hssi3/0/0
   Queueing strategy: VIP-based fair queueing
   Packet drop strategy: VIP-based random early detection (DWRED)
   Exp-weight-constant: 9 (1/512)
   Mean queue depth: 0
   Queue size: 0       Maximum available buffers: 5649
   Output packets: 118483  WRED drops: 800  No buffer: 0

   Class   Random    Tail   Minimum   Maximum    Mark       Output
           drop      drop   threshold threshold  probability Packets
     0      23        0      1412      2824      1/10        116414
     1       0        0      1588      2824      1/10             0
     2       0        0      1764      2824      1/10         12345
     3       0        0      1940      2824      1/10         20031
     4       0        0      2116      2824      1/10         45670
     5       0        0      2292      2824      1/10             0
     6       0        0      2468      2824      1/10          2345
     7       0        0      2644      2824      1/10             0
```

When running WRED in a distributed mode on VIP-based 7500 routers, WRED processing for an interface line card is done locally and not on the route processor. Hence, distributed WRED operates on the queue on the VIP and not on the interface transmit queue.

Distributed WRED uses Cisco Express Forwarding (CEF)-based inter-process communication to propagate configuration and statistics information between the Route Switch Processor (RSP) and the VIP. (CEF is discussed in Appendix B, "Packet Switching Mechanisms.") Hence, CEF should be enabled when operating WRED in a distributed mode. The interface drop statistics include Distributed WRED (DWRED) drops.

DWRED calculates the default maximum threshold based on the pool size (loosely speaking, VIP queue size), the interface maximum transmission unit (MTU) size, and the interface bandwidth. Pool size is, in turn, dependent on the memory size on the VIP and other factors and, therefore, difficult to pin down to a fixed number. Therefore, the pool size information only helps to estimate the burst size that can be accommodated. You can configure the DWRED maximum threshold to a value different from the default, if necessary.

Case 6-2: WRED Based on Traffic Classes Using Modular QoS CLI

A service provider is interested in running WRED in its routers because the interface queues in the routers often exhibit symptoms of global synchronization. The service provider carries critical User Datagram Protocol (UDP)-based application traffic on its network and hence, it doesn't want to randomly drop any of its critical application traffic, although tail drop can be applied at the queue's maximum threshold.

Listing 6-3 excludes the critical UDP-based application traffic before applying WRED on the router's interface.

Listing 6-3   *Enable WRED Using Modular QoS CLI on the Noncritical Traffic Class Only*

```
class-map non-critical
 match access-group 101

policy-map wred
 match class non-critical
 random-detect exponential-weighting-constant 9
 random-detect precedence 0 112 375 1

interface Hssi0/0/0
service-policy output wred
```

As shown in Listing 6-3, you first define a noncritical traffic class that includes all traffic except the critical UDP traffic. Next, use an **access-list 101** command (not shown in Listing 6-3) to match all traffic, except the critical UDP application traffic. Follow this with the **match access-group 101** command, which matches all traffic that passed the **access-list 101** definition, and the **policy-map wred** command, which enables WRED on the noncritical traffic. In this Listing, WRED is enabled with an exponential weighting constant of 9. At the same time, minimum threshold, maximum threshold, and mark probability denominator values for IP precedence 0 packets are set to 112, 375, and 1, respectively. The **policy-map wred** is then enabled on the router's Hssi0/0/0 interface.

Flow WRED

Only adaptive TCP flows respond to a congestion signal and slow down, while nonadaptive UDP flows, which do not respond to congestion signals, don't slow down. For this reason, nonadaptive flows can send packets at a much higher rate than adaptive flows at times of congestion. Hence, greedy, nonadaptive flows tend to use a higher queue resource than the adaptive flows that slow down in response to congestion signals. *Flow WRED* modifies WRED such that it penalizes flows taking up more than their fair share of queue resources.

To provide fairness among the active traffic flows in the queue, WRED classifies all arriving packets into the queue based on their flow and precedence. It also maintains state for all *active flows*, or flows that have packets in the queue. This state information is used to determine the fair amount of queue resources for each flow (queue size/number of active flows), and flows taking more than their fair share are penalized more than the others are.

To accommodate for a flow's traffic burstiness, you can increase each flow's fair share by a scaling factor before it gets penalized using the following formulas:

Fair share of queue resources per active flow = queue size ÷ number of active flows
Scaled fair share of queue resources per flow = (queue size ÷ number of active flows) × scaling factor

A flow exceeding the scaled fair share of queue resources per flow in the queue is penalized by an increase in the non-zero drop probability for all the newly arriving packets in the queue.

As an example, consider a packet arriving on a queue running Flow WRED. Flow WRED considers both the IP precedence value in the packet and the flow state information to determine the packet's drop probability. The packet's IP precedence determines the configured (or the default) minimum and maximum WRED thresholds for the packet. If the average queue size is below the minimum threshold, the packet gets zero drop probability (in other words, it is not dropped). If the average queue size is in between the packet's minimum and maximum threshold (as determined by the packet's IP precedence), the flow state information is taken into consideration. If the packet belongs to a flow that exceeded the scaled fair share of queue resources per flow in the queue, you increase the packet's drop probability by decreasing the WRED maximum threshold as follows:

New Maximum threshold = Minimum threshold + ((Maximum threshold – Minimum threshold) ÷ 2)

The non-zero probability is then derived based on the minimum threshold and the new maximum threshold values. Because the drop probability curve is much steeper now, as shown in Figure 6-4, you apply a higher drop probability on the packet. If the flow is within its fair allocation of queue resources, the packet gets a non-zero drop probability determined by the normal WRED calculation.

If the average queue size exceeds the maximum threshold, continue to drop packets using a process similar to that used in the WRED operation.

Flow WRED increases the probability of a packet getting dropped only if the packet belongs to a flow whose packets in the queue exceed the scaled per-flow limit. Otherwise, Flow WRED operates similar to WRED.

NOTE   Flow WRED, as described previously, still applies non-zero drop probability for flows with a few packets in the queue when the average queue size is between the minimum and maximum thresholds. You can implement Flow WRED such that it doesn't drop packets of a flow with a few, specified number of packets in the queue by increasing the minimum threshold to be close to or equal to the maximum threshold. You apply tail-drop on the packet at the queue's WRED maximum threshold value.

Figure 6-4 *Packet Drop Probability with Flow WRED*

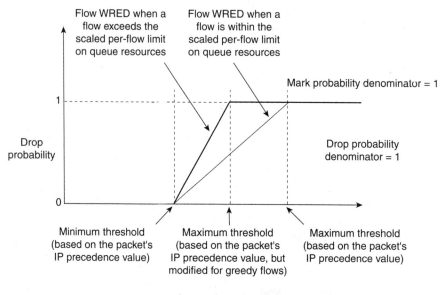

Case Study 6-3: Congestion Avoidance for Nonadaptive Flows
==

On a router transiting a considerable amount of UDP traffic along with TCP traffic, a network engineer wants to implement Flow WRED to avoid congestion and to control the average queuing delay seen by the traffic. The traffic seen by the router is expected to be bursty in nature.

Listing 6-4 shows how to enable Flow WRED with a scaling factor of 6 for the average queue depth.

Listing 6-4 *Enabling Flow WRED with Scaling Factor of 6*

```
random-detect flow
random-detect flow average-depth-factor 6
```

The **random-detect flow** command enables Flow WRED with a scaling factor of 4 and a flow count of 256. Because the traffic is expected to be bursty in nature, you can increase the scaling factor to 6 using the **random-detect flow average-depth-factor 6** command. You can modify the allowed active flow count to be any value between 0 and 2^{15} using the **random-detect flow count** command.

You can use the **show queueing random-detect** command to verify an interface's queuing strategy.

ECN

Thus far, in active queue management using WRED, packets have been dropped to signal congestion to a TCP source. ECN provides routers the functionality to signal congestion to a TCP source by marking a packet header rather than dropping the packet[4]. In the scenarios where a WRED-enabled router dropped a packet to signal congestion, it can now set the ECN bit in the packet, avoiding potential delays due to packet retransmissions caused by packet loss.

ECN functionality requires support for a Congestion Experienced (CE) bit in the IP header and a transport protocol that understood the CE bit. An ECN field of 2 bits in the IP header is provided for this purpose. The ECN-Capable Transport (ECT) bit is set by the TCP source to indicate that the transport protocol's end-points are ECN-capable. The CE bit is set by the router to indicate congestion to the end nodes.

Bits 6 and 7 in the IPv4 Type of Service (ToS) byte form the ECN field and are designated as the ECT bit and the CE bit, respectively. Bits 6 and 7 are listed in differentiated services architecture as currently unused.

For TCP, ECN requires three new mechanisms:

- **ECN Capability Negotiation**—The TCP endpoints negotiate during setup to determine if they are both ECN-capable.
- **ECN-Echo flag in the TCP header**—The TCP receiver uses the ECN-Echo flag to inform the TCP source that a CE packet has been received.
- **Congestion Window Reduced (CWR) flag in the TCP header**—The TCP source uses the CWR flag to inform the TCP receiver that the congestion window has been reduced.

ECN functionality is still under discussion in the standard bodies.

SPD

SPD helps differentiate important control traffic (such as routing protocol packets) over normal data traffic to the router. This enables the router to keep its Interior Gateway Protocol (IGP) and Border Gateway Protocol (BGP) routing information during congestion by enqueuing routing protocol packets over the normal data traffic.

SPD implements a selective packet drop policy on the router's IP process queue. Therefore, it applies to only process switched traffic. Even when the router is using route-cache forwarding (also called fast switching), some of the transit data traffic still needs to be process switched in order to create a route-cache entry. When a router is using CEF, though, all transit data traffic is usually CEF switched and the only packets that reach the IP process input queue are the important control packets such as routing and keepalives, normal data traffic destined to the router, and transit traffic that is not CEF supported. Process switching, route-cache forwarding, and CEF are discussed in Appendix B.

Traffic arriving at the IP process input queue is classified in three ways:

- Important IP control traffic (routing protocol packets), often called *priority traffic*.

- Normal IP traffic, such as telnet/ping packets to a router interface, IP packets with options, and any IP feature or encapsulation not supported by CEF.

- Aggressive dropable packets. These are IP packets that fail the IP sanity check; that is, they might have incorrect checksums, invalid versions, an expired Time-to-Live (TTL) value, an invalid UDP/TCP port number, an invalid IP protocol field, and so on. Most of these packets trigger an Internet Control Message Protocol (ICMP) packet to notify the sender of the bad packet. A small number of these packets are generated due to normal utilities such as a trace route. Such packets in large numbers, however, can be part of a malicious smurf attack intended to cripple the router by filling up the IP process queue. It is essential to selectively drop these packets without losing the important control information.

SPD operates in the following modes:

- **Disabled**—The SPD feature is disabled on the router.

- **Normal**—The IP input queue is less than the queue minimum threshold. No packets are dropped.

- **Random drop**—The IP input queue is more than the minimum threshold but less than the maximum threshold. Normal IP packets are dropped in this mode, with a drop probability shown in the following formula:

  drop probability = (queue length – min. threshold) ÷ (max. threshold – min. threshold)

  Random drops are called *SPD flushes*. Important IP control traffic is still enqueued.

- **Full drop**—The IP input queue is above the maximum threshold. All normal IP traffic is dropped. Important IP control traffic is still received to a special process level queue, termed the *priority queue*, that is drained before the normal one.

- **Aggressive drop**—This is a special aggressive drop mode for IP packets failing the sanity check. All bad IP packets are dropped when the input queue is above the minimum threshold. You can enable this special drop mechanism using the **ip spd mode aggressive** command.

Figure 6-5 illustrates SPD operation and its modes.

Figure 6-5   *SPD Packet Drop Modes*

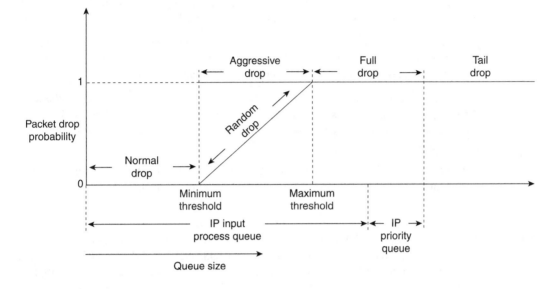

Case Study 6-4: Preventing Bad IP Packet Smurf Attacks by Using SPD

Your network is seeing a smurf attack of IP packets with expired TTL values. These bad IP packets are adversely affecting the router, as they need to be processed by the router in the process switching path because those packets trigger a TTL-exceeded ICMP packet. You should turn on the aggressive drop mechanism to drop such packets if they exceed the set SPD minimum threshold. This case study discusses SPD operation by using various **show** commands.

SPD can be enabled by using the **ip spd** enable command. When running IOS version 12.0 or higher, though, SPD is turned on by default. Listing 6-5 shows the enabled SPD parameters and the SPD mode of operation:

Listing 6-5   *SPD Parameters and Current Mode of Operation*

```
R3#sh ip spd
Current mode: normal.
Queue min/max thresholds: 73/74, Headroom: 100
IP normal queue: 20, priority queue: 20.
SPD special drop mode: none.
```

You use the **show ip spd** command to show the SPD operation mode, the minimum and maximum thresholds, and the IP process and priority queue sizes. The minimum and maximum input queue SPD thresholds are user-configurable.

IP normal queue and priority queue give the value of their respective queues at the time the **show ip spd** command is executed. IP normal queue is 20, which is below the minimum queue threshold of 73. Hence, SPD is currently operating in the normal mode.

A special queue, termed the *IP priority queue*, is used to hold the important IP traffic when the IP input process queue is full. The IP input process queue is a global queue that holds all IP packets waiting to be processed by the IP input process. These packets cannot be processed on a CPU interrupt.

You can configure the priority queue length using the **ip spd headroom** command. Any important IP traffic arriving on a full IP priority queue is dropped.

NOTE Note that some of the SPD command formats changed in 12.0 IOS releases when compared to the earlier 11.1 IOS versions. While all the 11.1 IOS version SPD commands started with **ip spd**, some of the SPD commands in 12.0 and later versions of IOS can only be configured as **spd** <> instead of **ip spd** <>. Refer to the appropriate Cisco documentation for clarification on the command formats.

Headroom shows the priority queue's depth. Priority queue holds the priority traffic. Presently, the priority queue has 20 packets to be processed. The default normal queue thresholds are derived from the input queue length. The **show interface** command shows the queue length of the input queue. All bad IP packets need to be process-switched. You should enable the SPD aggressive drop mechanism to drop bad or illegal IP packets when the normal IP queue exceeds the minimum threshold. You can enable the SPD aggressive drop mode using the **ip spd mode aggressive** command. Listing 6-6 shows the SPD operation with special SPD aggressive mode on.

Listing 6-6 *Aggressive SPD Drop Mechanism for Bad or Illegal IP Packets*

```
R3#sh ip spd
Current mode: normal.
Queue min/max thresholds: 73/74, Headroom: 100
IP normal queue: 20, priority queue: 5.
SPD special drop mode: aggressively drop bad packets
```

For detailed SPD packet statistics, refer to Listing 6-7.

Listing 6-7   *Detailed SPD Packet Statistics*

```
R3#show interface hssi0/0/0 switching
Hssi0/0/0
          Throttle count          10
          Drops       RP       13568       SP         0
    SPD Flushes     Fast      322684       SSE        0
    SPD Aggress     Fast      322684
    SPD Priority   Inputs      91719       Drops      4
```

You use the **show interfaces switching** command to view statistics on the SPD flushes and aggressive drops. It includes information on received important (priority) IP traffic and on any drops that occur when you exceed the headroom threshold.

Route Processor (RP) drops are categorized as those dropped by a processor on a full input queue. They match with the input drops shown in the **show interface Hssi0/0/0** command output.

Fast SPD flushes are the random, full drops as well as the special aggressive drops done by SPD when the input queue is not physically exhausted. No SPD drops occur when the normal queue is below the minimum threshold.

Fast SPD aggressive drops occur when SPD is operating in the special aggressive mode. They show the number of bad or illegal IP packets dropped by SPD. No SPD aggressive drops occur when the normal queue is below the minimum threshold.

The SPD priority queue carries the *priority traffic*. Priority traffic is control traffic tagged with a precedence of 6.

Summary

This chapter focuses on congestion avoidance and packet drop policy algorithms: RED, WRED, Flow WRED, and ECN.

RED is an active queue management algorithm that allows routers to detect congestion before the queue overflows. It aims to reduce the average queue size, hence reducing queuing delay and avoiding global synchronization by adopting a probability-based packet drop strategy between certain queue thresholds. Weighted version of RED, WRED allows different RED parameters based on a packet's IP precedence.

Flow WRED extends WRED to provide fairness in the packet drop behavior among the different flow types. ECN enables congestion notification for incipient congestion by marking packets rather than dropping them.

The chapter also discusses SPD, a selective packet drop policy that is used on the IP input queue of a Cisco router. SPD is used to differentiate between the data and control packets that are enqueued to the IP process in a Cisco router.

Frequently Asked Questions

Q — *What are some rule-of-thumb values for configuring RED parameters?*

A — You can calculate the exponential weighting factor based on the following formula[5]:

Exponential weighting factor = $10 \div B$

where B is the output link bandwidth in MTU-size packets.

Because it doesn't change the end result, use an MTU of 1500 bytes for all links, even on links with an actual MTU size of 4470 bytes.

For a DS3 (45 Mbps) link,

$B = (45 \text{ Mbps} \div 8) \div 1500 = 3750.$

Therefore, the exponential weighting factor

$= 10 \div B = 2.67 \text{ E} - 3$

which is approximately equal to 2^{-9}.

The exponential weighting factor for the other interfaces can be derived similarly.

You can set the minimum and maximum threshold values to 0.03B and 0.1B, respectively. For a DS3 link, these values are 112 and 375, respectively. The mark (drop) probability denominator should be set to 1.

Table 6-1 shows the recommended RED parameters for link speeds DS1, DS3, OC3, and OC12. When enabling WRED, these are the recommended values for IP precedence 0 packets.

Table 6-1 *Recommended RED Parameters*

Link Speed	Exponential Weighting Factor	Minimum Threshold	Maximum Threshold	Mark Probability Denominator
DS1	4	4	13	1
DS3	9	112	375	1
OC3	10	388	1292	1
OC12	12	1550	5167	1

Q — *Is Flow WRED bad for voice because it penalizes UDP traffic?*

A — Flow WRED is not bad for voice because it doesn't penalize all UDP traffic, only greedy UDP flows.

Q — *Should I be running SPD in all my routers?*

A — The SPD feature is critical in routers in any large-scale IP network, especially when they do route-cache-based forwarding. With CEF-based switching, the utility of SPD is a bit low because SPD applies only for process-switched traffic, but it is still useful in differentiating the routing protocol packets and keepalive packets from the other normal packets destined to the router.

SPD with the special aggressive drop mode is useful for minimizing potential denial-of-service attacks on a router by using bad IP packets such as packets with expired TTL values.

References

[1] "TCP Slow Start, Congestion Avoidance, Fast Recovery, and Fast Recovery Algorithms," RFC 2001.

[2] "Recommendations on Queue Management and Congestion Avoidance in the Internet," B. Braden, D. Clark, J. Crowcroft, B. Davie, S. Deering, D. Estrin, S. Floyd, V. Jacobson, G. Minshall, C. Partridge, L. Peterson, K.Ramakrishnan, S. Shenker, J. Wroclawski, L. Zhang, April 1998.

[3] "Random Early Detection Gateways for Congestion Avoidance," S. Floyd and V. Jacobson, *IEEE/ACM Transactions on Networking*, V.1 N.4, August 1993, pp. 397-413.

[4] "A Proposal to add Explicit Congestion Notification (ECN) to IP," K. Ramakrishnan, S. Floyd, RFC 2481.

[5] "RED in a Different Light," V. Jacobson, K. Nichols, K. Poduri, work in progress.

CHAPTER 7

Integrated Services: RSVP

The previous chapters discussed the Differentiated Services (diffserv) architecture and its enabling functions. They discussed how the Differentiated Services Code Point (DSCP) and Internet Protocol (IP) precedence in a packet's IP header are used to classify traffic based on the traffic's service level to indicate the required per-hop behavior within a network. Now, in the Integrated Services (intserv) architecture, we will discuss how the network is informed about the various traffic flows' divergent needs?

In intserv, a quality of service (QoS) signaling protocol, Resource Reservation Protocol (RSVP) is used for this purpose. RSVP is a QoS signaling protocol that enables end applications requiring certain guaranteed services to signal their end-to-end QoS requirements to obtain service guarantees from the network. The per-hop behavior in the network, however, is provided by network node scheduler functions, as discussed in Chapter 4, "Per Hop Behavior: Resource Allocation I," Chapter 5, "Per-Hop Behavior: Resource Allocation II, and Chapter 6, "Per-Hop Behavior: Congestion Avoidance and Packet Drop Policy."

This chapter discusses the RSVP protocol, its control messages, its operation, and other details. The two integrated service types—controlled load and guaranteed service—also are covered.

Subnet Bandwidth Manager (SBM), the Layer 2 version of RSVP and RSVP extensions that support traffic engineering in a Multiprotocol Label Switching (MPLS)-based network, is covered in Chapter 8, "Layer 2 QoS: Interworking with IP QoS," and in Chapter 10, "MPLS Traffic Engineering," respectively.

RSVP

The Internet Engineering Task Force (IETF) specified RSVP[1] as a signaling protocol for the intserv architecture. RSVP enables applications to signal per-flow QoS requirements to the network. Service parameters are used to specifically quantify these requirements for admission control.

RSVP is used in multicast applications such as audio/video conferencing and broadcasting. Although the initial target for RSVP is multimedia traffic, there is a clear interest in reserving bandwidth for unicast traffic such as Network File System (NFS), and for Virtual Private Network (VPN) management.

RSVP signals resource reservation requests along the routed path available within the network. It does not perform its own routing; instead, it is designed to use the Internet's current robust routing protocols. Like other IP traffic, it depends on the underlying routing protocol to determine the path for both its data and its control traffic. As the routing protocol information adapts to network topology changes, RSVP reservations are carried over to the new path. This modularity helps RSVP to function effectively with any underlying routing service. RSVP provides opaque transport of traffic control and policy control messages, and provides transparent operation through nonsupporting regions.

RSVP Operation

End systems use RSVP to request a specific QoS from the network on behalf of an application data stream. RSVP requests are carried through the network, visiting each node the network uses to carry the stream. At each node, RSVP attempts to make a resource reservation for the stream.

RSVP-enabled routers help deliver the right flows to the right locations. Figure 7-1 gives an overview of the important modules and the data and control flow information of a client and router running RSVP.

Figure 7-1   *Data and Control Flow Information of a Client and Router Running RSVP*

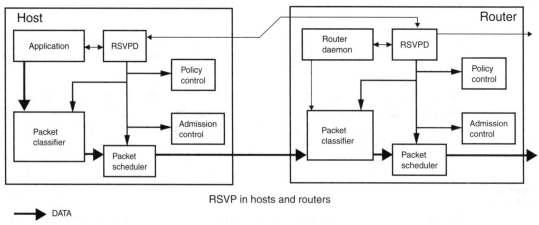

RSVP in hosts and routers

▶ DATA

▶ RSVP/Control packets

The RSVP daemon in a router communicates with two local decision modules—*admission control* and *policy control*—before making a resource reservation[2]. Admission control determines whether the node has sufficient available resources to supply the requested QoS.

Policy control determines whether the user has administrative permission to make the reservation. If either check fails, the RSVP daemon sends an error notification to the application process that originated the request. If both checks succeed, the RSVP daemon sets parameters in a *packet classifier* and a *packet scheduler* to obtain the desired QoS. The packet classifier determines the QoS class for each packet, and the packet scheduler orders packet transmission based on its QoS class. The Weighted Fair Queuing (WFQ) and Weighted Random Early Detection (WRED) disciplines provide scheduler support for QoS. WFQ and WRED are discussed in Chapters 4 and 6, respectively.

During the admission control decision process, a reservation for the requested capacity is put in place if sufficient capacity remains in the requested traffic class. Otherwise, the admission request is refused, but the traffic is still forwarded with the default service for that traffic's traffic class. In many cases, even an admission request that failed at one or more routers can still supply acceptable quality, as it might have succeeded in installing a reservation in all the routers suffering congestion. This is because other reservations might not be fully utilizing their reserved capacity.

Reservations must follow on the same unicast path or on the multicast tree at all times. In case of link failures, the router should inform the RSVP daemon so that RSVP messages are generated on a new route.

You can break down the process of installing a reservation into five distinct steps[3]:

1   Data senders send RSVP PATH control messages the same way they send regular data traffic. These messages describe the data they are sending or intend to send.

2   Each RSVP router intercepts the PATH messages, saves the previous hop IP address, writes its own address as the previous hop, and sends the updated message along the same route the application data is using.

3   Receiver stations select a subset of the sessions for which they are receiving PATH information and request RSVP resource reservations from the previous hop router using an RSVP RESV message. The RSVP RESV messages going from a receiver to a sender take an exact reverse path when compared to the path taken by the RSVP PATH messages.

4   The RSVP routers determine whether they can honor those RESV requests. If they can't, they refuse the reservations. If they can, they merge reservation requests being received and request a reservation from the previous hop router.

5   The senders receive reservation requests from the next hop routers indicating that reservations are in place. Note that the actual reservation allocation is made by the RESV messages.

Figure 7-2 shows the RSVP reservation setup mechanism.

As discussed in Chapter 3, "Network Boundary Traffic Conditioners: Packet Classifier, Marker, and Traffic Rate Management," an individual flow is made of packets going from an application on a source machine to an application on a destination machine. The FlowSpec parameterizes a flow's requirements for admission control.

Figure 7-2 *RSVP Reservation Setup Mechanism*

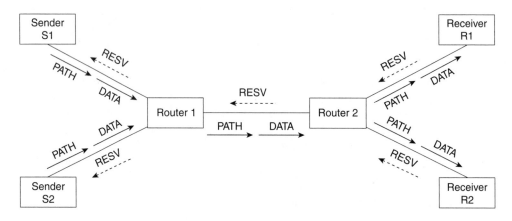

RSVP Components

The operational responsibilities of the three RSVP components are as follows:

- An *RSVP sender* is an application that originates traffic in an RSVP session. The flow specifications that RSVP senders can send across the RSVP network are:
  - Average data rate
  - Maximum burst size
- An *RSVP-enabled router network* provides the path between the RSVP senders and the RSVP receivers.
- An *RSVP receiver* is an application that receives traffic in an RSVP session. In conferencing and Voice over IP (VoIP) applications, an application can act as both an RSVP sender and receiver. The flow specifications that RSVP receivers can send across the RSVP network are:
  - Average data rate
  - Maximum burst size
  - QoS, including
    - **Guaranteed service**—PATH messages also describe the worst-case delays in the network.
    - **Controlled load service**—The routers guarantee only that network delays will be minimized.

RSVP Messages

RSVP uses seven message types for its operation: two required message types—PATH and RESV—and five optional message types—PATH ERROR, PATH TEARDOWN, RESV ERROR, RESV CONFIRM, and RSV TEARDOWN. The RSVP routers and clients use them to create and maintain reservation states.

RSVP usually runs directly over the IP. As such, RSVP messages are unreliable datagrams. They help create soft states within the routers, and a periodic refresh is needed.

The following are the sender message types:

- PATH messages are sent periodically by senders. The senders describe the flows in terms of the source and destination IP addresses, the IP protocol, and the User Datagram Protocol (UDP) or Transmission Control Protocol (TCP) ports, if applicable. They quantify the expected resource requirements for this data by specifying its mean rate and burst size.

  They are sent to the multicast group or unicast destination of the flow for which the reservation is being made; RSVP routers detect them because they are sent in UDP messages to a particular UDP port, or because they have the IP Router Alert option in their IP header. A router creates a Path State Block (PSB) when the PATH messages are received.

  PATH messages contain a periodic hello interval indicating how frequently the sender sends them. The default hello interval is 30 seconds. It is important to keep the hello interval small, or to have a fast retransmit scheme, because lost PATH messages can result in poor performance for VoIP, as that would delay the establishment of an RSVP reservation along the path of the VoIP call. The PSB is discarded upon a PATH TEARDOWN or ingress link failure, or when the PSB has not been refreshed by a new PATH message after four hello intervals.

- When error(s) in a PATH message are found, the optional PATH ERROR message is sent by the receiver or router, notifying the sender of the problem. Typically, this is a fundamental format or integrity check fault.

- PATH TEARDOWN messages are sent to the multicast group with the sender's source address when the PATH must be flushed from the database, either due to a link failure or because the sender is exiting the multicast group.

The following are the receiver message types:

- RESV messages are sent periodically by receivers. The receivers describe the flows and resource guarantees they need using information derived from the PATH messages, in terms of the source and destination IP addresses, the IP protocol, and the UDP or TCP ports, if applicable. They also describe the bit rate and delay characteristics they need, using flow specifications. They traverse through all RSVP routers along the routed path to the sender for which the reservation is being made. Routers create Reservation State Blocks (RSBs) when RESV messages (FlowSpec, FilterSpec) are granted.

RESV messages contain a periodic hello interval indicating how frequently the receiver sends them. The RSB is discarded upon a RESV TEARDOWN or ingress link failure, or when they have not been refreshed by a new RESV message after four hello intervals.

* When error(s) in an RESV message are found, an RESV ERROR message is sent by a sender or router informing the receiver of a problem. Typically, it is due to a fundamental format or integrity check fault, or because insufficient resources were available to make the requested guarantees.

* When the effect of an RESV message applies end to end and a receiver requests notification of the fact, RESV CONFIRM messages are sent to the receivers or merge point routers.

* RESV TEARDOWN messages are sent when an RSB must be flushed from the database, either due to a link failure or because the sender is exiting the multicast group.

Reservation Styles

You can categorize RSVP flow reservations into two major types—distinct and shared—which are discussed in the following sections.

Distinct Reservations

Distinct reservations are appropriate for those applications in which multiple data sources are likely to transmit simultaneously. In a video application, each sender emits a distinct data stream requiring separate admission control and queue management on the routers along its path to the receiver. Such a flow, therefore, requires a separate reservation per sender on each link along the path.

Distinct reservations are explicit about the sender and are installed using a Fixed Filter (FF) reservation style. Symbolically, you can represent an FF-style reservation request by FF (S,Q), where the S represents the sender selection and the Q represents the FlowSpec.

Unicast applications form the simplest case of a distinct reservation, in which there is one sender and one receiver.

Shared Reservations

Shared reservations are appropriate for those applications in which multiple data sources are unlikely to transmit simultaneously. Digitized audio applications, such as VoIP, are suitable for shared reservations. In this case, as a small number of people talk at any time, a limited number of senders send at any given time. Such a flow, therefore, does not require a separate reservation per sender; it requires a single reservation that you can apply to any sender within a set, as needed.

RSVP refers to such a flow as a *shared flow* and installs it using a shared explicit or wildcard reservation scope. These two reservation styles are discussed below.

- The Shared Explicit (SE) reservation style specifically identifies the flows that reserve network resources.

  Symbolically, you can represent an SE-style reservation request by SE((S1,S2){Q}), where the S1, S2, . . . represent specific senders for the reservation and the Q represents the FlowSpec.

- The Wildcard Filter (WF) reserves bandwidth and delay characteristics for any sender. It does not admit the sender's specification; it accepts all senders, which is denoted by setting the source address and port to zero.

  Symbolically, you can represent a WF-style reservation request by WF(* {Q}), where the asterisk represents the wildcard sender selection and the Q represents the FlowSpec.

Table 7-1 shows the different reservation filters based on the reservation styles and sender's scope, and Figure 7-3 illustrates the three reservation filter styles described previously.

Table 7-1 *Different Reservation Filters, Based on Style and Sender Scope*

Sender Selection Scope	Reservation Styles	
	Distinct	**Shared**
Explicit	FF	SE
Wildcard	None defined	WF

Figure 7-3 *Examples of the Three Reservation Filter Styles*

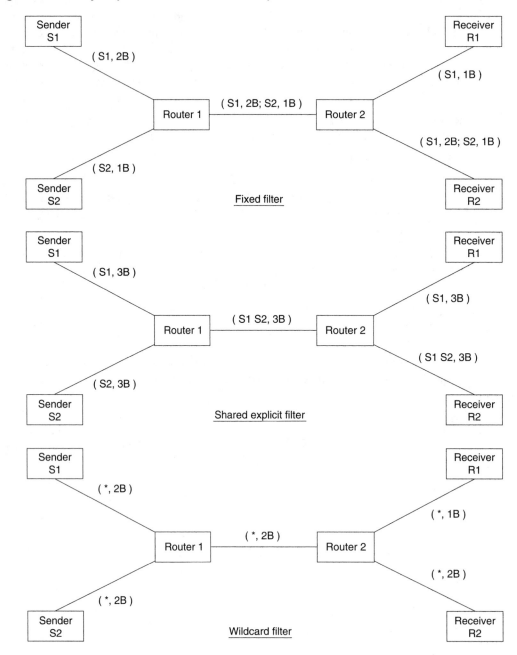

Service Types

RSVP provides two types of integrated services that the receivers can request through their RSVP RESV messages: controlled load service and guaranteed bit rate.

Controlled Load

Under *controlled load service*[4], the network guarantees that the reserved flow will reach its destination with a minimum of interference from the best-effort traffic. In addition, Cisco's implementation of the service offers isolation between the reserved flows. Flow isolation allows a flow reservation to operate unaffected by the presence of any other flow reservations that might exist in the network.

The controlled load service is primarily intended for a broad class of applications running on the Internet today that are sensitive to overloaded conditions. These applications work well on unloaded nets, but they degrade quickly under overloaded conditions. An example of such an application is File Transfer Protocol (FTP).

Guaranteed Bit Rate

Guaranteed bit rate service[5] provides a delay-bounded service with no queuing loss for all conforming datagrams, assuming no failure of network components or changes in routing during the life of the flow. Under this service, the network guarantees a minimum of interference from best-effort traffic, isolation between reserved flows, and a quantified worst-case delay.

Guaranteed service only guarantees the worst-case queuing delay, not the datagrams' minimal or average delay. Furthermore, to compute the maximum delay a datagram will experience, the path's fixed latency (propagation delay and transmission delay) must be determined and added to the guaranteed worst-case queuing delay. It is important to note that the guaranteed service guarantees maximum queuing delay, but not the maximum overall end-to-end delay, because the total delay's remaining components, such as propagation and transmission delay, depend entirely on the traffic path.

The worst-case queuing delay that the guaranteed service promises is the cumulative delay as seen by the PATH message before it reaches the receiver. PATH messages carry the delay information along the path from the source to the receiver and provide the receiver an accurate estimation of the exact delay conditions along the path at any time. A receiver uses this delay information while making a request for a guaranteed service.

Guaranteed service suits well for playback and real-time applications. Playback applications use a jitter buffer to offset the delay variations of the packet arrivals to function well. Guaranteed service, by guaranteeing the worst-case queuing delay, aids in the estimation of required jitter buffer size. Real-time applications get guaranteed bandwidth and delay service.

Both controlled load and guaranteed bit rate use a token bucket to describe a data flow's traffic parameters. The token bucket is a rate control mechanism that identifies a mean rate (how much can be sent or forwarded per unit time on average), a burst size (how much can be sent within a given unit of time without scheduling concerns), and a measurement interval (the time quantum). Details regarding the token bucket rate control mechanism are discussed in Chapter 3.

Under both services, a receiver requests for a certain bit rate and burst size in an RESV message. The WFQ scheduler and WRED queue management techniques with preferential weights assure that traffic to the receiver has a bounded latency. The latency bound is not specified, however. The controlled load service only promises "good service," and the guaranteed service provides information (in the PATH messages) from which the delay bounds can be calculated.

RSVP Media Support

Point-to-point media, such as serial lines, are well modeled for RSVP, but shared media, such as Ethernet, Asynchronous Transfer Mode (ATM), Frame Relay, and X.25, are not.

In shared media, there is no way to ensure that others on the same segment do not send traffic that might fill up the segment. It can work fine, however, in a segment that is lightly loaded or has only a few sources. To address this problem of resource reservation on shared media, SBM, a protocol for RSVP-based admission control over Institute of Electrical and Electronic Engineers (IEEE) 802-style networks, was developed. SBM defines some RSVP extensions that provide a method of mapping RSVP onto Layer 2 devices and networks. It is discussed further in Chapter 8.

In the Cisco-specific implementation, to support RSVP over ATM, RSVP creates a Variable Bit Rate (VBR) ATM switched virtual circuit (SVC) for every reservation across an ATM network. It then redirects all reserved traffic down the corresponding SVCs and relies on the ATM interface to police the traffic.

RSVP Scalability

One drawback of RSVP is that the amount of state information required increases with the number of per-flow reservations. As many hundreds of thousands of real-time unicast and multicast flows can exist in the Internet backbone at any time, state information on a per-flow granularity is considered a nonscalable solution for Internet backbones.

RSVP with per-flow reservations scales well for medium-size corporate intranets with link speeds of DS3 or less. For large intranets and for Internet service provider (ISP) backbones, you can make RSVP scale well when you use it with large multicast groups, large static classes, or an aggregation of flows at the edges rather than per-flow reservations. RSVP reservation aggregation[6] proposes to aggregate several end-to-end reservations sharing common ingress and egress routers into one large, end-to-end reservation. Another approach is to use RSVP at the edges and diffserv in the network backbone to address RSVP scalability issues in the core of a large network. RSVP-to-diffserv mapping is discussed in Chapter 2, "Differentiated Services Architecture."

The service provider networks and the Internet of the future are assumed to have, for the most part, sufficient capacity to carry normal telephony traffic. If a network is engineered with sufficient capacity, you can provision all telephony traffic as a single class. Depending on available network capacity, telephony traffic can require relatively modest capacity, which is given some fraction of the capacity overall, without the need for resource allocation per individual call.

Case Study 7-1: Reserving End-to-End Bandwidth for an Application Using RSVP

The sender and receiver applications need to signal over the network using RSVP so that they can reserve end-to-end network bandwidth for digital audio playback. The sender and receiver application traffic is made up of UDP packets with destination port number 1040. The network setup is shown in Figure 7-4 (note that the IP addresses in this figure indicate just the last octet of 210.210.210.X network address). Assume that the sender and receiver applications are not yet RSVP-compliant and rely on the end routers for RSVP signaling.

Figure 7-4   *RSVP Signaling and Reservations for Traffic FLows Between Two End-Hosts*

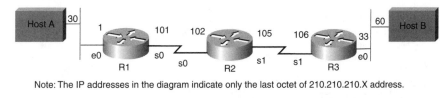

Note: The IP addresses in the diagram indicate only the last octet of 210.210.210.X address.

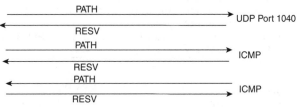

In case the applications are not RSVP-compliant, end routers should be set up to behave as though they are receiving periodic signaling information from the sender and the receiver. Another RSVP reservation should be configured for Internet Control Message Protocol (ICMP) packets to allow pinging between the sender and the receiver to troubleshoot end-to-end network connectivity issues.

NOTE   The use of RSVP for ICMP messages in this case study is meant primarily to illustrate RSVP operation, though the practical need might be limited.

To enable end-to-end RSVP signaling over the network, the inbound and outbound interfaces of the routers along the path of the sender to the receiver need to be configured for WFQ and RSVP. Note that WFQ is on by default on interfaces with bandwidths of 2 MB or less. The **show interface** command shows the queuing strategy being used by an interface.

In this case study, RSVP reservations are made for the following protocols:

- UDP Port 1040 application traffic from Host A to Host B.

- ICMP packets from Host A to Host B and vice versa to verify and diagnose connectivity issues at times of network congestion. This enables ping (ICMP Echo Request) packets from one end host to the other, and ICMP Echo Reply packets in response to the requests to work at all times.

Listing 7-1 shows a sample configuration for Router R1 for the RSVP setup.

Listing 7-1   *RSVP-Related Configuration on Router R1*

```
interface Ethernet0
 ip address 210.210.210.1 255.255.255.224
 fair-queue 64 256 234
 ip rsvp bandwidth 7500 7500
!
interface Serial0
 ip address 210.210.210.101 255.255.255.252
 fair-queue 64 256 36
 ip rsvp bandwidth 1158 1158

ip rsvp sender 210.210.210.60 210.210.210.30 1 0 0
210.210.210.30 Et0 1 1
ip rsvp sender 210.210.210.60 210.210.210.30 UDP 1040 0
210.210.210.30 Et0 32 32
ip rsvp reservation 210.210.210.60 210.210.210.30 1 0 0
210.210.210.30 Et0 ff 1 1
```

This configuration enables WFQ and RSVP on the router interfaces. The **fair-queue** command enables you to set up the queue's drop threshold and the maximum number of normal and reservable conversation queues. The **ip rsvp bandwidth** command sets up the maximum amount of reservable bandwidth on the interface and the maximum allowable reservable bandwidth for any particular reservation.

The **ip rsvp sender** command is used to set up the router as if it were receiving periodic RSVP PATH messages from a downstream sender, and enable it to send RSVP PATH messages upstream. Note that this command is needed only when the sender cannot send RSVP PATH messages.

Two **ip rsvp sender** commands are used in the configuration. They are used to simulate receipt of periodic RSVP PATH messages from sender 210.210.210.30 for ICMP and UDP Port 1040 traffic, respectively. Router R1 forwards the received RSVP PATH messages further downstream toward the destination 210.210.210.60.

The **ip rsvp reservation** command is used to set up the router as if it were receiving periodic RSVP RESV messages. The command in the configuration shows receipt of periodic RSVP RESV messages from 210.210.210.30 for the ICMP traffic. This is to enable RSVP reservation for ping (ICMP) packets from Host B to Host A. The RSVP RESV messages are forwarded toward source 210.210.210.60.

Listings 7-2 and 7-3 show the RSVP-related configuration for Routers R2 and R3, respectively.

Listing 7-2   *RSVP-Related Configuration on Router R2*

```
interface Serial0
 ip address 210.210.210.102 255.255.255.252
 fair-queue 64 256 36
 ip rsvp bandwidth 1158 1158
!
interface Serial1
 ip address 210.210.210.105 255.255.255.252
 fair-queue 64 256 36
 ip rsvp bandwidth 1158 1158
```

Note that this router doesn't need any RSVP sender and reservation statements, as they are needed only on edge routers. Edge routers dynamically propagate the RSVP messages to allow Router R2 to make reservations for the RSVP flows.

Listing 7-3   *RSVP-Related Configuration on Router R3*

```
interface Ethernet0
 ip address 210.210.210.33 255.255.255.224
 fair-queue 64 256 234
 ip rsvp bandwidth 7500 7500
!
interface Serial1
 ip address 210.210.210.106 255.255.255.252
 fair-queue 64 256 36
 ip rsvp bandwidth 1158 1158


ip rsvp sender 210.210.210.30 210.210.210.60 1   0 0
210.210.210.60 Et0 1 1
ip rsvp reservation 210.210.210.60 210.210.210.30 1   0 0
210.210.210.60 Et0 FF LOAD 1 1
ip rsvp reservation 210.210.210.60 210.210.210.30 UDP 1040 0
 210.210.210.60 Et0 FF LOAD 32 32
```

Listings 7-4 through 7-10 provide output of the different RSVP-related information from the router.

Listing 7-4   *Interface-Related RSVP Information of Router R1*

```
Router#show ip rsvp interface
interfac allocate i/f max  flow max  per/255 UDP  IP   UDP_IP
UDP M/C
Et0       1K       7500K    7500K    0  /255 0    1    0
  0
Se0       33K      1158K    1158K    7  /255 0    1    0
  0
```

The **show ip rsvp interface** command shows the total allocated bandwidth on an interface. By default, the maximum reservable bandwidth on an interface is 0.75 times the total interface bandwidth.

Listing 7-5   *RSVP Sender Information on Router R1*

```
Router#show ip rsvp sender
To              From            Pro DPort Sport
Prev Hop        I/F  BPS Bytes
210.210.210.30  210.210.210.60  1   0     0
     210.210.210.102 Se0   1K      1K
210.210.210.60  210.210.210.30  1   0     0
     210.210.210.30   Et0   1K      1K
210.210.210.60  210.210.210.30  UDP 1040  0
     210.210.210.30   Et0   32K     32K
```

The **show ip rsvp sender** command shows that Router R1 saw three different RSVP PATH messages.

Listing 7-6   *Received RSVP Reservation Requests by Router R1*

```
Router#show ip rsvp reservation
To             From           Pro DPort Sport
Next Hop       I/F   Fi Serv BPS Bytes
210.210.210.30 210.210.210.60 1   0     0
    210.210.210.30 Et0    FF LOAD 1K      1K
210.210.210.60 210.210.210.30 1   0     0
    210.210.210.102 Se0   FF LOAD 1K      1K
210.210.210.60 210.210.210.30 UDP 1040  0
    210.210.210.102 Se0   FF LOAD 32K     32K
```

The **show ip rsvp reservation** command shows that Router R1 received three RSVP RESV messages. As an example, for the UDP flow, Router R1 received the RSVP RESV message from Router R2 with a next-hop of 210.210.210.102.

Listing 7-7   *Installed RSVP Reservations on Router R1*

```
Router#show ip rsvp installed
RSVP: Ethernet0
BPS    To                  From            Protoc DPort  Sport
Weight Conv
1K     210.210.210.30  210.210.210.60  1      0      0
    4       264
RSVP: Serial0
BPS    To                  From            Protoc DPort  Sport
  Weight Conv
1K     210.210.210.60  210.210.210.30  1      0      0
    128     264
32K    210.210.210.60  210.210.210.30  UDP    1040   0
    4       265
```

The **show ip rsvp installed** command shows three active RSVP reservations in Router R1. It also shows the conversation number and weight assigned by WFQ for each reservation.

Note that the weight for the largest RSVP reservation is always 4. The weight for the reservation of ICMP packets on the serial0 interface is derived as:

$4 \times$ (RSVP reservation request) $\div$ (largest RSVP reservation allocated) $= 4 \times 32 \div 1 = 128$.

Listing 7-8   *RSVP Reservations Sent Upstream by Router R1*

```
Router#show ip rsvp request
To              From            Pro DPort Sport
Next Hop      I/F   Fi Serv BPS Bytes
210.210.210.30 210.210.210.60 1    0      0
   210.210.210.102 Se0   FF LOAD 1K     1K
210.210.210.60 210.210.210.30 1    0      0
   210.210.210.30 Et0   FF LOAD 1K     1K
210.210.210.60 210.210.210.30 UDP 1040  0
   210.210.210.30 Et0   FF LOAD 32K    32K
```

The **show ip rsvp request** command shows that Router R1 passed on three RSVP RESV messages. As an example, for the UDP flow, Router R1 sent the RSVP RESV message to the downstream host with a next-hop of 210.210.210.30.

Listing 7-9   *RSVP Neighbors of Router R1*

```
Router#show ip rsvp neighbor
Interfac Neighbor         Encapsulation
Et0       210.210.210.30  RSVP
Se0       210.210.210.102 RSVP
```

The **show ip rsvp neighbor** command shows the neighbor routers or hosts from which Router R1 received RSVP messages.

Listing 7-10 *Serial0 Queue Information of Router R1*

```
Router#show queue serial0
Input queue: 0/75/1071 (size/max/drops); Total output drops:
107516
Queueing strategy: weighted fair
Output queue: 41/1000/64/107516 (size/max total/threshold/drops)
   Conversations  1/4/256 (active/max active/max total)
   Reserved Conversations 1/1 (allocated/max allocated)

(depth/weight/discards/tail drops/interleaves) 1/4096/100054/0/0
Conversation 265, linktype: ip, length: 50
source: 210.210.210.30, destination: 210.210.210.60, id:
0x033D,
ttl: 254, TOS: 0 prot: 17, source port 38427,
destination port 1040

(depth/weight/discards/tail drops/interleaves) 40/4096/1131/0/0
Conversation 71, linktype: ip, length: 104
source: 210.210.210.30, destination: 210.210.210.60, id:
0x0023, ttl: 254, prot: 1

(depth/weight/discards/tail drops/interleaves) 1/128/65046/0/0
Conversation 264, linktype: ip, length: 104
source: 210.210.210.30, destination: 210.210.210.60, id:
0x0023, ttl: 254, prot: 1
```

The **show queue s0** command shows the capture of the packets in the output queue of the serial0 interface at the time the command was issued. Note that the conservation numbers of the RSVP flows in the queue match those shown in the **show ip rsvp installed** command output.

Case Study 7-2: RSVP for VoIP

Assume that Routers R1 and R3 in Figure 7-4 have dial-ports attached for analog phones for voice calls across the network. The voice call between the two phones needs resource reservation for guaranteed service from the network.

Adding to the discussion and configuration provided in Case Study 7-1 in setting up RSVP in a network, Listings 7-11 and 7-12 show sample configurations for enabling VoIP dial peers and RSVP reservations.

Listing 7-11 *VoIP QoS Configuration on Router R1*

```
dial-peer voice 1211 voip
  req-qos guaranteed-delay
```

Listing 7-12   *VoIP QoS Configuration on Router R3*

```
dial-peer voice 1212 voip
req-qos guaranteed-delay
```

The **req-qos guaranteed-delay** command sets up guaranteed delay as the desired (requested) QoS to a dial peer. Other QoS requests can be either controlled load or best effort. By default, the voice call gets only best-effort service.

NOTE   The retransmit time for RSVP messages can be too long for VoIP. Because lost RSVP PATH messages can result in poor performance for VoIP by delaying the establishment of an RSVP reservation along the VoIP call's path, it is important to keep hello interval for RSVP PATH messages small, or to have a fast retransmit scheme.

Summary

In intserv, RSVP is used to signal QoS information using control messages that are different from the actual data packets. RSVP signaling results in certain resource guarantees along the traffic's routed path.

Like diffserv, intserv using RSVP depends on the packet scheduler with QoS support (such as WFQ and WRED) in the router to offer the desired QoS for the RSVP reserved flows.

Frequently Asked Questions

Q — *What are some examples of applications with RSVP support?*

A — Microsoft NetShow and NetMeeting are examples of some popular desktop applications with RSVP support. Moreover, the new Microsoft Windows operating system, Windows 2000, has built-in RSVP support.

Q — *Is there any way to know which session, address, and port have reserved bandwidth on a certain interface?*

A — This information is displayed when the command **show ip rsvp installed** is issued on the router. Also, **show tech-support rsvp** displays the output of all RSVP-related commands, including **show ip rsvp**, installed.

Q — *How can you make sure RSVP control packets are prioritized over the rest of the traffic within the network?*

A — The network operator can set RSVP control packets with a high IP precedence value such that they are preferentially treated within the network.

Q — *Does RSVP run over IP or the UDP protocol layer?*

A — RSVP runs directly over IP using IP protocol field 46. UDP encapsulations are needed, however, in hosts that cannot do raw network I/O (in other words, send and receive IP datagrams). To use RSVP, such systems must encapsulate RSVP messages in UDP. Two well-known UDP ports, 1698 and 1699, are used for UDP encapsulation of RSVP.

Q — *I am issuing a static RSVP sender command, **ip rsvp sender 224.10.10.10 10.1.15.5 udp 0 0 10.1.15.5 Hssi 1/0 1200 4**, but the router gives the message RSVP: sender not accepted. Is my command not accepted?*

A — This error message could occur due to a number of reasons. The most common reason, however, is that WFQ is not enabled on the interface going to the sender (in this case, Hssi 1/0), though RSVP is enabled. Because RSVP depends on WFQ for resource allocation, an error message is produced.

Q — *Why doesn't the **show ip rsvp installed** command show the weight and conversation numbers for the installed reservation?*

A — The weight and conversation numbers are assigned by the WFQ algorithm. Make sure WFQ is enabled on the interface that has the reservation installed. WFQ is discussed in detail in Chapter 4.

Q — *The **show ip rsvp installed** command shows the conversation number 256 and weight 4 of an RSVP flow reservation on serial0. However, the **show queue s0** command output shows a weight of 4096 for conversation 256. How can you explain this discrepancy in weights given by these two commands?*

A — It is likely that the RSVP flow is sending more than the reserved bandwidth. If the flow is sending traffic at a rate that goes over the bandwidth reservation, the excess traffic is treated as best effort and is assigned a weight of 4096 in WFQ. Therefore, the packet with a weight of 4096 might be a nonconforming packet. Chapter 4 describes the WFQ algorithm in detail.

Q — *The router cannot install the RSVP reservation for the flow I just configured on the router. The* **debug ip rsvp** *command shows the following message: RSVP RESV: no path information for 207.2.23.1. What does this debug message mean?*

A — Generally, you should see this message on a router that has a static RSVP reservation configuration for a flow so that the router behaves as if it is receiving periodic RESV messages for this flow. The debug informs that the router didn't receive any PATH message for the corresponding flow. RSVP cannot send a RESV message without first receiving a corresponding PATH message for the flow. Troubleshoot over the path leading to the sender to find out why the router didn't receive any RSVP PATH message.

Q — *Are RSVP messages Cisco Express Forwarding (CEF)-switched?*

A — No. RSVP messages are control packets that need to be processed by the router. Hence, they are process-switched. Note, however, that the data packets belonging to an RSVP flow follow whatever switching path is configured in the router. Packet switching is discussed in Appendix B, "Packet Switching Mechanisms."

References

[1] "Resource ReSerVation Protocol (RSVP)—Version 1 Functional Specification," R. Branden and others, RFC 2205, 1997.

[2] "Resource Reservation Protocol (RSVP) Version 1 Applicability Statement, Some Guidelines on Deployment," A. Mankin and others, RFC 2208, 1997.

[3] RSVP home page: www.isi.edu/rsvp.

[4] "Specification of the Controlled-Load Network Element Service," J. Wroclawski, RFC 2211, 1997.

[5] "Specification of Guaranteed Quality of Service," S. Shenker, C. Partridge, and R. Guerin, RFC 2212, 1997.

[6] "Aggregation of RSVP for IPv4 and IPv6 Reservations," IETF Draft, Baker and others, 1999.

PART II

Layer 2, MPLS QoS—Interworking with IP QoS

Chapter 8   Layer 2 QoS: Interworking with IP QoS

Chapter 9   QoS in MPLS-Based Networks

Layer 2 QoS: Interworking with IP QoS

Most networks use diverse network technologies. Popular link-layer technologies, such as Asynchronous Transfer Mode (ATM), Frame Relay, and Ethernet, offer quality of service (QoS) functionality at Layer 2. This chapter discusses these multi-access Layer 2 technologies and their QoS offerings. Because QoS is only as good as its weakest link, it is necessary to ensure that Internet Protocol (IP) QoS is seamless across diverse link technologies. To provide end-to-end IP QoS, it is necessary that QoS at Layer 2 map to IP QoS, and vice versa.

ATM

ATM[1] is a fixed-size cell-switching and multiplexing technology. It is connection-oriented, and a virtual circuit (VC) must be set up across the ATM network before any user data can be transferred between two or more ATM attached devices. Primarily, ATM has two types of connections, or VCs: permanent virtual circuits (PVCs) and switched virtual circuits (SVCs). PVCs are generally static and need a manual or external configuration to set them up. SVCs are dynamic and are created based on demand. Their setup requires a signaling protocol between the ATM endpoints and ATM switches.

An ATM network is composed of ATM switches and ATM end nodes, or hosts. The cell header contains the information the ATM switches use to switch ATM cells. The data link layer is broken down into two sublayers: the ATM Adaptation Layer (AAL) and the ATM layer. You map the different services to the common ATM layer through the AAL. Higher layers pass down the user information in the form of bits to the AAL. User information gets encapsulated into an AAL frame, and then the ATM layer breaks the information down into ATM cells. The reverse is done at the receiver end. This process is known as *segmentation and reassembly (SAR)*.

ATM Cell Format

Each ATM cell contains 53 bytes—5 bytes of cell header information and 48 bytes of user information, or *payload*. Two ATM cell formats exist: User-to-Network Interface (UNI), which defines the format for cells between a user and an ATM switch; and Network-to-

Node Interface (NNI), which defines the format for cells between the switching nodes. The cell formats are shown in Figure 8-1.

Figure 8-1   *ATM Cell UNI and NNI Header Formats*

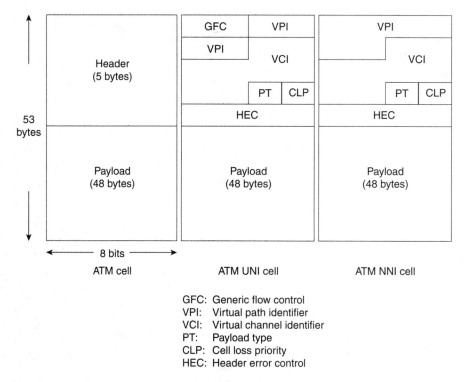

GFC: Generic flow control
VPI: Virtual path identifier
VCI: Virtual channel identifier
PT: Payload type
CLP: Cell loss priority
HEC: Header error control

Generic flow control (GFC) has local flow-control significance to the user for flow control. The GFC mechanism is used to control traffic flow from end stations to the network. The GFC field is not present in the NNI cell format. Two modes of operation are defined: uncontrolled access and controlled access. Traffic enters the network without GFC-based flow control in uncontrolled access mode. In controlled access mode, ATM-attached end nodes shape their transmission in accordance with the value present in GFC. Most UNI implementations don't use this field.

A virtual path (VP) consists of a bundle of VCs and is assigned to a virtual path identifier (VPI). ATM switches can switch VPIs, along with all the VCs within them. VCs are the paths over which user data is sent. Each VC within a VP is assigned a virtual channel identifier (VCI). VPI and VCI fields are used in ATM switches to make switching decisions.

Figure 8-2 shows a VC being set up between routers R1 and R2 through a network of ATM switches. All the cells leaving R1 for R2 are tagged with a VPI of 0 and a VCI of 64. The

ATM switch S1 looks at the VPI and VCI pair on Port 0 and looks them up in its translation table. Based on the lookup, the ATM switch switches the cells out of Port 1 with a VPI of 1 and a VCI of 100. Similarly, Switch S4 switches cells on Port 4 with a VPI of 1 and a VCI of 100 onto Port 3 with a VPI of 2 and a VCI of 100 based on its translation table.

Figure 8-2   *Connectivity Between Routers R1 and R2 Across an ATM Network*

PVC translation table on port 0 of Switch S1

PVC	Outgoing PVC	Outgoing port
0/64	1/100	1

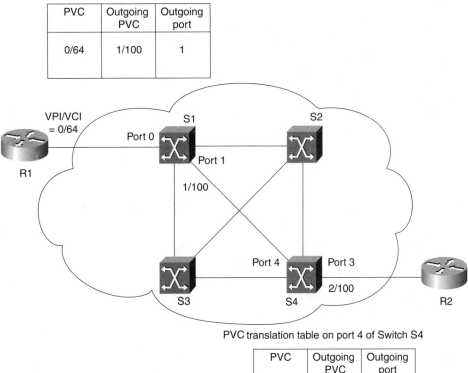

PVC translation table on port 4 of Switch S4

PVC	Outgoing PVC	Outgoing port
1/100	2/100	3

The remaining fields in the ATM header are as follows:

- **Payload type identifier (PTI)**—This 3-bit field is used to identify the kind of payload carried in the cell. It is used to differentiate between operation, administration, and maintenance (OAM) information and user data.

- **Cell loss priority (CLP)**—CLP defines a cell's priority. If CLP is not set (CLP = 0), it is considered at a higher priority than cells with CLP set (CLP = 1). With CLP set, the cell has a higher chance of being discarded at times of network congestion.

- **Header error control (HEC)**—HEC is used for detecting and correcting the errors in the ATM header.

ATM QoS

ATM offers QoS guarantees by making the ATM end system explicitly specify a traffic contract describing its intended traffic flow characteristics. The flow descriptor carries QoS parameters, such as Peak Cell Rate (PCR), Sustained Cell Rate (SCR), and burst size.

ATM end systems are responsible for making sure the transmitted traffic meets the QoS contract. The ATM end system shapes traffic by buffering data and transmitting it within the contracted QoS parameters. The ATM switches police each user's traffic characteristics and compare them to their QoS contract. If certain traffic is found to exceed the QoS contract, a switch can set the CLP bit on the nonconforming traffic. A cell with the CLP bit set has a higher drop probability at times of congestion.

ATM Service Classes

The AAL layer is what gives ATM the flexibility to carry entirely different traffic services within the same format. ATM defines five different AAL types based on the supported service type. AAL1 and AAL2 are designed for Constant Bit Rate (CBR) and Variable Bit Rate (VBR) services, respectively. AAL3 and AAL4, meant for connection-oriented and connectionless data traffic, respectively, have been absorbed by a more generalized AAL5 service for packetized data.

ATM services exist based on timing between source and destination, type of bit rate, and connection mode. The ATM Forum defines five service categories:

- **CBR**—CBR is meant for real-time data with tight constraints on delay and jitter and consistent bandwidth availability. CBR is synonymous with Circuit Emulation. This type of traffic requires reserved bandwidth that is available on demand. Examples include standard digitized voice at 64 Kbps and video (H.320 standard).

- **Real-Time Variable Bit Rate (RT-VBR)**—As the name implies, this service is meant for real-time data similar to CBR, but under this service, the sources are expected to be bursty. Packetized video and data traffic with real-time requirements, such as interactive multimedia traffic, fall into this category. RT-VBR is specified by PCR, SCR, and maximum burst size (MBS).

- **Non-Real Time Variable Bit Rate (nRT-VBR)**—nRT-VBR is intended for applications that have burst traffic characteristics and do not have tight constraints on delay and jitter. Interactive data transactions fall into this category. nRT-VBR is specified by PCR, SCR, and MBS.

- **Available Bit Rate (ABR)**—ABR sources regulate their sending rate according to feedback provided by the network. An ABR service doesn't make bandwidth reservations as such, but it adapts the traffic allowed into the network based on the feedback mechanism implemented by using the Resource Management (RM) cells. It uses a rate-based approach where the sending rate on each VC is adaptive to the explicit rate indications in the network as conveyed by the RM cells. Data cell transmission is preceded by sending ABR RM cells. The source rate is controlled by the return of these RM cells, which are looped back by the destination or by a virtual destination. RM cells introduce a new source of overhead. This service works well with Transmission Control Protocol (TCP) sources[2], which implement adaptive flow control.

  ABR service specifies a PCR and a guaranteed Minimum Cell Rate (MCR) per VC.

- **Unspecified Bit Rate (UBR)**—UBR is the ATM equivalent of best-effort service in IP. There is no bandwidth reservation, nor are there delay and jitter bounds. No congestion control is performed at the ATM layer. An example of such traffic is massive file transfers, such as system backups. TCP over UBR is not expected to perform well, because cell loss can occur on a UBR circuit, but you can improve the performance by using the cell discard strategies described in the next section.

Cell Discard Strategies

As discussed earlier in this chapter, the ATM header has a CLP bit to indicate CLP. Cells with CLP = 1 are dropped before a cell with CLP = 0. The ATM traffic policing mechanism can tag the CLP bit as 1 in a cell when a cell exceeds the VC's traffic contract specifications. When congestion occurs in some part of the ATM network, cells with a CLP bit of 0 or 1 might be dropped, though cells whose CLP bits are tagged will be dropped first. Partial packet discard (PPD) and early packet discard (EPD) are ATM cell discard strategies that increase the effective throughput in an ATM network.

The ATM SAR function takes care of segmenting larger packets into cells. When a dropped ATM cell is part of a larger packet, it is not necessary to send the remaining cells belonging to the segmented packet, because this would cause unnecessary traffic on an already congested link. In this case, reassembling the cells into the original packet at the destination is not possible, and the entire packet needs to be retransmitted anyway. Therefore, when a cell of a larger packet is discarded, PPD starts discarding the packet's remaining cells. The improvement is limited, however, because the switch begins to drop cells only when the buffer overflows.

Implementing PPD is straightforward with AAL5. PPD can be signaled on a per-VC basis. With PPD, after the switch drops cells from the VC, the switch continues dropping cells from the same VC until the switch sees the parameter set in the ATM cell header indicating the end of the AAL packet. The end-of-packet cell itself is not dropped. Because AAL5 does not support the simultaneous multiplexing of packets on a single VC, you can use this cell to delimit packet boundaries.

Because a cell discard of a larger packet (and, hence, PPD) can occur after some of the earlier cells of the larger packet find space in the output queue, PPD does only a partial packet discard. Thus, the congested link can still transmit a significant fraction of cells belonging to corrupted packets. Note, however, that if the discarded cell happens to be the packet's first cell, PPD is effectively doing a full packet discard. On the other hand, EPD[3] occurs before any cell is admitted into the output queue. When a new packet arrives, EPD checks the output buffer usage. If the buffer usage is below the configured threshold value, the ATM switch knows the buffer space is not about to be exhausted, and all the packet's cells can be queued. Otherwise, the switch assumes the buffer is close to exhaustion and the entire packet might not be queued; hence, the switch throws the entire packet away. Therefore, EPD either queues all the cells of a packet or drops the entire packet altogether. Because EPD does a full packet discard before any cell belonging to the packet is queued, this process is called *early packet discard*.

VP Shaping

Similar to the ATM services for an ATM VC, an ATM service—or shaping—can be applied on a VP for traffic contract restrictions on an entire VP. Within a shaped VP, all VCs still can be UBR without strict traffic constrictions carrying best-effort traffic. Figure 8-3 shows a logical diagram of how VCs are bundled within a VP.

Figure 8-3   *Bundling of Multiple VCs in a VP*

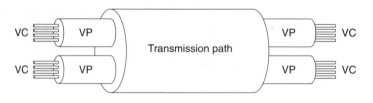

NOTE   A VP ATM service can support all the ATM service classes that can be supported at the VC level.

Case Study 8-1: A PVC with ABR Service

Say you're setting up an ABR PVC on a router with a VPI of 0 and a VCI of 34. The PCR and MCR parameters for the ABR service are 10 Mbps and 1 Mbps, respectively. The ABR rate needs to increase and decrease by a factor of 8 in response to the feedback from the network as received by the RM cells.

Listing 8-1 shows the configuration to enable the ABR PVC for this case study.

Listing 8-1   *ABR PVC Configuration on an ATM0/0/0 Interface*

```
interface atm 0/0/0
 ip address 225.225.255.2  255.255.255.252
 pvc 0/34
 abr 10000 1000
 atm abr rate-factor 8 8
```

The ABR service is configured with a PCR and MCR of 10 Mbps and 1Mbps, respectively. The **atm abr rate-factor 8 8** command configures the cell transmission rate increases and decreases in response to RM control information from the network.

Note that the PCR and MCR default values are the line rate and 0, respectively. The default rate factor is 16.

Case Study 8-2: VP Traffic Shaping

A Tier-1 ISP wants to collaborate with Competitive Local Exchange Carrier (CLEC) to offer a virtual ISP product. The CLEC provides physical DSL loops to the end users and the Tier-1 ISP provides the Internet connectivity. For example, ISP-1 buys a 6 Mbps Internet connection from the Tier-1 ISP. The Tier-1 ISP interfaces directly with the CLEC to access the DSL end users of ISP-1. Note that ISP-1 doesn't own any equipment; instead, they own the relationship with the end user. The CLEC will deliver to the Tier-1 ISP an ATM VC on a per-end-user basis.

The Tier-1 ISP imposes a general bandwidth constraint on the VP associated with ISP-1. Inside the VP, the VCs could do either CBR or have a free reign on bandwidth, as in a UBR service, as long as the aggregate is restricted by the VP CBR.

The CLEC uses a *Digital Subscriber Line Access Multiplexer (DSLAM)*, which is a rack of Asynchronous Digital Subscriber Line (ADSL) cards with data multiplexed into a backbone network interface/connection (T1, OC3 DS3, ATM, or Frame Relay). DSLAM is an ADSL equivalent of a modem rack in ISP dial environments. In this case, the DSLAM is owned by the CLEC. The DSLAM connects to the Tier-1 ISP router after going through an ATM-Frame switch at their PoP, as shown in Figure 8-4.

Figure 8-4 *VP Traffic Shaping Example*

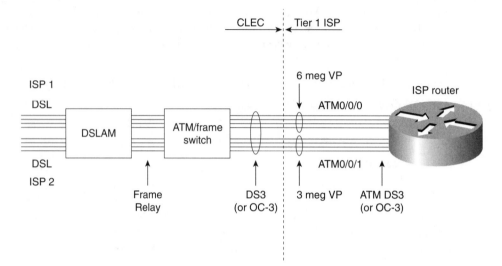

Each ISP connected by the CLEC is assigned an interface on the Tier-1 ISP router, and all its VCs fall under the same VP. In the sample configuration on the Tier-1 ISP router shown in Listing 8-2, the CLEC's ISP 1 is assigned interface ATM0/0/0 and VP 2. The VP traffic shaping is configured under the main ATM interface. All VCs use the same VP, and each is assigned its own subinterface under the main interface.

Listing 8-2 *VP Traffic Shaping Configuration on the ATM0/0/0 interface of the Tier 1 ISP Router*

```
interface ATM0/0/0
 atm pvp 2 6000000
!
interface ATM0/0/0.1 point-to-point
 ip address 212.12.12.1 255.255.255.252
 atm pvc 101 2 101 aal5snap
!
interface ATM0/0/0.2 point-to-point
 ip address 212.12.12.4 255.255.255.252
 atm pvc 102 2 102 aal5snap

interface ATM 0/0/0.3 point-to-point
ip address 212.12.12.8 255.255.255.252
 atm pvc 103 2 103 aal5snap
```

As shown in Listing 8-2, the **atm pvp** configuration command sets up VP traffic shaping for all the VCs of the specified VP to the stipulated peak rate.

To examine the VP groups' configuration, you can use the **show atm vp** command, which shows the VP traffic shaping parameters of all VP groups in the router. The user can create up to 256 different VP groups. It also shows the number of VCs in a VP group. Listing 8-3 shows the ATM VP traffic shaping parameters.

Listing 8-3   *ATM VP Traffic Shaping Parameters*

```
Router#show atm vp
                     Data  CES    Peak      CES
Interface     VPI    VCs   VCs    Kbps      Kbps     Status
ATM0/0/0      2      3     0      6000000 0          ACTIVE
```

You can obtain detailed information on VP 2 by using the **show atm vp 2** command. This command shows information about all the VCs with a VPI of 2 in the router. Two management virtual channels are created automatically by the router per each VP group configured for the segment OAM F4 flow cells and for the end-to-end OAM F4 flow cells. Listing 8-4 shows detailed information on the VCs with VPI 2.

Listing 8-4   *Information on VP Traffic Shaping Parameters for VPI 2*

```
Router#show atm vp 2
ATM0/0/0  VPI: 2, PeakRate: 6000000, CesRate: 0, DataVCs: 3, CesVCs: 0,
Status: ACTIVE

  VCD    VCI    Type    InPkts    OutPkts    AAL/Encap    Status
  1      3      PVC     0         0          F4 OAM       ACTIVE
  2      4      PVC     0         0          F4 OAM       ACTIVE
  101    101    PVC     0         0          AAL5-SNAP    ACTIVE
  102    102    PVC     0         0          AAL5-SNAP    ACTIVE
  103    103    PVC     0         0          AAL5-SNAP    ACTIVE

TotalInPkts: 0, TotalOutPkts: 0, TotalInFast: 0, TotalOutFast: 0,
TotalBroadcasts: 0
```

The **show atm vc** command shows information on all the VCs in the router without regard to the VPI information. Listing 8-5 displays information on all ATM VCs enabled on the router.

Listing 8-5   *ATM VC Parameters*

Interface Sts	VCD / Name	VPI	VCI	Type	Encaps	SC	Peak Kbps	Avg/Min Kbps	Burst Cells
0/0/0 UP	1	2	3	PVC	F4-OAM	UBR	6000000		
0/0/0 UP	2	2	4	PVC	F4-OAM	UBR	6000000		
0/0/0.1 UP	101	2	101	PVC	SNAP	UBR	6000000		
0/0/0.2 UP	102	2	102	PVC	SNAP	UBR	6000000		
0/0/0.3 UP	103	2	103	PVC	SNAP	UBR	6000000		

ATM Interworking with IP QoS

In an IP network where a certain part of the network uses ATM as the underlying Layer 2 technology (as in Figure 8-5), the IP traffic is carried across the ATM backbone using a VC provisioned with certain ATM QoS, which suits the IP traffic it carries. Due to congestion at the ingress to the ATM network, however, queues can build up and certain packets might be tail-dropped. Without IP QoS, such packet drops are random and happen without any knowledge of the packet's IP precedence value, which fails to deliver end-to-end IP QoS across an ATM network. Hence, a need exists for IP QoS in an ATM network. You can apply the Weighted Random Early Detection (WRED) and Weighted Fair Queuing (WFQ) IP QoS techniques on the queues at the ingress to an ATM network, so the packet drops and scheduling on the output queue are based on the packets' IP QoS. Chapter 4, "Per-Hop Behavior: Resource Allocation I," and Chapter 6, "Per-Hop Behavior: Congestion Avoidance and Packet Drop Policy," discuss WFQ and WRED functions, respectively.

Figure 8-5   *IP over ATM*

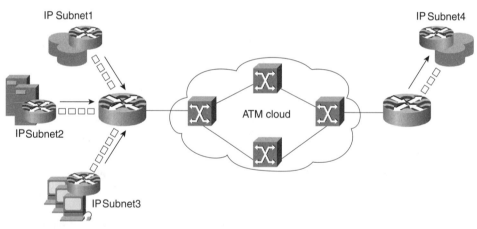

Note that from the IP QoS perspective, the IP traffic is transported across the ATM network without any loss (as any drops in the ATM network are IP QoS-unaware) by using an ATM service that suits the traffic's IP service needs. For IP QoS, each VC in an ATM network maintains a separate queue. You can apply the WRED and WFQ IP QoS functions on each VC queue.

Two scenarios are discussed in this section as a way to preserve IP QoS over an ATM network:

   1 **A single PVC carrying all the IP traffic to its destination**—IP traffic exceeding the ATM PVC parameters and service at the ingress to the ATM network gets queued, and IP QoS techniques such as WRED and WFQ are applied on the queue as it builds up due to congestion conditions.

WRED ensures that high-precedence traffic has low loss relative to lower-precedence traffic. WFQ ensures that high-precedence traffic gets a higher bandwidth relative to the lower-precedence traffic, because it schedules high-precedence traffic more often. Note that when Class-Based Weighted Fair Queuing (CBWFQ) is run on a PVC, you can make bandwidth allocations based on traffic class. CBWFQ is discussed in Chapter 4.

2 **A VC bundle (made of multiple PVCs) carrying IP traffic to its destination**— When carrying traffic with different QoS (real-time, non-real-time, best-effort) to the same destination, it is a good idea to provision multiple PVCs across the ATM network to the destination so that each IP traffic class is carried by a separate PVC. Each PVC is provisioned to an ATM service class based on the IP traffic it is mapped to carry. Figure 8-6 depicts IP-ATM QoS using a VC bundle. Some VC bundle characteristics are as follows:

— Each VC in the bundle is mapped to carry traffic with certain IP precedence value(s). You can map a VC to one or more IP precedence values. Note, however, that only one routing peering or adjacency is made per PVC bundle.

— You can monitor VC integrity by using ATM OAM or Interim Local Management Interface (ILMI). If a bundle's high-precedence VC fails, you can either "bump" its traffic to a lower-precedence VC in the bundle, or the entire bundle can be declared down.

— A separate queue exists for each VC in the bundle. You can apply the WRED and WFQ IP QoS techniques on each VC queue.

Figure 8-6   *ATM VC Bundle: IP Precedence to VC Mapping*

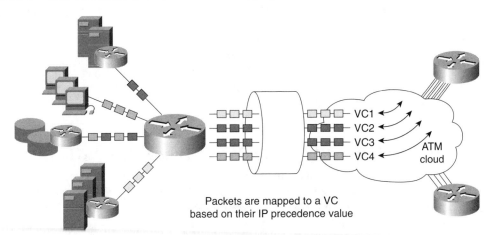

Packets are mapped to a VC
based on their IP precedence value

ATM service for the IP traffic is expected to be above UBR (best-effort) class so that no packets (cells) are dropped as part of ATM QoS within the ATM network. Figure 8-7 illustrates the two IP-ATM QoS scenarios.

Figure 8-7   *IP-ATM QoS Interworking*

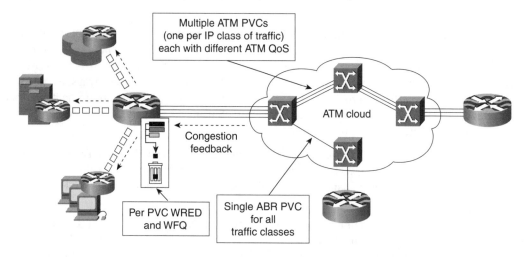

The difference between using a single PVC or a PVC bundle for IP QoS interworking depends on the cost and traffic needs in the network. Although a PVC bundle can be more expensive than a single PVC, a PVC bundle provides traffic isolation for critical traffic classes such as voice. On the other hand, a PVC bundle requires prior traffic engineering so that all the PVCs in the bundle are utilized optimally. Otherwise, you can run into conditions in which the PVC in the bundle carrying the high-precedence traffic gets congested while the PVC carrying the lower-precedence traffic is running relatively uncongested. Note that you cannot automatically bump high-precedence traffic to a different member PVC when the PVC carrying high precedence gets congested. When using a single PVC, you can enable CBWFQ with a priority queue on it so that voice traffic is prioritized over the rest of the traffic carried by the PVC. CBWFQ with a priority queue is discussed in Chapter 4.

Case Study 8-3: Differentiated IP Packet Discards at ATM Edges

Say an ISP backbone engineer implements IP-based differentiated services across the IP network offering three service classes: gold, silver, and bronze. Traffic entering the ISP is tagged into the three service classes by using a mapping to the IP precedence value according to Table 8-1. A certain part of the ISP backbone uses ATM as the underlying transport technology. The engineer wants to use the WFQ and WRED IP QoS functions at the ingress to the ATM network—WFQ for allocating bandwidth per service class, and WRED so that any packet drops are based on the knowledge of the IP precedence values in the packet.

Table 8-1   *Service Classes Based on IP Precedence*

	Control	Gold	Silver	Bronze
Normal Traffic	Precedence 7	Precedence 5	Precedence 3	Precedence 1
Excess Traffic	Precedence 6	Precedence 4	Precedence 2	Precedence 0

The ATM PVC is engineered to be lossless because drops in the ATM network are without regard to the IP precedence value in the packet. The ATM network just functions as a lossless physical transport mechanism offering a service required by the underlying traffic.

To begin with, the different traffic classes and the policies are defined for each class. The defined policy is then applied to the ingress interface to the ATM network. Listing 8-6 is a sample configuration for this functionality.

Listing 8-6   *Configuration for IP-ATM QoS Interworking*

```
interface ATM0/0/0.1 point-to-point
 ip address 200.200.200.1 255.255.255.252
 pvc 0/101
 abr 10000 1000
 encapsulation aal5nlpid
 service-policy output atmpolicy

class-map control
 match precedence 7
 match precedence 6

class-map gold
 match precedence 5
 match precedence 4

class-map silver
 match precedence 3
 match precedence 2

class-map bronze
 match precedence 1
 match precedence 0

policy-map atmpolicy
 class control
   bandwidth 10000
   random-detect
 class gold
   bandwidth 40000
   random-detect
 class silver
   bandwidth 30000
   random-detect
```

Listing 8-6 *Configuration for IP-ATM QoS Interworking (Continued)*

```
class bronze
 bandwidth 20000
 random-detect
```

Note that the configuration uses modular QoS command-line interface (CLI). Modular QoS CLI is discussed in Appendix A, "Cisco Modular QoS Command-Line Interface."

The configuration shown in Listing 8-6 defines three class maps—gold, silver, and bronze—to classify data traffic based on precedence. A fourth class map, control, is defined to match all network control traffic that can carry an IP precedence of 6 and 7.

After the initial traffic classification step, the atmpolicy policy map is defined to stipulate a bandwidth and WRED policy for the four traffic classes. The gold class, for example, is allocated a bandwidth of 40 Mbps and a WRED drop policy. Finally, the atmpolicy policy is applied to the ATM subinterface carrying the ATM PVC to the destination across the ATM cloud by using the **service-policy** configuration command. The **show policy-map** command shows the policies for each class of a policy map. The atmpolicy policy map information is shown in Listing 8-7.

Listing 8-7 *The atmpolicy Policy Map Information*

```
Router#show policy-map atmpolicy
Policy Map atmpolicy
  Weighted Fair Queueing
Class control
      Bandwidth 20000 (kbps)
    exponential weight 9
    class    min-threshold    max-threshold    mark-probability
    ------------------------------------------------------------

    0        -                -                1/10
    1        -                -                1/10
    2        -                -                1/10
    3        -                -                1/10
    4        -                -                1/10
    5        -                -                1/10
    6        128              512              1/10
    7        256              512              1/10
    rsvp     -                -                1/10

Class gold
      Bandwidth 10000 (kbps)
    exponential weight 9
    class    min-threshold    max-threshold    mark-probability
    ------------------------------------------------------------

    0        -                -                1/10
    1        -                -                1/10
    2        -                -                1/10
```

Listing 8-7   *The atmpolicy Policy Map Information (Continued)*

```
      3          -                -                1/10
      4          128              512              1/10
      5          256              512              1/10
      6          -                -                1/10
      7          -                -                1/10
      rsvp       -                -                1/10
Class silver
      Bandwidth 30000 (kbps)
      exponential weight 9
      class    min-threshold    max-threshold    mark-probability
      ------------------------------------------------------------

      0          -                -                1/10
      1          -                -                1/10
      2          128              512              1/10
      3          256              512              1/10
      4          -                -                1/10
      5          -                -                1/10
      6          -                -                1/10
      7          -                -                1/10
      rsvp       -                -                1/10
Class bronze
      Bandwidth 20000 (kbps)
      exponential weight 9
      class    min-threshold    max-threshold    mark-probability
      ------------------------------------------------------------

      0          128              512              1/10
      1          256              512              1/10
      2          -                -                1/10
      3          -                -                1/10
      4          -                -                1/10
      5          -                -                1/10
      6          -                -                1/10
      7          -                -                1/10
      rsvp       -                -                1/10
```

Case Study 8-4: Differentiated Services

Similar to Case Study 8-3, a service provider wants to implement precedence-based differentiated services offering three service classes—gold, silver, and bronze—within the IP network. Traffic entering the network is tagged into the three service classes by using a mapping to the IP precedence value according to Table 8-1. A part of the service provider network uses ATM as the transport technology, and the network's backbone engineer wants to map traffic with the three precedence levels on different VCs across the ATM cloud.

A PVC bundle (with multiple PVCs) is used to carry traffic to London, the PVCs' remote destination. Listing 8-8 shows the sample configuration of the PVC bundle to deliver IP-based differentiated services across an ATM network.

Listing 8-8   *Configuration for an ATM PVC Bundle*

```
interface atm0/0.1 multipoint
ip address 222.21.123.1 255.255.255.252
bundle london
 oam-bundle manage 5
 encapsulation aal5snap
 protocol ip 192.1.103.20 broadcast
 pvc-bundle control 1/107
  vbr-nrt 4000 2000 200
  precedence 6-7
  protect vc
  random-detect
 pvc-bundle gold 1/105
  vbr-nrt 2000 1000 100
  precedence 4-5
  protect group
  random-detect
pvc-bundle silver 1/103
 vbr-nrt 1000 500 50
 precedence 2-3
 random-detect
 protect group
pvc-bundle bronze 1/102
 ubr
 precedence 0-1
 random-detect
 protect group
```

Initially, a PVC bundle london is defined. The bundle definition is followed by the definition of its member PVCs—control, gold, silver, and bronze. Each member PVC belongs to an ATM service class based on the IP traffic it is mapped to carry. A silver PVC bundle member, for example, carries traffic requiring better service than a bronze PVC, which carries best-effort traffic.

The PVC bundle member control is defined as a protect VC because the control PVC is crucial for the entire PVC bundle to operate properly. Hence, if the control PVC goes down, the entire PVC bundle is brought down.

The bundle members gold, silver, and bronze form a protect group. All the member VCs in the protect group need to go down before the bundle is brought down. If a protect group's member VC goes down, its traffic is bumped to a lower-precedence VC.

Case Study 8-5: Setting an ATM CLP Bit Based on IP Precedence

A network administrator implementing IP precedence-based differentiated services in the company's IP network wants to map the IP precedence to the ATM CLP bit. Because one-to-one mapping is not possible between IP precedence and the ATM CLP bit, the network administrator for the site wants to map the IP packets with a precedence value of 0 with a CLP flagged (set to 1) on the ATM network. This is to ensure that best-effort precedence 0 traffic is dropped before any higher-precedence traffic when transported over an ATM network during times of congestion. Listing 8-9 shows the configuration required for this functionality.

Listing 8-9   *Configuration to Set an ATM CLP Bit to 1 for Best-Effort Traffic*

```
class-map best-effort
 match ip precedence 0

policy-map lossok
 class best-effort
 set atm-clp 1

interface atm0/0/0.1 point-to-point
 service-policy output lossok
```

Initially, IP precedence 0 traffic is classified as best-effort. Then, a policy lossok is defined on the best-effort class to set the ATM CLP bit to 1. Finally, the policy lossok is applied on the ATM interface.

Frame Relay

Frame Relay is a popular wide-area network (WAN) packet technology well suited for data traffic. It is a simple protocol that avoids link-layer flow control and error correction functions within the Frame Relay network. These functions are left for the applications in the end stations. The protocol is best suited for data traffic, because it can carry occasional bursts.

Frame Relay operates using VCs. A VC offers a logical connection between two end points in a Frame Relay network. A network can use a Frame Relay VC as a replacement for a private leased line. You can use PVCs and SVCs in Frame Relay networks. A PVC is set up by a network operator through a network management station, whereas an SVC is set up dynamically on a call-by-call basis. PVCs are most commonly used, and SVC support is relatively new.

A user frame is placed in a Frame Relay header to be sent on a Frame Relay network. The Frame Relay header is shown in Figure 8-8.

The 10-bit data-link connection identifier (DLCI) is the Frame Relay VC number corresponding to a logical connection to the Frame Relay network. A DLCI has only local significance. A Frame Relay switch maintains the VC mapping tables to switch a frame to its destination DLCI.

The Address Extension (AE) bit indicates a 3- or 4-byte header. It is not supported under the present Cisco Frame Relay implementation. The Command and Response (C/R) bit is not used by the Frame Relay protocol and is transmitted unchanged end to end.

Figure 8-8 *An Example of a Frame Relay Header*

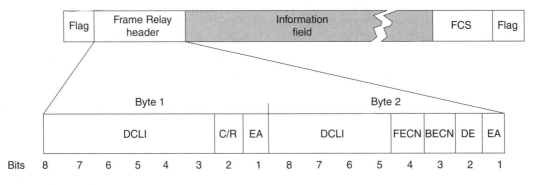

DCLI: Data-link connection identifier
C/R: Common/response field bit (application specific—not modified by network)
FECN: Forward Explicit Congestion Notification
BECN: Backward Explicit Congestion Notification
DE: Discard eligibility indicator
EA: Extension bit (allows indication of 3- or 4-byte header)

The Frame Check Sequence (FCS) is used to verify the frame's integrity by the switches in the Frame Relay network and the destination station. A frame that fails the FCS test is dropped. A Frame Relay network doesn't attempt to perform any error correction. It is up to the higher-layer protocol at the end stations to retransmit the frame after discovering the frame might have been lost.

Frame Relay Congestion Control

Three bits in the Frame Relay header provide congestion control mechanisms in a Frame Relay network. These 3 bits are referred to as *Forward Explicit Congestion Notification (FECN), Backward Explicit Congestion Notification (BECN)*, and *Discard Eligible (DE)* bits.

You can set the FECN bit to a value of 1 by a switch to indicate to a destination data terminal equipment (DTE) device, such as a router, that congestion was experienced in the direction of the frame transmission from source to destination.

The BECN bit is set to a value of 1 by a switch to indicate to the destination router that congestion was experienced in the network in the direction opposite the frame transmission from source to destination.

The primary benefit of the FECN and BECN congestion notification bits is the capability of higher-layer protocols to react intelligently to these congestion indicators. The use of FECN and BECN is shown in Figure 8-9.

Figure 8-9   *Use of FECN and BECN Bits*

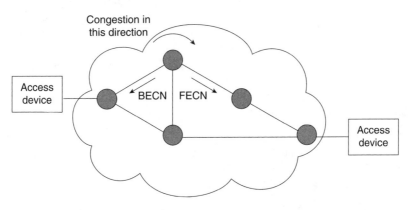

The DE bit is set by the router or other DTE device to indicate that the marked frame is of lesser importance relative to other frames being transmitted. It provides a basic prioritization mechanism in Frame Relay networks. Frames with the DE bit set are discarded first, before the frames without the DE bit flagged.

Frame Relay Traffic Shaping (FRTS)

FRTS shapes traffic going out on a Frame Relay VC in accordance with the rate configured. It tries to smooth the bursty traffic by buffering packets exceeding the average rate. The buffered packets are de-queued for transmission when enough resources are available according to the queuing mechanism configured. A queuing algorithm is configurable on a per-VC basis. It can be configured only for outbound traffic on an interface.

FRTS can do traffic shaping to a peak rate configured to be either the Committed Information Rate (CIR) or some other defined value, such as the Excess Information Rate (EIR), on a per-VC basis.

FRTS in adaptive mode also permits output on Frame Relay VCs to be throttled based on received network BECN congestion indicators. It shapes traffic going out on a PVC in accordance with the bandwidth available in a Frame Relay network. It is able to run at rate X, and when the network sees BECNs, it drops down to rate Y.

VC Traffic Shaping

A token bucket, similar to the one used for traffic shaping in Chapter 3, "Network Boundary Traffic Conditioners: Packet Classifier, Marker, and Traffic Rate Management," is used as a traffic descriptor to measure conforming traffic. The contracted average rate is called the Committed Information Rate (CIR). Burst size (B_C) is the amount of data added to the token bucket of size ($B_C + B_E$) at each measuring time interval, T_C. T_C is defined as $B_C \div CIR$. Excess burst size (B_E) is the amount of excess burst of data allowed to be sent during the first interval when the token bucket is full. When a new packet arrives, it is queued into the output queue and scheduled for transmission based on the queue scheduler used, such as WFQ or first-in, first-out (FIFO). A packet scheduled for transmission by the scheduler is transmitted only if enough tokens are available in the bucket equivalent to the scheduled packet. After a conforming packet is transmitted, an equivalent amount of tokens are removed from the bucket.

If not all B_C bytes are sent in a T_C interval, you can transmit the unused bytes in the subsequent interval along with the new credit for B_C bytes. Hence, in a T_C interval during which there is less than B_C traffic, the credit can increase to an upper bound of $B_C + B_E$ for the next subsequent interval.

If serious load sets in and the token bucket is full, you can send $B_E + B_C$ bytes in the first interval and B_C bytes in each subsequent interval until congestion conditions ease. As you can see, you can throttle to the CIR equation at times of congestion.

This relationship between the traffic shaping parameters is shown in Figure 8-10.

Frame Relay traffic shaping allows occasional bursts over the CIR on a PVC, although the rate throttles to the CIR at times of congestion. A PVC can also be configured for a fixed data rate equal to the CIR ($B_E = 0$).

Adaptive FRTS

At every time interval T_C, a process checks if any BECN was received from the Frame Relay network. If BECN was received in the last T_C interval, the transmission rate is dropped by 25 percent of the current rate. It might continue to drop until the lower limit is reached, which is the minimum CIR (MINCIR). No matter how congested the Frame Relay network is, the router does not drop its transmission rate below MINCIR. The default value for MINCIR is half of the CIR.

Figure 8-10 *Relationship Between Traffic Shaping Parameters*

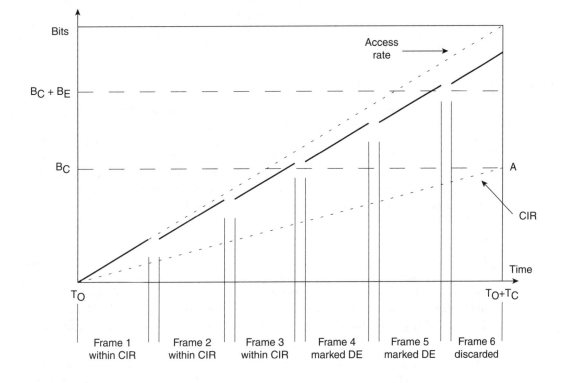

After the traffic rate has adapted to the congestion in the Frame Relay network, it takes 16 T_C intervals without BECN to start increasing the traffic rate back to the configured CIR.

FECN/BECN Integration

A UDP- or IP-based application can result in a unidirectional traffic flow, but the application might not necessarily have data flowing in the opposite direction because both IP and UDP do not use any acknowledging scheme. If you enable traffic shaping on UDP data, the only congestion notification set by the network is the FECN bit received in the frames arriving at the destination router. The router sourcing all this traffic does not see any BECNs because there's no return traffic. FECN/BECN integration implemented a command to send a Q.922 test frame with the BECN bit set in response to a frame that has the FECN set. Note that you need to clear the DE bit in a BECN frame you send in response to a received FECN. The source router gets a test frame, which is discarded, but the BECN bit is used to throttle the data flow. To have this interaction, traffic shaping commands need to be present on the ingress and egress ports.

NOTE	In case of unidirectional traffic, the **traffic-shape adaptive** command is needed on the router sourcing the traffic, and the **traffic-shape fecn-adapt** command is used to send a Q.922 test frame[4] with the BECN bit set in response to an FECN.

Frame Relay Fragmentation

At the output queue of a PVC on a router, large packets that were queued ahead of small, delay-sensitive packets contribute to increased delay and jitter for the small packets. This behavior is due to the larger transmission delay for a large packet compared to a small packet. Transmission delay is discussed in Chapter 1, "Introducing IP Quality of Service." Fragmenting the large data frames into smaller frames, interleaving small, delay-sensitive packets between the fragments of large packets before putting them on the queue for transmission, and reassembling the frame at the destination eases the problem for the small packets. The Frame Relay Forum (FRF)[5] has ratified a new standard for Frame Relay fragmentation: FRF.12.

FRF.12 ensures that voice and similar small packets are not unacceptably delayed behind large data packets. This standard also attempts to ensure that the small packets are sent in a more regular fashion, thereby reducing jitter. This capability is important in enabling a user to combine voice and other delay-sensitive applications, such as Enterprise Resource Planning (ERP)-based, mission-critical applications with non-time-sensitive applications or other data on a single PVC.

The same standard is applicable at the UNI interface (between the router or a Frame Relay Access Device [FRAD] and the Frame Relay cloud), at the NNI interface (between the switches within the Frame Relay cloud), and between the routers (or FRADs) for end-to-end transmissions, where fragmentation is transparent to the Frame Relay cloud.

Because fragmentation is most useful on slow lines, and the slower links tend to be access links to an FRAD or a router, UNI fragmentation becomes the widely used application. UNI fragmentation is local to the router, and you can optimize its network interface and fragment size based on the DTE device's speed.

NNI and end-to-end fragmentation are not commonly used applications. Fragmentation might not be a good idea across high-speed trunk lines in the Frame Relay cloud because it can carry relatively large frames when compared to the slow speed access links without delaying the voice packets drastically. A speed mismatch between the two end FRAD systems can also preclude running end-to-end fragmentation between the DTE devices. UNI fragmentation can also be used to run fragmentation end to end. For an end DTE that doesn't implement end-to-end fragmentation, UNI fragmentation enables the network to proxy the DTE.

An important driving application for FRF.12 is to enable voice over Frame Relay technology for service approaching toll voice quality. Fragmentation, especially when used with QoS functionality such as WFQ and WRED, is used to ensure a consistent flow of voice information.

Prior to FRF.12, in an IP environment the only way to fragment frames was to set the IP maximum transmission unit (MTU) to a small value. This action introduces undesirable inefficiencies in the system in terms of increased processor overhead and packet overhead, however. In addition, FRF.12 operates below Layer 3 of the Open System Interconnection (OSI) model, and hence it fragments not only IP, but other frames as well. With Voice over IP (VoIP), fragmentation becomes an absolute necessity in low-bandwidth environments.

In addition to FRF.12 fragmentation, Cisco supports FRF.11 Annex C fragmentation and a Cisco proprietary fragmentation. Frame Relay fragmentation is part of Cisco's traffic-shaping functionality. Figure 8-11 illustrates Frame Relay fragmentation when carrying voice and data traffic on a PVC.

Figure 8-11 *Frame Relay Fragmentation*

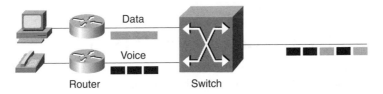

Enabling FRTS is a prerequisite to turning on FRF.12 fragmentation. For voice, FRTS uses a flow-based Weighted Fair Queuing (WFQ) with a priority queue (PQ) on the shaping queue. Each Frame Relay PVC has its own PQ-WFQ structure that is used to schedule packets based on their IP precedence values as per the flow-based WFQ algorithm discussed in Chapter 4. FRTS uses dual FIFO queues at the interface level—the first queue for priority packets such as voice, Local Management Interface (LMI), and related high-priority packets and the second queue for the rest of the traffic. Note that FRTS disallows any queuing other than dual FIFO at the interface level.

In Figure 8-12, three different flows—two data flows and one voice flow—arrive for transmission on an interface. The flows are routed to their respective PVC structures based on the flow header information. In this case, flows 1 and 2 belong to PVC 1, and flow 3 belongs to PVC 2. Each PVC has its own shaping queue. In this case, PQ-WFQ is enabled on PVC 1 such that all voice flow packets are scheduled first, and all voice packets go to the priority interface FIFO queue. Data packets scheduled by the shaping queue are fragmented based on the fragment threshold value and are put in the normal FIFO interface queue. It is assumed that the fragment threshold is set such that none of the voice packets need to be fragmented. Though a separate shaping queue exists for each PVC, all the PVCs on the interface share the dual FIFO interface queues. Packets are transmitted from the priority FIFO queue with a strict priority over the packets in the normal FIFO interface queue.

Figure 8-12 *A Conceptual View of FRF.12 Operation with Multiple PVCs*

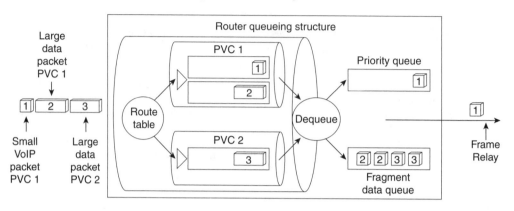

Frame Relay Interworking with IP QoS

Similar to IP-ATM QoS, IP Frame Relay QoS is necessary to provide end-to-end IP QoS. At the ingress to a Frame Relay network, IP traffic queues are maintained for each Frame Relay VC. On each VC queue, you can apply the WFQ and WRED IP QoS techniques. In addition to WFQ, PQ-WFQ, priority, and custom queuing can also be configured as a scheduling mechanism for traffic queued on a VC.

As discussed previously, the Frame Relay uses the DE bit to provide a basic prioritization scheme for its traffic. A frame with a DE bit flagged has a higher drop probability than a frame with the DE bit at 0.

Because IP uses 3 bits to indicate its precedence, there can't be a one-to-one map between the Frame Relay DE bit setting and IP precedence levels. A fairly basic mapping can be worthwhile, however. For example, you can map IP best-effort traffic indicated by an IP precedence of 0 over Frame Relay with a DE bit set, whereas you can send other, better-than-best-effort traffic without flagging the DE bit. This ensures that the best-effort traffic is dropped before the other, more important traffic.

Case Study 8-6: Frame Relay Traffic Shaping with QoS Autosense

Say the network administrator of a nationwide network wants his Frame Relay-connected routers to shape traffic according to the contracted QoS (CIR, B_C, B_E) information. Instead of an explicit configuration, the administrator wants to use extended LMI so that the routers get their per-VC QoS information directly from the connected switch in the Frame Relay network.

For the QoS autosense to work, extended LMI must be configured on both the router and its connected switch. The router dynamically gets the QoS information from the switch for each VC.

Based on the QoS (CIR, B_C, B_E) information received by the router, the router shapes the traffic on the VC.

Listing 8-10 shows an example configuration needed in a router to enable FRTS with QoS autosense. Only the configuration on the router is shown.

Listing 8-10   *An FRTS Configuration with QoS Autosense*

```
interface Serial0/0
encapsulation frame-relay
frame-relay lmi-type ansi
frame-relay traffic-shaping
frame-relay qos-autosense

interface Serial0/0.1 point-to-point
ip address 202.12.12.1 255.255.255.252
frame-relay interface-dlci 17 IETF protocol ip 202.12.12.2
```

The **frame-relay qos-autosense** command enables extended LMI to dynamically learn QoS information for each VC on the interface. The **frame-relay traffic-shaping** command shapes the traffic on each VC based on the received QoS information.

Listings 8-11 and 8-12 show the output of a few relevant **show** commands for this feature. As shown in Listing 8-11, the **show frame-relay qos-autosense** command also shows the values received from the switch. As shown in Listing 8-12, the **show traffic-shape** command shows the QoS parameters and the traffic descriptor parameters.

Listing 8-11   *Frame Relay QoS Autosense Information*

```
Router#show frame-relay qos-autosense
ELMI information for interface Serial1
 Connected to switch:FRSM-4T1   Platform:AXIS   Vendor:cisco
              (Time elapsed since last update 00:00:03)


 DLCI = 17
 OUT:   CIR 64000      BC 9600       BE 9600      FMIF 4497
 IN:    CIR 32000      BC 30000      BE 20000     FMIF 4497
 Priority 0     (Time elapsed since last update 00:00:03)
```

Listing 8-12 *Frame Relay Traffic Shaping Parameters*

```
Router#show traffic-shape

         access Target   Byte  Sustain  Excess    Interval
I/F      list   Rate     Limit bits/int bits/int  (ms)
Se0/0           64000    2400  9600     9600       150
```

The *Byte Limit* value is the size of the bucket in bytes (Size of bucket = B_C + B_E = 9600 + 9600 = 19200 bits = 2400 bytes). *Interval* is the T_C interval ($T_C = B_C \div CIR = 9600/64000$ = 150 ms).

Case Study 8-7: Adaptive Traffic Shaping and BECN/FECN Integration

For this case study, assume that an e-business site connects to the Internet by using Frame Relay at a physical rate of T1. The access rate provided by the service provider is 256 Kbps, and the CIR is 64 Kbps. The e-business site wants to send traffic at the access rate of 256 Kbps and throttle back to the CIR of 64 Kbps if it receives BECNs. Also, the e-business site wants the remote service provider router to be configured with an outbound CIR of 32 Kbps to reflect any FECNs it receives as BECNs because the traffic is mostly UDP-based and is unidirectional from the e-business site to the remote router.

Listings 8-13 and 8-14 show the sample configuration required on the e-business site's interface to the service provider, using FRTS and DTS features, respectively. DTS is introduced in Chapter 3.

Listing 8-13 *E-Business Site FRTS Configuration on the Interface Connecting to the Service Provider*

```
interface Serial 0/0/0
 encapsulation frame-relay

interface Serial0/0/0.1 point-to-point
ip address 202.12.12.1 255.255.255.252
frame-relay interface-dlci 17 IETF protocol ip 202.12.12.2
frame-relay class adaptivefrts

map-class frame-relay adaptivefrts
 frame-relay traffic-shape rate 256000
 frame-relay traffic-shape adaptive 64000
```

Listing 8-14 *E-Business Site DTS Configuration on the Interface Connecting to the Service Provider*

```
interface Serial 0/0/0
 encapsulation frame-relay

class-map myclass
  match any
```

Listing 8-14   *E-Business Site DTS Configuration on the Interface Connecting to the Service Provider (Continued)*

```
policy-map mypolicy
  class-map myclass
    shape peak 256000 8000 8000
    shape adaptive 64000

interface serial0/0/0.1 point-to-point
ip address 202.12.12.1 255.255.255.252
frame-relay interface-dlci 17 IETF protocol ip 202.12.12.1
service-policy output mypolicy
```

The router at the e-business site is set up to send at a CIR of 256000 and dynamically adapts the rate at which it receives BECNs. The minimum CIR with continued receipt of BECNs (congestion) is 64 Kbps.

Listings 8-15 and 8-16 show the FRTS and DTS configurations needed on the service provider router.

Listing 8-15   *FRTS Configuration on the Service Provider Router Interface*

```
interface Serial 0/0
encapsulation frame-relay
frame-relay traffic-shaping

interface Serial0/0/0.1 point-to-point
ip address 202.12.12.2 255.255.255.252
frame-relay interface-dlci 20 IETF protocol ip 202.12.12.1
frame-relay class BECNforFECN

map-class frame-relay BECNforFECN
frame-relay traffic peak 32000
frame-relay bc out 8000
frame-relay be out 8000
```

Listing 8-16   *DTS Configuration on the Service Provider Router Interface*

```
interface Serial 0/0
 encapsulation frame-relay

class-map myclass
  match any

policy-map mypolicy
  class-map myclass
    shape peak 32000 8000 8000
    shape fecn-adapt

interface serial0/0/0.1 point-to-point
ip address 202.12.12.2 255.255.255.252
frame-relay interface-dlci 17 IETF protocol ip 202.12.12.1
service-policy output mypolicy
```

Because the traffic from the e-business router to the remote router is UDP-based and unidirectional, the e-business site router does not receive any BECNs from the service provider router to adaptively shape its traffic to the adaptive rate in case of congestion. Hence, the service provider router needs to be made to reflect a frame with a BECN bit set in response to a frame with an FECN bit for the e-business router to shape adaptively.

The configuration sets the router to send with a CIR of 32 Kbps and respond with a BECN to any received FECNs.

DTS uses modular QoS CLI, which is discussed in Appendix A.

Case Study 8-8: Using Multiple PVCs to a Destination Based on Traffic Type

Imagine that the network architect at an e-commerce site connecting to a service provider backbone wants to use multiple PVCs to carry traffic of different priority. The network currently carries IP traffic at four precedence levels: 0–3. The e-commerce site orders four PVCs to carry traffic at the four precedence levels. Each PVC is provisioned according to the precedence of the traffic it carries.

Listing 8-17 is the sample configuration for this application.

Listing 8-17   *Configuration to Route Traffic to a PVC Based on Traffic Type*

```
interface Serial5/0
 encapsulation frame-relay

interface Serial 5/0.1 multipoint
 frame-relay priority-dlci-group 1 203 202 201 200
 frame-relay qos-autosense

access-list 100 permit ip any any precedence routine
access-list 101 permit ip any any precedence priority
access-list 102 permit ip any any precedence immediate
access-list 103 permit ip any any precedence flash
priority-list 1 protocol ip high list 103
priority-list 1 protocol ip medium list 102
priority-list 1 protocol ip normal list 101
priority-list 1 protocol ip low list 100
```

The four PVCs configured to the destination have 203, 202, 201, and 200 as their DLCI numbers. The **frame-relay priority-dlci-group** command configures these four DLCIs to carry traffic of high, medium, normal, and low priority, respectively. Note that the command doesn't enable priority queuing, it only assigns different DLCIs to carry different traffic classes. The command uses priority-list 1 to categorize traffic into the four classes that carry traffic with IP precedence 0–3. The high-priority traffic is carried on the high-priority DLCI, the medium-priority traffic on the medium-priority DLCI, and so on.

Listings 8-18 and 8-19 display the output of two relevant **show** commands. The **show frame-relay pvc** command in Listing 8-18 shows all the known PVC/DLCI and priority DLCI group information on the router. This command also displays each DLCI's packet statistics. The **show queueing priority** command in Listing 8-19 displays the configured priority lists on the router.

Listing 8-18   *show frame-relay pvc Command Output*

```
Router#show frame-relay pvc
PVC Statistics for interface Serial5/0 (Frame Relay DTE)
               Active      Inactive     Deleted       Static
  Local        4           0            0             0
  Switched     0           0            0             0
  Unused       0           0            0             0

DLCI = 200, DLCI USAGE = LOCAL, PVC STATUS = ACTIVE, INTERFACE = Se5/0

  input pkts 0              output pkts 0          in bytes 0
  out bytes 0              dropped pkts 0          in FECN pkts 0
  in BECN pkts 0           out FECN pkts 0         out BECN pkts 0
  in DE pkts 0             out DE pkts 0
  out bcast pkts 0          out bcast bytes 0
  pvc create time 00:05:31, last time pvc status changed 00:05:31

DLCI = 201, DLCI USAGE = LOCAL, PVC STATUS = ACTIVE, INTERFACE = Se5/0

  input pkts 0              output pkts 0          in bytes 0
  out bytes 0              dropped pkts 0          in FECN pkts 0
  in BECN pkts 0           out FECN pkts 0         out BECN pkts 0
  in DE pkts 0             out DE pkts 0
  out bcast pkts 0          out bcast bytes 0
  pvc create time 00:05:55, last time pvc status changed 00:05:55

DLCI = 202, DLCI USAGE = LOCAL, PVC STATUS = ACTIVE, INTERFACE = Se5/0

  input pkts 0              output pkts 0          in bytes 0
  out bytes 0              dropped pkts 0          in FECN pkts 0
  in BECN pkts 0           out FECN pkts 0         out BECN pkts 0
  in DE pkts 0             out DE pkts 0
  out bcast pkts 0          out bcast bytes 0
  pvc create time 00:04:36, last time pvc status changed 00:04:36

DLCI = 203, DLCI USAGE = LOCAL, PVC STATUS = ACTIVE, INTERFACE = Se5/0

  input pkts 0              output pkts 0          in bytes 0
  out bytes 0              dropped pkts 0          in FECN pkts 0
  in BECN pkts 0           out FECN pkts 0         out BECN pkts 0
  in DE pkts 0             out DE pkts 0
  out bcast pkts 0          out bcast bytes 0
  pvc create time 00:04:37, last time pvc status changed 00:04:37
  Priority DLCI Group 1, DLCI 203 (HIGH), DLCI 202 (MEDIUM)
  DLCI 201 (NORMAL), DLCI 200 (LOW)
```

Listing 8-19 *show queueing priority Command Output*

```
Router#show queueing priority
Current priority queue configuration:
List   Queue  Args
1      high   protocol ip          list 103
1      medium protocol ip          list 102
1      normal protocol ip          list 101
1      low    protocol ip          list 100
```

Case Study 8-9: Per-VC WFQ

For this case study, assume that a network uses different QoS traffic classes based on precedence. The network administrator wants the packets sent on each VC of the Frame Relay network to be scheduled using WFQ so that a traffic class with high IP precedence gets a higher relative bandwidth corresponding to traffic with a lower IP precedence.

Listing 8-20 shows a sample configuration for per-VC WFQ.

Listing 8-20 *Enabling Per-VC WFQ*

```
interface Serial 0/0/0
 encapsulation frame-relay
 frame-relay class pervcwfq

interface Serial0/0/0.1 point-to-point
 ip address 220.20.20.1 255.255.255.252
 frame-relay interface-dlci 17 IETF protocol ip 220.20.20.2

map-class frame-relay pervcwfq
 frame-relay fair-queue
```

Case Study 8-10: Mapping Between Frame Relay DE Bits and IP Precedence Bits

Say a finance company is using a Frame Relay network as a backbone for its nationwide network. The company categorizes traffic at the edges so that priority traffic is serviced preferentially over any background, lower-priority traffic. Its traffic falls into two classes: high priority and low priority, indicated by IP precedence levels 3 and 0, respectively. The company wants to map the low-priority, background traffic with the DE bit set so that nonpriority traffic is discarded when necessary without affecting the priority traffic. The egress traffic at the Frame Relay network is mapped back with IP precedence levels of 3 and 0 based on whether the DE bit is set.

Listing 8-21 shows a configuration for mapping IP precedence 0 packets with the DE bit flagged on the Frame Relay circuit.

Listing 8-21 *Sample Configuration to Map Precedence 0 IP Packets with the DE Bit Set to 1 on the Frame Relay Network*

```
frame-relay de-list 1 protocol ip list 101

interface serial 1/0/0
encapsulation frame-relay

interface serial1/0/0.1 point-to-point
frame-relay interface-dlci 18 broadcast
frame-relay de-group 101 18

access-list 101 permit ip any any precedence routine
```

The **de-group** command defines the packet class and the DLCI on which the DE bit mapping occurs. The **de-list** command defines the packet class that needs to be sent on the Frame Relay network with the DE bit set. In the preceding example, all IP packets with precedence 0 that need to go on the Frame Relay DLCI have the DE bit set. All other IP traffic goes on the Frame Relay without the DE bit flagged (DE = 0).

Case 8-11: Frame Relay Fragmentation

Say the network administrator of a Frame Relay-based IP data network wants the network to carry VoIP traffic. He wants the VoIP traffic to experience minimal delays and low jitter.

The network administrator is aware that VoIP has time constraints and uses IP precedence 5 for it. The data traffic uses IP precedence levels 0–4. Although the network uses WFQ, some of the VoIP traffic sees unusually high delay, causing jitter. The administrator notices that the data traffic on average is 1024 bytes, and the VoIP traffic is 64 bytes. Because large packet sizes of the data traffic can cause delays for the VoIP traffic, it is necessary to fragment the data packets exceeding a certain size so that VoIP traffic sees only minimum delays and low jitter. In addition, PQ-WFQ is used to reduce delay and jitter for voice traffic.

Listing 8-22 is a sample configuration for enabling Frame Relay fragmentation.

Listing 8-22 *Enable Frame Relay Fragmentation with PQ-WFQ Shaping Queue*

```
interface Serial 1/0
ip address 220.200.200.2 255.255.255.252
encapsulation frame-relay
frame-relay traffic-shaping
ip rtp priority 16384 16383 640
frame-relay interface-dlci 110
 class frag


map-class frag
 fromo relay cir 64000
```

Listing 8-22   *Enable Frame Relay Fragmentation with PQ-WFQ Shaping Queue (Continued)*

```
frame-relay bc 8000
frame-relay fragment 64
frame-relay fair-queue
```

Class frag is defined under the Frame Relay interface to configure Frame Relay fragment-ation along with traffic shaping. The **frame-relay fragment** command defines the fragment size. According to the configuration, any packet bigger than 64 bytes is fragmented. Frame Relay traffic shaping needs to be enabled on the Frame Relay interface to enable fragmentation. A CIR of 64 Kbps and a B_C of 8000 bytes is defined for traffic shaping. On the queue used to buffer frames for traffic shaping, WFQ scheduling is used to decide which buffered packet to transmit next. The **ip rtp priority** command is used to enable a priority queue within WFQ. By default, end-to-end fragmentation based on the FRF.12 specification is used. Other types of fragmentation also are supported on the Cisco router. Fragmentation based on the FRF.11 Annex C specification is used if the **vofr** command is used on the Frame Relay interface. The command **vofr cisco** is used to enable Cisco proprietary fragmentation.

The IEEE 802.3 Family of LANs

Ethernet is the most common LAN technology used today. The original Ethernet operates at 10 Mbps using carrier sense media access, collision detect (CSMA/CD) for media access. Today, the term "Ethernet" is used to refer to all extensions of the original Ethernet specification that continue to use CSMA/CD.

Ethernet operating at 10 Mbps is standardized as part of the IEEE 802.3 specification. Ethernet Version 2.0, which is compatible with IEEE 802.3, is also commonly used. The higher-speed version of the Ethernet family LANs—100 Mbps fast Ethernet (100BaseT) and Gigabit Ethernet—continue to use the existing IEEE 802.3 CSMA/CD specification or an extension of it. 100BaseT and Gigabit Ethernet are standardized as the IEEE 802.3u and 802.3x specifications, respectively. As a result, all the 802.3 family of Ethernets retain the IEEE 802.3 frame format, size, and error-detection mechanism. The IEEE 802.3 and Ethernet frame formats are shown in Figure 8-13.

Expedited Traffic Capability

Expedited traffic capability provides the ability for network prioritization on an Ethernet, virtual LAN (VLAN)-based or otherwise.

The expedited traffic capability for Ethernet is defined as part of the 802.1p standard. 802.1p uses 3 bits within the 4-byte tag defined by 802.1Q[6] to support VLANs. The 4-byte 802.1Q and the 802.1p bits are shown is Figure 8-14.

Figure 8-13 *Ethernet and IEEE 802.3 Frame Formats*

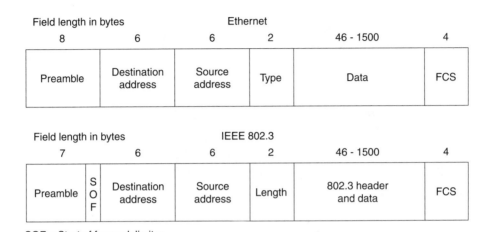

SOF = Start of frame delimiter
FCS = Frame check sequence

Figure 8-14 *802.1Q Frame Showing 802.1p Bits*

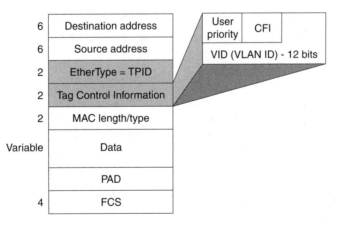

802.1Q defines a new tagged frame type by adding a 4-byte tag, which is made up of the following:

- 2 bytes of Tagged Protocol Identifier (TPID)
  - 0x8100 is used to indicate an 802.1Q packet
- 2 bytes of Tagged Control Information (TCI)
  - 3-bit 802.1p bits
  - 1-bit canonical format identifier (CFI)
  - 12-bit VLAN Identifier (ID)

Figure 8-15 shows how the original Ethernet/802.3 frame is changed into a tagged 802.1Q frame. The FCS needs to be recalculated after introducing the 4-byte tag.

Figure 8-15 *An Ethernet Frame to a Tagged 802.1Q Frame*

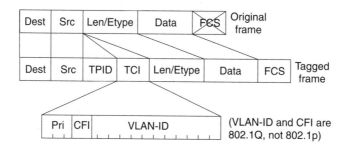

802.1p provides a way to maintain priority information across LANs. It offers eight priorities from the three 802.1p bits. To support 802.1p, the link layer has to support multiple queues—one for each priority or traffic class. The high-priority traffic is always preferred over lower-priority traffic. A switch preserves the priority values while switching a frame.

NOTE   You can easily map the 3-bit IP precedence field to the three priority bits of IEEE 802.1p, and vice versa, to provide interworking between IP QoS and IEEE 802.1p.

Cisco's Catalyst family of switches uses 802.1p class of service (CoS) bits for prioritizing traffic based on QoS features such as Weighted Round Robin (WRR) and WRED. WRR and WRED are discussed in detail in Chapter 5, "Per-Hop Behavior: Resource Allocation II," and in Chapter 6, respectively. Though 802.1p uses the tag defined by IEEE 802.1Q, a standard for VLANs, the 802.1p can still be used in the absence of VLANs, as shown in Figure 8-16. A VLAN ID of 0 is reserved and is used to indicate the absence of VLANs.

Figure 8-16 *Use of 802.1p in the Absence of VLANs*

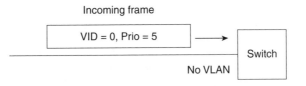

With the addition of the 4-byte tag introduced by the 802.1Q and 802.1p specifications, an Ethernet frame can now exceed the maximum frame size of 1518 bytes. Hence, IEEE 802.3ac is tasked with modifying the 802.3 standard to extend the maximum frame size from 1518 to 1522 bytes.

NOTE   IEEE 802.1Q "Standard for Virtual Bridged Local Area Networks" defines a method of establishing VLANs.

Expedited traffic capabilities are defined as part of the 802.1p standard. 802.1p is part of the recently modified version of 802.1D[7], a standard for transparent bridging. Expedited traffic capabilities define traffic classes to allow user priorities at frame level.

IETF's Integrated Services over Specific Lower Layers (ISSLL) Working Group[8] is defining a way to map Layer 3 Resource Reservation Protocol (RSVP) requests to 802.1p priorities through a Subnet Bandwidth Manager (SBM). SBM is covered in the next section.

SBM

SBM[9] is a signaling protocol that supports RSVP-based admission control over the Ethernet family of 802.3-style networks. As discussed in Chapter 7, "Integrated Services: RSVP," RSVP is an end-to-end signaling mechanism used to request specific resource reservation from the network. Across an Ethernet, guaranteed bandwidth reservation is not possible by any single station on the segment because the Ethernet segment is a shared medium. A station on the Ethernet segment has no idea of the reservations guaranteed by the other stations on the segment and can send traffic to the segment at a rate that might compromise the reservations existing on the other stations. SBM is a means of supporting RSVP-based reservations on 802.3-style networks.

An Ethernet segment with one or more SBM-capable devices is referred to as a *managed Ethernet segment*. A managed segment can be either a shared segment with one or many SBM stations or a switched segment with up to two SBM stations. On a managed segment, one of the SBM-capable devices acts as a *designated SBM (DSBM)*. You can elect a DSBM dynamically, or you can stipulate it by static configuration on SBM stations.

All other SBM-capable stations other than the DSBM on a managed segment act as DSBM clients. A DSBM is responsible for admission control for all resource reservation requests originating from DSBM clients in its managed segment. Cisco routers and Windows NT 5.0 are examples of stations with DSBM functionality.

A station with SBM functionality is called an *SBM-capable station*. An SBM-capable station configured to participate in DSBM election is called a *candidate DSBM station*.

Initialization

SBM uses two multicast addresses for its operation:

- **AllSBMAAddress**—This address is used for DSBM election and all DSBM messages. All SBM-capable stations listen on this address. A DSBM sends its messages on this address.

- **DSBMLogicalAddress**—This address is used for RSVP PATH messages from DSBM clients to DSBM. Only candidate DSBM stations listen to this address.

When RSVP is enabled on an SBM-capable station on a shared segment, RSVP registers the interface on the shared segment to listen to the AllSBMAddress multicast address. If the station receives a message I_AM_DSBM on the AllSBMAddress, the interface is considered to be on a managed segment. RSVP on a managed segment should operate according to SBM protocol. A DSBM client on a managed segment will listen for RSVP PATH messages destined to it through the DSBM on AllSBMAddress.

A station configured as a candidate DSBM listens to DSBMLogicalAddress along with AllSBMAddress. A candidate DSBM sends a DSBM_WILLING message on the managed segment. All RSVP PATH messages originated by the SBM clients are sent to the DSBMLogicalAddress. A DSBM does not listen for PATH messages on the AllSBAAddress.

Broadly, an SBM-capable station adds the following functionality:

- **DSBM Election**—A mechanism to elect a DSBM on a managed segment

- **RSVP Extensions**—Extensions for incoming and outgoing RSVP PATH and PATH TEAR message processing

The following two sections discuss these requirements.

DSBM Election

A new SBM station on a managed segment initially listens for a period of time to see if a DSBM is already elected for that segment. If it receives an I_AM_DSBM message on AllSBMAddress, it doesn't participate in the DSBM election until the DSBM goes down and a new DSBM election process becomes necessary.

A DSBM sends an I_AM_DSBM message every DSBMRefreshInterval seconds. If a DSBM client doesn't see an I_AM_DSBM message after DSBMDeadInterval (a multiple of DSBMRefreshInterval) seconds, it assumes the DSBM is probably down and starts a new DSBM election process if it is configured to be a candidate DSBM.

During DSBM election, each candidate DSBM station sends a DSBM_WILLING message to DSBMLogicalAddress listing its interface address and SBM priority. SBM priority determines the precedence of a candidate DSBM to become a DSBM. A higher-priority candidate DSBM station wins the election. If the SBM priority is the same, the tie is broken by using the IP addresses of the candidate DSBMs. A candidate DSBM with the highest IP address wins the election.

RSVP Extensions

Under SBM, a DSBM intercepts all incoming and outgoing RSVP PATH and PATH-TEAR messages, adding an extra hop to the normal RSVP operation.

All outgoing RSVP PATH messages from the SBM client on a managed segment are sent to the segment's DSBM device (using DSBMLogicalAddress) instead of to the RSVP session destination address. After processing, the DSBM forwards the PATH message to the RSVP session destination address. As part of the processing, the DSBM builds and updates a Path State Block (PSB) for the session and maintains the previous hop L2/L3 addresses of the PATH message.

An incoming RSVP PATH message on a DSBM requires parsing of the additional SBM objects and setting up the required SBM-related information in the PSB. An RSVP PATH-TEAR message is used to tear down an established PSB for an RSVP session.

RSVP RESV messages don't need any changes as part of SBM. An SBM client wanting to make a reservation after processing an incoming RSVP PATH message follows the standard RSVP rules and sends RSVP RESV messages to the previous hop L2/L3 addresses (the segment's DSBM) of the incoming PATH message based on the information in the session's PSB.

A DSBM processes the RSVP RESV message from an SBM client based on available bandwidth. If the request cannot be granted, an RSVP RESVERR message is sent to the SBM client requesting the reservation. If the reservation request can be granted, the RESV message is forwarded to the previous hop address of the incoming PATH message based on the session's PSB. Similar to standard RSVP, a DSBM can merge reservation requests when possible.

Summary

ATM provides rich QoS functionality that offers a variety of services. PPD and EPD cell discard techniques improve the effective throughput relative to a random cell discard in an ATM network carrying IP traffic. When a cell needs to be dropped in an ATM network, PPD can send a partial packet (not all packet cells can be dropped), whereas EPD drops all the packet cells.

For running IP QoS end to end across an ATM network, packet drops and scheduling at the ingress to the ATM network should be done based on the packet's IP precedence. For this purpose, the IP QoS technologies WFQ and WRED are used. Within the ATM cloud, the ATM VC carrying the IP traffic is provisioned to be lossless and offers a service meeting the IP traffic's service requirements.

When all the traffic to a destination is carried over a single PVC, you can apply IP QoS on a per-VC basis. In the case of a PVC bundle where multiple PVCs exist to the destination, you can map certain IP precedence to each PVC and apply per-VC IP QoS for each VC in the bundle.

Frame Relay offers a CIR-based QoS with a capability to burst above the committed QoS when the network is not congested. It also offers extensive congestion control parameters. Frame Relay fragmentation enables real-time traffic to be carried on the same PVC as the data packets made up of relatively large packet sizes.

On a shared or a switched Ethernet, you can prioritize traffic using 802.1p on an 802.1Q frame. A high-priority frame gets precedence over a lower-priority frame. RSVP-based bandwidth reservation on an Ethernet becomes a problem because it is a shared medium. SBM designates a single station to make RSVP-type bandwidth reservations for the entire Ethernet segment.

Frequently Asked Questions

Q — *What are the multicast addresses reserved for SBM?*

A — SBM uses two multicast addresses for its operation. All SBM systems listen on 224.0.0.17. In addition, candidate DSBMs listen on 224.0.0.16.

Q — *What kinds of scheduling algorithms can I run on the shaping queue for the FRTS feature?*

A — The priority queue (PQ), custom queue (CQ), WFQ, and CBWFQ scheduling algorithms can run on the FRTS shaping queue. WFQ and CBWFQ are supported with and without a strict PQ. These scheduling algorithms are discussed in detail in Chapter 4.

Q — *When doing Frame Relay traffic shaping, what is the difference between an interface queue and a shaping queue?*

A — In shaping traffic, traffic in excess of the allowed rate is queued for transmission at a later time in a shaping queue. You can run any of the scheduling algorithms— PQ, CQ, WFQ, or PQ-WFQ—on the shaping queue based on the traffic requirements. Packets scheduled from the shaping queue are put on the interface dual FIFO queue for transmission. Note that FRTS disallows any queuing mechanism other than FIFO at the interface level. FRTS uses dual-interface FIFO queues. Packets from the first queue are transmitted at a strict priority over the packets in the second queue.

Q — *What is the difference between Generic Traffic Shaping (GTS) and FRTS?*

A — Table 8-2 lists the various differences between GTS and FRTS. GTS is discussed in Chapter 3.

Table 8-2 *Comparison Between GTS and FRTS Functions*

	GTS	**FRTS**
Intended application	Generic across interfaces.	Frame Relay-specific.
Granularity of application	Enabled on an interface basis.	Enabled based on a Frame Relay PVC or DLCI.
Internal shaping queue	Supports only flow-based WFQ, CBWFQ on its internal shaping queue.	Supports PQ, CQ, WFQ, and CBWFQ on its internal shaping queue.
	WFQ and CBWFQ are supported with and without a strict priority queue.	WFQ and CBWFQ are supported with and without a strict priority queue.

Table 8-2 *Comparison Between GTS and FRTS Functions (Continued)*

	GTS	FRTS
FRF.12 fragmentation	Not supported.	Works only with FRTS.
Interface queue	Supports any queuing at the interface level.	Supports only a dual-FIFO queue at the interface level.

References

[1] The ATM Forum, www.atmforum.com/.

[2] "Dynamics of TCP Traffic over ATM Networks," A. Romanow and S. Floyd, IEEE JSAC, V. 13 N. 4, May 1995, pp. 633-641.

[3] Early Packet Discard (EDP) Page, www.aciri.org/floyd/epd.html.

[4] "ISDN Data Link Layer Specification for Frame Mode Bearer Services," International Telegraph and Telephone Consultative Committee, CCITT Recommendation Q.922, 19 April 1991.

[5] Frame Relay Forum (FRF), www.frforum.com.

[6] "Virtual Bridged Local Area Networks," IEEE 802.1Q, grouper.ieee.org/groups/802/1/vlan.html.

[7] "MAC Bridges," IEEE 802.1D, grouper.ieee.org/groups/802/1/mac.html.

[8] "Integrated Services over Specific Link Layers (ISSLL)," IETF Working Group, www.ietf.org/html.charters/issll-charter.html.

[9] "SBM: A Protocol for RSVP-Based Admission Control over IEEE 802-Style Networks," Ed. Yavatkar and others, "draft-ietf-issll-is802-sbm-08.txt," search.ietf.org/internet-drafts/draft-ietf-issll-is802-sbm-08.txt.

QoS in MPLS-Based Networks

Multiprotocol Label Switching (MPLS) is an Internet Engineering Task Force (IETF) standard for a new switching paradigm that enables packet switching at Layer 2 while using Layer 3 forwarding information. Thus, MPLS combines the high-performance capabilities of Layer 2 switching and the scalability of Layer 3-based forwarding.

At the ingress to the MPLS network, Internet Protocol (IP) precedence information can be copied as class of service (CoS) bits, or can be mapped to set the appropriate MPLS CoS value in the MPLS Layer 2 label. Within the MPLS network, MPLS CoS information is used to provide differentiated services. Hence, MPLS CoS enables end-to-end IP quality of service (QoS) across an MPLS network.

MPLS-based forwarding enables a service provider network to deploy new services, particularly Virtual Private Networks (VPNs) and traffic engineering.

This chapter introduces MPLS and MPLS-based VPNs and discusses their QoS offerings. Traffic engineering is covered in Chapter 10, "MPLS Traffic Engineering."

MPLS

MPLS[1] is an IETF standard for label-swapping-based forwarding in the presence of routing information. It consists of two principal components: control and forwarding. The *control component* uses a label distribution protocol to maintain label-forwarding information for all destinations in the MPLS network. The *forwarding component* switches packets by swapping labels using the label information carried in the packet and the label-forwarding information maintained by the control component.

MPLS, as the name suggests, works for different network layer protocols. As such, the forwarding component is independent of any network layer protocol. The control component has to support label distribution for different network layer protocols to enable MPLS use with multiple network layer protocols.

Forwarding Component

MPLS packet forwarding occurs by using a label-swapping technique. When a packet carrying a label arrives at a Label Switching Router (LSR), the LSR uses the label as the index in its Label Information Base (LIB). For an incoming label, LIB carries a matching entry with the corresponding outgoing label, interface, and link-level encapsulation information to forward the packet. Based on the information in the LIB, the LSR swaps the incoming label with the outgoing label and transmits the packet on the outgoing interface with the appropriate link-layer encapsulation.

A Label Edge Router (LER) is an edge router in the MPLS cloud. Some LER interfaces perform non-MPLS-based forwarding and some run MPLS. An LER adds an MPLS label to all packets entering the MPLS cloud from non-MPLS interfaces. On the same token, it removes the MPLS label from a packet leaving the MPLS cloud. The forwarding behavior in an MPLS network is depicted in Figure 9-1.

Figure 9-1   *MPLS Network*

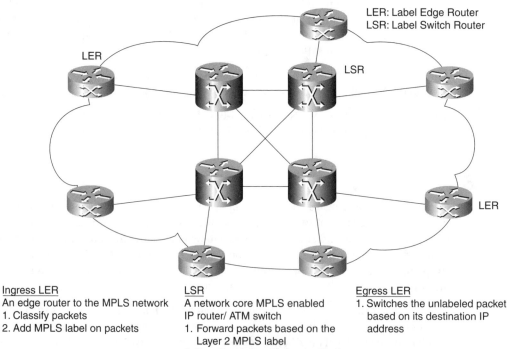

LER: Label Edge Router
LSR: Label Switch Router

Ingress LER
An edge router to the MPLS network
1. Classify packets
2. Add MPLS label on packets

LSR
A network core MPLS enabled
IP router/ ATM switch
1. Forward packets based on the
   Layer 2 MPLS label
2. Penultimate hop to the destination
   removes the label before sending it
   to the egress LER

Egress LER
1. Switches the unlabeled packet
   based on its destination IP
   address

The preceding procedure simplifies a normal IP router's forwarding behavior. A non-MPLS router performs destination-based routing based on the longest match from the entries in the routing-table-based forwarding table. An MPLS router, on the other hand, uses a short label, which comes before the Layer 3 header, to make a forwarding decision based on an exact match of the label in the LIB. As such, the forwarding procedure is simple enough to allow a potential hardware implementation.

Control Component

The control component is responsible for creating label bindings and then distributing the label binding information among LSRs.

Label binding is an association between a label and network layer's reachability information or a single traffic flow, based on the forwarding granularity. On one end, a label can be associated to a group of routes, thereby providing MPLS good-scaling capabilities. On the other end, a label can be bound to a single application flow, accommodating flexible forwarding functionality. MPLS network operation is shown in Figure 9-2.

Figure 9-2   *MPLS Network Operation*

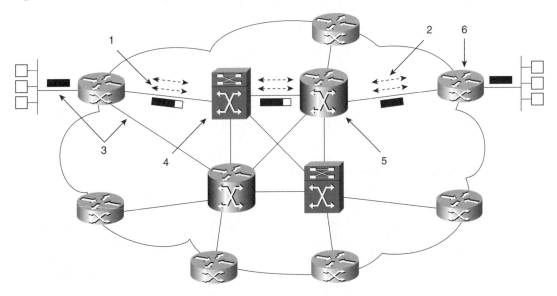

1. Existing routing protocols (e.g., OSPF, ISIS) establish reachability to destination networks.
2. Label Distribution Protocol (LDP) establishes tag to destination network mappings.
3. Ingress label switch router receives packet, performs Layer 3 value-added services, and tags packets.
4. Core LSR switches packets by using label swapping.
5. The penultimate hop to the destination removes the label and sends an unlabeled packet towards the last hop LER.
6. Egress LER switches an unlabeled packet based on its destination IP address.

When label binding is based on routing information, MPLS performs destination-based forwarding. Destination-based forwarding is not amenable to more granular and flexible routing policies, however. For cases involving flexible forwarding policies, the label binding might not be based on routing information. MPLS provides flexible forwarding policies at a granularity of a flow or group of flows. You can use this aspect of MPLS to offer a new service called *traffic engineering*. Traffic engineering is discussed in Chapter 10.

The next section discusses label-binding procedures for achieving destination-based forwarding.

Label Binding for Destination-Based Forwarding

Cisco Express Forwarding (CEF) is the recommended packet switching mechanism for IP networks today. CEF is discussed in Appendix B, "Packet Switching Mechanisms." A CEF table carries forwarding information based on the routing table; as such, it forwards packets on the basis of the destination. MPLS extends the CEF table to accommodate label allocation for each entry. LIB binds each CEF table entry with a label.

MPLS allows three methods for label allocation and distribution:

- Downstream label allocation
- Downstream label allocation on demand
- Upstream label allocation

For all the different types of label allocations, a protocol called *Label Distribution Protocol (LDP)* is used to distribute labels between routers. Note that the terms "downstream" and "upstream" are used with respect to the direction of the data flow.

Downstream Label Allocation

Downstream label allocation occurs in the direction opposite the actual data flow's direction. The label carried in a packet is generated and bound to a prefix by an LSR at the link's downstream end. As such, each LSR originates labels for its directly connected prefixes, binds them as an incoming label for the prefixes, and distributes the label association to its prefixes to all the upstream routers. An upstream router puts the received label binding as an outgoing label for the prefix in the CEF table and, in turn, creates an incoming label to it and advertises it to a router further upstream.

In independent label distribution mode, each downstream router binds an incoming label for a prefix independently and advertises it as an outgoing label to all its upstream routers. It is not necessary to receive an outgoing label for a prefix before an incoming label is created and advertised. When a router has both the incoming and outgoing labels for a prefix, it can start switching packets by label swapping.

The other label distribution mode is termed *ordered control mode*. In this mode, a router waits for the label from its downstream neighbor before sending its label upstream.

Downstream Label Allocation on Demand

This label allocation process is similar to downstream allocation, but it is created on demand by an upstream router. The upstream router identifies the next hop for each prefix from the CEF table and issues a request to the next hop for a label binding for that route. The rest of the allocation process is similar to downstream label allocation.

Upstream Label Allocation

Upstream label allocation occurs in the direction of the actual data flow. The label carried in the data packet's header is generated and bound to the prefix by the LSR at the upstream end of the link. For each CEF entry in an LSR, an outgoing label is allocated and distributed as an incoming label to downstream routers. In this case, incoming labels are allocated to prefixes.

When an LSR has both the incoming and the outgoing labels for a prefix, it can start switching packets carrying a label by using label swapping.

When an LSR creates a binding between an outgoing labels and a route, the switch, in addition to populating its LIB, also updates its CEF with the binding information. This enables the LSR to add labels to previously unlabeled packets it is originating. Table 9-1 compares downstream and upstream label distribution methods.

Table 9-1 *Comparison Between Downstream and Upstream Label Distribution*

	Downstream Allocation	**Upstream Allocation**
Direction of Label Allocation	Occurs in the direction opposite the data flow.	Occurs in the direction of the data flow.
Label Allocation and Distribution	Allocates the incoming prefix for all entries in the CEF table and distributes the outgoing label to the upstream routers.	Allocates the outgoing label for all entries in the CEF table and distributes the incoming label to the downstream routers.
Label Distribution Protocol	Allocates outgoing labels.	Distributes incoming labels.
Applicability	Applicable for non-ATM-based IP networks.	Downstream label allocation on demand and upstream label allocation are most useful in Asynchronous Transfer Mode (ATM) networks.

NOTE   Some important points to note regarding the MPLS control component:

- The total number of labels used in an LSR is no greater than the number of its CEF entries. Actually, in most cases, you can associate a single label with a group of routes sharing the same next hop; hence, the number of labels used is much less than the number of CEF entries. This provides a scalable architecture.

- Label allocation is driven by topology information as reflected by CEF, which is based on the routing information and not on actual data traffic.

- MPLS doesn't replace IP routing protocols. The MPLS control component depends on the existence of routing information in a router, but it is independent of the kind of IP routing protocol used in an MPLS network. For that matter, you can use any or multiple routing protocols in an MPLS network.

Label Encapsulation

A packet can carry label information in a variety of ways:

- **As a 4-byte label inserted between the Layer 2 and network layer headers**—This applies to Point-to-Point Protocol (PPP) links and Ethernet (all flavors) LANs. A single MPLS label or a label stack (multiple labels) can be carried in this way. Figure 9-3 shows how the label is carried over PPP links and over an Ethernet-type LAN.

Figure 9-3   *MPLS Label in Ethernet and PPP Frame*

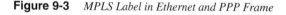

PPP header	MPLS label	Layer 3 header
MAC header	MPLS label	Layer 3 header

- **As a part of the Layer 2 header**—This applies to ATM, where the label information is carried in the VPI/VCI fields, as shown in Figure 9-4.

Figure 9-4   *MPLS Label Carried in the VPI/VCI Fields in an ATM Header*

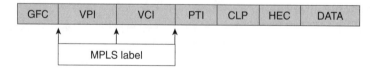

- **As part of the ATM Adaptation Layer 5 (AAL5) frame before segmentation and reassembly (SAR)**—This occurs in an ATM environment for label information made up of a label stack (multiple MPLS label fields).

NOTE   An addition of an MPLS label or a label stack to a 1492-byte packet might lead to packet fragmentation. Transmission Control Protocol (TCP) path maximum transmission unit (MTU) discovery packets carrying the MPLS label, if sent, detect the need to fragment across an MPLS network.

Note, however, that many Ethernet links actually support 1500- or 1508-byte packets. In addition, in most network designs, labeled packets are usually carried over ATM or PPP links and not on local-area network (LAN) segments.

An MPLS label field consists of a label header and a 20-bit label. The label header consists of three fields: CoS, S bit, and Time-to-Live (TTL). The 4-byte MPLS label field format is shown in Figure 9-5.

Figure 9-5   *MPLS Label Format*

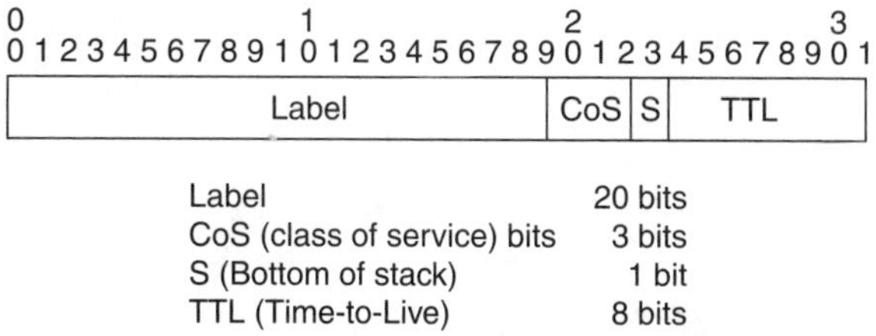

```
0                   1                   2                   3
0 1 2 3 4 5 6 7 8 9 1 0 1 2 3 4 5 6 7 8 9 0 1 2 3 4 5 6 7 8 9 0 1
+-------------------------------------+-----+-+---------+
|                Label                | CoS |S|   TTL   |
+-------------------------------------+-----+-+---------+

    Label                        20 bits
    CoS (class of service) bits   3 bits
    S (Bottom of stack)           1 bit
    TTL (Time-to-Live)            8 bits
```

- **CoS (3 bits)**—This field is used to deliver differentiated services in an MPLS network. To deliver end-to-end IP QoS, you can copy the IP precedence field to the CoS field at the edge of the MPLS network.

NOTE   The CoS field in the MPLS header has only 3 bits. As such, it can carry only the 3-bit IP precedence field and not the 6-bit Differentiated Services Code Point (DSCP) field. Therefore, as needed, the CoS information can be carried as one of the labels in an MPLS label stack. The label field is 20 bits in length and can fit in either the IP precedence field or the DSCP field.

- **S bit**—Indicates a label entry at the bottom of the label stack. It is set to 1 for the last entry in the label stack and to zero for all other label stack entries. This allows binding a prefix with multiple labels, also called a *label stack*. In the case of a label stack, each label has its own associated CoS, S, and TTL values.

- **TTL (8 bits)**—Indicates the time to live for an MPLS packet. The TTL value, when set at the edge of the MPLS network, is decremented at each MPLS network hop.

NOTE   The IP TTL field is copied into the MPLS TTL field during label imposition by default. It enables the *traceroute* utility to show all the MPLS hops when the destination lies within or across the MPLS cloud.

The **no mpls ip propagate-ttl** command is used to disallow copying of IP TTL into the MPLS TTL field at the ingress to the MPLS network. In this case, the MPLS TTL field is set to 255. Hence, the *traceroute* output does not show any hops within the MPLS network. It shows only one IP hop to transit the entire MPLS domain.

MPLS with ATM

An ATM switch already has the MPLS-type forwarding component, as it performs VPI/VCI field swapping similar to MPLS label swapping. As such, it needs only the control component to support MPLS. For the forwarding component, the VPI/VCI field is leveraged to carry the label information. For all instances when a single label can be used, the VCI field is used to carry the label within an ATM-based MPLS network. The VPI field can be leveraged when a second label becomes necessary.

To support the MPLS control component, an ATM switch needs to run routing protocols such as OSPF or IS-IS to peer with the other connected LSRs so that it can obtain IP layer reachability information and populate its CEF table based on it. An ATM LSR might not need to run BGP because, in most cases, it can't be an LER anyway. In addition, it needs to run label distribution protocols such as LDP and Resource Reservation Protocol (RSVP) with traffic engineering modifications (TE-RSVP), discussed in Chapter 10, to distribute the label information to the peer LSRs.

MPLS on an ATM switch might require that the switch maintain several labels associated with a route (or a group of routes with the same next hop). This is necessary to avoid the interleaving of packets arriving from different upstream label switches but sent concurrently to the same next hop. Either the downstream label allocation on demand or the upstream label allocation scheme can be used for the label allocation and LIB maintenance procedures with ATM switches.

Case Study 9-1: Downstream Label Distribution

This case study discusses the label binding, distribution, and label-based switching operations for the prefix 222.222.222.3 on Router NewYork in the network shown in Figure 9-6. It does so by looking into the NewYork, Chicago, Dallas, and SanFrancisco routers.

Figure 9-6 *Downstream Label Distribution*

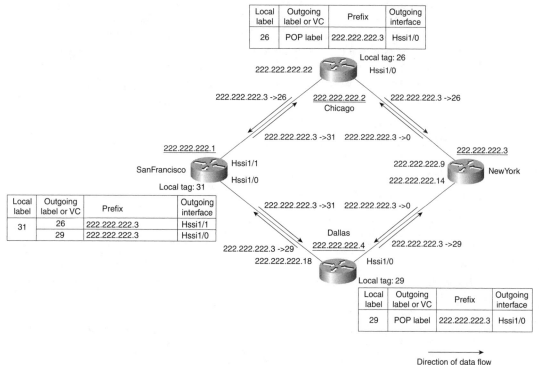

The **mpls ip** command is used to enable MPLS on a router. One prerequisite for label distribution is CEF, which you can enable by using the global **ip cef** command.

In downstream label allocation, an MPLS router allocates an incoming label for each CEF entry and distributes it on all its interfaces. An upstream router receives a label binding and uses it as an outgoing label for its associated CEF prefix. In this method of label allocation, the incoming label is allocated locally and the outgoing label is received remotely from a downstream router.

This case study concentrates on studying the behavior of downstream label distribution for one prefix, 222.222.222.3. The following Listings show information on the prefix 222.222.222.3 from the CEF table, the label bindings, and the label forwarding table from each router. The **show ip cef**, **show mpls ldp bindings**, and **show mpls forwarding-table** commands are used to fetch information on CEF, label binding, and label-based forwarding, respectively. Listings 9-1, 9-2, and 9-3 show information on CEF, label binding, and the label distribution protocol from Router NewYork.

Listing 9-1   *Information on the 222.222.222.3 Prefix in the CEF Table of Router NewYork*

```
NewYork#show ip cef 222.222.222.3
222.222.222.3/32, version 170, connected, receive
```

Listing 9-2   *Label Binding Information for Prefix 222.222.222.3 on Router NewYork*

```
NewYork#show mpls ldp bindings
  LIB entry: 222.222.222.3/32, rev 118
      local binding:  label: imp-null
      remote binding: lsr: 222.222.222.2:0, label: 26
      remote binding: lsr: 222.222.222.4:0, label: 29
```

Listing 9-3   *Label Distribution Protocol Parameters*

```
NewYork#show mpls ldp parameters
 Protocol version: 1
 Downstream label pool: min label: 10; max_label: 100000; reserved labels: 16
 Session hold time: 180 sec; keep alive interval: 60 sec
 Discovery hello: holdtime: 15 sec; interval: 5 sec
 Discovery directed hello: holdtime: 180 sec; interval: 5 sec
```

MPLS performs label binding for all prefixes in the CEF table and distributes them to all established LDP neighbors. The **show mpls ldp bindings** command shows the label bindings. A local binding is advertised upstream by a router. In this case, the local binding for prefix 222.222.222.3 is NULL because it is a directly connected IP address on the router. Router NewYork advertises the null label binding to its LDP adjacent routers, Chicago and Dallas. A router receiving a null label binding for a prefix *pops* the label out when forwarding a packet destined to this prefix.

The remote bindings are the label bindings advertised by the respective routers. The remote LSR routers 222.222.222.2 and 222.222.222.4 have a local label of 26 and 29, respectively. A local label binding is advertised to all LDP adjacent routers. The **show mpls ldp parameters** command displays the LDP protocol and label binding information.

Because Router New York receives packets destined to its directly connected 222.222.222.3 prefix without a label, the label forwarding table does not carry any information on prefix 222.222.222.3.

Listings 9-4, 9-5, and 9-6 display CEF, label binding, and label forwarding information for prefix 222.222.222.3 from Router Chicago.

Listing 9-4 *CEF Information on Prefix 222.222.222.3 in Router Chicago*

```
Chicago#show ip cef 222.222.222.3
222.222.222.3/32, version 179, cached adjacency to Hssi1/0
0 packets, 0 bytes
  via 210.210.210.9, Hssi1/0, 0 dependencies
    next hop 210.210.210.9, Hssi1/0
    valid cached adjacency
```

Listing 9-5 *Label Binding Information for Prefix 222.222.222.3 in Router Chicago*

```
Chicago#show mpls ldp bindings
 LIB entry: 222.222.222.3/32, rev 90
       local binding:  label: 26
       remote binding: lsr: 222.222.222.3:0, label: imp-null
       remote binding: lsr: 222.222.222.1:0, label: 31
```

Listing 9-6 *Label Forwarding Information on Prefix 222.222.222.3 in Router Chicago*

```
Chicago#show mpls forwarding-table
Local  Outgoing     Prefix          Bytes label  Outgoing    Next Hop
label  label or VC  or Tunnel Id    switched     interface
26     Pop label    222.222.222.3/32 63          Hs1/0       point2point
```

The local label 26 is the label binding for 222.222.222.3 on Router Chicago. This local binding is triggered by the presence of 222.222.222.3 in the CEF table, and it is distributed to all its LDP neighbors. LSR SanFrancisco has a local binding of label 31 for 222.222.222.3, which it advertised to all its LDP neighbors. The **show mpls forwarding-table** command shows the information required to switch packets by label swapping. The outgoing label is the *pop* label because it received a null label from the remote New York LSR on its outgoing interface (because the prefix is a directly connected address on the remote LSR). In this example, any incoming packet with a label of 26 is switched to the outgoing interface Hssi1/0 after removing or *popping* the label. The label is removed because the packet is switched to its ultimate destination router. This phenomenon for popping the label at the penultimate hop to the destination is termed penultimate hop popping (PHP).

Listings 9-7, 9-8, and 9-9 give CEF, label binding, and label-based forwarding information for the 222.222.222.3 prefix in Router Dallas.

Listing 9-7   *CEF-related Information on Prefix 222.222.222.3 in Router Dallas*

```
Dallas#show ip cef 222.222.222.3
222.222.222.3/32, version 18, cached adjacency to Hssi1/0
0 packets, 0 bytes
  via 210.210.210.14, Hssi1/0, 0 dependencies
    next hop 210.210.210.14, Hssi1/0
    valid cached adjacency
```

Listing 9-8   *Label Bindings for Prefix 222.222.222.3 in Router Dallas*

```
Dallas#show mpls ldp bindings
LIB entry: 222.222.222.3/32, rev 18
        local binding:  label: 29
        remote binding: lsr: 222.222.222.3:0, label: imp-null
        remote binding: lsr: 222.222.222.1:0, label: 31
```

Listing 9-9   *Label-based Forwarding Information for Prefix 222.222.222.3 in Router Dallas*

```
Dallas#show mpls forwarding-table
Local  Outgoing     Prefix          Bytes label  Outgoing    Next Hop
label    label or VC   or Tunnel Id     switched   interface
29     Pop label    222.222.222.3/32 1190         Hs1/0        point2point
```

Explanations for the preceding listings from Router Dallas are largely similar to the discussion on the listings from Router Chicago.

Listings 9-10, 9-11, and 9-12 display CEF, label binding, and label-based forwarding information on prefix 222.222.222.3 in Router SanFrancisco.

Listing 9-10   *CEF Entry for Prefix 222.222.222.3 in Router SanFrancisco*

```
SanFrancisco#show ip cef 222.222.222.3
222.222.222.3/32, version 38, per-destination sharing
0 packets, 0 bytes
  via 210.210.210.22, Hssi1/1, 0 dependencies
    traffic share 1
    next hop 210.210.210.22, Hssi1/1
    valid adjacency
```

Listing 9-10 *CEF Entry for Prefix 222.222.222.3 in Router SanFrancisco (Continued)*

```
    via 210.210.210.18, Hssi1/0, 0 dependencies
      traffic share 1
      next hop 210.210.210.18, Hssi1/0
      valid adjacency
    0 packets, 0 bytes switched through the prefix
```

Listing 9-11 *Label Binding Information on Prefix 222.222.222.3 in Router SanFrancisco*

```
SanFrancisco#show mpls ldp bindings
  LIB entry: 222.222.222.3/32, rev 8
      local binding:  label: 31
      remote binding: lsr: 222.222.222.2:0, label: 26
      remote binding: lsr: 222.222.222.4:0, label: 29
```

Listing 9-12 *Label-Based Forwarding Information on Prefix 222.222.222.3 in Router SanFrancisco*

```
SanFrancisco#show mpls forwarding-table
Local  Outgoing    Prefix          Bytes label  Outgoing    Next Hop
label    label or VC   or Tunnel Id    switched    interface
31     26          222.222.222.3/32  0              Hs1/1      point2point
       29          222.222.222.3/32  0              Hs1/0      point2point
```

The CEF table shows two equal cost paths taken to reach 222.222.222.3. The local binding for the prefix is 31, and it distributes to all its LDP neighbors. The remote bindings show the local label bindings distributed by the LDP adjacent routers. The MPLS router label switches packets received with a local label with an outgoing label based on the received remote binding information.

MPLS QoS

QoS is an important component of MPLS. In an MPLS network, QoS information is carried in the label header's MPLS CoS field.

Like IP QoS, MPLS QoS is achieved in two main logical steps, as shown in Table 9-2, and uses the same associated QoS functions. Figure 9-7 depicts the QoS functions used in an MPLS network.

MPLS uses the same IP QoS functions to provide differentiated QoS for traffic within an MPLS network. The only real difference is that MPLS QoS is based on the CoS bits in the MPLS label, whereas IP QoS is based on the IP precedence field in the IP header.

On an ATM backbone with an MPLS-enabled ATM switch, the switch can support MPLS CoS in two ways:

- Single Label Switched Path (LSP) with Available Bit Rate (ABR) service
- Parallel LSPs with Label Bit Rate (LBR) service

Table 9-2 *MPLS QoS*

Step	Place of Application	Applicable QoS Functions	QoS action
1	Ingress (edge) router to the MPLS cloud	Committed Access Rate (CAR)	(Option 1) CAR polices traffic on the ingress router for all incoming IP traffic entering the MPLS cloud. It sets an IP precedence value for traffic according to the traffic profile and policies. The IP packet's IP precedence value is copied into the MPLS CoS field.
			(Option 2) CAR polices traffic on the ingress router for all incoming IP traffic entering the MPLS cloud. It sets an MPLS CoS value for traffic according to the traffic profile and contract.
			The precedence value in the IP header is left unchanged end-to-end, unlike Option 1.
2	Entire MPLS network	Weighted Fair Queuing (WFQ), Weighted Random Error Detection (WRED)	Traffic differentiation based on the MPLS CoS field in the MPLS backbone using the IP QoS functions WFQ and WRED.

A single LSP using ATM ABR service can be established through LDP. All MPLS traffic uses the same ABR LSP, and the differentiation is made on the ingress routers to the ATM cloud by running WFQ and WRED algorithms on traffic going over an LSP.

Multiple LSPs in parallel can be established through LDP to support traffic with multiple precedence values. Each established LSP is mapped to carry traffic of certain MPLS CoS values. The LSPs use the LBR ATM service. LBR is a new ATM service category that relies on scheduling and discarding in the ATM switch based on WFQ and WRED, respectively, and hence is more appropriate for IP.

Figure 9-7   *QoS in an MPLS Network*

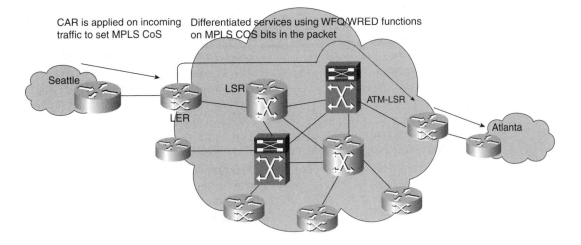

When an ATM switch doesn't support MPLS, you can use ATM QoS using the ATM Forum traffic class (Constant Bit Rate [CBR], Variable Bit Rate [VBR], and ABR) and its IP interworking, as discussed in Chapter 8, "Layer 2 QoS: Interworking with IP QoS."

End-to-End IP QoS

You can set the MPLS CoS bits at the edge of the network to provide traffic classification so that the QoS functions within the network can provide differentiated QoS. As such, to deliver end-to-end IP QoS across a QoS-enabled MPLS network, you map or copy the IP precedence value to the MPLS CoS bits at the edge of the MPLS network. The IP precedence value continues to be used after the packet exits the MPLS network. Table 9-3 shows the various QoS functions for delivering end-to-end IP QoS across an MPLS network.

Case Study 9-2: MPLS CoS

A service provider MPLS network offers varied service classes for its traffic. The four service classes based on the CoS bit settings are shown in Table 9-4.

Table 9-3   *End-to-End IP QoS Across an MPLS Network*

Step	Place of Application	Type of QoS	QoS Function
1	IP cloud (before entering the MPLS network)	IP QoS	Standard IP QoS policies are followed. At the network boundary, incoming traffic is policed and set with an IP precedence value based on its service level. Differentiated service is based on the precedence value in the IP network.
2	Ingress router to the MPLS cloud	IP/MPLS QoS Interworking	Packet's IP precedence value is copied into the MPLS CoS field. Note that the MPLS CoS field can also be set directly based on the traffic profile and service contract.
3	MPLS network	MPLS QoS	Traffic differentiation is based on the MPLS CoS field in the MPLS backbone using the IP QoS functions WFQ and WRED.
4	IP network (after traversing the MPLS network)	IP QoS	IP precedence in the IP header continues to be the basis for traffic differentiation and network QoS.

Two sites, Seattle and Atlanta, in the IP network are connected through the MPLS network as shown previously in Figure 9-7. Discuss the MPLS CoS functionality needed in the MPLS network to offer a standard service class for the traffic from Seattle to Atlanta.

Table 9-4   *Four Service Classes Using MPLS CoS*

Class	IP Precedence Bits (Value in Decimals)	Type of Service (ToS) Class Bits	Drop Priority
Class 0 (Available)	000 (0)	00	0
	100 (4)	00	1
Class 1 (Standard)	001 (1)	01	0
	101 (5)	01	1
Class 2 (Premium)	010 (2)	10	0
	110 (6)	10	1
Class 3 (Control)	011 (3)	11	0
	111 (7)	11	1

LER

IP traffic from the Seattle site going to the Atlanta site enters the MPLS network on the LER router.

On the LER router interface that connects to the Seattle site, enable CAR to police incoming traffic according to the service contract. In Listing 9-13, the incoming traffic on the interface is contracted at standard CoS, with traffic of 20 Mbps getting an IP precedence of 5 and any exceeding traffic getting an IP precedence of 1.

Listing 9-13 *Enable CAR to Classify Traffic for Standard CoS*

```
interface Hssi0/0/0
 ip address 221.221.221.254 255.255.255.252
rate-limit input 20000000 2000000 8000000 conform-action set-mpls-exp-transmit
  transmit 5
exceed-action set-mpls-exp-transmit 1
```

As part of IP/MPLS QoS Interworking, IP precedence is copied into the MPLS CoS field.

From the LER, the Atlanta-bound traffic goes via the LSR. On the LER POS3/0/0 interface connecting to the LSR, WRED and WFQ are enabled to differentiate traffic based on the MPLS CoS value carried in the MPLS packet.

LSR

Traffic going to the Atlanta site goes via an MPLS ATM network. On the LSR, parallel LSPs with LBR service are set up such that separate LSPs are used to carry traffic belonging to each IP precedence. It enables traffic differentiation based on IP precedence. Listing 9-14 shows a sample configuration to enable MPLS-based parallel LSPs with LBR service. On each LSP, WRED is enabled.

Listing 9-14 *Enable Parallel LSPs with LBR Service on an LSR*

```
interface ATM1/1/0
!
interface ATM 1/1/0.1 mpls
ip unnumbered Loopback0
mpls multi-vc
mpls random detect
```

MPLS VPN

One important MPLS application is the VPN[2] service. A client with multiple remote sites can connect to a VPN service provider backbone at multiple locations. The VPN backbone offers connectivity among the different client sites. The characteristics of this connectivity make the service provider cloud look like a private network to the client. No communication is allowed between different VPNs on a VPN service provider backbone.

Any device at a VPN site can communicate only with a device at a site belonging to the same VPN.

In a service provider network, a Provider Edge router connects to the Customer Edge router at each VPN site. A VPN usually has multiple geographically distributed sites that connect to the service provider's local Provider Edge routers. A VPN site and its associated routes are assigned one or more *VPN colors*. Each VPN color defines the VPN a site belongs to. A site can communicate with another site connected to the VPN backbone only if it belongs to the same VPN color. A VPN intranet service is provided among all sites connected to the VPN backbone using the same color. A site to one VPN can communicate to a different VPN or to the Internet by using a VPN extranet service. A VPN extranet service can be provided by selectively leaking some external routes of a different VPN or of the Internet into a VPN intranet.

Provider Edge routers hold routing information only for the VPNs to which they are directly connected. Provider Edge routers in the VPN provider network are fully meshed using multiprotocol internal BGP (IBGP)[3] peerings.

Multiple VPNs can use the same IP version 4 (IPv4) addresses. Examples of such addresses are IP private addresses and unregistered IP addresses. The Provider Edge router needs to distinguish among such addresses of different VPNs. To enable this, a new address family called VPN-IPv4 is defined. The VPN-IPv4 address is a 12-byte value; the first eight bytes carry the route distinguisher (RD) value, and the last four bytes consist of the IPv4 address. The RD is used to make the private and unregistered IPv4 addresses in a VPN network unique in a service provider backbone. The RD consists of a 2-byte autonomous system (AS) number, followed by a 4-byte value that the provider can assign. VPN-IPv4 addresses are treated as a different address family and are carried in BGP by using BGP multiprotocol extensions. In these BGP extensions, label-mapping information is carried as part of the Network Layer Reachability Information (NLRI)[4]. The label identifies the output interface connecting to this NLRI.

The extended community attribute[5] is used to carry Route Target (RT) and Source of Origin (SOO) values. A route can be associated with multiple RT values similar to the BGP community attribute that can carry multiple communities for an IP prefix. RT values are used to control route distribution, because a router can decide to accept or reject a route based on its RT value. The SOO value is used to uniquely identify a VPN site. Table 9-5 lists some important MPLS VPN terminology.

Table 9-5   *MPLS VPN Terminology*

Term	Definition
Customer Edge Router	A customer router that interfaces with a Provider Edge router.
Provider Edge Router	A provider router that interfaces with a Customer Edge router.
Provider Router	A router internal to the provider network. It doesn't have any knowledge of the provisioned VPNs.
VPN Routing and Forwarding (VRF) Instance	A routing and forwarding table associated with one or more directly connected customer sites. A VRF is assigned on the VPN customer interfaces. VPN customer sites sharing the same routing information can be part of the same VRF. A VRF is identified by a name, and it has local significance only.
VPN-IPv4 Address	Includes 64-bit RD and 32-bit IPv4 addresses.
SOO	Identifies the originating site.
RD	64-bit attribute used to uniquely identify VPN and customer address space in the provider backbone.
RT	64-bit identifier to indicate which routers should receive the route.

Case Study 9-3: MPLS VPN

Discuss VPN service deployment between enterprise customer sites in San Francisco and New York across a service provider backbone, as shown in Figure 9-8. The customer San Francisco site connects to the service provider's local SanFrancisco router and the New York site to the service provider's NewYork router in New York.

This case study discusses how MPLS VPNs are implemented in a service provider backbone. It studies the configuration used for VPN service implementation and discusses VPN operation across a provider network using various commands in the provider backbone's router.

Figure 9-8   *MPLS VPN*

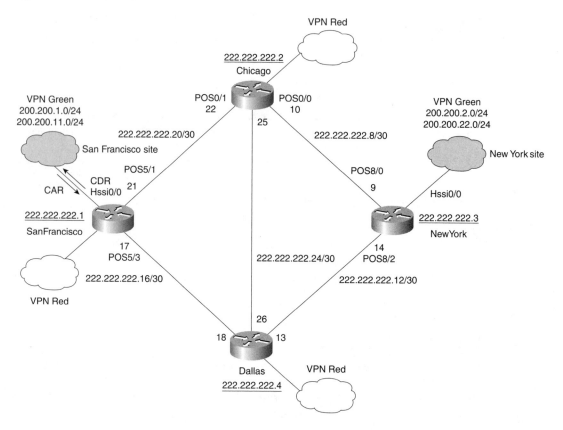

A VRF instance green for VPN service to the enterprise customer is defined. An RD of 200:100 is used to distinguish this customer's routes in the service provider backbone. The VPN configuration on Router SanFrancisco and the VPN operation between the customer San Francisco site and New York site across the service provider network is discussed next. Listing 9-15 gives the MPLS VPN-related configuration on the SanFrancisco router.

Listing 9-15   *Setting Up MPLS VPN on Router SanFrancisco*

```
ip vrf green
rd 200:100
route-target export 200:1
route-target import 200:1
route-target import 200:2
ip cef
```

Listing 9-15   *Setting Up MPLS VPN on Router SanFrancisco (Continued)*

```
clns routing
!
interface Loopback0
 ip address 222.222.222.1 255.255.255.255
 ip router isis isp
!
interface Hssi0/0
 ip vrf forwarding green
 ip address 222.222.222.25 255.255.255.252
 ip router isis isp
 mpls ip
!
interface POS5/1
 ip address 222.222.222.21 255.255.255.252
 ip router isis isp
 mpls ip
!
interface POS5/3
 ip address 222.222.222.17 255.255.255.252
 ip router isis isp
 mpls ip
!
!
router isis isp
 net 50.0000.0000.0000.0001.00
 metric-style wide
 mpls traffic-eng router-id Loopback0
 mpls traffic-eng level-1
!
router bgp 200
 no synchronization
 neighbor 222.222.222.2 remote-as 200
 neighbor 222.222.222.2 update-source Loopback0
 neighbor 222.222.222.3 remote-as 200
 neighbor 222.222.222.3 update-source Loopback0
 neighbor 222.222.222.4 remote-as 200
 neighbor 222.222.222.4 update-source Loopback0
 no auto-summary
 !
 address-family ipv4 vrf green
 no auto-summary
 no synchronization
 network 200.200.1.0
 network 200.200.11.0
 exit-address-family
 !
 address-family vpnv4
 neighbor 222.222.222.2 activate
 neighbor 222.222.222.2 send-community extended
 neighbor 222.222.222.3 activate
```

continues

Listing 9-15   *Setting Up MPLS VPN on Router SanFrancisco (Continued)*

```
 neighbor 222.222.222.3 send-community extended
 neighbor 222.222.222.4 activate
 neighbor 222.222.222.4 send-community extended
 no auto-summary
 exit-address-family
 !
ip route vrf green 200.200.1.0 255.255.255.0 Hssi0/0
ip route vrf green 200.200.11.0 255.255.255.0 Hssi0/0
 !
```

VRF green is enabled on interface Hssi0/0 that connects to the customer San Francisco site on Router SanFrancisco. Listing 9-16 shows the RD and the interfaces used for VRF green.

Listing 9-16   *Information on VRF Instance Green*

```
SanFrancisco#sh ip vrf green
  Name               Default RD         Interfaces
  green              200:100            Hssi0/0
```

In the first section of the BGP configuration, Router SanFrancisco peers with the other routers through BGP in the service provider backbone. The loopback0 interface addresses are used for this peering because such interfaces never go down.

The next section of the BGP configuration specifies the routes belonging to VRF green. Such routes can be learned dynamically using the VRF green instance of protocols, such as BGP and Routing Information Protocol version 2 (RIPv2). A VRF green instance of a protocol runs only on the VRF green interfaces. Hence, all VRF green routes are learned dynamically through the VRF green interfaces or are specified statically as VRF green routes that point to a VRF green interface.

On Router SanFrancisco, the customer routes belonging to the San Francisco site are specified using static routes into VRF green. These static routes point to the point-to-point interface connecting to the San Francisco site. You can see static VRF green routes by using the **show ip route vrf green** command.

The last section of the BGP configuration specifies the BGP peering to exchange the VPN-IPv4 address route family. BGP's extended community attribute is used to carry the export RT values. Local VRF routes are installed in the local BGP VPN-IPv4 table if their import RT value matches their specified export RT value. A VRF in a router has to specify an import RT value equal to one of the export RT values carried by a route for the route to be installed in the BGP VPN routing table.

On Router SanFrancisco, an export RT of 200:1 is specified for VRF green. All local routes belonging to VRF green on this router are exported through BGP with an RT of 200:1 in the BGP extended community attribute. A router that needs the SanFrancisco routes belonging to the VRF green should import routes with an RT of 200:1 by using the command **route-target import 200:1**. Router SanFrancisco itself should have this command because its import RT should match its export RT for the router to carry the routes through BGP.

VRF green specifies an RT of 200:2 in addition to 200:1. Therefore, Router SanFrancisco can import any BGP VPN routes that have an RT of either 200:1 or 200:2 into the VRF green routing table. You can show the VRF green routes carried in BGP by using the **show ip bgp vpn vrf green** command. You can see the routing table for VRF green by using the **show ip router vrf green** command. The IP routes and BGP routes belonging to VRF green in Router SanFrancisco are shown in Listings 9-17 and 9-18, respectively.

Listing 9-17 *SanFrancisco Routes in the VRF Routing Table Green*

```
SanFrancisco#show ip route vrf green
Codes: C - connected, S - static, I - IGRP, R - RIP, M - mobile, B - BGP
       D - EIGRP, EX - EIGRP external, O - OSPF, IA - OSPF inter area
       N1 - OSPF NSSA external type 1, N2 - OSPF NSSA external type 2
       E1 - OSPF external type 1, E2 - OSPF external type 2, E - EGP
       i - IS-IS, L1 - IS-IS level-1, L2 - IS-IS level-2, ia - IS-IS inter area
       * - candidate default, U - per-user static routeo - ODR

Gateway of last resort is not set

     222.222.222.0/30 is subnetted, 1 subnets
C       222.222.222.24 is directly connected, Hssi0/0
B    200.200.22.0/24 [200/0] via 222.222.222.3, 00:01:19
S    200.200.1.0/24 is directly connected, Hssi0/0
B    200.200.2.0/24 [200/0] via 222.222.222.3, 00:01:19
S    200.200.11.0/24 is directly connected, Hssi0/0
```

The VRF green instance of the routing table shows all the dynamically learned or statically specified VRF green routes. It also shows the BGP VPN-IPv4 that is imported into the local VRF green routing table as it matches the import RT 200:2.

Listing 9-18 *SanFrancisco BGP VPN-IPv4 Routes That Belong to VRF Green*

```
SanFrancisco#sh ip bgp vpn vrf green
BGP table version is 57, local router ID is 222.222.222.1
Status codes: s suppressed, d damped, h history, * valid, > best, i - internal
Origin codes: i - IGP, e - EGP, ? - incomplete

   Network          Next Hop          Metric LocPrf Weight Path
Route Distinguisher: 200:100 (default for vrf green)
*> 200.200.1.0      0.0.0.0                0            32768 i
*>i200.200.2.0      222.222.222.3          0       100     0 3456 i
*> 200.200.11.0     0.0.0.0                0            32768 i
*>i200.200.22.0     222.222.222.3          0       100     0 3456 i
```

BGP exchanges label bindings along with its VPN-IPv4 routes. A BGP label indicates the local output interface that can reach the route. Listing 9-19 shows the label bindings for the VPN-IPv4 routes carried by BGP.

Listing 9-19 *Label Bindings for the VPN-IPv4 Routes Carried by BGP*

```
SanFrancisco#sh ip bgp vpn vrf green label
    Network         Next Hop      In label/Out label
Route Distinguisher: 200:100 (green)
    200.200.1.0     0.0.0.0          26/nolabel
    200.200.2.0     222.222.222.3    nolabel/39
    200.200.11.0    0.0.0.0          27/nolabel
    200.200.22.0    222.222.222.3    nolabel/40
```

Listing 9-19 shows that 39 is the label the New York router with router ID 222.222.222.3 advertised as a label binding for the 200.200.2.0 route. The next several Listings show how an IP packet from the customer San Francisco site reaches the 200.200.2.1 address in the New York site across the service provider network.

Listing 9-20 shows label forwarding information for the prefix 222.222.222.3.

Listing 9-20 *Label Forwarding Information for the 222.222.222.3 Prefix*

```
SanFrancisco#show mpls forwarding-table 222.222.222.3
Local  Outgoing    Prefix           Bytes mpls  Outgoing   Next Hop
label     label or VC   or Tunnel Id    switched   interface
36     37          222.222.222.3/32 0           Po5/3      point2point
       30          222.222.222.3/32 7161        Po5/1      point2point
```

Depending on the nature of load balancing over parallel paths, the router can choose either label for 222.222.222.3. In this case, it chose label 30 through interface Po5/1.

After a packet for the 200.200.2.1 prefix arrives on Router SanFrancisco, the router attaches a label stack of two labels (30 and 39) and sends the packet on interface PO5/1 toward Router Chicago. An inner label takes the packet to the next hop 222.222.222.3 and the outer label switches the packet to its actual destination 222.222.2.1. Listing 9-21 shows the label forwarding information on Router Chicago for an incoming label of 30.

Listing 9-21 *The Label Forwarding Table for Prefix 222.222.222.3*

```
Chicago#sh mpls forwarding-table 222.222.222.3 32
Local  Outgoing    Prefix           Bytes label  Outgoing   Next Hop
label     label or VC   or Tunnel Id    switched   interface
30     Pop label   222.222.222.3/32 7161         Po0/0      point2point
```

Being a penultimate hop to the next-hop address 222.222.222.3, Router Chicago pops the inner label of 30 and sends the packet toward Router NewYork through interface Serial0, as shown in Listing 9-22.

Listing 9-22   *Debug Output Showing How the Router Chicago Label-Switched an MPLS Packet from the Customer San Francisco Site to 200.200.2.1 Address of the Customer New York Site*

```
MPLS: Po0/1: recvd: CoS=0, TTL=255, Label(s)=30/39
MPLS: Po0/0: xmit: CoS=0, TTL=254, Label(s)=39
```

On arrival to Router NewYork, the packet still carries the second label, 39. Listing 9-23 shows the label forwarding table in Router NewYork for an incoming label of 39.

Listing 9-23   *Router NewYork's Label Forwarding Table for VRF Green*

```
NewYork#sh mpls forwarding-table  vrf green
Local  Outgoing     Prefix             Bytes mpls  Outgoing    Next Hop
label    label or VC   or Tunnel Id      switched   interface
39     Unlabelged   200.200.2.0/24[V] 520         Hs0/0       point2point
40     Unlabelged   200.200.22.0/24[V] 0          Hs0/0       point2point
```

Based on the label forwarding information, Router NewYork removes the incoming label 39 and sends the packet out on interface Hssi0/0, which connects to the New York site. This label-switching action is depicted in Listing 9-24 by using debug commands in Router NewYork.

Listing 9-24   *Debug Output Showing How Router NewYork Label-Switched an MPLS Packet from SanFrancisco to the 200.200.2.1 Address*

```
MPLS: Po8/0: recvd: CoS=0, TTL=254, Label(s)=39
 MPLS: Hs0/0: xmit: (no label)
```

Listing 9-25 gives the VPN-related configuration on Router NewYork.

Listing 9-25   *VPN Setup on Router NewYork*

```
!
ip vrf green
 rd 200:100
 route-target export 200:2
 route-target import 200:1
 route-target import 200:2
ip cef
clns routing
!
!
!
interface Loopback0
 ip address 222.222.222.3 255.255.255.255
 ip router isis isp
```

continues

Listing 9-25 *VPN Setup on Router NewYork (Continued)*

```
!
interface POS8/0
 ip address 222.222.222.9 255.255.255.252
 ip router isis isp
 mpls ip
!
interface Hssi0/0
 ip vrf forwarding green
 ip address 222.222.222.37 255.255.255.252
 ip router isis isp
 mpls ip
!
interface POS8/2
 ip address 222.222.222.14 255.255.255.252
 ip router isis isp
 mpls ip
!
router isis isp
 net 50.0000.0000.0000.0003.00
 metric-style wide
 mpls traffic-eng router-id Loopback0
 mpls traffic-eng level-1
!
router bgp 200
 no synchronization
 neighbor 222.222.222.1 remote-as 200
 neighbor 222.222.222.1 update-source Loopback0
 neighbor 222.222.222.2 remote-as 200
 neighbor 222.222.222.2 update-source Loopback0
 neighbor 222.222.222.4 remote-as 200
 neighbor 222.222.222.4 update-source Loopback0
 no auto-summary
 !
 address-family ipv4 vrf green
 neighbor 222.222.222.38 remote-as 3456
 neighbor 222.222.222.38 activate
 no auto-summary
 no synchronization
 exit-address-family
 !
 address-family vpnv4
 neighbor 222.222.222.1 activate
 neighbor 222.222.222.1 send-community extended
 neighbor 222.222.222.2 activate
 neighbor 222.222.222.2 send-community extended
 neighbor 222.222.222.4 activate
 neighbor 222.222.222.4 send-community extended
 no auto-summary
 exit-address-family
 !
```

In Router NewYork, the second section of the BGP configuration shows that you use BGP peering to learn the VRF green routes from New York site. Note that on Router SanFrancisco discussed earlier, you configured the San Francisco site VRF green routes statically.

MPLS VPN QoS

QoS is a key component of a VPN service. Similar to IP QoS discussed in Part I of the book, the MPLS VPN QoS can be a differentiated service or a guaranteed service. You can use the same IP QoS functionality discussed in Part I, "IP QoS," to deliver MPLS VPN QoS. The coarse-grained differentiated QoS is provided by use of the CAR, WFQ, and WRED functions, whereas the fine-grained guaranteed service is provided by use of the RSVP protocol.

Differentiated MPLS VPN QoS

This QoS model delivers capabilities that, in some ways, look similar to Committed Information Rate (CIR) in a Frame Relay network.

Each VPN site is offered a CAR and a Committed Delivery Rate (CDR) for each port at which they access the network. In a Frame Relay network, CIR applies to both the incoming and the outgoing traffic from a device connected to the network. In a connectionless IP VPN environment, however, two different rates exist for each port connected to the network offering VPN service:

- CAR for all incoming traffic from the site into the VPN service network's access port
- CDR for all outgoing traffic from the rest of the VPN network to the site connected through the access port

The traffic on an MPLS VPN-enabled network's access port is said to be committed if the access port's incoming and outgoing traffic falls below the contracted CAR and CDR, respectively. Committed packets are delivered with a probability higher than that of uncommitted traffic.

Because of the connectionless nature of an IP VPN service, you can send packets from any site to any site within a VPN, but you must specify the committed traffic rate for a site's outgoing and incoming traffic separately. Because Frame Relay is connection-oriented, the same traffic rate applies for both ends of the circuit.

To implement CAR and CDR service on an access port, a traffic policing function for both incoming and outgoing traffic is applied. A policing function applies a higher IP precedence value for committed traffic than uncommitted traffic. In the service provider VPN backbone, the WFQ and WRED differentiated QoS functions are applied to deliver committed traffic at a probability higher than uncommitted traffic. Table 9-5 illustrates the QoS functions applied on traffic from one VPN site to the other through an MPLS VPN provider network.

Table 9-6   *MPLS VPN QoS Functions*

Step	Place of Application	QoS Function
1	Ingress router	(Option 1) CAR polices traffic on the Provider Edge router at the service provider for the incoming traffic from the Customer Edge router. Sets the IP precedence value for traffic according to the traffic profile and contract. The IP packet's IP precedence value is copied into the MPLS CoS field.
		(Option 2) CAR polices traffic on the Provider Edge router at the service provider for the incoming traffic from the Customer Edge router. Sets the MPLS CoS value for traffic according to the traffic profile and contract.
2	Service provider backbone	Traffic differentiation based on the MPLS CoS field in the MPLS backbone by using the WFQ and WRED IP QoS functions.
3	Egress router	CoS field on the MPLS label is copied to the IP precedence field in the IP header.
4	Egress router	CAR does outbound traffic policing on the Provider Edge router interface connecting to the destination Customer Edge router based on CDR.

The service provider for the VPN customer provides the CAR and CDR services for each access port, as shown in Figure 9-9. The VPN service provider provisions its network to deliver its access ports' CAR and CDR rates. Any traffic over the committed rates is dropped at a higher probability over the committed traffic.

Committed packets in a properly provisioned MPLS VPN network are delivered with a high probability and provide the same service level as CIR in Frame Relay networks.

Guaranteed QoS

Guaranteed QoS requires the use of RSVP end-to-end along the path, from the source to the destination at the VPN sites connected by the VPN service provider backbone. The extent and level of guaranteed QoS depends on which part of the network makes explicit reservations through RSVP PATH messages. The three levels of guaranteed QoS deployment are discussed next. Figure 9-10 depicts these three options, which vary primarily on the QoS offered from the VPN service provider.

Figure 9-9   *MPLS VPN Differentiated Services (Diff-Serv) QoS*

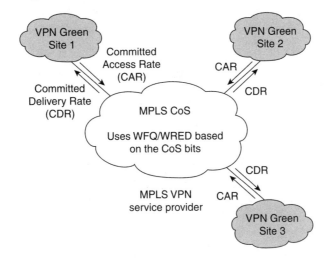

Figure 9-10   *Guaranteed MPLS VPN QoS*

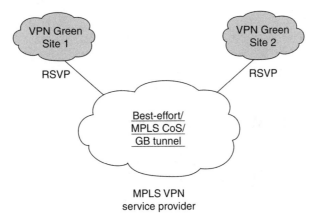

RSVP at VPN Sites Only

RSVP reservations are made only on the nodes in the VPN sites. A VPN service provider just passes any RSVP packet as it would any normal IP data packet.

This enables a customer to control resource allocation within the customer's sites to specific applications but has no effect on how the customer's traffic is handled in the service provider network.

RSVP at VPN Sites and Diff-Serv Across the Service Provider Backbone

RSVP reservations are made only on the nodes in the VPN sites. At the ingress to the VPN service provider, the guaranteed traffic is marked with a high MPLS CoS value, such that the guaranteed traffic is delivered across the MPLS VPN service provider with a high degree of probability across its network by IP QoS functions such as WFQ and WRED. The MPLS VPN service provider passes any RSVP packet as any normal IP data packet.

Thus, reserved traffic receives better service without the service provider having to keep any per-customer reservation state in the provider network.

End-to-End Guaranteed Bandwidth

Guaranteed bandwidth (GB) tunnels are used to carry traffic that requires resource reservations across a service provider backbone. The basis for a GB tunnel project is to mark a fraction of guaranteed bandwidth's queue weight as occupied.

RSVP reservations are made end-to-end from the source to the destination across the VPN service provider. Within the service provider network, these RSVP messages are carried along the GB tunnel as normal data packets.

Case Study 9-4: MPLS VPN QoS

An IP VPN service provider offers premium and standard service levels to its customers, similar to the service classes shown previously in Table 9-4. Depending on the service type, all incoming traffic from a customer is classified and differentiated in the VPN provider backbone.

Listing 9-26 shows the configuration to police traffic based on the CAR and CDR parameters on a customer VPN connection.

Listing 9-26   *Configuration for Classifying Input and Output Traffic Based on a CAR and CDR, Respectively*

```
interface Hssi2/0/0
ip vrf forwarding green
 ip address 200.200.1.1 255.255.255.252
 rate-limit input 1500000 8000 8000 conform-action set-mpls-exp-transmit 5
 exceed-action set-mpls-exp-transmit 1
 rate-limit output 1000000 8000 8000 conform-action set-mpls-exp-transmit 5
exceed-action set-mpls-exp-transmit 1
```

The incoming interfaces on the Provider Edge routers are configured to define the CAR and CDR parameters. The CAR and CDR values for the customer site are configured as 1.5 Mbps and 10 Mbps, respectively. All the VPN service provider backbone router interfaces have MPLS CoS defined to differentiate traffic based on CoS values carried in an MPLS packet.

Summary

MPLS enables packet switching based on the label information in the packet without the need to look into the packet's IP header. Packet switching is done using label swapping rather than best-match forwarding for the destination address in the IP forwarding table. An MPLS label carries three CoS bits to indicate packet precedence, similar to the precedence field in the IP header. You can use the MPLS CoS field to indicate packet precedence within the MPLS network and to deliver end-to-end IP QoS across an MPLS cloud.

One important MPLS application is MPLS-based VPNs. MPLS VPNs enable a scalable VPN solution with the help of routing protocols that restrict the topology information known to an incoming packet from a VPN site. MPLS VPNs can deliver QoS functionality based on CAR and CDR and differentiated QoS in the service provider core. GB tunnels are used to offer guaranteed VPN QoS.

Frequently Asked Questions

Q — *Does LSR and LER functionality exist in all routers?*

A — In a router environment, both LSR and LER functionality are built-in, and both functions are supported by any Cisco IOS image that supports MPLS. A router fulfills an LER or an LSR function based on its location on the edge or the core of an MPLS network.

Q — *How is label information distributed in an MPLS network?*

A — Label information is distributed in an MPLS network by using an LDP. This information also can be carried within BGP (as in MPLS VPNs), by RSVP (MPLS traffic engineering), or within Cisco's Tag Discovery Protocol (TDP), which is a precursor to LDP.

References

[1] "Multiprotocol Label Switching Architecture," E. Rosen, A. Viswanathan, and R. Callon, IETF Draft, Work in Progress.

[2] "BGP/MPLS VPNs," E. Rosen and Y. Rekhter, RFC 2547.

[3] "Multiprotocol Extensions for BGP4," T. Bates, R. Chandra, D. Katz and Y. Rekhter, RFC 2283.

[4] "Carrying Label Information in BGP4," Y. Rekhter and E. Rosen, Work in Progress.

[5] "BGP Extended Communities Attribute," R. Srihari, D. Tappan, draft-ramachandra-bgp-ext-communities.txt.

PART III

Traffic Engineering

Chapter 10   MPLS Traffic Engineering

MPLS Traffic Engineering

Traffic engineering (TE) provides the capability to specify an explicit path for certain traffic flows to take. Internet Protocol (IP) traffic is routed on a hop-by-hop basis and follows a path that has a lowest cumulative Layer 3 metric to the traffic destination. The path the IP traffic takes might not be optimal, because it depends on static link metric information without any knowledge of the available network resources or the requirements of the traffic that needs to be carried on that path.

Chapter 9, "QoS in MPLS-Based Networks," discusses Multiprotocol Label Switching (MPLS) label allocation and distribution for switching packets so that they follow the destination-based routing path. This chapter focuses on MPLS TE. In MPLS TE, a Label Switched Path (LSP) is established for carrying traffic along an explicit traffic-engineered path, which can be different from the normal destination-based routing path. Resource Reservation Protocol (RSVP) with TE modifications (TE-RSVP) is used as a signaling protocol for setting up the LSP.

For a service provider, the biggest challenge in deploying end-to-end quality of service (QoS) is the inability to determine the exact path the IP packets take. Any one router in the routed path does not predetermine the path the IP traffic takes; rather, it is a result of hop-by-hop routing decisions. IP routing behaves this way because IP is a connectionless protocol, unlike telephone networks, Frame Relay networks, or Asynchronous Transfer Mode (ATM) networks, which are connection-oriented. In Routing by Resource Reservation (RRR), MPLS circuit capabilities are exploited for IP TE. Hence, MPLS LSP-based tunnels are used for TE, and labels are used to provide forwarding along an explicit path different from the one resulting from destination-based forwarding[1].

Presently, the MPLS TE solution is limited to a single routing domain. Interior Gateway Protocols (IGPs) need extensions to support TE. At this time, only the Open Shortest Path First (OSPF) and Intermediate System-to-Intermediate System (IS-IS) protocols support extensions for TE.

The Layer 2 Overlay Model

Historically, Layer 2 overlay networks are used to engineer traffic and manage bandwidth. Layer 3 (IP) sees a logical full mesh across the Layer 2 (ATM or Frame Relay) cloud. Each router has a logical Layer 3 connection to every other router connected to the Layer 2 cloud.

Figure 10-1 shows a physical and logical Layer 3 view of such overlay models. The physical model shows Layer 3 devices—routers connected through Layer 2 (Frame Relay or ATM) switches. The switches in the network help define the exact physical path taken by any Layer 3 traffic entering the Frame Relay or the ATM cloud.

Figure 10-1 *Layer 2 Overlay Model for TE*

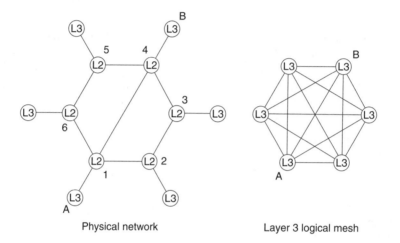

Physical network   Layer 3 logical mesh

For the traffic from Router A to Router B, for example, the Layer 2 cloud offers three physical paths: A->1->4->B, A->1->2->3->4->B, and A->1->6->5->4->B. The actual path the IP traffic takes, however, is determined by the path predetermined by the Layer 2 switches in the network. The use of the explicit Layer 2 transit layer gives you exact control over how traffic uses the available bandwidth in ways not currently possible by adjusting the Layer 3 IP routing metrics.

Large mesh networks mean extra infrastructure costs. They might also cause scalability concerns for the underlying IGP routing protocol, such as OSPF and IS-IS, as the normal IGP flooding mechanism is inefficient in large mesh environments.

RRR

Routing protocols such as OSPF and IS-IS route traffic using the information on the network topology and the link metrics. In addition to the information supplied by a routing protocol, RRR routes an IP packet taking into consideration its traffic class, the traffic class' resource requirements, *and* the available network resources.

Figure 10-2 shows two paths from San Francisco to New York in a service provider network—one through Dallas and another through Chicago. The service provider noticed that the traffic from San Francisco to New York usually takes the San Francisco->Chicago ->New York path. This path becomes heavily congested during a certain period of the day, however. It also was noted that during this period of congestion on the path from San Francisco to New York through Chicago, the path from San Francisco to New York through Dallas is heavily underutilized. The need is to engineer the traffic such that it is routed across a network by best utilizing all the available network resources. In this case, all the traffic between San Francisco and New York is getting poor performance because the network cannot use the available alternate path between these two sites during a certain period of the day. This scenario typifies the application and the need for TE. Case Study 10-1 discusses a more detailed scenario to illustrate the workings of MPLS TE.

Figure 10-2 *TE Tunnel from the San Francisco Router to the New York Router*

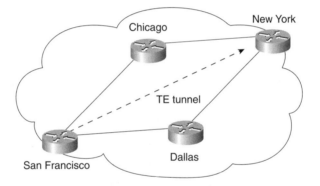

After some traffic analysis, it was clear that if all New York-bound traffic from San Francisco is carried along the path through Dallas rather than Chicago during its period of congestion, both the paths will be optimally utilized. Therefore, a TE tunnel is established between San Francisco and New York. It is called a tunnel because the path taken by the traffic is predetermined at the San Francisco router and not by a hop-by-hop routing decision. Normally, the TE tunnel takes the path through Chicago. During the period of congestion at Chicago, however, the TE path changes to the path through Dallas. In this case, TE resulted in optimal utilization of the available network resources while avoiding points of network congestion. You can set up the TE path to change back to the path through Chicago after sufficient network resources along that path become available.

RRR TE requires the user to define the traffic trunk, the resource requirements and policies on the traffic tunnel, and the computation or specification of the explicit path the TE tunnel will take. In this example, the traffic trunk is New York-bound traffic from San Francisco, the resource requirements are the TE tunnel's bandwidth and other policies, and the explicit path is the path from San Francisco to New York through Dallas.

An RRR operational model is shown in Figure 10-3. It depicts the various operational functional blocks of the TE in a flowchart format. The following sections discuss each function in detail.

Figure 10-3 *Block Diagram of TE Operation*

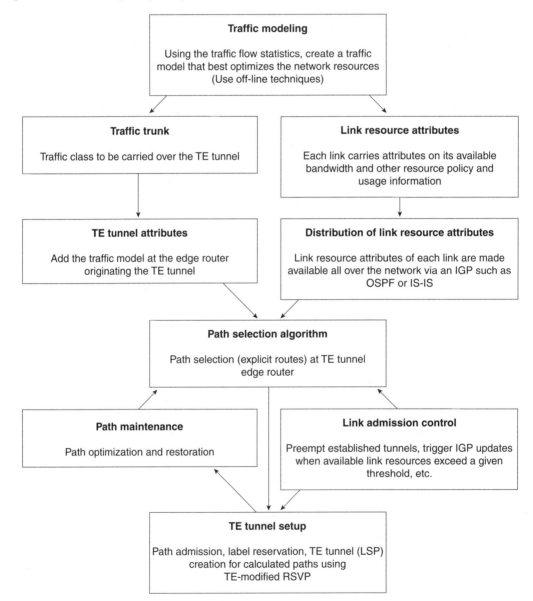

NOTE	Prior to deploying TE in a network, it is important to profile the traffic flow patterns and statistics at various points in the network. You can do this using offline tools and techniques that are beyond the scope of this book. The goal is to come up with a traffic model that best optimizes the network resources.

TE Trunk Definition

The *TE trunk* defines the class of packets carried on a TE tunnel. This policy is local to the head-end router originating the TE tunnel setup.

As discussed in Chapter 3, "Network Boundary Traffic Conditioners: Packet Classifier, Marker, and Traffic Rate Management," a traffic class is defined flexibly based on the Transmission Control Protocol/Internet Protocol (TCP/IP) traffic headers. A traffic class can be based on a single parameter, such as the IP destination or the MPLS Class of Service (CoS) field, or on a number of parameters, such as all File Transfer Protocol (FTP) traffic going from a certain sender to a specific destination. In RRR, all packets of a traffic class take a specified defined or dynamically determined common path across a network. For this reason, RRR traffic classes are also termed *traffic trunks*.

TE Tunnel Attributes

A TE tunnel is given attributes to describe the traffic trunk's requirements and to specify various administrative policies. This section discusses the various tunnel attributes.

Bandwidth

The *bandwidth* attribute shows the end-to-end bandwidth required by a TE tunnel. You can define it based on the requirements of the traffic class being carried within the TE tunnel.

Setup and Holding Priorities

The *setup* and *holding priorities* are used for admission control. *Holding priority* determines priority for holding a resource, whereas *setup priority* determines priority for taking a resource.

When resources are in *contention*, a new tunnel with a high setup priority can preempt all established tunnels in the path with a holding priority less than the new tunnel's setup priority. An established TE tunnel with the highest holding priority cannot be preempted.

Table 10-1 shows the implications of the low and high values for TE tunnel setup and holding priorities.

Table 10-1   *Implications of the Low and High Values for the TE Tunnel Setup and Holding Priorities*

	High Value	Low Value
Setup Priority	Likely to preempt established TE tunnels *(preemptor)*.	Less likely to preempt established TE tunnels *(nonpreemptor)*.
Holding Priority	Less likely to be preempted by a newly established TE tunnel *(non-preemptable)*.	Likely to be preempted by a newly established TE tunnel *(preemptable)*.

Resource Class Affinity

The *resource class affinity* attribute provides a means to apply path selection policy by administratively including or excluding specific links in the network. This resource class affinity attribute consists of a 32-bit resource affinity attribute and a 32-bit resource class mask. The *resource affinity* attribute indicates whether to include or exclude a specific link in the path computation process. Each link carries a resource class attribute, which defaults to 0x00000000 unless it is explicitly specified. The *resource class mask* shows the interesting bits of the resource class link attribute. The *resource class*, the *resource class mask,* and the *resource class affinity* attributes are related to each other as follows:

> Resource Class & Resource Class Mask == Resource Class Affinity
> where
> & indicates a bit-wise logical AND operation and
> == indicates a bit-wise logical equality.

Table 10-2 tabulates the link inclusion or exclusion policy in a TE tunnel path selection based on the resource attributes.

Table 10-2   *Policy on Including or Excluding a Link in a TE Tunnel Path Selection*

Resource Class Attribute of a Link	Resource Class Affinity of a TE Tunnel		Policy on Including or Excluding the Link in a Possible TE Tunnel Path
	Resource Class Mask	Resource Affinity	
1	1	1	Explicit inclusion
0	1	0	Explicit exclusion
1 or 0	0	0	Don't care

Path Selection Order

Path selection order specifies the order in which an edge route selects explicit paths for TE tunnels. The *explicit path* is a source route specified as a sequence of IP addresses that is either administratively specified or dynamically computed based on the shortest path meeting the constraints. Path selection order shows the order in which the administratively specified paths or the dynamically derived path is used to establish a TE tunnel.

Adaptability

The *adaptability* attribute specifies whether an existing TE tunnel needs to be reoptimized when a path better than the current TE tunnel path comes up. Reoptimization is discussed later in this chapter.

Resilience

The *resilience* attribute specifies the desired behavior if the current TE tunnel path no longer exists. This typically occurs due to network failures or preemption. Restoration of a TE tunnel when the current path doesn't work is addressed later in this chapter.

Link Resource Attributes

All links in an RRR network are described by attributes showing the available resource information and link usage policy for RRR path computation.

Available Bandwidth

The *available bandwidth* attribute describes the amount of bandwidth available at each setup priority. The available bandwidth might not be the actual available bandwidth. In certain situations, a network operator can choose to oversubscribe a link by assigning it to a value that is higher than its actual bandwidth.

NOTE   Available bandwidth for a higher setup priority should always be more than or equal to that for a lower setup priority.

Resource Class

The *resource class* attribute colors the link. As was discussed earlier in this chapter, a tunnel decides to include or exclude a link in its path selection computation based on the link's resource class attribute and its own resource class affinity attribute.

Distribution of Link Resource Information

An important underlying requirement for TE is the distribution of local link resource information throughout the RRR network. The link resource attributes are flooded across the network using extensions of the OSPF and IS-IS link-state routing protocols.

Existing link layer routing protocols flood the metric information for all the links in the network, along with the network topology information, to calculate the shortest path to a destination. In an RRR network, a routing protocol is extended to flood the resource attributes in addition to the metric information for each link.

Resource attribute flooding is independent of metric information. Link resource information flooding happens when a link state changes, the link's resource class changes, or the amount of available bandwidth crosses a preconfigured threshold. User-configurable timers control flooding frequency.

Path Selection Policy

A TE path needs to obey both the link constraints along a path and the TE tunnel requirements. The TE path computation takes the following steps:

Step 1 Considers the following attributes and information:

— TE tunnel attributes specified on the head-end router originating this tunnel.

— Link resource attributes from the entire network. They are learned through the IGP.

— Network topology information from the IGP.

— The TE tunnel's current path if the TE tunnel is being reoptimized.

Step 2 Prunes links with insufficient bandwidth or fail resource policy.

Step 3 Runs a separate Shortest Path First (SPF) algorithm to compute the shortest (minimum metric) path on the IGP protocol's link state database after removing any pruned links.

This instance of the SPF algorithm is specific to the TE path in question and is different from the SPF algorithm a router uses to build its routing table based on the entire link-state database.

An explicit path for the TE tunnel is computed from the SPF run. The computed explicit path is expressed as a sequence of router IP addresses. Upon request to establish a TE tunnel, an explicit path is used in establishing the TE tunnel based on the path selection order.

TE Tunnel Setup

TE-RSVP is used to signal TE tunnels[2]. It uses the same original RSVP messages as the generic signaling protocol, with certain modifications and extensions to support this new application. TE-RSVP helps build an explicitly routed LSP to establish a TE tunnel.

TE-RSVP adds two important capabilities that enable it to build an Explicitly Routed Label Switched Path (ER-LSP): a way to bind labels to RSVP flows and explicitly route RSVP messages. On an ER-LSP-based TE tunnel, the only sender to the TE tunnel is the LSP's first node, and the only destination is the LSP's last node. All intermediate nodes in the LSP do normal label switching based on the incoming label. The first node in the LSP initiates ER-LSP creation. The first node in the LSP is also referred to as the *head-end router*.

The head-end router initiates a TE tunnel setup by sending an RSVP PATH message to the tunnel destination IP address with a Source Route Object (SRO) specifying the explicit route. The SRO contains a list of IP addresses with a pointer pointing to the next hop in the list. All nodes in the network forward the PATH message to the next-hop address based on the SRO. They also add the SRO to their path state block. When the destination receives the PATH message, it recognizes that it needs to set up an ER-LSP based on the Label Request Object (LRO) present in the PATH message and generates an RSVP reservation request (RESV) message for the session. In the RSVP RESV message that it sends toward the sender, the destination also creates a label and sends it as the LABEL object. A node receiving the RESV message uses the label to send all traffic over that path. It also creates a new label and sends it as a LABEL object in the RSVP RESV message to the next node toward the sender. This is the label the node expects for all incoming traffic on this path.

NOTE   The RSVP RESV message follows exactly the reverse path as the RSVP PATH message because the SRO in the path state block established at each node by the PATH message defines how the RSVP RESV message is forwarded upstream.

An ER-LSP is formed and the TE tunnel is established as a result of these operations. Note that no resource reservations are necessary if the traffic being carried is best-effort traffic. When resources need to be allocated to an ER-LSP, the normal RSVP objects, Tspec and Rspec, are used for this purpose. The sender Tspec in the PATH message is used to define the traffic being sent over the path. The RSVP PATH message destination uses this information to construct appropriate receiver Tspecs and Rspecs used for resource allocation at each node in the ER-LSP.

Link Admission Control

Link admission control decides which TE tunnels can have resources. It performs the following functions:

- **Determines resource availability**—It determines if resources are available.
- **Tears tunnels when required**—It must tear down existing tunnels when new tunnels with a high setup priority preempt existing tunnels with a lower holding priority.
- **Maintains local accounting**—It maintains local accounting to keep track of resource utilization.
- **Triggers IGP updates**—It triggers IGP flooding when local accounting information shows that the available resources exceeded the configured thresholds.

TE Path Maintenance

TE path maintenance performs path reoptimization and restoration functions. These operations are carried out after the TE tunnel is established. *Path reoptimization* describes the desired behavior in case a better potential TE path comes up after a TE path has already been established. With path reoptimization, a router should look for opportunities to reoptimize an existing TE path. It is indicated to the router by the TE tunnel's adaptability attribute.

Path restoration describes how a TE tunnel is restored when the current path doesn't work. The TE tunnel's resilience attribute describes this behavior.

TE-RSVP

TE-RSVP extends the available RSVP protocol to support LSP path signaling. TE-RSVP uses RSVP's available signaling messages, making certain extensions to support TE. Some important extensions include the following:

- **Label reservation support**—To use RSVP for LSP tunnel signaling, RSVP needs to support label reservations and installation. Unlike normal RSVP flows, TE-RSVP uses RSVP for label reservations for flows without any bandwidth reservations. A new type of FlowSpec object is added for this purpose. TE-RSVP also manages labels to reserve labels for flows.
- **Source routing support**—LSP tunnels use explicit source routing. Explicit source routing is implemented in RSVP by introducing a new object, SRO.
- **RSVP host support**—In TE-RSVP, RSVP PATH and RESV messages are originated by the network head-end routers. This is unlike the original RSVP, in which RSVP PATH and RESV messages are generated by applications in end-hosts.

  Hence, TE-RSVP requires RSVP host support in routers.

- **Support for identification of the ER-LSP-based TE tunnel**—New types of Filter_Spec and Sender_Template objects are used to carry the tunnel identifier. The Session Object is also allowed to carry a null IP protocol number because an LSP tunnel is likely to carry IP packets of many different protocol numbers.

- **Support for new reservation removal algorithm**—A new RSVP message, RESV Tear Confirm, is added. This message is added to reliably tear down an established TE tunnel.

A summary of the RSVP objects that were added or modified to support TE is tabulated in Table 10-3.

Table 10-3 *New or Modified RSVP Objects for TE and Their Functions*

RSVP Object	RSVP Message	Purpose
Label	RESV	Performs label distribution.
Label Request	PATH	Used to request label allocation.
Source Route	PATH	Specifies the explicit source route.
Record Route	PATH, RESV	Used for diagnosis. This object is used to record the path taken by the RSVP message.
Session Attribute	PATH	Specifies the holding priority and setup priority.
Session	PATH	Can carry a null IP protocol number.
Sender_Template	PATH	Sender_Template and
Filter_Spec	RESV	Filter_Spec can carry a tunnel identifier to enable ER-LSP identification.

IGP Routing Protocol Extensions

The OSPF and IS-IS interior routing protocols have been extended to distribute link resource attributes along with IP reachability information. IS-IS uses a new tuple, consisting of a Type, a Length, and a Value commonly known as TLV[3], and OSPF uses Opaque Link State Advertisement (LSA)[4] to carry the link resource information. Note that the existing dynamics of IS-IS and OSPF remain the same. Only now, OSPF and IS-IS send the current constraint information whenever it needs to flood the IP reachability information. TE link admission control on a router requests reflooding of the constraint information when it sees significant changes in the available resource information, as determined by the configured threshold values.

IS-IS Modifications

The IS reachability TLV is extended to carry the new data for link resource information. The extended IS reachability TLV is TLV type 22. Within this TLV, various sub-TLVs are used to carry the link attributes for TE.

OSPF Modifications

Because the baseline OSPF Router LSA is essentially nonextensible, OSPF extensions for TE use the Opaque LSA[5]. Three types of Opaque LSAs exist, each having a different flooding scope. OSPF extensions for TE use only Type 10 LSAs, which have a flooding scope of an area.

The new Type 10 Opaque LSA for TE is called the *TE LSA*. This LSA describes routers and point-to-point links (similar to a Router LSA). For TE purposes, the existing Network LSA suffices for describing multiaccess links, so no additional LSA is defined for this purpose.

TE Approaches

The example discussed in the beginning of this chapter typifies one approach to TE— engineering traffic around points of congestion. This approach to scope TE to only a few paths might not work when other traffic in the network is carried without TE, however.

A commonly recommended approach for TE uses the full mesh of LSP-based TE tunnels between all the edge routers in a service provider network. Generally, these edge routers are customer Points of Presence (POP) routers, or routers with peer connections to other providers.

Case Study 10-1: MPLS TE Tunnel Setup and Operation

On the network shown in Figure 10-4, set up an MPLS TE tunnel from San Francisco to New York based on an explicit path and a fail-over dynamically determined path. Supply the configuration needed on all the routers in this network for establishing this tunnel. Investigate what happens if a link along the explicit path is no longer usable. In addition, study how the TE tunnel path reconverges when an established dynamic path becomes no longer usable.

Figure 10-4 *MPLS TE from the SanFrancisco Router to the NewYork Router*

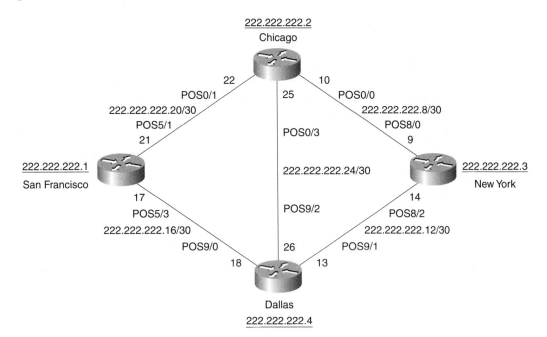

Discuss the operation of the TE tunnel and the TE extensions of IS-IS and RSVP based on the various **show** and **debug** commands in the router.

All four routers are configured with the addressing scheme and connectivity, as shown in Figure 10-4. Integrated IS-IS is used as the IGP. IS-IS is set up for 32-bit-wide metric values, as opposed to normal 6-bit metrics. The loopback0 interface IP address is enabled as the router-id for MPLS TE.

To enable MPLS TE, the **mpls traffic-eng tunnels** command at both the global and interface levels is enabled. RSVP is enabled on all the interfaces to facilitate RSVP signaling to establish the TE tunnels. RSVP performs two major tasks: It distributes labels to establish a label-switched path along an explicit path for the tunnel, and it makes any necessary bandwidth reservations along the label-switched path. Weighted Fair Queuing (WFQ) is enabled on the interfaces because RSVP depends on WFQ to provide bandwidth guarantees.

Router SanFrancisco initiates the TE tunnel to the New York router. Interface tunnel0 is configured for this purpose. The tunnel mode is set to TE by the **tunnel mode mpls traffic-eng** command. A bandwidth reservation of 10 kbps is requested along the tunnel path. The setup and holding priority for the tunnel are set at 7, the highest possible priority value.

An explicit TE tunnel path through the Chicago router is specified by an explicit path named *sfny*. A path option of 1 is used to indicate that the explicitly specified path is the preferred path to establish the TE tunnel. A dynamically determined TE path is specified as the fail-over path. Note that the path option specifies a path's order of preference to be the TE tunnel path.

Listings 10-1 through 10-4 list the configuration required on each router. Note that the listings show only the MPLS-related configuration, removing any extraneous information.

Listing 10-1 *Configuration on Router SanFrancisco*

```
ip cef
clns routing
mpls traffic-eng tunnels
!
!
!
interface Loopback0
 ip address 222.222.222.1 255.255.255.255
 ip router isis isp
!
interface Tunnel0
 ip unnumbered Loopback0
 tunnel destination 222.222.222.3
 tunnel mode mpls traffic-eng
 tunnel mpls traffic-eng autoroute announce
 tunnel mpls traffic-eng priority 7 7
 tunnel mpls traffic-eng bandwidth 10
 tunnel mpls traffic-eng path-option 1 explicit name sfny
 tunnel mpls traffic-eng path-option 2 dynamic
 tunnel mpls traffic-eng record-route
!
!
interface POS5/1
 ip address 222.222.222.21 255.255.255.252
 ip router isis isp
 mpls traffic-eng tunnels
 fair-queue 64 256 36
 ip rsvp bandwidth 1158 1158
!
interface POS5/3
 ip address 222.222.222.17 255.255.255.252
 ip router isis isp
 mpls traffic-eng tunnels
 fair-queue 64 256 36
 ip rsvp bandwidth 1158 1158
!
```

Listing 10-1 *Configuration on Router SanFrancisco (Continued)*

```
router isis isp
 net 50.0000.0000.0000.0001.00
 metric-style wide
 mpls traffic-eng router-id Loopback0

mpls traffic-eng level 1
!
ip explicit-path name sfny enable
 next-address 222.222.222.22
 next-address 222.222.222.9
```

Listing 10-2 *Configuration on Router Chicago*

```
ip cef
clns routing
mpls traffic-eng tunnels
!
!
interface Loopback0
 ip address 222.222.222.2 255.255.255.255
 ip router isis isp
!
interface POS0/0
 ip address 222.222.222.10 255.255.255.252
 ip router isis isp
 mpls traffic-eng tunnels
 fair-queue 64 256 468
 ip rsvp bandwidth 1158 1158
!
interface POS0/1
 ip address 222.222.222.22 255.255.255.252
 ip router isis isp
 mpls traffic-eng tunnels
 fair-queue 64 256 36
 ip rsvp bandwidth 1158 1158
!
interface POS0/3
 ip address 222.222.222.25 255.255.255.252
 ip router isis isp
 mpls traffic-eng tunnels
 fair-queue 64 256 36
 ip rsvp bandwidth 1158 1158
!
router isis isp
 net 50.0000.0000.0000.0002.00
 metric-style wide
 mpls traffic-eng router-id Loopback0
 mpls traffic-eng level-1
```

Listing 10-3 *Configuration on Router NewYork*

```
interface Loopback0
 ip address 222.222.222.3 255.255.255.255
 ip router isis isp
 !
interface POS8/0
 ip address 222.222.222.9 255.255.255.252
 ip router isis isp
 mpls traffic-eng tunnels
 fair-queue 64 256 36
 ip rsvp bandwidth 1158 1158
 !
interface POS8/2
 ip address 222.222.222.14 255.255.255.252
 ip router isis isp
 mpls traffic-eng tunnels
 fair-queue 64 256 36
 ip rsvp bandwidth 1158 1158
 !
router isis isp
 net 50.0000.0000.0000.0003.00
 metric-style wide
 mpls traffic-eng router-id Loopback0
 mpls traffic-eng level-1
 !
```

Listing 10-4 *Configuration on Router Dallas*

```
clns routing
mpls traffic-eng tunnels
 !
interface Loopback0
 ip address 222.222.222.4 255.255.255.255
 ip router isis isp

interface POS9/0
 ip address 222.222.222.18 255.255.255.252
 ip router isis isp
 mpls traffic-eng tunnels
 fair-queue 64 256 36
 ip rsvp bandwidth 1158 1158
 !
interface POS9/1
 ip address 222.222.222.13 255.255.255.252
 ip router isis isp
 mpls traffic-eng tunnels
 fair-queue 64 256 36
 ip rsvp bandwidth 1158 1158
 !
interface POS9/2
 ip address 222.222.222.26 255.255.255.252
 ip router isis isp
```

Listing 10-4 *Configuration on Router Dallas (Continued)*

```
mpls traffic-eng tunnels
fair-queue 64 256 36
ip rsvp bandwidth 1158 1158
!
router isis isp
net 50.0000.0000.0000.0004.00
metric-style wide
mpls traffic-eng router-id Loopback0
mpls traffic-eng level-1
!
```

After enabling the preceding configurations on the routers, check the TE tunnel's status by using the **show mpls traffic-eng tunnel tunnel0** command. Listing 10-5 shows the output of this command. The output shows the tunnel's status and the path option used in setting up the tunnel. In addition, it shows the tunnel configuration and the RSVP signaling information.

Listing 10-5 *The show mpls traffic-eng tunnel tunnel0 Command Output When the Tunnel Is Taking the Path of the Administratively Defined Explicit Route*

```
SanFrancisco#sh mpls tr tun t0

Name: SanFrancisco_t0                    (Tunnel0) Destination: 222.222.222.3
  Status:
    Admin: up        Oper: up      Path: valid      Signalling: connected

    path option 1, type explicit sfny (Basis for Setup, path weight 20)
    path option 2, type dynamic

  Config Paramters:
    Bandwidth:  10       Priority: 7  7    Affinity: 0x0/0xFFFF
    AutoRoute:  enabled    LockDown: disabled

  InLabel  :  -
  OutLabel : POS5/1, 26
  RSVP Signalling Info:
      Src 222.222.222.1, Dst 222.222.222.3, Tun_Id 0, Tun_Instance 1
    RSVP Path Info:
      My Address: 222.222.222.1
      Explicit Route: 222.222.222.22 222.222.222.9
      Record    Route:
      Tspec: ave rate=10 kbits, burst=1000 bytes, peak rate=10 kbits
    RSVP Resv Info:
      Record    Route: 222.222.222.9 222.222.222.22
      Fspec: ave rate=10 kbits, burst=1000 bytes, peak rate=Inf
```

As is evident from the output shown, the tunnel was set up by using the user-given explicit path through Chicago. RSVP signaling shows the label 26 and the outgoing interface POS5/1 used to send packets on the tunnel path. Because the Record Route option was enabled using the **tunnel mpls traffic-eng record-route** command on the TE tunnel, the RSVP RESV information records the route taken by it.

After the tunnel has been operational, assume that the link from Chicago to New York becomes no longer usable in the tunnel path. The Chicago-to-New York link can be made unusable by just bringing down the link, or by changing the local link resource class attribute. In this case study, the resource class attribute on the link from the Chicago router to the NewYork router is changed to 0x1. Therefore, a bit-wise logical AND operation between the link resource class (0x1) and the tunnel resource class mask (0x0000FFFF) is not logically equal to the tunnel resource affinity value (0x0000). Hence, the link cannot be used in the tunnel path.

The resource class attribute on the link from the Chicago router to the NewYork router is changed to 0x1 by using the **mpls traffic-eng attribute-flag 0x1** configuration command on the Chicago router's POS0/0 interface.

This local link resource attribute change on the Chicago router makes the explicit path unusable because it fails the resource affinity test.

Hence, the TE tunnel path falls over to a dynamically selected path. While selecting a dynamic path, the router removes the Chicago-to-NewYork link for the network topology based on its local link resource policy. The router recomputes the TE tunnel path to run through Dallas by running an instance of the SPF algorithm for the tunnel.

Listing 10-6 shows the output of the **show mpls traffic-eng tunnel tunnel0** command when the tunnel path is taking the dynamic path through the Dallas router.

Listing 10-6   *The **show mpls traffic-eng tunnel tunnel0** Command Output When the Tunnel Path Is Taking the Dynamic Path Through the Dallas Router*

```
SanFrancisco#sh mpls tr tun t0

Name: SanFrancisco_t0                        (Tunnel0) Destination: 222.222.222.3
  Status:
    Admin: up          Oper: up     Path: valid       Signalling: connected

    path option 2, type dynamic (Basis for Setup, path weight 20)
    path option 1, type explicit sfny

  Config Paramters:
    Bandwidth: 10       Priority: 7  7   Affinity: 0x0/0xFFFF
    AutoRoute:  enabled    LockDown: disabled

  InLabel  :  -
  OutLabel : POS5/3, 26
  RSVP Signalling Info:
      Src 222.222.222.1, Dst 222.222.222.3, Tun_Id 0, Tun_Instance 2
    RSVP Path Info:
      My Address: 222.222.222.1
      Explicit Route: 222.222.222.18 222.222.222.14 222.222.222.3
      Record   Route:
```

Listing 10-6   *The **show mpls traffic-eng tunnel tunnel0** Command Output When the Tunnel Path Is Taking the Dynamic Path Through the Dallas Router (Continued)*

```
    Tspec: ave rate=10 kbits, burst=1000 bytes, peak rate=10 kbits
  RSVP Resv Info:
    Record    Route: 222.222.222.14 222.222.222.18
    Fspec: ave rate=10 kbits, burst=1000 bytes, peak rate=Inf
```

After the path through Chicago is established, once again a link in the tunnel path becomes unusable. The local resource attribute on the link from the SanFrancisco router to the Dallas router is changed to 0x1, making the established TE path no longer usable. Hence, taking into consideration the new local link resource attributes, the SanFrancisco router chooses the TE path through the Chicago and Dallas routers for the path to the NewYork router.

Listing 10-7 shows the output of the **show mpls traffic-eng tunnel tunnel0** command when the tunnel path is taking the dynamic path through the Chicago and Dallas routers to go to the NewYork router.

Listing 10-7   *The **show mpls traffic-eng tunnel tunnel0** Command Output on the SanFrancisco Router When the Tunnel Path Is Taking the Dynamically Determined Path via Chicago and Dallas to Go to New York*

```
SanFrancisco#sh mpls traffic-eng tunnel t0

Name: SanFrancisco_t0                    (Tunnel0) Destination: 222.222.222.3
  Status:
    Admin: up         Oper: up     Path: valid      Signalling: connected

    path option 2, type dynamic (Basis for Setup, path weight 30)
    path option 1, type explicit sfny

  Config Paramters:
    Bandwidth:  10        Priority: 7  7   Affinity: 0x0/0xFFFF
    AutoRoute:  enabled   LockDown: disabled

  InLabel  :  -
  OutLabel : POS5/0, 26
  RSVP Signalling Info:
       Src 222.222.222.1, Dst 222.222.222.3, Tun_Id 0, Tun_Instance 2
    RSVP Path Info:
      My Address: 222.222.222.1
      Explicit Route: 222.222.222.22 222.222.222.26 222.222.222.14 222.222.222.3
      Record    Route:
      Tspec: ave rate=10 kbits, burst=1000 bytes, peak rate=10 kbits
    RSVP Resv Info:
      Record    Route: 222.222.222.14 222.222.222.26 222.222.222.22
      Fspec: ave rate=10 kbits, burst=1000 bytes, peak rate=Inf
SanFrancisco#
```

The preceding example on the SanFrancisco router shows that the TE tunnel path to NewYork is now established through the Chicago and Dallas routers.

To learn more about how the MPLS TE tunnel operates, look at Listing 10-8. It shows the relevant beginning section of the **show interface tunnel0** command output. The **show isis mpls traffic tunnel** command can also be used to check on the established TE tunnels. Its output is shown in Listing 10-9.

Listing 10-8   *The **show interface tunnel0** Command Output*

```
SanFrancisco#sh interface tunnel 0
Tunnel0 is up, line protocol is up
  Hardware is Tunnel
  Interface is unnumbered.  Using address of Loopback0 (222.222.222.1)
  MTU 1496 bytes, BW 9 Kbit, DLY 500000 usec, rely 255/255, load 1/255
  Encapsulation TUNNEL, loopback not set
  Keepalive set (10 sec)
  Tunnel source 222.222.222.1, destination 222.222.222.3
  Tunnel protocol/transport Label Switching, key disabled, sequencing disabled
  Checksumming of packets disabled,  fast tunneling enabled
```

Listing 10-9   *The **show isis mpls traffic tunnel** Command Output*

```
SanFrancisco# sh isis mpls traffic-eng tunnel
System Id           Tunnel Name   Bandwidth    Nexthop          Metric   Mode
NewYork.00          Tunnel0       100000       222.222.222.3
```

Listings 10-10 and 10-11 use commands that show the operation of IS-IS with TE extensions. IS-IS with TE extensions not only gives the network topology with the link metric information, but also carries TE attributes of all the links in the network. Listing 10-10 shows the output of a command to show the MPLS TE attributes of all the MPLS-enabled links on the Chicago router with a router-id of 222.222.222.2.

Listing 10-10   *A Display of the MPLS Traffic Engineering Attributes of All the MPLS-Enabled Links on the Chicago Router with a router-id of 222.222.222.2*

```
4c7507=R1#sh mpls traffic-eng topology 222.222.222.2

IGP Id: 0000.0000.0002.00, MPLS TE Id:222.222.222.2 Router Node, Internal Node_id 3
     link[0 ]:Nbr IGP Id: 0000.0000.0004.00, nbr_node_id:2
         Intf Address:222.222.222.25, Nbr Intf Address:222.222.222.26
         admin_weight:10, affinity_bits:0x0
         max_link_bw:1544 max_link_reservable: 1158
               allocated     reservable       allocated     reservable
               ---------     ----------       ---------     ----------
         bw[0]: 0            1158       bw[1]: 0            1158
         bw[2]: 0            1158       bw[3]: 0            1158
         bw[4]: 0            1158       bw[5]: 0            1158
         bw[6]: 0            1158       bw[7]: 10           1148

     link[1 ]:Nbr IGP Id: 0000.0000.0001.00, nbr_node_id:1
         Intf Address:222.222.222.22, Nbr Intf Address:222.222.222.21
         admin_weight:10, affinity_bits:0x0
         max_link_bw:1544 max_link_reservable: 1158
               allocated     reservable       allocated     reservable
```

Listing 10-10 *A Display of the MPLS Traffic Engineering Attributes of All the MPLS-Enabled Links on the Chicago Router with a router-id of 222.222.222.2 (Continued)*

```
           ---------   ----------      ---------   ----------
      bw[0]: 0             1158      bw[1]: 0          1158
      bw[2]: 0             1158      bw[3]: 0          1158
      bw[4]: 0             1158      bw[5]: 0          1158
      bw[6]: 0             1158      bw[7]: 0          1158

   link[2 ]:Nbr IGP Id: 0000.0000.0003.00, nbr_node_id:4
      Intf Address:222.222.222.10, Nbr Intf Address:222.222.222.9
      admin_weight:10, affinity_bits:0x1
      max_link_bw:1544 max_link_reservable: 1158
           allocated   reservable     allocated   reservable
           ---------   ----------      ---------   ----------
      bw[0]: 0             1158      bw[1]: 0          1158
      bw[2]: 0             1158      bw[3]: 0          1158
      bw[4]: 0             1158      bw[5]: 0          1158
      bw[6]: 0             1158      bw[7]: 0          1158
SanFrancisco#
```

Each router in MPLS TE advertises its own link attributes to the rest of the network using IS-IS extensions. The **show isis mpls traffic-eng advertise** command shows the TE attributes being advertised by a router. Listing 10-11 shows the output of this command on the SanFrancisco router.

Listing 10-11 *TE Attributes Being Advertised by the SanFrancisco Router*

```
SanFrancisco#sh isis mpls traffic-eng advertise
  System ID: SanFrancisco.00
  Router ID: 222.222.222.1
  Link Count: 2
    Link[1]
      Neighbor System ID: W1-R2c4500m=R2.00 (broadcast link)
      Interface IP address: 222.222.222.21
      Neighbor IP Address: 222.222.222.22
      Admin. Weight: 10
      Physical BW: 1544000 bits/sec
      Reservable BW: 1158000 bits/sec
      BW unreserved[0]: 1158000 bits/sec, BW unreserved[1]: 1158000 bits/sec
      BW unreserved[2]: 1158000 bits/sec, BW unreserved[3]: 1158000 bits/sec
      BW unreserved[4]: 1158000 bits/sec, BW unreserved[5]: 1158000 bits/sec
      BW unreserved[6]: 1158000 bits/sec, BW unreserved[7]: 1148000 bits/sec
      Affinity Bits: 0x00000000
    Link[2]
      Neighbor System ID: Y1-R5c7513=R4.00 (broadcast link)
      Interface IP address: 222.222.222.17
      Neighbor IP Address: 222.222.222.18
      Admin. Weight: 10
      Physical BW: 1544000 bits/sec
      Reservable BW: 1158000 bits/sec
      BW unreserved[0]: 1158000 bits/sec, BW unreserved[1]: 1168000 bits/sec
      BW unreserved[2]: 1158000 bits/sec, BW unreserved[3]: 1158000 bits/sec
```

continues

Listing 10-11 *TE Attributes Being Advertised by the SanFrancisco Router (Continued)*

```
        BW unreserved[4]: 1158000 bits/sec, BW unreserved[5]: 1158000 bits/sec
        BW unreserved[6]: 1158000 bits/sec, BW unreserved[7]: 1158000 bits/sec
        Affinity Bits: 0x00000001
SanFrancisco#
```

By default, an operational TE tunnel is not installed in the routing table or announced by IS-IS. The **tunnel mpls traffic-eng autoroute announce** command is used to install the MPLS tunnel in the routing table and announce it through IS-IS. Listing 10-12 shows output of the **show ip route** command to the tunnel destination before and after enabling the **autoroute announce** command.

Listing 10-12 *Route to the Tunnel Destination 222.222.222.3 Before and After the Tunnel Is Installed in the Routing Table*

```
SanFrancisco#show ip route 222.222.222.3
Routing entry for 222.222.222.3/32
  Known via "isis", distance 115, metric 30, type level-1
  Redistributing via isis
  Last update from 222.222.222.22 on POS5/1, 00:02:07 ago
  Routing Descriptor Blocks:
  * 222.222.222.22, from 222.222.222.3, via POS5/1
      Route metric is 30, traffic share count is 1
    222.222.222.18, from 222.222.222.3, via POS5/3
      Route metric is 30, traffic share count is 1

SanFrancisco(config)#int t0
SanFrancisco(config-if)#tunnel mpls traffic-eng autoroute announce

SanFrancisco#sh ip route 222.222.222.3
Routing entry for 222.222.222.3/32
  Known via "isis", distance 115, metric 30, type level-1
  Redistributing via isis
  Last update from 222.222.222.3 on Tunnel0, 00:00:01 ago
  Routing Descriptor Blocks:
  * 222.222.222.3, from 222.222.222.3, via Tunnel0
      Route metric is 30, traffic share count is 1
```

Listing 10-13 shows the information on the tunnel destination 222.222.222.3 in the Cisco Express Forwarding (CEF) table by using the **show ip cef 222.222.222.3 internal** command. This command output shows the label imposed on the traffic to the tunnel destination.

Listing 10-13 *Information on the Tunnel Destination 222.222.222.3 in the CEF Table*

```
SanFrancisco#sh ip cef 222.222.222.3 internal
222.222.222.3/32, version 253
0 packets, 0 bytes
  has label information: local label: tunnel head
  fast label rewrite: Tu0, point2point, labels imposed 26
  via 222.222.222.3, Tunnel0, 0 dependencies
    next hop 222.222.222.3, Tunnel0
    valid adjacency
```

RSVP establishes labels to create a label-switched MPLS tunnel path. Each router keeps a label forwarding table to switch packets based on their incoming label. Listing 10-14 shows the label forwarding tables on the routers in the TE tunnel path to the destination. Note that the Dallas router removes the MPLS label before sending the packet to the destination NewYork router. Hence, the NewYork router's label forwarding table is not shown in this example.

Listing 10-14 *Information on the Label Forwarding Table on the SanFrancisco, Chicago, and Dallas Routers*

```
SanFrancisco#sh mpls forwarding-table 222.222.222.3 32 detail
Local  Outgoing     Prefix            Bytes mpls  Outgoing   Next Hop
label  label or VC  or Tunnel Id       switched   interface
Tun hd Unlabeled    222.222.222.3/32  0            Tu0       point2point
          MAC/Encaps=4/8, MTU=1500, Label Stack{26}, via POS5/1
          0F008847 0001A000

Chicago#sh mpls forwarding-table
Local  Outgoing     Prefix            Bytes mpls  Outgoing   Next Hop
label  label or VC  or Tunnel Id       switched   interface
26     30           222.222.222.1 0 [1] 0          POS0/3    point2point
Chicago#

Dallas#sh mpls forwarding-table
Local  Outgoing     Prefix            Bytes mpls  Outgoing   Next Hop
label  label or VC  or Tunnel Id       switched   interface
30     Pop label    222.222.222.1 0 [1] 0          POS9/1    point2point
```

Figure 10-5 shows how packets are label-switched along the TE tunnel's path. The SanFrancisco router imposes a label of 26 and sends all traffic destined to or through the tunnel destination on interface POS5/1. The Chicago router receives the packet with an incoming label of 26. Based on its label forwarding table, the Chicago router swaps the incoming label in the packet with an outgoing label of 30 and sends it on interface POS0/3. The packet now arrives on the Dallas router with an incoming label of 30. Because Dallas is the penultimate hop before the destination, it removes the MPLS label and sends it toward the destination through interface POS9/1.

Figure 10-5 *LSP for the TE Tunnel from San Francisco to New York*

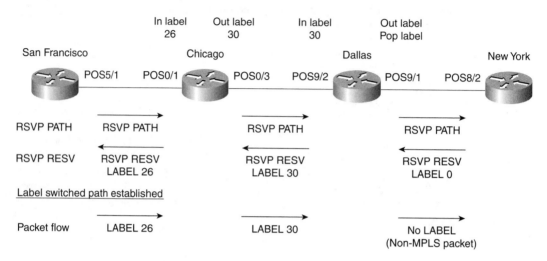

As noted previously, RSVP is used to establish TE tunnels. On the Chicago router, debug information is captured to show the contents of the RSVP messages used to establish the tunnel. Listings 10-15 and 10-16 display the contents of the RSVP PATH and RESV messages, respectively, as seen by the Chicago router. Note the new and modified RSVP objects and the information they carried.

Listing 10-15 *RSVP PATH Message That the Chicago Router Receives from the SanFrancisco Router*

```
RSVP: version:1 flags:0000 type:PATH cksum:0000 ttl:254 reserved:0 length:248
  SESSION              type 7 length 16:
      Destination 222.222.222.3, TunnelId 0, Source 222.222.222.1
  HOP                  type 1 length 12: DEDEDE15
                                       : 00000000
  TIME_VALUES          type 1 length 8 : 00007530
  EXPLICIT_ROUTE       type 1 length 28:
      (#1) Strict IPv4 Prefix, 8 bytes, 222.222.222.22/32
      (#2) Strict IPv4 Prefix, 8 bytes, 222.222.222.26/32
      (#3) Strict IPv4 Prefix, 8 bytes, 222.222.222.14/32
  LABEL_REQUEST        type 1 length 8 : 00000800
  SESSION_ATTRIBUTE    type 7 length 24:
      setup_pri: 7, reservation_pri: 7 MAY REROUTE
      SESSION_NAME:SanFrancisco_t0
  SENDER_TEMPLATE      type 7 length 12:
      Source 222.222.222.1, tunnel_id 1
  SENDER_TSPEC         type 2 length 36:
      version=0, length in words=7
      service id=1, service length=6
      parameter id=127, flags=0, parameter length=5
      average rate=1250 bytes/sec, burst depth=1000 bytes
```

Listing 10-15 *RSVP PATH Message That the Chicago Router Receives from the SanFrancisco Router (Continued)*

```
           peak rate    =1250 bytes/sec
           min unit=0 bytes, max unit=0 bytes
    ADSPEC                 type 2 length 84:
    version=0  length in words=19
    General Parameters  break bit=0  service length=8
                                        IS Hops:0
                   Minimum Path Bandwidth (bytes/sec):2147483647
                        Path Latency (microseconds):0
                                       Path MTU:-1
    Guaranteed Service  break bit=0  service length=8
                         Path Delay (microseconds):0
                         Path Jitter (microseconds):0
             Path delay since shaping (microseconds):0
             Path Jitter since shaping (microseconds):0
    Controlled Load Service  break bit=0  service length=0
    RECORD_ROUTE          type 1 length 12:
        (#1) IPv4 address, 222.222.222.21/32
```

Note the Explicit Route object in the RSVP PATH message that gives the exact path to be taken by the RSVP PATH message to establish the label-switched tunnel path. It also carries a LABEL REQUEST object to request label distribution and a RECORD ROUTE object to record the path taken by the message.

Listing 10-16 *RSVP RESV Message Sent by the Chicago Router to the SanFranciso Router*

```
RSVP: version:1 flags:0000 type:RESV cksum:D748 ttl:255 reserved:0 length:136
SESSION           type 7 length 16:
     Destination 222.222.222.3, TunnelId 0, Source 222.222.222.1
  HOP              type 1 length 12: DEDEDE16
                                   : 00000000
  TIME_VALUES      type 1 length 8 : 00007530
  STYLE            type 1 length 8 :
     RSVP_SE_OPTION
  FLOWSPEC         type 2 length 36:
     version = 0 length in words = 7
     service id = 5, service length = 6
     tspec parameter id = 127, tspec flags = 0, tspec length = 5
     average rate = 1250 bytes/sec, burst depth = 1000 bytes
     peak rate    = 2147483647 bytes/sec
     min unit = 0 bytes, max unit = 0 bytes
  FILTER_SPEC      type 7 length 12:
     Source 222.222.222.1, tunnel_id 1
  LABEL            type 1 length 8 : 0000001A
  RECORD_ROUTE     type 1 length 28:
     (#1) IPv4 address, 222.222.222.14/32
     (#2) IPv4 address, 222.222.222.26/32
     (#3) IPv4 address, 222.222.222.22/32
```

Note that the RSVP RESV message carries the LABEL 0x1A (26 in decimal) and the FLOWSPEC information. Its RECORD ROUTE object recorded the path taken by the message. The RSVP session and the installed reservation are shown in Listing 10-17.

Listing 10-17 *The RSVP Session and Installed Reservation Information from the SanFrancisco Router*

```
SanFrancisco#show ip rsvp host sender
To              From            Pro DPort Sport Prev Hop      I/F  BPS  Bytes
222.222.222.3   222.222.222.1   0   0     1                        10K   1K


SanFrancisco#show ip rsvp installed
RSVP: POS5/1
BPS   To              From            Protoc DPort  Sport  Weight Conversation
10K   222.222.222.3   222.222.222.1   0      0      1      4      264
```

By default, the Time-to-Live (TTL) value in the IP header is copied to the TTL value on the MPLS header at the edge router to a label-switched path. Hence, a trace route utility would normally show all the hops in a label-switched tunnel path. You can mask the label-switched hops in a network from outside users, however, by not copying the TTL value of the IP header into the MPLS header at the edge of the MPLS network. Listing 10-18 shows the output of a trace route utility on the SanFrancisco router before and after enabling the **no mpls ip propagate-ttl** command.

Listing 10-18 *The traceroute Utility Output With and Without Setting the IP Header TTL Value in the MPLS Label*

```
SanFrancisco#trace 222.222.222.3

Type escape sequence to abort.
Tracing the route to 222.222.222.3

  1 222.222.222.22 12 msec 8 msec 8 msec
  2 222.222.222.26 12 msec 8 msec 12 msec
  3 222.222.222.14 12 msec 8 msec *

SanFrancisco(config)#no  mpls ip propagate-ttl

SanFrancisco#trace 222.222.222.3

Type escape sequence to abort.
Tracing the route to 222.222.222.3

  1 222.222.222.14 8 msec 8 msec *
SanFrancisco#
```

Summary

MPLS TE uses MPLS' circuit-switching properties to engineer TE tunnels with adequate reserved resources along the tunnel path based on the traffic carried by the tunnel. TE-RSVP is used to establish the LSP-based TE path for a TE tunnel. TE extensions for OSPF and IS-IS enable them to carry the available link resource information all over the network.

The famous quote on TE by Mike O'Dell of UUNET—"The efficacy with which one uses the available bandwidth in the transmission fabric directly drives the fundamental 'manufacturing efficiency' of the business and its cost structure"—eloquently captures the reasoning for TE.

Frequently Asked Questions

Q — *What is the tie-breaking mechanism to determine the path of a TE tunnel if two multiple paths to the tunnel destination exist in the routing table?*

A — If multiple paths are available to the tunnel destination, the tunnel path is chosen based on the following criteria, in the order in which they are listed here:

- **Metric**—The lowest metric (cost) path always wins.
- **Bandwidth**—The path with the most available bandwidth.
- **Hops**—The path with the least number of hops.
- **First path**—The first path it finds.

Q — *What is the difference between a TE trunk, a TE tunnel, and a TE path?*

A — A TE trunk defines the class of packets carried on a TE tunnel. A TE tunnel is an MPLS-based unidirectional IP tunnel between a source and a destination. A TE path is the path taken by the TE tunnel. It is determined by RRR and established by TE-RSVP.

Q — *What are the differences between the application and operation of RSVP and TE-RSVP?*

A — The application of the original RSVP and TE-RSVP differs greatly. Table 10-4 attempts to capture some of the important differences between their application and operation.

Table 10-4   *Comparison Between the Operation of RSVP and TE-RSVP*

	RSVP	TE-RSVP
Application	Signals resource requirements for resource allocations along the path.	Establishes a label-switched path with or without resource allocations.
State Information	Per-flow basis.	Per traffic trunk.
Path Taken by the RSVP Messages	RSVP messages take the path of the normal destination-based routed path taken by the data packets.	Messages not bound by destination-based routing.
Control of Resource Allocations	Receiver-controlled.	Sender-controlled.
RSVP Session	Between hosts.	Between routers.

References

[1] "Requirements for Traffic Engineering Over MPLS," D. Awduche et al., draft-ietf-mpls-traffic-eng-00.txt, work in progress.

[2] "Extensions to RSVP for LSP Tunnels," D. Awduche et al., draft-ietf-mpls-rsvp-lsp-tunnel-04.txt, work in progress.

[3] "IS-IS Extensions for Traffic Engineering," H. Smit and T. Li, draft-ietf-isis-traffic-00.txt, work in progress.

[4] "Traffic Engineering Extensions to OSPF," D. Katz and D. Yueng, draft-katz-yeung-ospf-traffic-00.txt, work in progress.

[5] "The OSPF Opaque LSA Option," R. Coltun, RFC 2370, July 1998.

PART IV

Appendixes

Appendix A Cisco Modular QoS Command-Line Interface

Appendix B Packet Switching Mechanisms

Appendix C Routing Policies

Appendix D Real-time Transport Protocol (RTP)

Appendix E General IP Line Efficiency Functions

Appendix F Link-Layer Fragmentation and Interleaving

Appendix G IP Precedence and DSCP Values

Cisco Modular QoS Command-Line Interface

Modular quality of service (QoS) command-line interface (CLI) defines a new modular CLI-based QoS configuration in Cisco IOS Software. This new framework for defining QoS policies divides the QoS configuration into three modules: traffic class definition, policy definition, and policy application.

Modular QoS CLI applies equally well for various Internet Protocol (IP) QoS, Multi-protocol Label Switching (MPLS) QoS, and the Asynchronous Transfer Mode (ATM) and Frame Relay virtual circuit (VC)-based QoS models. In terms of policy definition, all QoS models share a common thread of policies. They include rate-shaping or rate-limiting policies, such as Committed Access Rate (CAR), Generic Traffic Shaping (GTS), and Frame Relay Traffic Shaping (FRTS); packet scheduling policies, such as Weighted Fair Queuing (WFQ); and packet drop policies, such as Weighted Random Early Detection (WRED).

The primary difference between the various QoS models is their traffic classification policy. IP precedence-based and Differentiated Services Code Point (DSCP)-based IP QoS differ, for example, in terms of the bits they use to define a traffic class. After a traffic class is defined, the same standard policies are used to deliver differentiated service among the classes. Similarly, IP and MPLS QoS differ only in terms of the bits in the packet header they use to define a traffic class. Frame Relay- and ATM-based QoS models differ from IP QoS in terms of their level of policy application. IP QoS policies are applied at the interface level, whereas in ATM and Frame Relay models, QoS is applied at the VC level.

In the modular QoS CLI model, you can configure QoS policies in a router in three steps, one step for each module in the new CLI model:

Step 1 **Traffic class definition**—Configuring the traffic classification policy. This is achieved using a **class-map** configuration command.

Step 2 **Policy definition**—Configuring policies on the various traffic classes defined. This is achieved using a **policy-map** configuration command.

Step 3 **Policy application**—Enabling the policy to an interface or a VC in the ATM or Frame Relay QoS models. This is achieved using the **service-policy** configuration command.

Traffic Class Definition

Traffic differentiation or classification is the first step in providing QoS differentiated services. The modular QoS CLI uses a **class-map** command to define a traffic class. Within a traffic class definition using the **class-map** command, a **match** subcommand is used to define the packets belonging to that class.

The **class-map** command is similar to the **route-map** command available in Cisco IOS. A **route-map** command is used to match packets based on packet header information such as IP address, IP precedence, and so on, and on IP routes based on information such as IP prefix, Border Gateway Protocol (BGP) autonomous system (AS) number, BGP community attribute, and so on. The **class-map** command extends **route-map** functionality by adding new packet classification means, such as matching based on Media Access Control (MAC) addresses and input interfaces.

In Listing A-1, the traffic classes *class1*, *class2*, *class3*, *class4*, and *class5* are defined based on IP precedence, DSCP, destination MAC address, input interface, and protocol information, respectively.

Listing A-1   *Traffic Class Definition Examples*

```
class-map class1
 match ip precedence 5

class-map class2
 match ip dscp EF

class-map class3
 match destination <mac-address>

class-map class4
 match input-interface Hssi0/0/0

class-map class5
 match protocol https
```

Another necessary element in the traffic classification definition is the ability to define a traffic class such that it matches all packets meeting the criteria of any or all of the previously defined classes. Two keywords—**match-any** and **match-all**—are added for this purpose. These keywords define a logical OR and a logical AND operation, respectively, on the **match** subcommands defined under the **class-map** definition. Listing A-2 defines a *class-any* traffic class that matches any traffic matching either of the previously defined *class1* and *class2* traffic classes.

Listing A-2   *Example of **match-any class-map** Keyword Usage*

```
class-map class1
 match <>

class-map class2
```

Listing A-2   *Example of* **match-any class-map** *Keyword Usage (Continued)*

```
 match <>

class-map match-any class-any
 match class1
 match class2
```

Listing A-3 defines a *class-all* traffic class that matches traffic matching both of the previously defined *class1* and *class2* traffic classes.

Listing A-3   *Example of* **match-all class-map** *Keyword Usage*

```
class-map class1
 match <>

class-map class2
 match <>

class-map match-all class-all
 match class1
 match class2
```

Policy Definition

After traffic class configuration, the next step is defining the QoS policies on the previously defined traffic classes. Policies are defined using the **policy-map** command. You can implement any QoS function as a subcommand under the **policy-map** definition. They include all edge QoS features, such as rate-limiting, rate-shaping, and IP precedence or DSCP settings, as well as core QoS features, such as WFQ and WRED.

Listings A-4 and A-5 show examples of policies meant for network boundary and core network interfaces, respectively.

Listing A-4   *Examples of Policies Meant for Network Boundary Interfaces*

```
policy-map epolicy1
 match class1
  rate-limit <>

policy-map epolicy2
 match class2
  set ip dscp EF

policy-map epolicy3
 match class3
  shape <>
  set ip precedence 4
```

In Listing A-4, **epolicy1** defines a rate-limiting policy on the *class1* traffic class, **epolicy2** sets the DSCP field to EF on the *class2* traffic class, and **epolicy3** enables traffic shaping as well as sets the IP precedence value to 4 for all traffic belonging to the *class3* class.

Listing A-5 *Examples of Policies Meant for Core Network Interfaces*

```
policy-map cpolicy1
 match class1
  bandwidth <>
  random-detect <>
```

In Listing A-5, **cpolicy1** defines a certain minimum bandwidth and WRED policies on the *class1* traffic class.

An example of a multidimensional policy configuration is shown in Listing A-6. In this example, **epolicy1** defines a traffic rate-limiting policy on traffic class *class1* and sets the IP precedence value to 3 for traffic belonging to the *class2* class.

Listing A-6 *Multidimensional Policies*

```
policy-map epolicy1
 match class1
  rate-limit <>
 match class2
   set ip precedence 3
```

Policy Application

After configuring all relevant **class-map**s and **policy-map**s, the final step is enabling the policy on an interface by associating a **policy-map** command to an interface using a **service-policy** command. An additional keyword, **input** or **output**, is used to specify whether the policy applies to incoming or outgoing packets on an interface, respectively.

Listing A-7 shows examples for enabling a policy on an interface. A **policy1** policy is applied on all the input traffic arriving on interface HSSI0/0/0. A **policy2** policy is applied on the output traffic of interface POS0/0/0.

Listing A-7 *Examples of Enabling a Policy on an Interface*

```
interface HSSI0/0/0
 service-policy input policy1

interface POS0/0/0
 service-policy output policy2
```

The **service-policy** command is also available on a per-VC basis on ATM and Frame Relay interfaces, and on a per-interface basis on logical interfaces such as Tunnel and Fast EtherChannel interfaces, provided the policies specified by the associated **policy-map** are supported over a VC or logical interface.

Hierarchical Policies

For certain applications, it is necessary to allow definition of hierarchical policies.

Given that service policies can be attached to interfaces as well as to individual VCs on a Frame Relay or ATM interface, there is already an implied hierarchy of policies that you can configure by attaching policies at different layers of the hierarchy. (You can attach one **service-policy** command to a Frame Relay interface and a different **service-policy** command to a permanent virtual circuit [PVC] on the Frame Relay interface.) In a real sense, an interface or PVC, though not defined by means of a **class-map** command, represents a traffic class that shares a common attribute. Hence, you also can configure a **service-policy** command not only on an interface or PVC, but also on a traffic class under a **policy-map** command.

Listing A-8 shows how you can apply a **service-policy** command on a traffic class to define a policy.

Listing A-8   *Attaching a Service Policy Directly to a Class*

```
policy-map policy-hierarchy
        class class1
            service-policy <>
```

To illustrate hierarchical policies, consider a policy that polices aggregate Transmission Control Protocol (TCP) traffic to 10 Mbps but simultaneously polices certain TCP application traffic, such as aggregate Telnet and File Transfer Protocol (FTP) traffic, each to 1 Mbps. Listing A-9 shows a hierarchical policy configuration for this application.

Listing A-9   *Hierarchical Rate-Limiting Policy Example*

```
class-map tcp
 match <all tcp traffic>

class-map telnet
 match <all telnet traffic>

class-map ftp
 match <all  ftp traffic>

policy-map telnet-ftp-police
 class telnet
  rate-limit 1000000
 class ftp
  rate-limit 1000000

policy-map TCP-police-hierarchical
 class tcp
   rate-limit 10000000
   service-policy telnet-ftp-police
```

In the preceding listing, the classes *tcp*, *telnet*, and *ftp* define the traffic belonging to TCP and TCP-based applications, Telnet, and FTP, respectively. A **telnet-ftp-police** policy is defined to rate-limit traffic belonging to Telnet and FTP applications to 1 Mbps each.

Finally, the **TCP-police-hierarchical** policy is defined to enable hierarchical policy configuration. This hierarchical policy rate-limits traffic belonging to the *tcp* class to 10 Mbps, while at the same time uses the **telnet-ftp-police** policy to rate-limit individual TCP-based application traffic belonging to Telnet and FTP traffic to 1 Mbps each.

Order of Policy Execution

An important issue to note in defining various QoS policies is the order (in time) of policy execution. It is necessary for a well-defined ordering among the policy features so that a user can know the effect of various QoS policy configurations.

Inter-Policy Feature Ordering

The order of policy execution in Cisco IOS with or without using modular QoS CLI (also known as inter-policy feature ordering) is shown here:

1 Input access-lists (input packet filtering)

2 Source-based QoS-label or precedence setting

3 Destination-based QoS-label or precedence setting

4 Input rate-limiting

5 Policy-based routing

6 Output access-lists (output packet filtering)

7 Output rate-limiting

8 Output drop policy (for example, WRED)

9 Output scheduling (for example, WFQ) and shaping

Apart from the QoS policies, the input packet accounting occurs immediately after the input access-lists are applied, and the output packet accounting occurs immediately before the packet goes on the wire.

Intra-Feature Execution Order

Another order of policy execution is intra-feature ordering. In intra-feature ordering (such as rate-limiting), a sequence number option is available to enable users to specify the order in which matches are applied. The sequence number also enables easy insertion of new classes into the ordering.

Consider Listing A-10, where a match against *class1* is performed prior to the match against *class2* (sequence number 10 before 20) for **policy-map** *policy1*.

Listing A-10 *Intra-Policy Execution Order*

```
policy-map policy1
 class class1
  rate-limit 10 input <>
 class class2
  rate-limit 20 input <>
```

In Listing A-11, the *policy2* **policy-map** policy matches traffic against *class2* before *class1* (sequence number 5 before 10). It illustrates how you can change the order in which policies are executed.

Listing A-11 *Intra-Policy Execution Order Changed by Modifying Sequence Number*

```
policy-map policy1
 class class1
  rate-limit 10 input <>
 class class2
  rate-limit 5 input <>
```

Packet Switching Mechanisms

A router's primary function is to switch packets efficiently and accurately. Cisco IOS supports several switching methods. Three of them—process switching, route-cache forwarding, and Cisco Express Forwarding (CEF)—are discussed in this appendix.

CEF is the recommended switching mechanism in routers of today's networks that carry thousands of short-duration flows. CEF plays a vital role in policy-routing functions requiring a route table lookup. CEF is also a prerequisite switching mechanism for certain QoS functions, such as QoS Policy Propagation using BGP (QPPB). Policy-based routing and QPPB are discussed in Appendix C, "Routing Policies."

Process Switching

In *process switching*, a packet arrives on an incoming interface and is enqueued on the input queue of the process that switches the packet. When the process is scheduled to run by the scheduler, the process looks in the routing table for a route to the destination address. If a route is found, the next-hop address is retrieved from the routing table. The Layer 2 Media Access Control (MAC) rewrite information for this next hop is derived from the Address Resolution Protocol (ARP) table, and the packet is now enqueued on the outbound interface for transmission. Process switching is slow, inefficient, and processor-intensive because every packet-switching decision involves lookups in the routing table and in the ARP table. Process switching does per-packet load balancing when multiple equal cost paths exist to a destination. Process-switching operation is depicted in Figure B-1.

Route-Cache Forwarding

Route-cache forwarding addresses some of the problems with process switching. In this method, after the first packet to a destination is process-switched, the destination address, next-hop interface, and MAC address encapsulation to that next hop are all stored in a single table called the *route cache*. You can quickly switch subsequent packets to the destination by looking up the destination in this route cache. In this method, the switching decision is made on the same receive interrupt that fetched the incoming packet. Route-cache forwarding is also commonly referred to as *fast switching*. The route-cache forwarding mechanism for packet forwarding is depicted in Figure B-2.

Figure B-1   *Process Switching Packets by Doing Internet Protocol (IP) Routing Table and ARP Table Lookups*

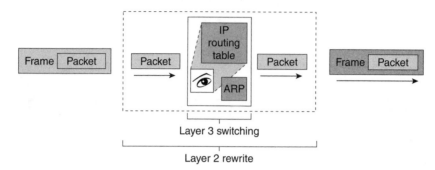

Figure B-2   *Route-Cache Forwarding Packets by Doing IP Cache Lookup*

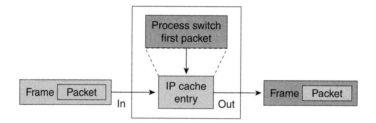

Route-cache forwarding populates a fast lookup cache on demand for destination prefixes. A route-cache entry for a destination is created only after the router receives the first packet to that destination. This first packet to a destination is process-switched, but any subsequent packets to the same destination are switched by looking them up in the faster and more efficient route cache. Route-cache entries are periodically aged out. In addition, network topology changes can immediately invalidate these entries.

This demand-caching scheme is efficient for scenarios in which most of the traffic flows are associated with a subset of the destinations in the routing table. Traffic profiles in the Internet core and in large intranets, however, no longer fit this description. Traffic characteristics have changed toward an increased number of short-duration flows, typically sourced by Web-based and interactive applications. This changed pattern of Internet traffic calls for a paradigm change in the switching mechanism—one that reduces the increased cache-maintenance activity caused by a greater number of short-duration flows and network topology changes, as reflected by the routing table.

When multiple equal cost paths exist to a destination subnet, route-cache forwarding caches /32 host prefixes for all traffic going to that subnet to accomplish load balancing.

CEF

CEF is a scalable, Layer 3 switching mechanism designed to accommodate the changing traffic characteristics and network dynamics of the Internet and of large intranets. CEF provides a number of improvements over the traditional route-cache switching approach.

CEF Advantages

CEF avoids the potential overhead of continuous cache activity by using a topology-driven CEF table for the destination switching decision. The CEF table mirrors the entire contents of the routing information; there is a one-to-one correspondence between CEF table entries and routing table prefixes. Any route recursion is also resolved while creating a CEF entry. This translates into significant benefits in terms of performance, scalability, network resilience, and functionality. CEF's benefits are most apparent in large, complex networks that have dynamic traffic patterns.

CEF also avoids performance hits during times of network instability by dropping packets without trying to process switch a packet based on the routing table when a CEF entry is missing. Because CEF is based on routing information, a missing CEF entry automatically implies a missing route entry, which itself might be due to lost peering sessions or network instability.

An *adjacency table* is maintained along with the CEF table. The adjacency table keeps the Layer 2 header information separate from the CEF table and is populated by any protocol— ARP, Open Shortest Path First (OSPF), BGP, and so on—that discovers an adjacency. Each adjacent node's link layer header is precomputed and stored along with the adjacency.

The CEF table is populated by callbacks from the routing table. After a route is resolved, its corresponding CEF entry points to a next hop, which should be an adjacency. If an adjacency is found in the adjacency table, a pointer to the appropriate adjacency is cached in the CEF entry. Figure B-3 depicts a CEF switching operation.

Figure B-3 *CEF Switching Packets by Doing CEF Table Lookup*

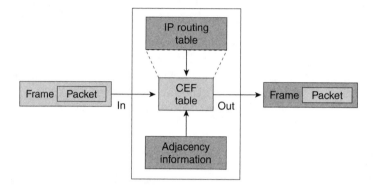

In addition to regular physical adjacencies, some special handling is also required for special adjacency types. CEF entries with prefixes that need special processing are cached with the appropriate special adjacency type. Table B-1 shows examples of these adjacency types.

Table B-1 *Examples of Certain Common Special Adjacency Types*

Adjacency Type	Reason for Special Handling
Receive	Packets to these prefixes are intended for the router. CEF entries with this adjacency are /32 prefixes of the router's IP addresses, and direct and normal broadcast addresses.
Null	Packets to these prefixes are destined to the router's Null0 interface. CEF entries with this adjacency are created for prefixes destined to the router's Null0 interface. Packets to CEF entries pointing to Null adjacency are dropped by CEF.
Glean	CEF entries with Glean adjacency are created for subnet prefixes that are directly connected to one of the router's non-point-to-point interfaces. For packets that need to be forwarded to an end station, the adjacency database is gleaned for the specific prefix.
Punt	CEF entries with Punt adjacency are created for prefixes that can't be CEF-switched because certain features might require special handling or are not yet CEF-supported.

NOTE   The Null0 interface is a pseudo-interface that functions similarly to the null devices available on most operating systems. This interface is always up and can never forward or receive traffic. It provides an alternative method of filtering traffic.

Unlike the route-cache model, which caches /32 prefixes to accomplish load balancing, CEF uses an efficient hash function lookup to provide per-source/destination pair load balancing. A hash function points to a unique adjacency for each source and destination address. In addition, CEF can do per-packet load balancing by using a pointer that moves among the equal-cost adjacencies to a destination in a round-robin manner.

Other significant advantages of CEF are extensive CEF packet accounting statistics and QoS policy propagation. Appendix C discusses QoS policy propagation.

Distributed CEF (DCEF)

CEF switching can operate in a distributed mode in routers supporting interface line cards with built-in processors. When operating in the distributed mode, the CEF table is downloaded to the router interface line cards so that the packet-switching decision can be made on the individual line cards rather than on a centralized processor card. DCEF is a prerequisite switching mechanism for all distributed QoS functions operating on the interface line cards.

NOTE   Route-cache forwarding can also operate on a distributed mode by downloading the IP cache information to the interface line cards.

Case Study B-1: Deploying CEF in a Backbone Router

Currently, an Internet service provider (ISP) has all routers in its network doing route-cache-based forwarding. The service provider network is shown in Figure B-4. The ISP wants to implement CEF-based packet forwarding in the network.

NOTE   This case study is intended to illustrate how CEF works and to differentiate it from the route-cache model. By enabling route-cache and CEF forwarding one after the other, this case study discusses the route-cache and the CEF forwarding tables on Router R2 to foster a better understanding of both route-cache forwarding and CEF. The case study also discusses the various types of CEF entries.

Figure B-4   *ISP Network Example*

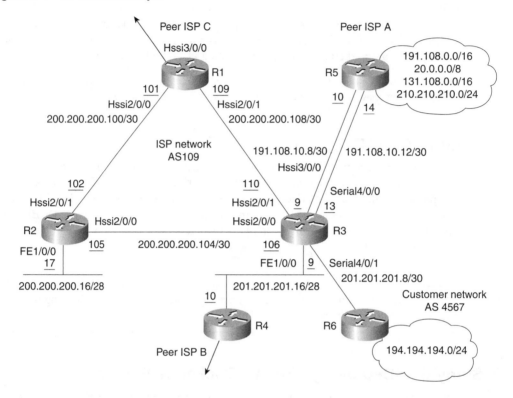

Because both CEF and route-cache model switch packets are based on routing information, first look into the routing table in Router R2. Listing B-1 shows the routing information in Router R2 by using the **show ip route** command.

Listing B-1   *Routing Table of Router R2*

```
R2#sh ip route
Codes: C - connected, S - static, I - IGRP, R - RIP, M - mobile,
B - BGP
       D - EIGRP, EX - EIGRP external, O - OSPF, IA - OSPF inter area
       N1 - OSPF NSSA external type 1, N2 - OSPF NSSA external type 2
       E1 - OSPF external type 1, E2 - OSPF external type 2, E - EGP
       i - IS-IS, L1 - IS-IS level-1, L2 - IS-IS level-2, * - candidate
default
U - per-user static route, o - ODR, P - periodic downloaded
static route
T - traffic engineered route
Gateway of last resort is not set
     200.200.200.0/24 is variably subnetted, 8 subnets, 4 masks
C        200.200.200.104/30 is directly connected, Hssi2/0/0
O        200.200.200.108/30 [110/20] via 200.200.200.101, Hssi2/0/1
```

Listing B-1   *Routing Table of Router R2 (Continued)*

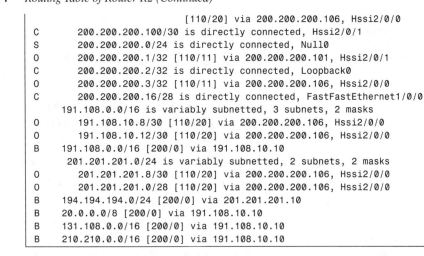

```
                              [110/20] via 200.200.200.106, Hssi2/0/0
C       200.200.200.100/30 is directly connected, Hssi2/0/1
S       200.200.200.0/24 is directly connected, Null0
O       200.200.200.1/32 [110/11] via 200.200.200.101, Hssi2/0/1
C       200.200.200.2/32 is directly connected, Loopback0
O       200.200.200.3/32 [110/11] via 200.200.200.106, Hssi2/0/0
C       200.200.200.16/28 is directly connected, FastFastEthernet1/0/0
        191.108.0.0/16 is variably subnetted, 3 subnets, 2 masks
O          191.108.10.8/30 [110/20] via 200.200.200.106, Hssi2/0/0
O          191.108.10.12/30 [110/20] via 200.200.200.106, Hssi2/0/0
B       191.108.0.0/16 [200/0] via 191.108.10.10
        201.201.201.0/24 is variably subnetted, 2 subnets, 2 masks
O          201.201.201.8/30 [110/20] via 200.200.200.106, Hssi2/0/0
O          201.201.201.0/28 [110/20] via 200.200.200.106, Hssi2/0/0
B       194.194.194.0/24 [200/0] via 201.201.201.10
B       20.0.0.0/8 [200/0] via 191.108.10.10
B       131.108.0.0/16 [200/0] via 191.108.10.10
B       210.210.0.0/16 [200/0] via 191.108.10.10
```

The IP routing table is independent of the packet switching mechanism, CEF or route-cache forwarding. It is populated mainly by dynamic routing protocols, connected subnets, and static routes.

Before enabling CEF on Router R2, use the **show ip cache verbose** command to look at the cache table used in the route-cache model. Listing B-2 shows a snapshot of Router R2's route cache table.

Listing B-2   *A Snapshot of Router R2 Doing Route-Cache Forwarding*

```
R2#sh ip cache verbose
IP routing cache 7 entries, 1196 bytes
   1967 adds, 1960 invalidates, 0 refcounts
Minimum invalidation interval 2 seconds, maximum interval 5 seconds,
   quiet interval 3 seconds, threshold 0 requests
Invalidation rate 0 in last second, 0 in last 3 seconds

Prefix/Length          Age       Interface     Next Hop
20.0.0.0/8-8           00:01:14  Hssi2/0/0     200.200.200.106
   4    0F000800
131.108.0.0/16-16      00:00:49  Hssi2/0/0     200.200.200.106
   4    0F000800
191.108.1.0/30-30      00:01:47  Hssi2/0/0     200.200.200.106
   4    0F000800
191.108.10.8/30-30     00:03:19  Hssi2/0/0     200.200.200.106
   4    0F000800
200.200.200.1/32-32    00:03:22  Hssi2/0/1     200.200.200.101
   4    0F000800
200.200.200.3/32-32    00:03:22  Hssi2/0/0     200.200.200.106
   4    0F000800
200.200.200.101/32-30  00:03:19  Hssi2/0/1     200.200.200.101
```

continues

Listing B-2 *A Snapshot of Router R2 Doing Route-Cache Forwarding (Continued)*

```
 4    0F000800
200.200.200.20/32-28   00:00:29  FastEthernet1/0/0    200.200.200.106
14    00000C31DD8B00E0B0E2B8430800
210.210.210.0/24-16    00:02:57  Hssi2/0/0            200.200.200.106
 4    0F000800
```

The cache table is always in a state of flux, as it is traffic-driven. A cache entry to a prefix is created only after the first packet to that prefix address space is process-switched. Note the following characteristics of the route-cache-based forwarding table:

- The cache table is classful. Its prefix length can only be 0, 8, 16, 24, or 32.

- A Class A, B, or C network prefix cannot have a cache prefix length of other than 8, 16, or 24, respectively.

- The length of a prefix in the cache table is equal to the most specific subnet of that particular prefix's class network in the IP routing table. The cache prefix length of the 200.200.200.0/24 address space, for example, is /32 because at least one route in the 200.200.200.0/24 address space exists with a /32 mask in the routing table.

The length of a prefix is shown in the format *x-y* in the cache table. Here, *x* indicates the actual length of the cache entry, and *y* indicates the length of the matching prefix in the routing table. A cache entry to a prefix also shows the outgoing interface, the next-hop IP address, and the Layer 2 encapsulation.

CEF is enabled on Router R2 using the global command **ip cef**. Listings B-3 and B-4 show Router R2's CEF adjacency table and CEF forwarding table.

Listing B-3 *CEF Adjacency Table of Router R2*

```
R4506#show adjacency detail
Protocol Interface              Address
IP       Hssi2/0/0              point2point(26)
                                0 packets, 0 bytes
                                0F000800
                                CEF    expires: 00:02:47
                                       refresh: 00:00:47
IP       Hssi2/0/1              point2point(16)
                                0 packets, 0 bytes
                                0F000800
                                CEF    expires: 00:02:01
                                       refresh: 00:00:01
IP       FastEthernet1/0/0      200.200.200.20(16)
                                0 packets, 0 bytes
                                00000C31DD8B00E0B0E2B8430800
                                ARP        00:08:00
```

The adjacency table shows the Layer 2 encapsulation needed to reach various directly connected routers and end-hosts. Adjacencies are discovered by means of ARP, routing protocols, or **map** configuration commands used typically on ATM and Frame Relay interfaces. The adjacencies are periodically refreshed to keep them current.

Listing B-4   *CEF Forwarding Table of Router R2*

```
R2#sh ip cef
Prefix                Next Hop            Interface
0.0.0.0/32            receive
20.0.0.0/8            200.200.200.106     Hssi2/0/0
131.108.0.0/16        200.200.200.106     Hssi2/0/0
191.108.0.0/16        200.200.200.106     Hssi2/0/0
191.108.10.8/30       200.200.200.106     Hssi2/0/0
191.108.10.12/30      200.200.200.106     Hssi2/0/0
194.194.194.0/24      200.200.200.106     Hssi2/0/0
200.200.200.0/24      attached            Null0
200.200.200.1/32      200.200.200.101     Hssi2/0/1
200.200.200.2/32      receive
200.200.200.3/32      200.200.200.106     Hssi2/0/0
200.200.200.16/28     attached            FastEthernet1/0/0
200.200.200.16/32     receive
200.200.200.17/32     receive
200.200.200.31/32     receive
200.200.200.100/30    attached            Hssi2/0/1
200.200.200.100/32    receive
200.200.200.101/32    200.200.200.101     Hssi2/0/1
200.200.200.102/32    receive
200.200.200.103/32    receive
200.200.200.104/30    attached            Hssi2/0/0
200.200.200.104/32    receive
200.200.200.105/32    receive
200.200.200.107/32    receive
200.200.200.108/30    200.200.200.101     Hssi2/0/1
                      200.200.200.106     Hssi2/0/0
201.201.201.8/30      200.200.200.106     Hssi2/0/0
201.201.201.16/28     200.200.200.106     Hssi2/0/0
210.210.0.0/16        200.200.200.106     Hssi2/0/0
224.0.0.0/4           0.0.0.0
224.0.0.0/24          receive
255.255.255.255/32    receive
```

The CEF table is stable as long as the topology, as reflected by the routing table, stays the same. All routing table entries have a one-to-one matching entry in the CEF table. CEF entries of various adjacency types in the remaining part of the case study are discussed next. Listings B-5 through B-10 show examples of the various CEF entry types.

Listing B-5   *An Example of a CEF Entry with Receive Adjacency*

```
R4506#sh ip cef 200.200.200.105
200.200.200.105/32, version 6, receive
```

CEF, in addition to maintaining a matching CEF entry for each route in the routing table, carries CEF entries with a Receive adjacency for all connected IP addresses, directed broadcast addresses (the first and the last addresses of each connected subnet) of the router, and general broadcast addresses (0.0.0.0 and 255.255.255.255). 200.200.200.105 is the IP address of the router's Hssi2/0/0 interface.

Listing B-6   *An Example of a Recursive CEF Entry with Valid Cached Adjacency*

```
R4506#sh ip cef 131.108.0.0
131.108.0.0/16, version 20, cached adjacency to Hssi2/0/0
0 packets, 0 bytes
  via 191.108.10.10, 0 dependencies, recursive
    next hop 200.200.200.106, Hssi2/0/0 via 191.108.10.8/30
    valid cached adjacency
```

The routing table entry for 131.108.0.0 has a next-hop address of 191.108.10.10, which is not a directly connected next hop. It requires a recursive lookup for the next hop for 191.108.10.10 to arrive at a right-connected next hop of 200.200.200.106 for 131.108.0.0.

CEF does a recursive lookup prior to creating a CEF entry for 131.108.10.1. Hence, 131.108.0.0 gets a connected next hop 200.200.200.106 in the CEF table.

In the route-cache forwarding model, recursive lookup for a destination, if needed, is done in the process switch path for the first packet being switched to the destination appropriate to the cache entry created. CEF precomputes recursive lookups before packet arrival. This can save some CPU cycles.

Listing B-7   *An Example of a CEF Entry with Valid Cached Adjacency with Dependencies*

```
R2#sh ip cef 191.108.10.10
191.108.10.8/30, version 17, cached adjacency to Hssi2/0/0
0 packets, 0 bytes
  via 200.200.200.106, Hssi2/0/0, 4 dependencies
    next hop 200.200.200.106, Hssi2/0/0
    valid cached adjacency
```

This CEF entry denotes four dependencies. It indicates that four recursive entries (20.0.0.0/8, 131.108.0.0/16, 191.108.0.0/16, and 210.210.210.0/24) depend on this CEF entry to resolve their next hop.

Listing B-8   *An Example of a CEF Entry for Equal Cost Paths with Per-Destination Load Sharing*

```
R2#sh ip cef 200.200.200.108
200.200.200.108/30, version 12, per-destination sharing
0 packets, 0 bytes
  via 200.200.200.101, Hssi2/0/1, 0 dependencies
    traffic share 1
    next hop 200.200.200.101, Hssi2/0/1
    valid adjacency
  via 200.200.200.106, Hssi2/0/0, 0 dependencies
    traffic share 1
```

Listing B-8   *An Example of a CEF Entry for Equal Cost Paths with Per-Destination Load Sharing (Continued)*

```
     next hop 200.200.200.106, Hssi2/0/0
     valid adjacency
 0 packets, 0 bytes switched through the prefix
```

200.200.200.108/30 has two equal cost paths and load shares on a per source-destination pair basis. (Note that the term "per-destination sharing" in Listing B-8 is not entirely accurate. It is actually "per source-destination pair load sharing.") Load sharing on a per-packet basis is also supported under CEF.

Listing B-9   *An Example of CEF Entry with Glean Adjacency*

```
R2#sh ip cef 200.200.200.16 255.255.255.240
200.200.200.16/28, version 26, attached, connected
0 packets, 0 bytes
  via FastEthernet1/0/0, 0 dependencies
    valid glean adjacency
```

200.200.200.16/28 is a directly connected subnet on the Fast Ethernet interface. Instead of creating a CEF entry for each host on this broadcast/multiaccess subnet, the subnet is installed with a glean adjacency. When sending a packet using a glean adjacency, CEF gleans the adjacency table to get the destination host's MAC address before switching the packet.

Listing B-10   *An Example of a CEF Entry with Null Adjacency*

```
R4506#sh ip cef 200.200.200.0
200.200.200.0/24, version 14, attached
0 packets, 0 bytes
  via Null0, 0 dependencies
    valid null adjacency
```

Traffic matching this CEF entry is directed to the Null0 interface.

Route-Cache Switching and CEF Switching Compared

Table B-2 compares the route-cache and CEF switching schemes.

Table B-2   *Comparison Between Route-Cache and CEF Switching Schemes*

Route-Cache Switching	CEF Switching
A cache entry is created while the first packet is being process-switched. All subsequent packets are forwarded using the cache entry created while switching the first packet.	CEF builds a forwarding table based on the routes in the routing table. A CEF entry is always available to CEF-switch a packet, as long as a routing entry is available.
Traffic-driven. Created on demand.	Topology-driven. Created to be a replica of the routing table.

continues

Table B-2 *Comparison Between Route-Cache and CEF Switching Schemes (Continued)*

Route-Cache Switching	CEF Switching
Efficient for traffic characteristics where there is a small number of long-duration flows, typically sourced by file transfer applications.	Efficient for traffic characteristics where there is a large number of short-duration flows, typically sourced by Web-based and interactive applications.
Any recursive lookup for a route is done when an initial packet to a destination triggers cache creation. The limit on depth of recursion is six.	CEF resolves any recursive lookup required for routes in the table before it installs it in the forwarding table. There is no limit on depth of recursion.
Periodic CPU spikes of cache-based forwarding mechanism and its performance hit during network instability.	No activity that causes periodic CPU spikes. Doesn't take performance hit during network instability. CEF either switches a packet or drops it.
Does destination-based load balancing. Accomplished by creating /32 cache entries for a routing entry that has multiple equal cost paths.	Does load balancing per source-destination pair. Done by a hash algorithm that takes both source and destination into consideration.
No per-packet load balancing.	Does per-packet load balancing. Accomplished by using a hash algorithm that points to possible paths in a round-robin manner.
Packets that need to be forwarded to the Null0 interface are not supported under route-cache forwarding. Such packets go through the inefficient process-switching path.	Packets that need to be forwarded to the Null0 interface can be CEF-switched and can be dropped efficiently by means of a CEF special Null adjacency.
Features such as policy routing, which need occasional route lookup, can't be supported cleanly.	Because CEF is an exact replica of the routing table, policy routing can be efficiently supported through CEF.
Doesn't provide hooks for QoS policy propagation.	Allows QoS policy information tagged to a CEF entry. A packet can be CEF-switched, taking the tagged QoS policy into consideration.

Summary

CEF is the recommended switching mechanism in today's large-scale IP networks and ISP networks. Support for some of the QoS functions can be limited to specific packet-switching modes. In particular, all distributed QoS functions, where QoS functions run on a router's individual line cards instead of on the central processor card, require distributed CEF.

Routing Policies

This appendix discusses policy routing and quality of service (QoS) policy propagation using the Border Gateway Protocol (BGP). Policy routing is used to override a router's traditional, destination-based routing function with flexible policies. QoS policy propagation uses BGP to propagate policy information over a service provider network. This appendix also briefly discusses QoS-based routing.

Using QoS Policies to Make Routing Decisions

Apart from the destination address, routing decisions should be made based on flexible policies and on the resource requirements in the network whenever appropriate. Such routing decision mechanisms provide tools for the network administrator to more efficiently route traffic across a network.

QoS-Based Routing

QoS-based routing is a routing mechanism under which paths for flows are determined based on some knowledge of the resource availability in the network as well as the QoS requirements of flows[1].

QoS-based routing calls the following significant extensions:

- A routing protocol carries metrics with dynamic resource (QoS) availability information (for example, available bandwidth, packet loss, or delay).

- A routing protocol should calculate not only the most optimal path, but also multiple possible paths based on their QoS availability.

- Each flow carries the required QoS in it. The required QoS information can be carried in the Type of Service (ToS) byte in the Internet Protocol (IP) header. The routing path for a flow is chosen according to the flow's QoS requirement.

QoS-based routing also involves significant challenges. QoS availability metrics are highly dynamic in nature. This makes routing updates more frequent, consuming valuable network resources and router CPU cycles. A flow could oscillate frequently among alternate QoS paths as the fluid path QoS metrics change. Furthermore, frequently changing routes can increase *jitter*, the variation in the delay experienced by end users. Unless these concerns are addressed, QoS-based routing defeats its objective of being a value add-on to a QoS-based network.

Open Shortest Path First (OSPF) and Intermediate System-to-Intermediate System (IS-IS), the common Interior Gateway Protocols (IGPs) in a service provider network, could advertise a ToS byte along with a link-state advertisement. But the ToS byte is currently set to zero and is not being used. QoS routing is still a topic under discussion in the standards bodies.

In the meantime, OSPF and IS-IS are being extended for Multiprotocol Label Switching (MPLS) traffic engineering (TE) to carry link resource information with each route. These routing protocols still remain destination-based, but each route carries extra resource information, which protocols such as MPLS can use for TE. TE-extended OSPF and IS-IS protocols provide a practical trade-off between the present-day destination-based routing protocols and QoS routing. MPLS-based TE is discussed in Chapter 10, "MPLS Traffic Engineering."

Policy-Based Routing

Routing in IP networks today is based solely on a packet's destination IP address. Routing based on other information carried in a packet's IP header or packet length is not possible using present-day dynamic routing protocols. Policy routing is intended to address this need for flexible routing policies.

For traffic destined to a particular server, an Internet service provider (ISP) might want to send traffic with a precedence of 3 on a dedicated faster link than traffic with a precedence of 0. Though the destination is the same, the traffic is routed over a different dedicated link for each IP precedence. Similarly, routing can be based on packet length, source address, a flow defined by the source destination pair and Transmission Control Protocol (TCP)/User Datagram Protocol (UDP) ports, ToS/precedence bits, batch versus interactive traffic, and so on. This flexible routing mode is commonly referred to as *policy-based routing*.

Policy-based routing is not based on any dynamic routing protocol, but it uses the static configuration local to the router. It allows traffic to be routed based on the defined policy, either when specific routing information for the flow destination is unavailable, or by totally bypassing the dynamic routing information. In addition, for policy-routed traffic, you can configure a router to mark the packet's IP precedence.

NOTE   Some policy routing functions requiring a route table lookup perform well in the Cisco Express Forwarding (CEF) switching path. CEF is discussed in Appendix B, "Packet Switching Mechanisms." Because CEF mirrors each entry in the routing table, policy routing can use the CEF table without ever needing to make a route table lookup.

If *netflow* accounting is enabled on the interface to collect flow statistics, you should enable the **ip route-cache flow accelerate** command. For a trade-off of minor memory intake, flow-cache entries carry state and avoid the policy route-map check for each packet of an active flow. Netflow accounting is used to collect traffic flow statistics.

Because the policy routing configuration is static, it can potentially black-hole traffic when the configured next hop is no longer available. Policy routing can use the Cisco Discovery Protocol (CDP) to verify next-hop availability. When policy routing can no longer see the next hop in the CDP table, it stops forwarding the matching packets to the configured next hop and routes those packets using the routing table. The router reverts to policy routing when the next hop becomes available (through CDP). This functionality applies only when CDP is enabled on the interface.

Case Study C-1: Routing Based on IP Precedence

An e-commerce company connects to its ISP using a high-speed DS3 connection and a lower-speed T1 link. The e-commerce company uses IP precedence to differentiate the various types of traffic based on criteria such as type of application traffic, premium user traffic, and so on. The e-commerce company wants to use the faster DS3 link for only the premium traffic set with an IP precedence value of either 4, 5, 6, or 7. The rest of the traffic carrying a low IP precedence value uses the lower-speed T1 peering to the ISP. Figure C-1 shows policy-routing traffic.

Figure C-1   *Policy-Routing Traffic Based on IP Precedence*

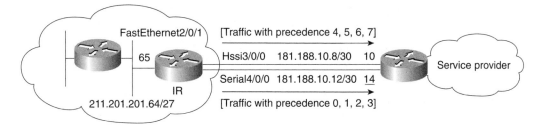

Listing C-1 shows the configuration on the Internet Router (IR) of the e-commerce company to enable the router to route packets based on their IP precedence value.

Listing C-1   *Configuration on the IR to Route Packets Based on Their IP Precedence Value*

```
interface FastEthernet 2/0/1
  ip address 211.201.201.65  255.255.255.224
  ip policy route-map  tasman

access list 101 permit ip any any precedence routine
```

continues

Listing C-1 *Configuration on the IR to Route Packets Based on Their IP Precedence Value (Continued)*

```
access-list 101 permit ip any any precedence priority
access-list 101 permit ip any any precedence immediate
access-list 101 permit ip any any precedence flash
access-list 102 permit ip any any precedence flash-override
access-list 102 permit ip any any precedence critical
access-list 102 permit ip any any precedence internet
access-list 102 permit ip any any precedence network

route-map tasman permit 10
 match ip address 101
 set ip next-hop 181.188.10.14

route-map tasman permit 20
 match ip address 102
 set ip next-hop 181.188.10.10
```

The interface FastEthernet2/0/1 is the input interface for all internal traffic. Policy routing is enabled on the input interface. All packets arriving on this interface are policy-routed based on route-map **tasman**.

access-list 101 and **access-list 102** are used to match packets with IP precedence values of 0, 1, 2, 3 and 4, 5, 6, 7, respectively.

All packets matching **access-list 101** are forwarded to the next-hop IP address of 181.188.10.14. All packets matching **access-list 102** are forwarded to the next-hop IP address of 181.188.10.10. Listing C-2 shows the relevant **show** commands for policy routing.

Listing C-2 *show Commands for Verifying Policy Routing Configuration and Operation*

```
IR#show ip policy

Interface       Route map
FastEthernet2/0/1    tasman

IR#show route-map tasman

route-map tasman, permit, sequence 10
  Match clauses:
    ip address (access-lists): 101
  Set clauses:
    ip next-hop 181.188.10.14
  Policy routing matches: 0 packets, 0 bytes
route-map tasman, permit, sequence 20
  Match clauses:
    ip address (access-lists): 102
  Set clauses:
    ip next-hop 181.188.10.10
  Policy routing matches: 0 packets, 0 bytes
```

The **show ip policy** command shows the interface(s) performing policy routing for incoming packets along the associated route map for each policy-routed interface. The **show route-map tasman** command shows the details of the route map **tasman** and the policy-routed packet statistics for each element (sequence number) of the route map.

Case Study C-2: Routing Based on Packet Size

An Internet banking company finds that certain application traffic using large packet sizes is slowing its mission-critical traffic composed of small packets (of 1000 bytes or less). Hence, the company decides to mark all its IP packets that are of size 1000 bytes or less with an IP precedence of 5.

Listing C-3 shows the router configuration to set the IP precedence value of a packet based on its size.

Listing C-3   *Router Configuration to Set Precedence Value Based on the Packet Size*

```
interface FastEthernet 4/0/1
  ip address 201.201.201.9  255.255.255.252
  ip policy route-map  tasman

route-map  tasman permit 10
  match length 32 1000
  set ip precedence 5
```

All packets with a minimum and maximum packet size of 32 and 1000 bytes, respectively, are set with an IP precedence of 5.

NOTE   A few handy pieces of information on policy-routing configuration are given here:

- Only one policy route map is allowed per interface. You can enter multiple route-map elements with different combinations of **match** and **set** commands, however.

- You can specify multiple **match** and **set** statements in a policy-routing route map. When all **match** conditions are true, all **set**s are performed.

- When more than one parameter is used for a **match** or a **set** statement, a **match** or **set** happens when any of the parameters is a successful match or a successful set, respectively.

  match ip address 101 102 is true, for example, when the packet matches against either IP **access list 101** or **102**. **set ip next-hop X Y Z** sets the IP next hop for the matched packet to the first reachable next hop. X, Y, and Z are the first, second, and third choices for the IP next hop.

- The **ip policy route-map** command is used to policy-route incoming traffic on a router interface. To policy-route router-generated (nontransit) traffic, use the **ip local policy route-map** command.

- At this time, policy routing matches packets only through IP access lists or packet length.

- Here is the evaluation order of commands defining policy routing:

```
set precedence/tos
set ip next-hop
set interface
set ip default next-hop
set default interface
```

QoS Policy Propagation Using BGP

The IP precedence value in a packet indicates its intended QoS policy. But how and when does a packet get its desired QoS policy?

In a simplistic scenario, the source machine sets the packet's IP precedence, and the packet is sent unaltered by its service provider and any other intermediate service provider domains until the packet reaches the destination. This is not entirely a practical or even desirable option, however. In most situations, the source service provider polices the incoming traffic and its service level to make sure they are within the negotiated traffic profile.

A source's own service provider can guarantee a certain service level specified by the IP precedence value within its network. After the packet leaves the service provider network to another peer service provider network that connects to the destination, however, the service provider cannot guarantee a certain service level unless it has negotiated specific Service Level Agreements (SLAs) for its traffic with its peer service providers.

This section does not go into interservice-provider QoS policy propagation, as it depends on the negotiated SLAs between service providers, but it does concentrate on propagating QoS policy information for customer networks all over the service provider network. All traffic to or from a customer gets its QoS policy (IP precedence) at the point of entry into the service provider network. As discussed earlier, an edge router of the service provider connecting to a customer can simply set with a QoS policy by writing the packet's IP precedence value based on its service level. The precedence value is used to indicate the service level to the service provider network.

Because Internet traffic is asymmetrical, traffic intended for a premium customer might arrive to its service provider network on any of the service provider's edge routers. Therefore, the question here is, how do all the routers in a service provider network recognize incoming traffic to a premium customer and set the packet's IP precedence to a value based on its service level? This section studies ways you can use BGP for QoS policy propagation in such situations.

QoS policy propagation using BGP[2] is a mechanism to classify packets based on IP prefix, BGP community, and BGP autonomous system (AS) path information. The supported classification policies include the IP precedence setting and the ability to tag the packet with a QoS class identifier, called a *QoS group*, internal to the router. After a packet is classified, you can use other QoS features such as Committed Access Rate (CAR) and Weighted Random Early Detection (WRED) to specify and enforce business policies to fit your business model. CAR and WRED are discussed in detail in Chapter 3, "Network Boundary Traffic Conditioners: Packet Classifier, Marker, and Traffic Rate Management," and in Chapter 6, "Per-Hop Behavior: Congestion Avoidance and Packet Drop Policy."

QoS policy propagation using BGP requires CEF. CEF switching is discussed in Appendix B. Any BGP QoS policy from the BGP routing table is passed to the CEF table through the IP routing table. The CEF entry for a destination prefix is tagged with the BGP QoS policy. When CEF-switching a packet, the QoS policy is mapped to the packet as per the CEF table.

Case Study C-3: QoS for Incoming and Outgoing Traffic

An ISP with QoS policies in the network starts offering premium service to its customers. The premium service offers priority for the premium customers' incoming or outgoing traffic over the other best-effort traffic in the network.

The ISP's QoS policies in the network offer precedence-based traffic differentiation, with the highest priority given to traffic with a precedence of 7 and the lowest priority given to best-effort (precedence 0) traffic. The intended premium service intends to tag premium customer traffic with a precedence of 4. Figure C-2 illustrates this operation in the service provider network.

In this case study, the service provider needs to be configured such that:

1 The premium customer traffic to the Internet gets premium service within the service provider's network. Premium customer traffic is set with an IP precedence value of 4 on its entry into the provider network so that the premium traffic gets premium service in the entire service provider network.

2 Internet traffic going to the premium customer network gets a precedence of 4 at its point of entry into the service provider's network, whether it is through routers BR-1, BR-2, or BR-3. Traffic with an IP precedence of 4 gets premium service within the entire service provider network.

Figure C-2 *IP QoS for Incoming and Outgoing Internet Traffic*

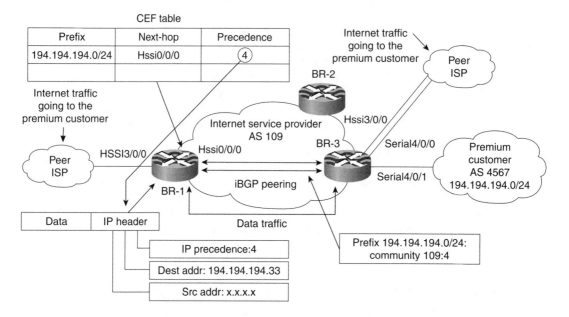

In Figure C-2, Router BR-3 connects to the premium customer. Therefore, all traffic coming from the premium customer connection gets premium service with the provider network. Premium service is identified by an IP precedence of 4 within the packet header. Internet traffic for the premium customer can arrive on either Router BR-1 or BR-3, as both routers peer with the rest of the Internet. All such Internet traffic on Router BR-1 and Router BR-3 going to the premium customer network needs to be given an IP precedence of 4.

Listing C-4 shows how to enable Router BR-3 for a premium customer and BGP policy propagation functionality for premium service.

Listing C-4 *Enable Router BR-3 with BGP Policy Propagation Functionality for Premium Service and a Premium Customer Connection*

```
ip cef

interface loopback 0
ip address 200.200.200.3  255.255.255.255

interface Serial4/0/1
ip address 201.201.201.10  255.255.255.252
bgp-policy source ip-prec-map

interface Hssi3/0/0
bgp-policy destination ip-prec-map

interface Serial4/0/0
```

Listing C-4   *Enable Router BR-3 with BGP Policy Propagation Functionality for Premium Service and a Premium Customer Connection (Continued)*

```
bgp-policy destination ip-prec-map

ip bgp-community new-format

router bgp 109
table-map tasman
neighbor 200.200.200.1 remote-as 109
neighbor 201.201.201.10  remote-as 4567
neighbor 201.201.201.10  route-map premium in

route-map tasman  permit 10
match as-path 1
set ip precedence 4

route-map premium permit 10
set community 109:4

ip as-path access-list 1 permit ^4567$
```

The **route-map tasman** command on router BR-3 sets a precedence of 4 for all routes with a AS path of 4567. In this case, it is only route 194.194.194.0/24 that belongs to AS 4567. Hence, IP precedence 4 is set on this route in the IP routing table, which is carried over to the CEF table. In addition, routes received on this peering with the premium customer are assigned a community of 109:4 using the **route-map premium** command such that routers elsewhere can use the community information to assign a policy.

Note that the **bgp-policy source ip-prec-map** command is used on interface Serial4/0/1 so that BGP policy propagation is applied on all premium customer packets. Here, IP precedence mapping is done based on the arriving packet's source address using the precedence value tagged to the source IP address's matching CEF entry. Internet traffic going to the premium customer can enter its service provider network on any of its edge routers with peering connection to other service providers. Hence, QoS policy information regarding a premium customer should be propagated all over the provider network so that the edge routers can set IP precedence based on the QoS policy information. In this example, Internet traffic for the premium customer can arrive on either Router BR-1 or BR-3.

Premium customer traffic arriving on interface Hssi3/0/0 and on Serial4/0/0 of Router BR-3 is assigned a precedence of 4. The **bgp-policy destination ip-prec-map** command is needed on the packets' input interface so that BGP policy propagation is applied on all incoming packets. Here, IP precedence mapping is done based on the packet's destination address using the matching CEF entry's precedence value for the destination address.

Listing C-5 shows the relevant BR-1 configuration that enables BGP policy propagation for premium service.

Listing C-5   *Enable Router BR-1 with BGP Policy Propagation Functionality for Premium Service*

```
ip cef


interface hssi 3/0/0
bgp-policy destination ip-prec-map
ip bgp-community new-format

router bgp 109
table-map tasman
neighbor 200.200.200.3   remote-as 109

route-map tasman   permit 10
match community 101
set ip precedence 4

ip community-list 101 permit :4$
```

In Listing C-5 of router BR-1, the **table-map** command uses route-map tasman to assign a precedence of 4 for all BGP routes in the routing table that have a BGP community whose last two bytes are set to 4. Because router BR-3 tags the premium customer route 194.194.194.0/24 with a community 109:4 and exchanges it via IBGP with routers BR-1 and BR-2, the router BR-1 tags the 194.14.194.0/24 in its IP routing table and CEF table with an IP precedence value of 4

The **bgp-policy destination ip-prec-map** command is needed on the input interface HSSI3/0 of router BR-1 for BGP policy propagation to be applied on the incoming packets from the Internet based on their destination IP address.

Summary

There is a growing need for QoS and traffic engineering in large, dynamic routing environments. The capability of policy-based routing to selectively set precedence bits and route packets based on a predefined flexible policy is becoming increasingly important. At the same time, routing protocols such as OSPF and IS-IS are being addressed for QoS support. TE extends OSPF and IS-IS to carry available resource information along with its advertisements, and it is a step toward full QoS routing. The viability of full QoS routing is still under discussion in the standards bodies.

BGP facilitates policy propagation across the entire network. CEF gets this BGP policy information from the routing table and uses it to set a packet policy before forwarding it.

References

[1] RFC 2386, "A Framework for QoS-Based Routing in the Internet," E. Crawley, et al.

[2] RFC 1771, "Border Gateway Protocol 4 (BGP-4)," Y. Rekhter and T. Li.

APPENDIX D

Real-time Transport Protocol (RTP)

Real-time Transport Protocol (RTP) is a transport protocol for carrying real-time traffic flows, such as packetized audio and video traffic, in an Internet Protocol (IP) network.[1] It provides a standard packet header format, which gives sequence numbering, media-specific timestamp data, source identification, and payload identification, among other things. RTP is usually carried using User Datagram Protocol (UDP).

RTP is supplemented by the Real-time Transfer Control Protocol (RTCP), which carries control information about the current RTP session. RTCP packets are used to carry status information on the RTP channel, such as the amount of data transmitted and how well the data is received. RTP can use this information on current packet loss statistics provided by RTCP and can request the source to adapt its transmission rate accordingly.

RTCP provides support for real-time conferencing for large groups. RTP allows flows from several sources to be mixed in gateways to provide a single resulting flow. When this happens, each mixed packet contains the source identifications of all the contributing sources.

RTP timestamps are flow-specific and, therefore, the timestamps used are in units appropriate for that media flow. Hence, when multiple flows are mixed to form a single flow, the RTP timestamps cannot ensure interflow synchronization by themselves. RTCP is used to provide the relationship between the real-time clock at a sender and the RTP media timestamps. RTCP also can carry descriptive textual information on the source in a conference.

Note that RTP does not address the issue of resource reservation or quality of service (QoS); instead, it relies on resource allocation functions such as Weighted Fair Queuing (WFQ) and on reservation protocols, such as Resource Reservation Protocol (RSVP).

Reference

[1] "RTP: A Transport Protocol for Real-Time Applications," RFC 1889, V. Jacobson, January 1996.

General IP Line Efficiency Functions

This appendix discusses the following Internet Protocol (IP) line efficiency functions: the Nagle Algorithm, Path maximum transmission unit (MTU) Discovery, Transmission Control Protocol/Internet Protocol (TCP/IP) header compression, and Real-time Transport Protocol (RTP) header compression.

The Nagle Algorithm

Terminal applications such as *telnet* and *rlogin* generate a 41-byte packet (a 40-byte IP length and a 1-byte TCP header) for each 1 byte of user data. Such small packets, referred to as *tinygrams*, are not a problem on local-area networks (LANs), but they can be inefficient in using the available bandwidth on slower or congested links. The Nagle Algorithm[1] aims to improve the use of available bandwidth for TCP-based traffic.

With the Nagle Algorithm, a TCP session works as follows. Each TCP connection can have only one outstanding (in other words, unacknowledged) segment. While waiting for the acknowledgment (ACK), additional data is accumulated, and this data is sent as one segment when the ACK arrives. Instead of sending a single character at a time, the TCP session tries to accumulate characters into a larger segment and send them after an ACK for the previous segment is received. The rate at which data is sent depends on the rate at which ACKs are received for the previous segments. This self-clocking mechanism enables a TCP session to send fewer segments on a slower or a congested link when compared to a faster, uncongested link.

You enable the Nagle Algorithm using the **service nagle** command. Though it is particularly beneficial for terminal application traffic on slower or congested links, it can be useful for most TCP-based traffic.

Path MTU Discovery

Path MTU Discovery[2] is used to dynamically determine the MTU along the path from the network's source to its destination. It helps eliminate or reduce packet fragmentation in a network that uses diverse link-layer technologies, thus maximizing the use of available bandwidth.

To determine the Path MTU, the source station sends out large packets with a DF (Don't Fragment) bit set in the IP header to the destination. When a router or a switch along the path needs to switch the packet to a link that supports a lower MTU, it sends back a "Can't Fragment" Internet Control Message Protocol (ICMP) message to the sender. A sender that receives a "Can't Fragment" ICMP message lowers the packet size and tries to discover the Path MTU once again. When a sender no longer receives the "Can't Fragment" ICMP message, the MTU size used by the sender becomes the Path MTU.

The **ip tcp path-mtu-discovery** command is used to enable TCP MTU path discovery for TCP connections initiated by the router.

TCP/IP Header Compression

TCP/IP header compression[3] is designed to improve the efficiency of bandwidth utilization over low-speed serial links. A typical TCP/IP packet includes a 20-byte IP and 20-byte TCP header. After a TCP connection is established, the header information is redundant and need not be repeated in its entirety in every packet that is sent. By reconstructing a smaller header that identifies the connection and indicates the fields that changed and the amount of change, fewer bytes can be transmitted. The average compressed TCP/IP header is 10 bytes long instead of the usual 40 bytes.

The **ip tcp header compression** command is used to enable TCP header compression on an interface.

RTP Header Compression

The RTP packets for audio application are typically small, ranging from approximately 20 to 150 bytes when carrying compressed payloads. For a typical payload, the overhead of the IP, User Datagram Protocol (UDP), and RTP headers can be relatively large. The minimum IP/UDP/RTP header is 40 bytes, considering the minimum IP, UDP, and RTP headers of 20, 12, and 8 bytes, respectively.

RTP header compression[4], using an implementation similar to the TCP header compression scheme of Request For Comments (RFC) 1144, compresses the 40-byte header, on average, to 10 bytes.

References

[1] RFC 896, "Congestion Control in IP/TCP Internetworks," John Nagle, 1984.

[2] RFC 1191, "Path MTU Discovery," S. Deering, and others, 1990.

[3] RFC 1144, "Compressing TCP/IP Headers for Low-Speed Serial Links," V. Jacobson, 1990.

[4] RFC 2508, "Compressing IP/UDP/RTP Headers for Low-Speed Serial Links," S. Casner, V. Jacobson, 1999.

Link-Layer Fragmentation and Interleaving

This appendix studies the Link-Layer Fragmentation and Interleaving (LFI) function using the Multi-link Point-to-Point (MLPP) protocol. LFI is a link-layer efficiency mechanism that improves the efficiency and predictability of the service offered to certain critical, application-level traffic.

MLPP[1] provides the functionality to spread traffic over multiple wide-area network (WAN) links running the Point-to-Point Protocol (PPP) while providing multi-vendor interoperability as well as packet fragmentation and sequencing. Chapter 8, "Layer 2 QoS: Interworking with IP QoS," discusses the Frame Relay fragmentation standard FRF.12, which performs link-layer fragmentation and interleaving functions over a Frame Relay network.

Even with scheduling algorithms such as Class-Based Weighted Fair Queuing (CBWFQ) with a priority queue and Resource Reservation Protocol (RSVP), real-time interactive traffic can still run into blocking delays due to large packets, especially on slow serial connections. When a voice packet arrives just after a large packet has been scheduled for transmission, the voice packet needs to wait until the large packet is transmitted before it can be scheduled. This blocking delay caused by the large packet can be prohibitive for real-time applications such as interactive voice. Interactive voice requires an end-to-end delay of 100 ms to 150 ms to be effective.

LFI fragments the large data frames into smaller frames, interleaving the small, delay-sensitive packets between the fragments of large packets before putting them on the queue for transmission, thereby easing the delay seen by the small-size, real-time packets. The fragmented data frame is reassembled at the destination.

You can use LFI in conjunction with CBWFQ with a priority queue for achieving the needs of real-time voice traffic, as shown in Figure F-1.

Figure F-1 *Link Layer Fragmentation and Interleaving Illustration*

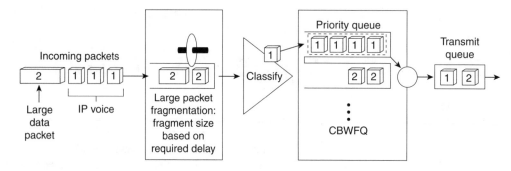

As you can see in Figure F-1, the real-time voice traffic is placed in the priority queue. The other non–real-time data traffic can go into one or more normal Weighted Fair Queuing (WFQ) queues. The packets belonging to the non–real-time traffic are fragmented to secure a minimal blocking delay for the voice traffic. The data traffic fragments are placed in the WFQ queues. Now, CBWFQ with a priority queue can run on the voice and data queues. The maximum blocking delay seen by a voice packet is equal to a fragment's serialization delay. Table F-1 shows the fragment size for a maximum blocking delay of 10 ms based on link speed.

Table F-1 *Fragment Size for a Maximum Blocking Delay of 10 ms Based on Link Speed*

Link Speed (in Kbps)	Fragment Size (in Bytes)
56	70
64	80
128	160
256	320
512	640
768	1000

LFI ensures that voice and similar small-size packets are not unacceptably delayed behind large data packets. It also attempts to ensure that the small packets are sent in a more regular fashion, thereby reducing jitter. This capability allows a network to carry voice and other delay-sensitive traffic along with non–time-sensitive traffic.

NOTE   MLPP link-layer fragmentation and interleaving are used in conjunction with CBWFQ using a priority queue to minimize the delay seen by the voice traffic. Listing F-1 shows the configuration for this purpose.

Listing F-1   *MLPP Link-Layer Fragmentation Configuration*

```
class-map premium
 match <voice packets>

policy-map premiumpolicy
 class premium
 priority 500

interface serial0
bandwidth 128
no fair-queue
ppp multilink

interarface serial1
 bandwidth 128
 no fair-queue
 ppp multilink

interface virtual-template 1
 service-policy output premiumpolicy
 ppp multilink
 ppp multilink fragment-delay 20
 ppp multilink interleave
```

In this example, an MLPP bundle configuration is added on the **virtual-template** interface. Interfaces Serial0 and Serial1 are made part of the MLPP bundle using the **ppp multilink** command. Note that CBWFQ with the priority queue is enabled on the **virtual-template** interface and not on the physical interfaces that are part of MLPP. The **ppp multilink fragment-delay 20** command is used to provide a maximum delay bound of 20 ms for the voice traffic. To interleave the voice packets among the fragments of larger packets on an MLPP bundle, the **ppp multilink interleave** command is used. The CBWFQ policy **premiumpolicy** is used to provide a strict priority bandwidth for the voice traffic.

Reference

[1] RFC 1717, "The PPP Multilink Protocol (MP)," K. Sklower et al., 1994.

IP Precedence and DSCP Values

Figure G-1 *Internet Protocol (IP) Precedence Bits in the Type of Service (ToS) Byte*

| P2 | P1 | P0 | T3 | T2 | T1 | T0 | CU |

IP precedence: 3 bits (P2-P0)
Type of service (ToS): 4 bits (T3-T0)
Currently unused (CU): 1 bit

Table G-1 *IP Precedence Table*

IP Precedence Value	IP Precedence Bits	IP Precedence Names	ToS Byte Value
0	000	Routine	0 (0x00)
1	001	Priority	32 (0x20)
2	010	Immediate	64 (0x40)
3	011	Flash	96 (0x60)
4	100	Flash Override	128 (0x80)
5	101	Critical	160 (0xA0)
6	110	Internetwork Control	192 (0xC0)
7	111	Network Control	224 (0xE0)

Figure G-2 *Differentiated Services Code Point (DSCP) Bits in the Differentiated Services (DS) Byte*

| DS5 | DS4 | DS3 | DS2 | DS1 | DS0 | CU | CU |

Differentiated services code point (DSCP): 6 bits (DS5-DS0)
Currently unused (CU): 2 bits

Defined DSCPs:

Default DSCP: 000 000.

Class Selector DSCPs:

Table G-2   *Class Selector DSCPs*

Class Selector	DSCP
Precedence 1	001 000
Precedence 2	010 000
Precedence 3	011 000
Precedence 4	100 000
Precedence 5	101 000
Precedence 6	110 000
Precedence 7	111 000

Expedited Forwarding (EF) per-hop behavior (PHB) DSCP: 101110.

Assured Forwarding (AF) PHB DSCPs:

Table G-3   *Assured Forwarding (AF) PHB DSCPs*

Drop Precedence	Class 1	Class 2	Class 3	Class 4
Low	001010	010010	011010	100010
Medium	001100	010100	011100	100100
High	001110	010110	011110	100110

Mapping between IP precedence and DSCP:

Table G-4 shows how IP precedence is mapped to DSCP values.

Table G-4   *IP Precedence to DSCP Mapping*

IP Precedence	DSCP
0	0
1	8
2	16
3	24
4	32
5	40
6	48
7	56

Table G-5 shows how DSCP is mapped to IP precedence values.

Table G-5   *DSCP to IP Precedence Mapping*

DSCP	IP Precedence
0–7	0
8–15	1
16–23	2
24–31	3
32–39	4
40–47	5
48–55	6
56–63	7

INDEX

A

AAL (ATM Adaptation Layer), 169, 172–173
ABR (Available Bit Rate), 173–175
access rates, case study, 56–60
access-list 101 command, 136
ACK (acknowledgement), 315
action policies, traffic, 47
active flows, 136
adaptability, TE tunnels, 253
adaptive FRTS, 188
adaptive traffic shaping, Frame Relay, 194
Address Resolution Protocol (ARP), 287
Address Extension (AE), 186
adjacency tables, 289
AE (Address Extension), 186
AF (Assured Forwarding), 25, 28
algorithms
    MDRR, 122
    Nagle, 315
    scheduling, 67–72
allocation
    bandwidth, 82, 91, 121–123
    case study, 87
    downstream label, 214
    upstream label, 216
alternate priority mode, 115
application-level traffic, LFI, 319–321
application-specific integrated circuit
    (ASIC), 48
applications, 190
    identification, 34
    levels of QoS, 6
    multicast, 147–151
    policies, 282–283
    RSVP, 148–152
approaches, TE, 258
architecture
    diffserv, 22–28
    intserv, 21

ARP (Address Resolution Protocol), 287
ASIC (application-specific integrated
    circuit), 48
assignment of bandwidth per ToS class, 88
Assured Forwarding (AF), 25
Asynchronous Transfer Mode (ATM), 279
ATM (Asynchronous Transfer Mode), 172, 279
    CLP bit based on IP Precedence, 185
    differentiated services, 183–184
    interworking, 178–179
    Layer 2, 169–184
    MPLS, 218
atm abr rate-factor 8 8 command, 175
ATM Adaptation Layer (AAL), 169
atm pvp configuration command, 176
atmpolicy Policy/Map information, 182
attacks
    denial-of-service, 51
    smurf, 141–142
attributes
    available bandwidth, 253
    link resource, 253
    resource class, 253
    TE path selection policies, 254
    TE tunnels, 251–253
audio, 313
    RSVP, 147–152
    RTP header compression, 316
autoroute announce command, 268
Autosense, FRTS, 192, 194
available bandwith attribute, 253
Available Bit Rate (ABR), 173
average queue size computation, 131
avoidance, congestion, 13, 130–132
    SPD, 139–140
    TCP, 127–128

B

backbone routers, deployment, 291–297
Backward Explicit Notification (BECN), 54
bandwidth, 10, 316
    allocation, 82
    assignment per ToS class, 88
    commands, 86
    custom queuing, 94–97
    end-to-end, 157–162, 240
    higher allocation case study, 86
    QoS-group classification case study, 91
    TE tunnels, 251
BECN (Backward Explicit Notification), 54,
    186–187
    Frame Relay case study, 194–195
    integration, 189
behavior
    PHB, 26–28
    TCP, 129
Best-Effort service, 6
BGP (Border Gateway Policy), 35, 301, 307
bgp-policy destination ip-prec-map
    command, 309
bgp-policy source ip-prec-map command, 309
binding labels, 213–216
Border Gateway Protocol. *See* BGP
boundaries
    network interfaces, 281
    traffic conditioners, 25–26
bumping traffic, 179
burst size, 172
business-site FRTS configuration, 194
byte-by-byte round-robin GPS Scheduler
    simulation, 73–74
byters, 95

C

C/R (Command and Response), 186
caches, route-cache forwarding, 287–288
CAR (Committed Access Rate), 35, 279
    configuring, 37, 40
    rate-limiting function, 43–48
case studies, 183–184
    ABR PVC, 175
    ATM CLP bit based on IP Precedence, 185
    bandwidth
        assignment per ToS class, 88
        QoS-group classification, 91
        for voice traffic, 121–123
    class-based MWRR scheduling, 113–114
    congestion avoidance, 133–135
    differentiated IP packet discards, 180
    downstream label ditribution, 219–222
    enforcing public exchange point traffic,
        52–53
    flow-based WFQ, 80–82
    fragmentation (Frame Relay), 199
    Frame Relay adaptive traffic shaping, 194
    FRTS with Autosense, 192
    high bandwidth, 86
    IP Precedence, 41
    limiting traffic, 48–50
    mapping Frame Relay, 198
    minimum interface bandwidth with
        different protocols, 95–98
    MPLS
        CoS, 225–227
        TE tunnel configuration, 258–272
        VPN QoS, 240–241
    multiple PVCs (Frame Relay), 196, 198
    packets
        classification, 37–39
        prioritization, 93
    per-VC WFQ (Frame Relay), 198
    preventing denial-of-service attacks, 51

priority queuing, 92
RSVP, 157–163
smurf attacks, 141–142
subrate IP services, 50
traffic shaping, 56–61
VP traffic shaping, 176
WFQ scheduling, 82–83
CBFWQ (Class-Based Weighted Fair
  Queuing), 76, 89–91, 319
CBR (Constant Bit Rate), 172–173
CDP (Cisco Discovery Protocol), 303
CDR (Committed Delivery Rate), 237
CE (Congestion Experienced), 139
CEF (Cisco Express Forwarding), 13, 287
  backbone routers, 291–297
  Cell Loss Priority (CLP), 171
  route-cache switching, 297–298
CIR (Committed Information Rate), 187, 237
Cisco Discovery Protocol (CDP), 303
Cisco Express Forwarding. *See* CEF
Class Based Weighted Fair Queuing
  (CBWFQ), 76, 89–91, 319
class-based distributed WFQ, 89–91
class-based MWRR scheduling, 113
class-based WFQ, 85–86
class-map configuration command, 279
classes, 172–173
  bandwidth assignment per ToS class, 88
  MWRR ToS allocation, 112–113
  traffic, 280
classification, packets, 34–39
classifiers, 12, 26
  packets, 12
CLI (command line interface), 279
CLP (Cell Loss Priority), 171
coloring packets, 34
Command and Response (C/R), 186
command line interface (CLI), 279
commands, 142, 193, 268
  access-list 101, 136
  atm abr rate-factor, 175
  atm pvp, 176
  bgp-policy source ip-prec-map, 309

class-map, 86, 279
cos-queue group cos-a, 122
de-group, 199
de-list, 199
fair-queue, 86, 158
fair-queue interface, 80
fair-queue qos-group, 91
frame-relay fragment, 200
frame-relay priority-dlci-group, 196
ip cef, 219, 294
ip local policy route-map, 306
ip policy route-map, 306
ip route-cache flow accelerate, 303
ip rsvp resrvation, 159
ip rsvp sender, 158
ip rtp priority, 99, 200
ip spd headroom, 142
ip spd mode aggressive, 142
ip tcp path-mtu-discovery, 316
map, 295
match, 305
match access-group 101, 136
max-reserved bandwidth, 99
mpls traffic-eng attribute-flag 0x1, 264
mpls traffic-eng tunnels, 259
no mpls ip propagate-ttl, 218, 272
policy-map, 281
policy-map wred, 136
ppp mulitlink, 321
ppp multilink fragement-delay 20, 321
ppp multilink interleave, 321
priority keyword, 100
qos switching, 114
random-detect, 134
random-detect flow, 138
random-detect flow average-depth-factor
  6, 138
random-detect flow count, 138
req-qos guaranteed-delay, 163
route-map, 280
route-target import 200;1, 233
rx-cos slot, 122
service nagle, 315

service-policy, 182, 282
service-policy output febandwidth, 87
set, 305
shape average, 58
show, 49, 304
show atm vc, 177
show atm vp, 176
show atm vp 2, 177
show class, 86
show controllers fefab/tofab cos-queue
   length/parameters/variables, 123
show frame-relay pvc, 196
show frame-relay qos-autosense, 193
show interface Hssi0/0/0, 143
show interface rate, 49
show interface shape, 58
show interface tunnel0, 266
show interfaces switching, 143
show ip cache verbose, 293
show ip cef 222.222.222.3 internal, 268
show ip policy, 305
show ip route, 292
show ip routre vrf green, 232
show ip rsvp installed, 161–162
show ip rsvp interface, 160
show ip rsvp neighbor, 161
show ip rsvp request, 161
show isis mpls traffic tunnel, 266
show isis mpls traffic-eng advertise, 267
show mpls forwarding-table, 220–221
show mpls idp bindings, 220
show mpls idp parameters, 221
show mpls traffic-eng tunnel tunnel0,
   263–264
show policy, 86
show policy-map, 182
show queue, 81
show queue interface, 81
show queue s0, 162
show queue serial0, 87
show queueing custom, 97
show queueing fair, 82
show queueing priority, 93, 197

show queueing random-detect, 134, 138
show route-map tasman, 305
show traffic-shape statistics, 58
show-traffic shape, 193
shpae peak, 58
slot-table_cos, 122
table-a slot-table cos, 122
traffic-shape fecn-adapt, 190
traffic-shape_adaptive, 190
tunnel mode mpls traffic-en, 259
tunnel mpls traffic-eng autoroute
   announce, 268
tunnel mpls traffic-eng record route, 264
tx-queue-limit, 78
vofr, 200
Committed Access Rate (CAR), 35, 279
Committed Delivery Rate (CDR), 237
Committed Information Rate (CIR), 187, 237
Common Open Policy Service (COPS), 30
comparisons, CEF switching/route-cache
   switching, 297–298
components
   control, 213–216
   forwarding, 212
   RSVP, 150
compression, RTP headers, 316
computation, 131
conditioners, network boundary traffic, 25–26
conferencing RSVP, 147–152
configuration
   ABR PVC, 175
   ATM CLP bit based on IP Precedence, 185
   business-site FRTS, 194
   CAR, 37–38
   CoS, 123
   FRTS with Autosense, 193
   IP Precedence case study, 41
   IP-ATM QoS interworking, 181
   MLPP link-layer fragmentation, 321
   multiple PVC bundles, 184
   per-VC WFQ, 198
   QoS-based DWFQ, 90
   QPPB, 40

RSVP-related, 159
TE tunnel, 258–272
voice traffic, 121–123
confirm-action statement, 47
congestion
    avoidance, 13
        ECN, 139
        enhancing link utilization with
            WRED, 133–135
        Frame Relay, 186–187
        RED, 130–132
        support, 67–70, 72
        TCP, 127–128
Congestion Avoidance Policy, 121–123
Congestion Experienced (CE), 139
connections
    performance, 9, 11
    TCP (Nagle Algorithm), 315
    traffic shaping, 56, 58–60
Constant Bit Rate (CBR), 172–173
contract restrictions, VP shaping, 174
control
    Frame relay congestion, 186–187
    MPLS, 211–217
controlled load service, 155
conversation queues, 80
COPS (Common Open Policy Service), 30
core network interfaces, 282
CoS
    configuring, 123
    MPLS case study, 225–227
cos-queue group cos-a command, 122
critical traffic, higher bandwidth allocation, 86–87
CU (currently unused), 24
currently unused (CU), 24
custom queuing, 94–100

D

data terminal equipment (DTE), 187
data-link connection identifier (DLCI), 185
DCEF (Distributed Cisco Express
    Forwarding), 83, 291
DE (Discard Eligible), 186–187, 198
Deficit Round Robin (DRR), 84, 106
definitions
    policies, 281
    traffic class, 280
    QoS policies, 279
    TE trunks, 251
de-group command, 199
de-list command, 199
deleting labels, 222
denial-of-service attacks, preventing, 51
deploying CEF backbone routers, 291–297
designated SBM (DSBM), 204
differentiated IP packet discards, 180
differentiated MPLS VPN QoS, 237–238
Differentiated Service Code Point (DSCP), 279
differentiated services, ATM case study,
    183–184
differentiated services byte (DS byte), 22
Differentiated Services Code Point (DSCP),
    12, 22–28
diffserv architecture, 22–28
Discard Eliglible (DE), 186–187
discard strategies, cells, 173–174
distinct reservations, 152
Distributed Cisco Express Forwarding
    (DCEF), 83, 291
Distributed Traffic Shaping (DTS), 55
distributed WFQ (DWFQ), 83–85
distribution
    downstream label case study, 219–222
    local link resource information, 254

DLCI (data-link connection identifier), 185
domains, 22
downstream label allocation, 214
drop probability, 132–135
dropper function, 26
DRR (Deficit Round Robin), 84, 106
DS byte (differentiated services byte), 22
DSBM (designated SBM), 204
DSCP (Differentiated Services Code Point), 12, 22, 85, 323–325
DTE (data terminal equipment), 187
DTS (Distributed Traffic Shaping), 55
DWFQ (distributed WFQ), 83–84
    QoS-based, 90
    ToS-based, 89–90

E

early packet discard (EPD), 173–174
ECN routers, 139
EF (Expedited Forwarding), 25
EIR (Excess Information Rate), 187
election, DSBM, 205
enabling
    Frame relay fragmentation, 199
    Nagle Algorithm, 315
    Path MTU Discovery, 316
    polices, 282–283
encapsulation, labels, 216–217
end-tend guaranteed bandwith, 240
end-to-end bandwidth, reserving with, 157–160, 162
end-to-end IP QoS, 225
end-to-end QoS, 15
enforcing
    IP Precedence setting case study, 41
    public exchange point traffic, 52–53
engineering traffic, 214
enhancing link utilization with WRED, 133–135
Enterprise Resource Planning (ERP), 190
EPD (early parket discard), 173–174

ER-LSP (Explicitly Routed Label Switched Path), 255
ERP (Enterprise Resource Planning), 190
exceed-action statement, 47
Excess Infromation Rate (EIR), 187
execution, order of policies, 284
expanded traffic capability, LANs, 200–203
Expedited Forwarding (EF), 25
Explicitly Routed Label Switched Path (ER-LSP), 255
extensions
    IGP routing protocol, 257
    RSVP, 205

F

fair allocation schemes, 69–70
Fair Queuing (FQ), 67
fair-queue command, 86, 158
fair-queue interface command, 80
fair-queue qos-group command, 91
fast switching, 287
FCS (Frame Check Sequence), 186
FDDI (Fiber Distributed Data Interface), 52
FECN (Forward Explicit Congestion Notification), 54, 186–187
    Frame Relay case study, 194–195
    integration, 189
FF (Fixed Filter), 152
Fiber Distributed Data Interface (FDDI), 52
FIFO (first-in, first-out), 9, 68–69
File Transfer Protocol (FTP), 6, 155, 283
first-in, first-out (FIFO), 9, 68–69
Fixed Filter (FF), 152
flow WRED, 136–138
flow-based DWFQ (distributed WFQ), 83–85
flow-based WFQ, 75–78
    case study, 80–82
    strict priorty queue for voice, 100
FlowSpec, 152
formats, ATM cells, 169–170

Forward Explicit Congestion Notification
(FECN), 54
forwarding
CEF, 289
MPLS, 211–212, 214–217
route-cache, 287–288
FQ (Fair Queuing), 67, 73
FRAD (Frame Relay Access Device), 190
fragmentation
Frame Relay, 190–191, 199
LFI, 319
sizes, 320
Frame Check Sequence (FCS), 186
Frame Relay, 185–199
fragmentation, 190–191
interwoking, 192
traffic shaping, 60–61
Frame Relay Access Device (FRAD), 190
Frame Relay Forum (FRF), 190
Frame Relay Traffic Shaping (FRTS), 187–
189, 279
Frame Relay virtual circuit (VC), 279
frame-relay fragment command, 200
frame-relay priority-dlci-group command, 196
frame relay qos-autosense, 193
frame-relay qos autosense command, 193
frame-relay traffic-shaping, 193
frame-relay traffic-shaping command, 193
FRF (Frame Relay Forum), 190
FRTS (Frame Relay Traffic Shaping), 192, 279
FTP (File Transfer Protocol), 82–83, 155, 283
functional blocks in diffserv architecture, 22
functions, 12. *See also* commands
congestion avoidance, 13
dropper, 26
identification, 34–35
LFI (Link Layer and INterleaving),
319–321
metering, 26
packet classifier and marker, 12

policing, 42
QoS Signaling Protocol, 13
rate-limiting, 43–48
resource allocation, 12
routing, 13
shaper, 26
shaping, 42
switching, 13

G

GB (guaranteed bandwidth), 240
generalized processor sharing (GPS), 71–72
Generic Traffic Shaping (GTS), 55, 279
global synchronization, 129
goldservice, 86
GPS (generalized processor sharing), 71–73
GTS (Generic Traffic Shaping), 55, 279
guaranteed bandwidth (GB), 240
guaranteed bit rate service, 155
guaranteed QoS, 238–239
guaranteed services, 7

H

hard QoS, 7
head-end router, 255
headers, 316
HEC (Header Error Control), 171
hierarchical policies, 283
high bandwidth allocation case study, 86
High-Speed Serial Interface (HSSI), 37, 88
histories, 8–9
holding priorities, TE tunnels, 251
hosting, Web services, 51
HSSI (High-Speed Serial Interface), 37, 88

I

ICMP (Internet Control Message Protocol), 51
identification function, 34–35
IEEE (Institute of Electronic Engineers), 14,
    200–203
IETF (Internet Engineering Task Force), 9, 21
IGPs (Interior Gateway Protocols), 257, 302
ILMI (Interim Local Manement Interface), 179
implementation
    MDRR, 119, 121
    MWRR, 112–113
    queuing, 68
    traffic measurement, 44, 54
    WFQ, 79–80
incoming traffic, 307–309
initialization, SBM, 204
input, interface queues, 119
Institute of Electronic Engineers (IEEE), 14,
    200–203
integrated services, 155
Integrated Services (intserv), 9
Integrated Services over Specifiuc Lower
    Layers (ISSLL), 203
integration, BECN/FECN, 189
interfaces
    network boundary, 281
    policies, 282
    virtual-template, 321
Interim Local Management Interface
    (ILMI), 179
Interior Gateway Protocols (IGPs), 302
Intermediate System-to-Intermediate System
    (IS-IS), 302
Internet Control Message Protocol (ICMP), 51
Internet Engineering Task Force (IETF), 9, 21
Internet Router (IR), 303
Internet service provider (ISP), 113, 291
inter-policy feature ordering, 284

interworking
    ATM, 178–179
    Frame Relay, 192
intra-feature execution orders, 284
intserv, 9, 21
IP (Internet Protocol), 30
    flow-based WFQ, 75–78
    Precedence, 34–35, 323–325
        case study, 37–41
        DSCP, 36
        limiting traffic, 49–50
        mapping Frame Relay DE bits, 198
        QPPB, 39
    networks, 302–303
    priority queuing case study, 92
    QoS history, 8–9
    services, 50
ip cef command, 219, 294
ip local policy route-map command, 306
ip policy route-map command, 306
ip priority queue, 142
ip route-cache flow accelerate command, 303
ip rsvp reservation command, 159
ip rsvp sender command, 158
ip rtp priority command, 99, 200
ip spd headroom command, 142
ip spd mode aggressive command, 142
ip tcp path-mtu-discovery command, 316
IR (Internet Router), 303
IS-IS (Intermediate System-to-Intermediate
    System), 302
IS-IS modifications, 258
ISP (Internet service provider), 113, 291
    backbone, 240
    CEF based packet forwarding, 291–297
ISSLL (Integrated Services over Specific
    Lower Layers), 203
its, 306

J-K-L

jitter
    minimum, 121–123
    packet, 10

Label Edge Router (LER), 212
Label Information Base (LIB), 212
Label Switched Path (LSP), 247
Label Switching Router (LSR), 212
labels
    binding, 213–216
    downstream distribution, 219–222
    encapsulation, 216–217
    switching, 14
LANs (local-area networks), 200–203
Layer 2
    ATM, 169–170–184
    overlay model, 247–248
    QoS technologies, 14
LER (Label Edge Router), 212, 227
levels of QoS, 6
LIB (Label Information Base), 212
limiting traffic, 48–50
link admission control, TE tunnels, 256
link resource attributes, 253
Link State Advertisement (LSA), 257
links, enhancing utilization, 133–135
local link resource information,
    distribution of, 254
lookups, process switching, 287
loss, packet, 11
low-latency queues, 98, 115
LSA (Link State Advertisement), 257
LSP (Label Switched Path), 247
LSR (Label Switching Router), 212, 227

M

MAC (Media Access Control), 280
maintenance, TE path, 256
management
    policies, 301–305
    queues, 130–132
    traffic rate, 42–48
managers, policy, 29
map commands, 295
mapping, Frame Relay, 198
mark probability denominator, 132
marking packets, 34–39
match access-group 101 command, 136
match commands, 305
match subcommand, 280
matching traffic specification, 44
max-min fair-share allocation scheme, 69–70
max-reserved bandwidth command, 99
maximum burst size (MBS), 172
maximum segment size (MSS), 127
MBS (maximum burst size), 172
MCR (Minimum Cell Rate), 173
MDRR (Modified Deficit Round Robin),
    114–121
measuring traffic, 42, 54
mechanisms, voice traffic, 98–101
Media Access Control (MAC), 280
media support, RSVP, 156
messages, RSVP, 151
metering function, 26
Minimum Cell rate (MCR), 173
MINCIR (minimum CIR), 188
minimum jitter, 121–123
MLPP (Multilink Point-to-Point), 99
models, Layer 2 overlay, 247–248

modes
    alternate priority, 115
    strict priority, 115
modification
    custom queues, 100
    IS-IS, 258
Modified Deficit Round Robin (MDRR),
    114–121
Modified Weighted Round Robin (MWRR),
    105–113
modular CLI (command-line interface), 89–91
MPLS (Multi Protocol Label Switching), 14,
    211, 247, 302
    ATM, 218
    case study, 258–272
    CoS case study, 225–227
    QoS, 223
    VPN, 227–237
    VPN QoS, 237–241
mpls traffic-eng attribute-flag 0x1
    command, 264
mpls traffic-eng tunnels command, 259
MSS (maximum segment size), 127
Multi Protocol Label Switching. *See* MPLS
multicast applications, RSVP, 147
multidimensional policies, 282
Multilink Point-to-Point (MLPP), 99
multimedia, RSVP, 147–152
multiple PVCs
    case study, 196
    configuring bundles, 184
MWRR (Modified Weighted Round Robin),
    105–114

N

Nagle Algorithm, 315
NBAR (Network Based Application
    recognition), 34
Network Based Application Recoginition
    (NBAR), 34
Network File System (NFS), 148

Network Layer Reachability Information
    (NLRI), 228
Network-to-Node Interface (NNI), 169–170
networks
    ATM
        interworking, 178–179
        Layer 2, 169–184
    boundary interfaces, 281
    boundary traffic conditioners, 25–26
    end-to-end IP QoS, 225
    Frame Relay, 185–199
    LANs, 200–203
    Layer 2 overlay, 247–248
    levels of QoS, 6
    Path MTU Discovery, 315
    perfomance, 9, 11
    policy-based routing, 302–303
    priority queuing, 91–92
    provisioning, 28
    RRR, 248–249
    support, 67–72
    traffic rate management, 42
    WAN (wide-area network), 8, 319
NFS (Network File System), 148
NLRI (Network Layer Reachability
    Information), 228
NNI (Network-to-Node Interface), 169–170
no mpls ip propagate-ttl command, 218, 272
nonadaptive flows, congestion avoidance, 138
nRT-VBR (Non-Real Time Variable
    Bit Rate), 172

O

Open Shortest Path First. *See* OSPF
optimization
    bandwidth, 316
    routing, 301, 303–305
    TE path, 256
order of policy execution, 284

OSPF (Open Shortest Path First), 258, 289
outgoing traffic, 307–309
output, interface queue, 119

P

packets
    cell discard strategies, 173–174
    classification, 34–39
    classifier and marker, 12
    coloring, 34
    delay and jitter, 10
    differentied IP discards, 180
    drop policy, 13
    drop probability, 132–135
    FIFO queuing, 68–69
    flow WRED, 136–138
    Frame Relay, 190–191
    label encapsulation, 216–217
    loss, 11
    marking, 34
    Path MTU Discovery, 315
    prioritization, 93
    priority queuing, 91–92
    process switching, 287
    route-cache forwarding, 287–288
    scheduling, 106
    size, 305
    TE trunks, 251
    traffic shaping, 53–60
    WRR (Weighted Round Robin), 106–108
parameters, 93
partial packet discard (PPD), 173–174
PATH messages, 151
Path MTU Discovery, 315
Path State Block (PSB), 151, 205
paths
    selection, 253–254
    TE maintenance, 256
Payload Type Identifier (PTI), 171
PBR (Policy-Based Routing), 35, 38
PCR (Peak Cell Rate), 172

PEP (Policy Enforcement Point), 30
performance, 9–11. *See also* optimization
Per-INterface Rate Configuration (PIRC), 48
permanent virtual circuits (PVCs), 54, 169
permium services, EF PHB, 27
per-VC WFQ, 198
PHB (per-hop behavior), 26–28
    MDRR, 114–121
    MWRR, 105–113
    resource allocation policy, 28–30
PIRC (Per-Interface Rate Configuration), 48
Point-to-Point Protocol (PPP), 319
Points of Presence (POP), 258
policies
    action, 47
    applications, 282–283
    defining, 281
    hierarchical, 283
    incoming traffic, 307–309managers, 29
    order of execution, 284
    outgoing traffic, 307–309
    packet drop, 13
    path selection, 254
    resource allocation, 28–30
    routing, 301–305
policing traffic, 43–48
Policy Enforcement Point (PEP), 30
Policy-Based Routing (PBR), 35, 302–303
policy-map command, 281
policy-map wred command, 136
POP (Points of Presence), 258
popping labels, 222
PPD (partial packet discard), 173–174
PPP (Point-to-Point Protocol), 319
ppp mulitlink command, 321
ppp multilink fragment-delay 20
    command, 321
ppp mulitlink interleave command, 321
PQ (priority queue), 83
precedence, 34–35, 303–304, 323–325.
    See also IP (Internet Protocol)

pre-hop behavior (PHB), 22
preventing
    denial-of-service attacks, 51
    smurf attacks, 141–142
priorities
    packets, 93
    TE tunnels, 251
priority keyword command, 100
priority queue (PQ), 83, 91–93
proactive queue management for congestion
    avoidance, 130–132
probability, packet drops, 132
process switching, 287–288
propagation, 307
protocols
    FTP (File Transfer Protocol), 6, 155
    ICMP (Internet Control Message
        Protocol), 51
    IGP routing extensions, 257
    IP (Internet Protocol), 8–9
    minimum interface bandwidth, 95–98
    MPLS (Multi Protocol Label
        switching), 14
    QoS Signaling Portocol, 13
    RSVP (Resource Reservation Protocol), 21
    RTP (Real-time Transport Protocol), 99
    SBM (Subnet Bandwidth Manager),
        203–205
    TCP (Transmissin Control Protocol), 151
    TCP/IP (Transmission Control Protocol/
        Internet Protocol), 8
    UDP (User Datagram Protocol), 151
Provider Edge routers, 228
provisioning networks, 28
PSB (Path State Block), 151, 205
PTI (Payload Type Identifier), 171
public exchange point traffic, enforcing, 52–53
PVCs (permanent virtual circuits), 54, 169

Q

QoS, 172
    end-to-end IP, 225
    MPLS, 223
    MPLS VPN, 237–241
    packet classification, 36
    policies, 279, 301–305, 307
    propagation, 307
QoS Policy Propagation BGP (QPPB), 287
QoS Signaling Protocol, 13
qos switching command, 114
QoS-based DWFQ, 90
QoS-based routing, 301–302
QPPB (QoS Policy Propagation BGP), 287
    IP Precedence, 39
    QoS groups, 40
quantum values, 114
queues
    ATM interworking, 178–179
    average size computation, 131
    conversation, 80
    input interface, 119
    IP priority, 142
    low-latency, 115
    output interface, 119
    RED, 130–132
    ToS-based DWFQ, 89–90
    WRR (Weighted Round Robin), 106
queuing
    custom, 94–97, 100
    FIFO, 68–69
    implementing, 68
    priority, 91–92

R

random-detect command, 134
random-detect flow average-depth-factor 6 command, 138
random-detect flow command, 138
random-detect flow count command, 138
rate-limiting function, 43–45, 47–48
rates
    access, 56–60
    ICMP, 51
    traffic, 48–50
    traffic management, 42–48
RD (route distinguisher), 228
Real-time Transfer Control Protocol (RTCP), 313
Real-time Transport Protocol (RTP), 99, 313
Real-Time Variable Bit Rate (RT-VBR), 172
receivers
    controlled load services, 155
    guaranteed bit rate services, 155
RED, congestion avoidance, 130–132
req-qos guaranteed-delay command, 163
reservation styles, RSVP, 152–162
resilience, TE tunnels, 253
resource allocation, 12
resource allocation policy, 28–30
resource class affinity, TE tunnel, 252
resource class attribute, 253
Resource Management (RM), 173
Resource Reservation Protocol (RSVP), 21, 313
RESV (RSVP reservation request), 79
retransmit timer (RTT), 128
RM (Resource Management), 173
round numbers, 72
round-robin, byte-by-byte GPS Scheduler simulation, 73–74
route distinguisher (RD), 228

route-cache
    forwarding, 287–288
    switching, 297–298
route-map command, 280
route-target import 200colon1 command (change in edit), 233
routers
    ABR PVC, 175
    backbone, 291–297
    class-based WFQ, 85–86
    ECN, 139
    head-end, 255
    Layer 2 overlay model, 247–248
    packets, 34
    Provider Edge, 228
    RSVP-related configuration, 159
    SPD, 139–140
    support, 67–72
    TE trunks, 251
    traffic rate management, 42–48
routing, 13
    IGP protocol extensions, 257
    IP precedence, 303–304
    packet size, 305
    policy-based, 302–303
    QoS, 301–305
RRR (Routing by Resource Reservation), 247–249, 253
RSVP (Resource Reservation Protocol), 21, 313, 147
    case study, 157–163
    controlled load service, 155
    extensions, 205
    guaranteed bit rate service, 155
    media support, 156
    resrvation styles, 152
    scalability, 156
    TE-RSVP, 256–257
    WFQ interaction, 79
    at VPN sites only, 239
RSVP reservation request (RESV), 79

RSVP-related configuration, 159
RT (Route Target), 228
RTCP (Real-time Transfer Control
    Protocol), 313
RTP (Real-time Transport Protocol), 99, 313
RTT (retransmit timer), 128
RT-VBR (Real-Time Variable Bit Rate), 172
rx-cos slot command, 122

S

SAR (segmentation and reassembly), 169
SBM (Subnet Bandwidth Manager), 203
scalability, RSVP, 156
schedulers, process switching, 287
scheduling
    class-based MWRR, 113–114
    GOS, 71–72
    MDRR, 114–121
    mechanisms for voice traffic, 98–101
    MWRR, 105–113
    sequence number computation-based
        WFQ, 72–73
    support, 67–72
    WFQ, 79, 82
schemes
    max-min fair-share allocation, 69–70
    switching, 297–298
    token buckert, 42
SCR (Sustained Cell Rate), 172
SE (Shared Explicit), 153
segmentation and reassembly (SAR), 169
self-clocking, 128
Sequence Number (SN), 73
sequence number computation-based WFQ,
    72–73
Service Level Agreements (SLAs), 306
service nagle command, 315
service-policy command, 182, 282
service-policy output febandwidth
    command, 87

services
    ABR case study, 175
    best-effort, 6
    controlled load, 155
    diffserv
        architecture, 22–26
        PHB, 26–28
        resource policy, 28–30
    guaranteed, 7
    guaranteed bit rate, 155
    IP subrate, 50
    Web hosting, 51
set commands, 305
setup priorities, TE tunnels, 251
shape average command, 58
shape peak command, 58
shaper function, 26
shaping
    FRTS (Frame Relay Traffic Shaping),
        187–189
    traffic, 53–60
        Frame Relay, 60–61
        VP case study, 176
    VP, 174
shaping functions, 42
Shared Explicit (SE), 153
shared reservations, 152
Shortest Path First (SPF), 254
show atm vc command, 177
show atm vp command, 176
show atm vp 2 command, 177
show class command, 86
show command, 49
show commands, 304
show controllers frfab/tofab cos-queue length/
    parameters/varaibles command, 123
show frame-relay pvc command, 196
show frame-relay qos-autosense
    command, 193
show interface Hssi0/0/0 command, 143
show interface rate commad, 49

show interface shape command, 58
show interface tunnel0 command, 266
show interfaces switching command, 143
show ip cache verbose command, 293
show ip cef 222.222.222.3 internal command, 268
show ip policy command, 305
show ip route, 268
show ip route command, 268, 292
show ip route vrf green command, 232
show ip rsvp installed command, 161–162
show ip rsvp interface command, 160
show ip rsvp neighbor command, 161
show ip rsvp request command, 161
show ip spd, 142
show ip spd command, 142
show isis mpls traffic tunnel command, 266
show isis mpls traffic-eng advertise command, 267
show mpls forward-table command, 220
show mpls forwarding-table command, 221
show mpls idp bindings command, 220
show mpls idp parameters command, 221
show mpls traffic-eng tunnel tunnel0 command, 263–264
show policy command, 86
show policy-map command, 182
show queue command, 81
show queue interface command, 81
show queue s0 command, 162
show queue serial0 command, 87
show queueing custom command, 97
show queueing fair command, 82
show queueing priority command, 93, 197
show queueing random-detect command, 134, 138
show route-map tasman command, 305
show traffic-shape command, 193
show traffic-shape statistics command, 58
signaled QoS, 29
simulation, byte-by-byte GPS Scheduler, 73–74

sizes
    fragements, 320
    packets, 305
SLAs (Service Level Agreements), 306
slot-table-cos_command, 122
slow start avoidance, TCP, 127–128
slow start threshold (ssthresh), 128
smurf attacks, 141–142
SN (Sequence Number), 73
SONET (Synchronous Optical Network), 121
SOO (Source of Origin), 228
Source Route Object (SRO), 255
specifications, traffic matching, 44
SPF (Shortest Path First), 254
SRAM (Static Random Access Memory), 85
SRO (Source Route Object), 255
ssthresh (slow start threshold), 128
statements
    confirm-action, 47
    exceed-action, 47
Static Random Access Memory (SRAM), 85
strategies, cell discard, 173–174
strict priority mode, 115
strict priority queue for voice, 100
studies, Frame Relay adaptive traffic shaping, 195
Subnet Bandwidth Manager (SBM), 203
subrate IP services, 50
support
    class-based WFQ, 85–86
    custom queuing, 101
    DWFQ (distributed WFQ), 83–85
    RSVP, 156
    scheduling, 67–72
Sustained Cell Rate (SCR), 172
SVCs (switched virtual circuits), 54, 169
switches, MPLS, 218
switching, 13
    fast, 287
    MPLS, 14, 211–217
    process, 287
Synchronous Optical Network (SONET), 121

T

table-a slot-table cos command, 122
tables, adjacency, 289
tail drop, 13
TCP (Tranmission Control Protocol), 127–128, 283, 315
  congestion, 139
  slow start avoidance, 127–128
  traffic, 129
TCP/IP (Transmission Control Protocol/Internet Protocol), 8, 316
TCP-police-hierarchical policies, 284
TE (traffic engineering), 258, 302
  path, 256
  trunks, 251
  tunnels, 251–272
telent-ftp-police policies, 284
TE-RSVP, 256–257
thresholds, packet drop probability, 132
Time-to-Live (TTL), 272
tinygrams, 315
token buckets, 42–44, 54
tools, routing decisions, 301–305
ToS (Type of Service), 22, 112–113
ToS-based DWFQ, 89–90
traffic
  action policies, 47
  ATM QoS, 172
  bandwidth assignment per ToS class, 88
  bumping, 179
  CAR, 37–40
  class definition, 280
  custom queuing, 94–97
  engineering, 214
  flow-based WFQ, 80–82
  Frame Relay, 186–189
  higher bandwidth allocation case study, 86–87
  incoming, 307–309
  IP precedence, 303–304
  LANs, 200–203
  Layer 2 overlay model, 247–248
  levels of QoS, 6
  limiting, 49–50
  measuring, 42, 54
  mechanisms, 99
  multimedia, 147–151
  network boundary conditioners, 25–26
  outgoing, 307–309
  PHB (per-hop behavior), 26
  policing, 43–48
  priority queuing, 91–92
  public exchange point, 52–53
  QPPB, 39
  rate management, 42–48
  rates, 48–50
  RRR, 248–249
  RTP, 313
  shaping, 53–54
    case study, 56–60
    Frame Relay, 60–61
  SPD, 139–140
  TCP behavior in tail-drop scenario, 129
  voice
    configuring, 121–123
    scheduling mechanisms, 98–101
  VP shaping, 174
  Web hosting services, 51
traffic engineering (TE), 302
traffic matching specification, 44
traffic shaping (TS), 42
traffic-shape fecn-adapt command, 190
traffic-shape_adaptive command, 190
Transmission Control Protocol. *See* TCP
Transmission Control Protocol/Internet Protocol. *See* TCP/IP
troubleshooting
  performance, 9, 11
  RSVP, 156
  scheduling, 67–72
  TE path, 256
  traffic rate management, 42–48
trunks, TE, 251
TS (traffic shaping), 42
TTL (Time-to-Live), 272

tunnel mode mpls traffic-eng command, 259
tunnel mpls traffic-eng autoroute announce
  command, 268
tunnel mpls traffic-eng record-route
  command, 264
tunnels, 251–272. *See also* TE
tx-queue-limit command, 78
Type of Service (ToS), 22
types of AAL, 172–173

U

UBR (Unspecified Bit Rate), 173
UDP (User Datagram Protocol), 151, 302
under, 301
UNI (User-to-Network Interface), 169–170
unicast traffic, 148
Universal Resource Locator (URL), 34
Unspecified Bit Rate (UBR), 173
upstream label allocation, 216
URL (Universal Resource Locator), 34
User Datagram Protocol (UDP), 151, 302
User-to-Network Interface (UNI), 169–170

V

values
    quantum, 114
    SOO, 228
VBR (Variable Bit Rate), 172–173
VC (virtual circuit), 185–199, 279
VCI (virtual channel identifier), 170
Versatile Interface Processor (VIP), 48, 83
video, 147–151, 313. *See also* RSVP
VIP (Versatile Interface Processor), 48, 83
virtual channel identifier (VCI), 170
virtual circuit (VC), 185–199, 279
virtual path (VP), 170
Virtual Private Network. *See* VPN
virtual-template interface, 321
vofr command, 200

voice, 100
    flow packets case study, 82–83
    traffic, 98
VoIP (Voice over IP), 93, 98, 162–163
VP (virtaul path), 170
VPN (Virtual Private Network), 148
    MPLS, 227–237
    RSVP, 240

W

WAN (wide area network), 185–199, 319
Web hosting services, 51
Weighted Fair Queuing. *See* WFQ
weighted flow classes, GPS, 71–72
Weighted Random Early Detection.
    See WRED
Weighted Round Robin (WRR), 105–108
WF (Wildcard Filter), 153
WFQ (weighted Fair Queuing), 83–85,
    279, 320
    case study, 82–83
    class-based, 85–86
    flow-based, 75–78
        bandwidth allocation case study, 82
        case study, 80–81
        strict priority queue for voice, 100
    implmenting, 79–80
    per-VC WFQ, 198
    sequence number computation-based,
        72–73
WG (Working Group), 21
wide area network (WAN), 185–199, 319
Wildcard Filter (WF), 153
Working Group (WG), 21
WRED (Weighted Random Early
    Detection), 279
    congestion avoidance, 133–135
    flow WRED, 136–138
WRR (Weighted Round Robin), 105–108

CCIE Professional Development

Routing TCP/IP, Volume I

Jeff Doyle, CCIE

1-57870-041-8 • **AVAILABLE NOW**

Routing TCP/IP, Volume I, takes the reader from a basic understanding of routers and routing protocols through a detailed examination of each of the IP interior routing protocols. Learn techniques for designing networks that maximize the efficiency of the protocol being used. Exercises and review questions provide core study for the CCIE Routing and Switching exam.

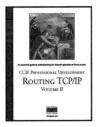

Routing TCP/IP, Volume II

Jeff Doyle, CCIE

1-57870-089-2 • **AVAILABLE NOW**

Routing TCP/IP, Volume II, presents a detailed examination of exterior routing protocols (EGP and BGP) and advanced IP routing issues such as multicast routing, quality of service routing, IPv6, and router management. Readers will learn IP design and management techniques for implementing routing protocols efficiently. Network planning, design, implementation, operation, and optimization are stressed in each chapter. Cisco-specific configurations for each routing protocol are examined in detail. Plentiful review questions and configuration and troubleshooting exercises make this an excellent self-study tool for CCIE exam preparation.

Inside Cisco IOS Software Architecture

Vijay Bollapragada, CCIE; Curtis Murphy, CCIE; and Russ White, CCIE

1-57870-181-3 • **AVAILABLE NOW**

Part of the Cisco CCIE Professional Development Series, *Inside Cisco IOS Software Architecture* offers crucial and hard-to-find information on Cisco's Internetwork Operating System (IOS) Software. The book begins with an overview of operating system concepts and the IOS Software infrastructure, and then delves into the intricate details of the design and operation of platform specific features, including the 1600, 2500, 4x00, 3600, 7200, 7500, and GSR Cisco Routers, and ending with an overview of IOS Quality of Service.

Cisco Press   **www.ciscopress.com**

CCIE Professional Development

Cisco LAN Switching

Kennedy Clark, CCIE; Kevin Hamilton, CCIE

1-57870-094-9 • AVAILABLE NOW

This volume provides an in-depth analysis of Cisco LAN switching technologies, architectures, and deployments, including unique coverage of Catalyst network design essentials. Network designs and configuration examples are incorporated throughout to demonstrate the principles and enable easy translation of the material into practice in production networks.

Advanced IP Network Design

Alvaro Retana, CCIE; Don Slice, CCIE; and Russ White, CCIE

1-57870-097-3 • AVAILABLE NOW

Network engineers and managers can use these case studies, which highlight various network design goals, to explore issues including protocol choice, network stability, and growth. *Advanced IP Network Design* also includes theoretical discussion on advanced design topics.

Large-Scale IP Network Design

Khalid Raza, CCIE; Salman Asad, CCIE; and Mark Turner

1-57870-084-1 • AVAILABLE NOW

Network engineers can find solutions as their IP networks grow in size and complexity. Examine all the major IP protocols in-depth and learn about scalability, migration planning, network management, and security for large-scale networks.

CCIE Fundamentals: Network Design and Case Studies, Second Edition

Cisco Systems, Inc., et al.

1-57870-167-8 • AVAILABLE NOW

CCIE Fundamentals: Network Design and Case Studies, Second Edition, offers a comprehensive collection of configuration scenarios and design recommendations. Each chapter is a self-contained solution that presents insights into the implementation of practical networking strategies flexible enough to fit a variety of situations. A broad range of networking technologies and protocols are discussed, creating an effective self-study tool for the CCIE examination.

Cisco Press   **www.ciscopress.com**

Cisco Press Solutions

Internet Routing Architectures, Second Edition
Sam Halabi and Danny McPherson
1-57870-233-x • **AVAILABLE NOW**

Internet Routing Architectures, Second Edition, explores the ins and outs of interdomain routing network designs with emphasis on BGP-4—the de facto interdomain routing protocol. The comprehensive resource provides you with real solutions for ISP connectivity issues. You will learn how to integrate your network on the global Internet and discover how to build large-scale autonomous systems. You will also learn to control expansion of interior routing protocols using BGP-4, design sound and stable networks, configure the required policies using Cisco IOS Software, and explore routing practices and rules on the Internet.

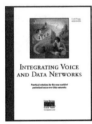

Integrating Voice and Data Networks
Scott Keagy
1-57870-196-1 • **AVAILABLE NOW**

Integrating Voice and Data Networks is both a conceptual reference and a practical how-to book that bridges the gap between existing telephony networks and the new world of packetized voice over data networks. Underlying technologies are explained in a context that gives a holistic understanding of voice/data integration. You'll then follow a complete process to design and implement a variety of network scenarios, leveraging author Scott Keagy's extensive experience with real voice/data networks. This book focuses on the implementation of Voice over Frame Relay, Voice over ATM, and Voice over IP using Cisco IOS voice gateways, including the Cisco MC3810, Cisco 2600/3600/7200/7500 series routers, and AS5300/AS5800 Access Servers.

MPLS and VPN Architectures
Ivan Pepelnjak and Jim Guichard
1-58705-002-1 • **AVAILABLE NOW**

This book provides an in-depth study of MPLS technology, including MPLS theory and configuration, network design issues, and case studies. The MPLS VPN architecture and all of its mechanisms are explained with configuration examples and suggested deployment guidelines. MPLS and VPNs provides the first in-depth discussion particular to Cisco's MPLS architecture. *MPLS and VPN Architectures* covers MPLS theory and configuration, network design issues, and case studies as well as one major MPLS application: MPLS-based VPNs. The MPLS VPN architecture and all of its mechanisms are explained with configuration examples, suggested design and deployment guidelines, and extensive case studies

Cisco Press   **www.ciscopress.com**

Cisco Press Solutions

Cisco Router Configuration, Second Edition
Allan Leinwand and Bruce Pinsky
1-57870-241-0 • AVAILABLE NOW

Cisco Router Configuration, Second Edition, takes an example-oriented and chronological approach to helping you implement and administer your internetworking devices. Starting with the configuration of devices out of the box, this book moves to configuring the Cisco IOS for the three most popular networking protocols used today: Transmission Control Protocol/Internet Protocol (TCP/IP), AppleTalk, and Novell InterPacket eXchange (IPX). You also will learn basic administrative and management configuration, including access control with TACACS+ and RADIUS, network management with SNMP, logging of messages, and time control with NTP. *Cisco Router Configuration,* Second Edition, is updated from the previous edition for many new features and configuration commands in Cisco IOS 12.1T. Updated in this edition are solutions for configuring Cisco IOS Software for Gigabit Ethernet LANs, Digital Subscriber Line (DSL) networks, DHCP services and Secure Shell (SSH) access IOS devices.

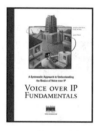

Voice over IP Fundamentals
Jonathan Davidson and Jim Peters
1-57870-168-6 • AVAILABLE NOW

This book will provide you with a thorough introduction to the voice and data technology. You will learn how the telephony infrastructure was built and how it works today. You will also gain understanding of the major concepts concerning voice and data networking, transmission of voice over data, and IP signaling protocols used to interwork with current telephony systems.

OpenCable Architecture
Michael Adams
1-57870-135-X • AVAILABLE NOW

This book explains key concepts in practical terms. It describes the digital headend, optical transport, distribution hub, hybrid-fiber coax, and set-top terminal equipment and how these components are interconnected. Whether you are a television, data communications, or telecommunications professional, or an interested layperson. *OpenCable Architecture* will help you understand the technical and business issues surrounding interactive television services. It will provide you with an inside look a the combined efforts of the cable, data, and consumer electronics industries to develop those new services.

Cisco Press   **www.ciscopress.com**

Cisco Press Solutions

Cisco IOS Releases

Mack Coulibaly

1-57870-179-1 • AVAILABLE NOW

This book is the first comprehensive guide to the more than three dozen types of Cisco IOS release being used today on enterprise and service provider networks. You will learn to select the best Cisco IOS release for your network and to predict the quality and stability of a particular release. You also will find out how to identify the content of an IOS Software image and to plan and predict software fixes that affect mission-critical applications. Also explained is how Cisco IOS interacts with various types of hardware and platforms. With the knowledge, you'll be able to design, implement, and manage world-class network infrastructures powered by Cisco IOS Software.

Internetworking Troubleshooting Handbook, Second Edition

Cisco Systems, et. al.

1-58705-005-6 • AVAILABLE NOW

Internetworking Troubleshooting Handbook, Second Edition, helps you diagnose and resolve specific and potentially problematic issues common to every network type. Created in conjunction with Cisco Systems' Technical Assistance Center, this book demonstrates proven troubleshooting solutions that will enable you to reduce downtime, improve network performance, and enhance network reliability. In addition, it is intended to help you make intelligent, timely, and cost-effective networking decisions for your networking environment. Each section of the book is devoted to problems common to a specific technology area. Sections are subdivided into symptoms, descriptions of environments, diagnosing and isolating problem causes, and problem-solution summaries. Specific protocols covered include TCP/IP, IPX, IBM AppleTalk, Transparent Bridging, DECnet, and ISO CLNS. This Second Edition includes brand-new troubleshooting advice for CiscoWorks 2000, cable, DSL, WAN switching, and security.

Cisco Press Solutions

Performance and Fault Management
Paul Della Maggiora, Christopher Elliott, et. al.
1-57870-180-5 • AVAILABLE NOW

Performance and Fault Management is a comprehensive guide to designing and implementing effective strategies for monitoring performance levels and correcting problems in Cisco networks. It provides an overview of router and LAN switch operations to help you understand how to manage such devices, as well as guidance on the essential MIBs, traps, syslog messages, and show commands for managing Cisco routers and switches.

Developing IP Multicast Networks, Volume I
Beau Williamson
1-57870-077-9 • AVAILABLE NOW

Developing IP Multicast Networks, Volume I, covers and area of networking that is rapidly being deployed in many enterprise and service provider networks to support applications such as audio and video conferencing, distance-learning, and data replication. This books provides a solid foundation of basic IP multicast concepts, as well as the information needed to actually design and deploy IP multicast networks.

Enhanced IP Services for Cisco Networks
Donald C. Lee
1-57870-106-6 • AVAILABLE NOW

Enhanced IP Services for Cisco Networks is a guide to the new enabling and advanced IOS services that build more scalable, intelligent, and secure networks. Networking professionals will gain an understanding of services that help networks support more users, more locations, and more applications. You will earn the technical details necessary to deploy quality of service and VPN technologies, as well as improved security and advanced routing features.

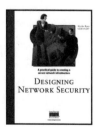

Designing Network Security
Merike Kaeo
1-57870-043-4 • AVAILABLE NOW

Designing Network Security is a practical guide designed to help you understand the fundamentals of securing your corporate network infrastructure. This book takes a comprehensive look at underlying security technologies, the process of crating a security policy, and the practical requirements necessary to implement a corporate security policy.

Cisco Press   **www.ciscopress.com**

Cisco Press Solutions

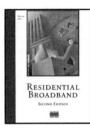

Residential Broadband, Second Edition
George Abe
1-57870-177-5 • AVAILABLE NOW

This book aims to provide a comprehensive, accessible introduction to the topics surrounding high-speed networks to the home. It is written for anyone seeking a broad-based familiarity with the issues of residential broadband (RBB) including product developers, engineers, network designers, business people, professionals in legal and regulatory positions, industry analysts, and the consumers using the RBB services will all find this book of interest. You will learn about the services that are driving the market, the technical issues shaping the evolution, and the network with the home and how it connects to the access network. Also explained are the technical concerns, accessibility, the current state, and potential future of cable TV, xDSL, FTTx, wireless access, and home networks.

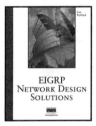

EIGRP Network Design Solutions
Ivan Pepelnjak
1-57870-165-1 • AVAILABLE NOW

EIGRP Network Design Solutions uses case studies and real-world configuration examples to help you gain an in-depth understanding of the issues involved in designing, deploying, and managing EIGRP-based network. It details proper designs that can be used to build large and scalable EIGRP-based networks and documents possible ways each EIGRP feature can be sued in network design, implementation, troubleshooting, and monitoring.

IP Routing Fundamentals
Mark Sportack
1-57870-071-X • AVAILABLE NOW

IP Routing Fundamentals is the definitive introduction to routing in IP networks. This comprehensive guide explores the mechanics of routers, routing protocols, network interfaces, and operating systems. This reference provides essential background information for network professionals who are deploying and maintaining LANs and WANs, as well as IT managers who are seeking information on how evolving internetworking technology will affect future networks.

Cisco Press   **www.ciscopress.com**

Cisco Press Solutions

Top-Down Network Design
Priscilla Oppenheimer
1-57870-069-8 • AVAILABLE NOW

Top-Down Network Design is a practical and comprehensive guide to designing enterprise networks that are reliable, secure, and manageable. Using illustrations and real-world examples, it teaches a systematic method for network design that can be applied to campus LANs, remote-access networks, WAN links, and large-scale internetworks.

OSPF Network Design Solutions
Thomas M. Thomas II
1-57870-046-9 • AVAILABLE NOW

This comprehensive guide presents a detailed, applied look into the workings of the popular Open Shortest Path First protocol, demonstrating how to dramatically increase network performance and security, and how to most easily maintain large-scale networks. OSPF is thoroughly explained through exhaustive coverage of network design, deployment, management, and troubleshooting.

Internetworking SNA with Cisco Solutions
George Sackett and Nancy Sackett
1-57870-083-3 • AVAILABLE NOW

This comprehensive guide presents a practical approach to integrating SNA and TCP/IP networks. It provides readers with an understanding of internetworking terms, networking architectures, protocols, and implementations for internetworking SNA with Cisco routers.

For the latest on Cisco Press resources and Certification and Training guides, or for information on publishing opportunities, visit **www.ciscopress.com**.

Cisco Press

Cisco Press books are available at your local bookstore, computer store, and online booksellers.

CISCO SYSTEMS

IF YOU'RE USING

CISCO PRODUCTS,

YOU'RE QUALIFIED

TO RECEIVE A

FREE SUBSCRIPTION

TO CISCO'S

PREMIER PUBLICATION,

PACKET™ MAGAZINE.

Packet delivers complete coverage of cutting-edge networking trends and innovations, as well as current product updates. A magazine for technical, hands-on Cisco users, it delivers valuable information for enterprises, service providers, and small and midsized businesses.

Packet is a quarterly publication. To start your free subscription, click on the URL and follow the prompts:

www.cisco.com/go/packet/subscribe

CISCO SYSTEMS/PACKET MAGAZINE
ATTN: C. Glover
170 West Tasman, Mailstop SJ8-2
San Jose, CA 95134-1706

Place
Stamp
Here

☐ YES! I'm requesting a **free** subscription to *Packet*™ magazine.

☐ No. I'm not interested at this time.

☐ Mr.
☐ Ms.

First Name (Please Print) _____ Last Name _____

Title/Position (Required) _____

Company (Required) _____

Address _____

City _____ State/Province _____

Zip/Postal Code _____ Country _____

Telephone (Include country and area codes) _____ Fax _____

E-mail _____

Signature (Required) _____ Date _____

☐ I would like to receive additional information on Cisco's services and products by e-mail.

1. Do you or your company:
- A ☐ Use Cisco products
- B ☐ Resell Cisco products
- C ☐ Both
- D ☐ Neither

2. Your organization's relationship to Cisco Systems:
- A ☐ Customer/End User
- B ☐ Prospective Customer
- C ☐ Cisco Reseller
- D ☐ Cisco Distributor
- E ☐ Integrator
- F ☐ Non-Authorized Reseller
- G ☐ Cisco Training Partner
- I ☐ Cisco OEM
- J ☐ Consultant
- K ☐ Other (specify): _____

3. How many people does your entire company employ?
- A ☐ More than 10,000
- B ☐ 5,000 to 9,999
- c ☐ 1,000 to 4,999
- D ☐ 500 to 999
- E ☐ 250 to 499
- f ☐ 100 to 249
- G ☐ Fewer than 100

4. Is your company a Service Provider?
- A ☐ Yes
- B ☐ No

5. Your involvement in network equipment purchases:
- A ☐ Recommend
- B ☐ Approve
- C ☐ Neither

6. Your personal involvement in networking:
- A ☐ Entire enterprise at all sites
- B ☐ Departments or network segments at more than one site
- C ☐ Single department or network segment
- F ☐ Public network
- D ☐ No involvement
- E ☐ Other (specify): _____

7. Your Industry:
- A ☐ Aerospace
- B ☐ Agriculture/Mining/Construction
- C ☐ Banking/Finance
- D ☐ Chemical/Pharmaceutical
- E ☐ Consultant
- F ☐ Computer/Systems/Electronics
- G ☐ Education (K–12)
- U ☐ Education (College/Univ.)
- H ☐ Government—Federal
- I ☐ Government—State
- J ☐ Government—Local
- K ☐ Health Care
- L ☐ Telecommunications
- M ☐ Utilities/Transportation
- N ☐ Other (specify): _____

CPRESS

PACKET

Packet magazine serves as the premier publication linking customers to Cisco Systems, Inc. Delivering complete coverage of cutting-edge networking trends and innovations, *Packet* is a magazine for technical, hands-on users. It delivers industry-specific information for enterprise, service provider, and small and midsized business market segments. A toolchest for planners and decision makers, *Packet* contains a vast array of practical information, boasting sample configurations, real-life customer examples, and tips on getting the most from your Cisco Systems' investments. Simply put, *Packet* magazine is straight talk straight from the worldwide leader in networking for the Internet, Cisco Systems, Inc.

We hope you'll take advantage of this useful resource. I look forward to hearing from you!

Cecelia Glover
Packet Circulation Manager
packet@external.cisco.com
www.cisco.com/go/packet

PACKET